THE ERASMUS READER

# The Erasmus Reader

edited by Erika Rummel

UNIVERSITY OF TORONTO PRESS
Toronto Buffalo London

Toronto / Buffalo / London
Printed in Canada

ISBN 0-8020-6806-5

Printed on acid-free paper

**Canadian Cataloguing in Publication Data**

Erasmus, Desiderius, d. 1536
The Erasmus reader

Based on the Collected works of Erasmus.
Includes bibliographical references.
ISBN 0-8020-6806-5

I. Rummel, Erika, 1942– . II. Title.

PA8502.E5R8 1990 199'.492 C90-094710-1

This volume is based on the *Collected Works of Erasmus* (CWE), the research and publication of which have been generously supported by the Social Sciences and Humanities Research Council of Canada.



COVER ILLUSTRATION: Hans Holbein, *Bildnis des Schreibenden Erasmus von Rotterdam / Portrait of Erasmus Writing.* Courtesy Oeffentliche Kunstsammlung Basel, Kunstmuseum. Colorfoto Hans Hinz, Allschwil, Switzerland.

# Contents

# THE ERASMUS READER

# Introduction

'Every day I receive letters from learned men which set me up as the glory of Germany and call me its sun and moon,' Erasmus wrote in 1515 when he was riding the crest of fame (Ep 237:12–14). His collection of proverbs, the *Adages*, had been reprinted by the prestigious Aldine Press; his *Praise of Folly* had caught the public eye, delighting humanists and disconcerting theologians; his *Enchiridion*, 'that small book of pure gold,' as one enthusiastic reader called it, had established his reputation as a Christian humanist. Erasmus was put on a pedestal by his admirers. Letters from his hand were considered treasures and shown around 'like some picture by Apelles' (Ep 493:114).

A decade later we find Erasmus in a markedly different situation. Once hailed as a hero, he was now 'greeted with silence or depicted in very different colours' (Ep 1352:37). By 1529 he was obliged to acknowledge that he was universally unpopular. 'There is no party that does not hate me bitterly,' he wrote (Allen Ep 2136:80–1). The turning point in Erasmus' career had come with the publication of his New Testament edition in 1516 and, on a larger plane, with the rise of Luther. The New Testament, undoubtedly Erasmus' *magnum opus*, brought him both fame and notoriety, involving him in endless polemics with conservative theologians; the Lutheran question drew all of Christendom into a battle that was fought with pen and sword alike. It was not possible to maintain scholarly detachment, as Erasmus had hoped. His books, written in more tranquil times, were given a new, radical meaning. 'It is no longer safe even to speak of Christ,' he protested (Allen Ep 1572:68). Unwilling to commit himself to either party in the religious debate, he was attacked by both. Reformers called him an opportunist, reactionary Catholics a heretic. Thus Erasmus' name stands for both greatness and tragedy.

Erasmus was born c 1469, the illegitimate son of a priest.[1] When his parents died of the plague, he came under the care of guardians who, anxious to dispose of their duties in the most expedient fashion, urged the youth to enter a monastery. With considerable reluctance and against his own inclinations, the young Erasmus joined the Augustinians at Steyn, professed his vows, and entered the priesthood in 1492. His views on monasticism were no doubt coloured by his personal experience. *On Disdaining the World*,[2] a rhetorical exercise in praise of the monastic life, composed at Steyn, may well have been an effort to rationalize his decision to join the order. Later works evince a more critical stance. In the *The Handbook of a Christian Soldier* and the *Praise of Folly* monasticism is disparaged and its status questioned. As Erasmus put it with epigrammatic flair: *Monachatus non est pietas* – being a monk does not amount to being pious.[3]

In 1493 Erasmus was made secretary to the bishop of Cambrai. Two years later he was sent to Paris to study theology, but the scholastic method taught at the university held no appeal for him. He described his teachers as pseudo-theologians with dull wits and uncultured tongues. 'They say that the secrets of this branch of learning cannot be grasped by a person who has anything at all to do with the Muses or the Graces,' he wrote to his friend Thomas Grey. On his own efforts he commented sarcastically: 'I am trying with might and main to say nothing in good Latin, or elegantly, or wittily; and I seem to be making progress; so there is some hope that eventually they will acknowledge me [as a theologian]' (Ep 64:84–90). In the eyes of his friends, however, Erasmus remained a poet.[4] 'Confound it,' he protested in a letter to his friend Hector Boece, 'who has put it into your head that Erasmus was a poet? That expression, by which you keep describing me in your letters, is in bad odour nowadays through the foolish ignorance of many of its practitioners.'[5] Erasmus was determined to project a scholarly image. To this purpose he wrote to his patron, the bishop of Cambrai, that he was immersed in theological studies and had lost all interest in his 'former darlings,' the Roman poets (Ep 49:107).

During his first year in Paris Erasmus lodged at the Collège de Montaigu, which he later described as a house of horrors: 'Our bedrooms on the groundfloor were cubicles with rotten plaster next to stinking latrines. No one ever lived there without either dying or getting a terrible disease. I'll say nothing about the savage floggings, even of the innocent. Thus, they declare, is "wildness" tamed – "wildness" being their name for unusual talent, which they zealously destroy, to render men more fit for monasteries! How many rotten eggs used to be eaten there! How much bad wine drunk! Perhaps those conditions have been corrected; but too late, obviously, for those who have died or who carry a diseased body about' (*Colloquies* 252–3).

Erasmus soon left the college and supported himself by tutoring private pupils. He created his own teaching materials which were eventually published to great acclaim. Among the handbooks conceived in the Paris years were anthologies of proverbs, similes, and anecdotes; manuals on style and letter-writing, and dialogues to teach boys conversational Latin.[6] His teaching experience also led Erasmus to formulate his own theories of education, which he expounded in *The Method of Study* and *On Education for Children*.[7]

In 1517 Erasmus sought and obtained a papal dispensation that allowed him to live the life of a secular priest. He explained his decision not to return to the monastery to his abbot, Servatius Rogerus: 'I have always regarded as the worst of my misfortunes the fact that I had been forced into the kind of profession which was utterly repugnant to my mind and body alike ... whenever I thought about rejoining your community, I envisaged the envy of many, the contempt of all, the conversations so cold and inept, with no savour of Christ, the banquets so profane in their spirit, in short the whole tenor of life such that, if the ceremonies were removed, I cannot see what would be left that was desirable' (Ep 296:29–31, 57–61). Erasmus' decision to abandon the monastic life was not a decision to abandon the pursuit of holiness. It was with sincerity that he had written in 1506: 'I am deeply preoccupied with pondering how I can wholly devote to religion and to Christ whatever life remains to me' (Ep 189:7–8). He had formulated for himself a *philosophia Christi*, a life centred on Christ and characterized by inner faith rather than external rites – a philosophy set forth in his *Handbook of the Christian Soldier*. The same message – though in a different manner – was also proffered in the *Praise of Folly*.[8] Here, too, we find praise for the simple, devout believer – the Christian fool – and scorn for those who are preoccupied with external things – the fools of the world. Using mordant satire, Erasmus pokes fun at quibbling theologians and hypocritical monks alike. He lampoons theologians playing dialectical games, spouting propositions, definitions, and conclusions. 'Such is the erudition and complexity they all display,' Erasmus quips, 'that I fancy the apostles themselves would need the help of the Holy Spirit, if they were obliged [to engage in debate] with our theologians (CWE 27 127). Foolish monks, who enjoy doing everything to rule, are similarly mocked: 'They work out the number of knots for a shoe-string, the colour and number of variations of a single habit, the material and width to a hair's breadth of a girdle, the shape and capacity (in sacksful) of a cowl, the length (in fingers) of a haircut, the number of hours prescribed for sleep ... There are others again who shrink from the touch of money as if it were deadly poison, but are less restrained when it comes to wine and contact with women' (ibid 131). After describing these pedants who are deaf to the call of Christ, Erasmus directs his readers to another kind of folly – the folly professed by St Paul and manifested in a rejection of human wisdom and in complete faith in Christ the Redeemer of souls.

For many years Erasmus led the life of a travelling scholar. Journeys to France, England, and Italy brought him in contact with the international community of humanists:[9] in Paris he found a mentor in the historian Robert Gaguin and a companion in the poet Fausto Andrelini; in England he formed lasting friendships with Thomas More and John Colet; in Italy he enjoyed the stimulating atmosphere of the Aldine Academy, the circle of scholars gathered around the printer Aldo Manuzio.

It was during his sojourn in Italy that news reached him of Henry VIII's accession to the throne. Lord Mountjoy, a former pupil turned benefactor, counselled Erasmus to come to England at once: 'All is milk and honey and nectar,' he reported, 'Tightfistedness is well and truly banished. Generosity scatters with unstinting hand' (Ep 215:16–18). Erasmus followed Mountjoy's advice, but was disappointed in his hopes for royal patronage. For five years he endured poverty but enjoyed a wealth of learning and the companionship of scholarly friends at London and Cambridge, where he taught Greek.

It was during the early 1500s that Erasmus laid the groundwork for his New Testament edition and turned from classical to biblical scholarship. Having acquired competence in Greek – a subject in which he was largely self-taught – Erasmus translated a number of classical Greek authors in what he considered a preliminary exercise preparing him for a greater task: 'While I linger within the garden of the Greeks I am gathering by the way many flowers that will be useful ... in sacred studies' (Ep 181:99–101). Convinced of the validity of a philological approach to biblical studies, Erasmus persevered and brought his work to fruition with an annotated bilingual edition of the New Testament in 1516. The edition was of historic significance. For the first time a Greek text of the New Testament was made available to the public in print; and the Latin version accompanying it was not the standard Vulgate text but a translation revised by Erasmus, purged of long-standing errors and solecisms.[10] Based on manuscript evidence, it represented a pioneering effort in textual criticism and helped to establish the role of philology in scriptural studies. While Erasmus was hailed as the 'champion of genuine theology' by progressive minds (Allen Ep 1352:36–7), conservative theologians were scandalized. Many questioned Erasmus' authority to undertake a revision of the Bible. The task, they said, had been entrusted to St Jerome by Pope Damasus – did Erasmus think he could improve on the inspired work of the Church Father? Erasmus in turn disputed that Jerome was the author of the Vulgate and insisted that the text the church was using had been corrupted by scribes. He was restoring rather than correcting the original text, he argued. In spite of letters of endorsement by Pope Leo x and other leading churchmen, Erasmus was unable to convince his critics of the merits of his undertaking and was soon engulfed in a storm of controversy.

For the time being, however, he was allowed to savour the sweet taste of fame. Young scholars undertook 'pilgrimages' to his house, which they considered a shrine of the Muses. Journeys turned into triumphal processions with guards of honour, speeches of welcome, and banquets drawn out into the night. Travelling down the Rhine in 1518, Erasmus was recognized by a customs official who immediately carried him off to his house: 'On his desk among the customs forms lay the works of Erasmus. He cried out on his good fortune, called for his children, his wife, and all his friends,' Erasmus reported (Ep 867:55–7). The official was delighted with his prominent guest, and Erasmus was equally delighted with the man's flattering attention. Public recognition also took more practical forms. Erasmus was given benefices, offered teaching posts, and in 1515 appointed councillor to Prince Charles (later Charles v). His connections with the imperial court yielded a number of 'political' writings: on the ideal prince (*The Education of a Christian Prince*), on the merits of peace (*A Complaint of Peace*), on the Turkish campaign (*On the War against the Turks*).[11] In all of his works on statescraft Erasmus promoted the idea of the prince as father of his country whose sacred obligation it was to look after the welfare of his subjects. Peace-loving, law-abiding, and morally upright, he was to be a source of inspiration to his subjects.

Erasmus' position as a councillor obliged him to reside within travelling distance of the court at Brussels. The nearest centre of learning was Louvain. Erasmus did not savour the idea of taking up residence there: 'I should have to pay my own way,' he told his friend Andrea Ammonio, 'and be the servant of the university people. The young men would be interrupting me all the time with their chatter ... and there is no one there whom it would be any credit or any help for me to know. On top of all this I should have to listen sometimes to the chatter of the theologians, the dreariest sort of men ... if only great Jupiter with his famous thunderbolt would plunge this whole race of men into Tartarus: they produce nothing that can make us better men or better scholars, and they are a perfect universal nuisance' (Ep 475:17–34). Erasmus' misgivings about the Louvain theologians were justified by subsequent events. Left without a feasible alternative, he moved to Louvain in July 1517, and for the next four years carried on a running battle with the faculty of theology. The vice-chancellor Jan Briart of Ath, the Paris graduate Jacques Masson, and the Carmelite Nicolaas Baechem were his chief enemies. They in turn suborned others to criticize Erasmus' work. The result was a number of polemics, a genre that came to dominate Erasmus' literary output during the twenties.

Several factors contributed to Erasmus' unpopularity with the theologians: his sharp criticism of the profession in the *Praise of Folly*; his active pursuit of biblical studies, which the theologians considered meddling since in their eyes Erasmus was a philologian rather than a theologian; and the appearance of writings by Luther who was said to have benefited from Erasmus' pen, if not from his inspiration.

Indeed Erasmus had at first welcomed Luther's initiatives, although from the beginning he was uncomfortable with that reformer's confrontational style.[12] Soon, however, he became alarmed by Luther's intransigence and feared for the peace and unity of the church. Erasmus eventually withdrew his support and, on the urging of Pope Adrian and other ecclesiastical leaders, engaged in a polemic with Luther on the subject of free will. Many conservative Catholics felt, however, that he had done too little too late. They regarded his contribution to the battle against Luther as ineffectual and alleged that his weak and unconvincing performance betrayed not only his ineptitude as a theologian but also a lack of commitment.

Undeterred by critics who questioned his motives and dismissed him as a 'theologizing humanist,' Erasmus continued his biblical studies, editing and translating patristic writings[13] and embarking on paraphrases of the New Testament.[14] He saw his *Paraphrases* as a 'kind of commentary' (Ep 1274) woven into a continuous narrative. He chose a style attractive to educated readers and hoped to foster in them an understanding of the *philosophia Christi* and a desire to live according to the precepts and example of Christ and the apostles. While the *Paraphrases* proved less controversial than his earlier exegetical work, Erasmus was nevertheless accused of introducing not only unorthodox ideas but also pagan rhetoric into the gospel doctrine. He insisted, however, that he was following traditional medieval and patristic exegesis and had at all times sought to be 'a Christian rather than a Ciceronian' (LB IX 530B).

By the mid-twenties suspicions that Erasmus was a Lutheran sympathizer and disseminator of unorthodox views hardened into a general perception. Erasmus became the target of popular witticisms, such as 'Erasmus laid the egg that Luther hatched' and 'Either Erasmus lutheranizes or Luther erasmianizes.' Not surprisingly his works came under investigation by the church. In 1527 the Spanish Inquisitor General convened a conference to examine Erasmus' writings. Although the meetings were adjourned because of an outbreak of the plague, the proceedings were soon public knowledge, and Erasmus felt obliged to defend his orthodoxy in an *apologia*. The prestigious faculty of theology at Paris also reviewed Erasmus' works and condemned a number of passages as scandalous and unorthodox. When their findings were published in 1531, Erasmus was once again obliged to justify his writings. In 1552, after Erasmus' death, the Louvain theologians joined their colleagues at the Sorbonne in condemning passages from Erasmus' writings as erroneous, scandalous, and heretical.

Ironically, Erasmus was also set upon by the Protestant camp. Keenly disappointed that he failed to join their cause, they unleashed numerous attacks on Erasmus. Ulrich von Hutten's *Expostulation* is representative of the bitterness felt by many of Erasmus' former champions. 'I am stupefied and shaken to know what has happened,' Hutten wrote, 'that you who once joined with us to demote the pope, you who detested bulls of indulgence, who damned ceremonies, expelled the papal courtiers, execrated the canon law and the decretals, in a word you who denounced universal hypocrisy, that you now turn completely around and join that enemy, that you now flatter ... Pope Adrian. Formerly you attacked the Dominicans, now you curry favour with them. You have been suborned by the lure of emoluments.'[15]

It is interesting to note that Erasmus returned to his scholarly roots toward the end of his career and once again focused his attention on language. In his mature work, however, the subject of language is inextricably linked with the *philosophia Christi*. In *The Tongue* (1525) he expounded the truly Christian use of language; in *The Ciceronian* (1528) he examined the question of a Christian style of speech; in the *Ecclesiastes* (1533) he proffered a manual of sacred oratory to complement *Copia: Foundations of the Abundant Style*, his manual for the student of secular rhetoric.[16]

The final years of Erasmus' life continued to be filled with controversy. While he had earlier on declined to become involved in the Reformation debate, protesting that 'not everyone has the strength needed for martyrdom' (Ep 1218:32–4), he found himself in that very position at the end of his life. His fate, he lamented, was harsher than St Sebastian's or St Stephen's. 'Stephen was overwhelmed with stones only once, Sebastian was transfixed with darts only once. Death put an end to their suffering, but my wounded soul survives to suffer a multitude of deaths' (Allen Ep 2136:92–5).

The attacks of the Louvain theologians prompted Erasmus to seek refuge in the more liberally minded Basel in 1521; seven years later religious unrest forced him to leave that city for imperial Freiburg im Breisgau. Burdened with illness and old age, he nevertheless returned to Basel when calm was restored. A few months later, in July 1536, he died in the city that had become his home. The contrasting reactions evoked by the news of his death are best seen through the magnifying glass of a contemporary satire, Ortensio Lando's *The Funeral of Desiderius Erasmus*. The scurrilous dialogue describes a group of monks who in a bacchantic frenzy break open Erasmus' grave, defile his body, and cast it into a sewer. This ghoulish scene is counterbalanced by a vision of Erasmus in heaven accompanied by a host of angels praying for the salvation of his foes who are suffering in hell.

In one of his last works, *On Establishing Concord in the Church,* Erasmus called for a universal council to restore the church to unity. He did not live to see the Council of Trent, but the doctrinalism that won the day there would hardly have been to his taste. One of the measures adopted by the council was the *Index of Forbidden Books*. In the original document (1559) Erasmus was placed in the first category of heretics whose works were to be shunned in their entirety; in the revised form approved by the council (1564) some of Erasmus' works were permitted in expurgated form, others such as the *Praise of Folly* and the *Colloquies* were suppressed.

Throughout the second half of the sixteenth century negative attitudes toward Erasmus prevailed. Protestants increasingly saw him as the man who had seen the better way but had chosen the worse; Catholics saw in him a corrosive influence and a proponent of unsound doctrine. The history of Erasmus' reputation 'has a simple shape,' as Bruce Mansfield puts it, 'it is a story of decline and fall.'[17] Erasmus recovered his position of authority only when the intellectual climate and religious sensibilities changed. In the Age of Enlightenment Erasmus' progressive spirit found a new appreciation. Just as first-generation Erasmians had seen in him a pioneer of the Reformation, so the eighteenth century saw in him a pioneer of the Enlightenment.

Of course Erasmianism had never been completely in abeyance. His legacy was cherished in Basel and in the Low Countries. It is fitting therefore that the first complete edition of Erasmus' works was published in Basel in 1538–40 and the second *Opera omnia*, the product of a renewed interest in the writings of the Dutch scholar in the eighteenth century, originated in Leiden (1703–6).[18] A first critical edition of Erasmus' correspondence had to wait until the beginning of the twentieth century when P.S. Allen devoted almost his entire scholarly life to this formidable task; the edition was published in Oxford, 1906–58.[19] A resurgence of interest in the second half of this century culminated in 1969 when the 500th anniversary of Erasmus' birth provided the focus for a number of international conferences. In the last two decades a concerted scholarly effort has made Erasmus' works more accessible to the modern reader. A new critical and annotated edition of his works in the original Latin is going forward in Amsterdam;[20] an English translation of Erasmus' works is under way in Toronto;[21] an eight-volume edition of selected works has appeared in a bilingual Latin/

German edition in Darmstadt,[22] and the complete correspondence is now available in a French translation.[23]

These publishing ventures demonstrate the relevance of Erasmus' writings to our generation. For today's student of sixteenth-century history their continued appeal lies in the fact that Erasmus, who coined the expression 'a man for all seasons,' was such a man himself. One cannot study early modern Europe without encountering Erasmus' authoritative voice. In the writings of his contemporaries as well as in modern literature his views continue to be cited on education, politics, and religion. In his correspondence especially, history comes alive. Indeed the list of Erasmus' correspondents reads like a *Who's Who* of the sixteenth century. He exchanged letters with princes and popes, bankers and scholars, poets and theologians, freely speaking his mind on a wide range of subjects. His concerns were essentially those of his time. He shared with contemporaries an admiration for antiquity, an active interest in the Reformation debate, a deep desire for peace, and a taste for the comforts of life. Of course Erasmus is not only instructive but also entertaining, and students of the period will enjoy his ready wit, his satirical vein, and his elegant style.

The selections in this book are designed to introduce readers to a broad range of Erasmian writings and to offer representative samples of his work. If certain areas appear to be neglected, it is because their appreciation requires more specialized knowledge. Erasmus' poetry and his translations from the Greek, for example, require a knowledge of the classical languages; his biblical exegesis and the polemics engendered by it require a background in patristic and scholastic theology. This book focuses on areas that are readily accessible to the general reader: education, ethics, politics, and social criticism.

The first section, which serves as an introduction, offers an autobiographical sketch and a descriptive catalogue of Erasmus' works.

Section 2 focuses on Erasmus the educator and contains selections from *The Antibarbarians*, a dialogue contrasting the medieval tradition with humanist ideals of education. This is followed by *On Education for Children*, an essay on early childhood education, and *On Good Manners*, Erasmus' guide to courteous behaviour.

Section 3 portrays Erasmus the Christian humanist. The selections come from two works, *The Ciceronian* and *The Handbook of the Christian*

*Soldier*, whose purpose is complementary. They offer instruction on being a true Christian in action, attitude, and speech.

Section 4 deals with Erasmus as a reformer and critic of the church. It includes a selection from the *Praise of Folly* and Erasmus' defence of that work in his letter to the Louvain theologian Maarten van Dorp. The course of Erasmus' involvement with Luther is traced in three letters from the years 1519–21. The next selection comes from *Julius Excluded from Heaven*, a lampoon ascribed to Erasmus, pitting St Peter, the true vicar of Christ, against the notorious Renaissance pope Julius II. The last piece is the colloquy 'Shipwreck,' a dialogue satirizing the superstitious veneration of saints.

The final section illustrates Erasmus' political theories. The *Education of a Christian Prince* and the adage 'One ought to be born a king or a fool' are essays on statecraft. *A Complaint of Peace* is Erasmus' celebrated plea for a general peace; *On the War against the Turks* discusses the concept of just war.

Each selection is preceded by a headnote explaining the significance of the piece and giving information on its genesis and publication history.[24] For brief biographical data readers may consult the chronological table at the end of the volume. The texts presented here are those already published or forthcoming in the *Collected Works of Erasmus*. For the contents of the headnotes and endnotes I am indebted to the translators and annotators of those volumes.

In the preface to his biography of Erasmus, Roland Bainton declares: 'Erasmus of Rotterdam has never had his due. The reason is in part that he founded no church to perpetuate his memory' (*Erasmus of Christendom* vii). Indeed, Erasmus defended the unity of the church and took pride in the fact that he had 'been neither a leader nor an adherent of any sect' (Allen Ep 2445:137). His congregation is the interdenominational community of scholars which continues to perpetuate the memory of the great Dutch humanist. In the words of Erasmus' friend John Colet: 'The name of Erasmus will never die.'

# ERASMUS: HIS LIFE AND WORKS 1

## Brief Outline of His Life / *Compendium vitae*

This autobiographical sketch was composed by Erasmus in 1524 when his health had been failing for some time. It was enclosed with a letter addressed to his friend and confidant Conradus Goclenius and was intended for the use of biographers after Erasmus' death. The *Outline* was first published in 1607 by Paul Merula, a scholar at the University of Leiden, from a manuscript he thought to be an autograph. The manuscript was still in existence in 1649 but has since disappeared. This circumstance and the occasionally jerky style of the narrative have prompted questions about the authenticity of the document. There is no doubt that the *Outline* is a highly tendentious account of Erasmus' life. However, parallels with contemporary letters argue for the substantial accuracy of the narrative and do not allow us to dismiss it as a pastiche without independent authority.

This extract is taken from CWE 4 403–10, translated by R.A.B. Mynors and D.F.S. Thomson, annotated by James K. McConica.

A BRIEF ACCOUNT OF THE LIFE OF ERASMUS OF ROTTERDAM ...
*The life to be kept secret*
Born in Rotterdam on the eve of SS Simon and Jude.[1] Reckons he is

about fifty-seven years of age.[2] His mother's name was Margaret, her father a physician named Pieter. She was from Septimontium, commonly known as Zevenbergen, and he saw two of her brothers at Dordrecht who were nearly ninety years old. His father's name was Gerard. He lay with Margaret secretly, in the expectation of marrying her. Some say they were already betrothed. This was received with indignation by Gerard's parents and his brothers. Gerard's father was called Elias and his mother Catharine; both lived to a very great age, Catharine till she was nearly ninety-five. There were ten brothers, but no sister, born of the same parents, all of them married. Gerard was the youngest but one. All agreed that out of so large a family one should be consecrated to God. You know how old men feel. And his brothers wished to have no reduction in their own patrimony, but someone with whom they could always be sure of a dinner. Gerard, finding himself entirely debarred by general consent from matrimony, did what men in despair often do: he ran away, and on his journey sent a letter to his parents and brothers, with two clasped hands on it, and the legend 'Farewell, I shall never see you more.'

Meanwhile the woman he had hoped to marry was left expecting a child. The boy was brought up by his grandmother. Gerard made his way to Rome. There he earned enough to live on as a copyist, for the art of printing as yet did not exist. He wrote a very expert hand. And he lived as young men will. Later he turned his mind to honourable studies. Of Greek and Latin he had a good knowledge. In the law too he was more than commonly proficient. Rome in those days was wonderfully blest with learned men. He heard Guarino lecture.[3] All the classical authors he had copied with his own hand. His parents, when they learned he was in Rome, wrote to him that the girl he hoped to marry was now dead. Supposing this to be true, in his grief he became a priest, and devoted his whole mind to religion. On returning home, he discovered this was a fraud. But she was never afterwards willing to marry, nor did he ever touch her.

For the boy he arranged to provide a liberal education, and when he was scarcely more than four years old he sent him to an elementary school. In his early years the child made very little progress in those tedious rudiments, for which he had no natural gift. In his ninth year he sent him to Deventer; his mother went with him as guardian and guide of his tender years. The school there was at that time in a state of barbarism (a standard text was the *Pater meus;* they were forced to learn the paradigms, the textbooks being Eberhard and John of Garland),[4] except that Alexander Hegius and Synthen had begun to introduce something of a higher standard as literature.[5] At length his playmates, of whom the older ones were in Synthen's class, gave him his first taste of better teaching, and later he sometimes heard Hegius, but only on feast days when he lectured to the whole school. Here he reached the third form; then the plague, which was raging there, carried off his mother, leaving her son now in his thirteenth year. As the plague grew daily more and more severe, the whole house in which he lived was deserted, and he returned to his native place. Gerard when he heard the sad news fell ill, and shortly afterwards died. Both were not much over forty. He set up three guardians, whom he thought most reliable. Of these the chief was Pieter Winckel, at that time master of the school of Gouda. He left a moderate estate, had his guardians managed it in good faith. And so the boy was removed to 's Hertogenbosch, being now old enough for the university. But they were afraid of a university, for they had already decided to bring up the boy for the life of a religious.

There he spent, or rather wasted, about three years in a house of the Brothers, as they call them, in which Rombold was then teaching.[6] This sort of men now spreads widely through the world, though it is disastrous for gifted minds and a mere nursery of monks. Rombold, who was much struck by the boy's gifts, began to work on him to join his flock. The boy pleaded the ignorance of his youth. At this point there was an outbreak of plague; and after suffering for a long time from a quartan fever, he returned to his guardians, having by now also acquired some fluency of style derived from a few good authors. One of the guardians had succumbed to the plague; the other two, who had not managed his affairs very skilfully, began to treat with him about the monastic life. The poor youth, who was weak from the fever which had held him for more than a year, felt no dislike of religion, but he did dislike a monastery. They therefore allowed him a day to think it over. All this time the guardian put up people to tempt and threaten him and bring pressure to bear on his innocent mind; and in the meanwhile he had found a place in a monastery of regular canons, as they are commonly called, in a house near Delft, called Sion, which is the chief house of that chapter. When the day arrived on which he had to answer, the youth answered sensibly, that he did not yet know what the world was, or what a monastery was, or what he was himself; and so it seemed, he said, a better plan that he should still spend some years attending lectures, until he might known his own mind better. When he saw the young man persist in this, Pieter suddenly lost his temper. 'I see,' he said; 'I have wasted my labour in securing you a place like that with so much entreaty. You are a worthless fellow, and have a spirit of perversity in you. I resign my office as your guardian. You can fend for yourself.' The youth replied that he accepted his resignation, being now of an age when guardians were no longer necessary. When the man saw that threats got him nowhere, he suborned his brother, who was also one of the trustees, and a man of business. He set to work with blandishments, and was supported on every hand by those who had put him up to it. The boy had a companion,[7] who betrayed his friend, and the fever still lay hard on him; but even so, a monastery had no appeal, until by some chance he visited a house of the same Order at Emmaus, or Steyn, near Gouda. There he found one Cornelis, who had been a friend of his and shared a room with him at Deventer. This man had not yet taken orders; he had visited Italy, but had returned without learning much. With an eye to his own advantage he began to draw a most eloquent picture of a very saintly way of life, with plenty of books, leisure, tranquillity, and a society like that of angels, everything you can think of. The young man was drawn to his old companion by fond memories of boyhood; he was lured on by some people and driven forward by others; the fever lay heavy on him. So he chose this place, being disgusted with the other, and of the moment all was made pleasant for him, until he should take the habit. Meanwhile, young as he was, he realized how far the place was from true religion; and yet he inspired the whole community to study harder. Though he made preparations to leave before his profession, he was restrained partly by natural shyness, partly by threats and partly by necessity.

He made his profession.[8] At length he had an opportunity of becoming known to Hendrik van Bergen, the bishop of Cambrai. The bishop was hoping for a cardinal's hat, and would have had one, had he not been short of ready money. For the purpose of this journey he needed a good Latin scholar. So our man was sent for by him, with authorization from the bishop of Utrecht, which was sufficient by itself, but he also secured the approval of the prior and of the general of the Order. He joined the bishop's household but none the less still wore his canonical habit. When the bishop had lost his hope of a hat, and perceived that the young man's devotion to them all left something to be desired, he arranged that he should go to Paris to study. He was promised an annual subvention, but nothing was ever sent. Great men are like that. There in the Collège de Montaigu, as a result of rotten eggs and infected lodgings, he contracted an illness, a morbid influence on a constitution until then quite free from taint. So he returned to the bishop. His reception was complimentary. He recovered his health at Bergen. He revisited Holland with the intention of remaining with his own people. But on their unsought encouragement he went back to Paris. There with no patron to support him it was a question of survival rather than study; and as the plague was continuous there for many years, he was obliged to return every year to his native country. Theology repelled him, for he felt himself not disposed to undermine all its foundations with the prospect of being branded as a heretic. At length, when the plague continued for a whole year, he was compelled to move to Louvain. He had previously visited England to oblige Mountjoy,[9] who was at that time his pupil and later his Maecenas, though more of a friend than a benefactor. In those days he won the good opinion of all men of standing in England, particularly because, although robbed on the coast at Dover,[10] he not only sought no revenge but published a short work not long after in praise of the king of England and the whole country. At length he was invited with generous offers to return from France to England, and it was at that time that he secured the friendship of the archbishop of Canterbury.[11] When the offers did not materialize, he set off for Italy, which he had always had a great desire to visit. He spent a little more than a year in Bologna, his life being already at its turning-point, for he was now about forty. Thence he moved to Venice, and published his *Adages*;[12] from there to Padua, where he spent the winter; thereafter to Rome, where a substantial and favourable reputation had preceded him. Raffaele[13] the cardinal of San Giorgio had a special feeling for him. Nor would he have failed to secure a lucrative position had he not been summoned back to England on the death of Henry VII[14] and accession of Henry VIII by letters from friends, full of generous promises. In England he had decided to spend the rest of his life; but as these promises were no more kept now than before, he retreated to Brabant, having been invited to the court of the present Emperor Charles, whose councillor he became through the efforts of the lord chancellor, Jean Le Sauvage.[15] The rest you know ...

His personal appearance you will describe yourself. His health was always delicate, and thus he was often attacked by fevers, especially in Lent on account of the eating of fish, the mere smell of which used to upset him. His character was straightforward, and his dislike of falsehood such that even as a child he hated other boys who told lies, and in old age even the sight of such people affected him physically. Among his friends he spoke freely – too freely sometimes, and though often deceived he never learned not to trust them. Having a touch of pedantry, he never wrote anything with which he was satisfied; he even disliked his own appearance, and his friends' entreaties barely prevailed on him to let himself be painted. For high office and for wealth he had a permanent contempt, and thought nothing more precious than leisure and liberty. A charitable judge of other men's learning, he would have been a supreme encourager of gifted minds had his resources run to it. In promoting the study of the humanities no one did more, and great was the unpopularity he had to suffer in return for this from barbarians and monks. Until his fiftieth year he had attacked no man, nor did any man attack him in print. This was his intention: to keep his pen absolutely innocent of what might wound. Lefèvre was the first to attack him; for Dorp's efforts were suppressed.[16] In reply he was always courteous. The sad business of Luther[17] had brought him a burden of intolerable ill will; he was torn in pieces by both sides, while aiming zealously at what was best for both.

# Catalogue of His Works / *Catalogus lucubrationum*

Erasmus sent this letter – a descriptive catalogue of his works – in response to a request from Johann von Botzheim (d 1535), a canon of Constance. It was published by Froben in April 1523 under the title *Catalogus omnium Erasmi Roterodami lucubrationum.* A second, much expanded edition appeared from the same press in September 1524. Following Erasmus' death in 1536, Froben issued a third, updated edition in February 1537. Revised once again, the catalogue was also included among the introductory material of the first volume of the Basel *Opera omnia* of 1540.

For the publication dates of individual works mentioned in the catalogue see the chronological table below 367. This extract is taken from CWE 9 293–363, translated by R.A.B. Mynors, annotated by James M. Estes.

ERASMUS OF ROTTERDAM TO THE LEARNED AND REVEREND JOHANN VON BOTZHEIM, OTHERWISE ABSTEMIUS,[1] DOCTOR OF CIVIL AND CANON LAW, AND CANON OF CONSTANCE

Unwilling as you are, dear Abstemius my lost learned friend, to think that any of my writings should be absent from your library, you complain that from time to time you have to buy the same book twice, when it has been either refurbished or enlarged or revised. You ask me therefore to make a list for you of all the trifles I have published (for that is a truer word for them than books) and to indicate which of them have received my final version, so that nothing may escape you which you do not possess, and at the same time you may buy nothing which you will soon be obliged to acquire in a new form. I will do as you wish, and render a service at the same time by your means, if I mistake not, to very many others. You love to add lustre to your library, you say, with Erasmus' works. For my part, I think your library adds lustre to my books, for it is one of the most illustrious I ever saw; one might call it a veritable home of the Muses. And so I pride myself more on your thinking my works good enough for a lodging in your library than I should if they were laid up in caskets of cedar-wood in the temple of Apollo. I do not suppose they will live; still less dare I hope they may be immortal; but if they have the good fortune to survive their creator by some few years, they will surely owe this to your library. Men will think there must be something in books which that sober judge Abstemius thought good enough for his shrine of the Muses. But in the meantime my own feelings towards the progeny of my nightly toils are much like those of parents towards their children when they have been unhappy in their offspring because they are either misshapen and sickly or likely in other ways to bring disgrace and disaster on their forebears. And in this regard I am the more dissatisfied with my performance; for children's failings cannot always be blamed upon their parents, but no one can answer for the faults of books except their authors – unless perhaps I choose to say in my defence that time and place have been unpropitious. When I was a boy, the humanities had begun to put forth fresh shoots among the Italians; but because the printer's art was either not yet invented or known to very few, nothing in the way of books came through to us, and unbroken slumber graced the universal reign of those who taught ignorance in place of knowledge. Rodolfus Agricola was the first to bring us a breath of more humane learning out of Italy;[2] in Deventer, as a boy of twelve or so, I was blessed with a sight of him, and that was all. Then again, the generation and the country in which you write make a great difference, the critical standards of your audience, and whom you compete with: even an opponent of some distinction puts an edge on your natural powers, and, as we all know, honour is the nursing mother of the arts. None of all this was vouchsafed me, and yet a kind of secret natural force swept me into liberal studies. My teachers might forbid it; even so, I furtively drank in what I could from such books as I had managed to acquire; I practised my pen, I used to challenge my companions to compete with me, with nothing further from my thoughts than the publication of trifles of this kind in print. These facts could not do away my responsibility, but they might well make it less heavy. There are however some points on which I am neither able nor desirous to defend myself. The chief thing is that the man who hopes to win a reputation by what he writes should choose a subject to which he is by nature suited, and in which his powers chiefly lie; all themes do not suit everyone. This I have never done; I have either stumbled on a subject unadvisedly or chosen one to comply with my friends' feelings rather than my own judgment. Next comes the importance, whatever you have chosen, of taking pains in the treatment of it, of keeping it by you for some time and often giving it further polish before it sees the light of day. But for my part, once I have embarked on a subject I generally run through to the finish without a break, and I have never been able to stomach the tedium of revision. So my experience has usually been, as Plato puts it, that I go too fast at the beginning, and am late in arriving at my goal. I publish in a hurry, and in the nature of things am sometimes obliged to refurbish the whole thing from top to toe. It surprises me therefore to find people, especially in so scholarly an age as ours, who read what I write. But they exist; if nothing else, the way the printers reproduce my works so often proves it.

But all this time you are waiting for a catalogue, not an apologia. So be it! And first I will recount what I have written in verse, for in boyhood my predilection for verse was such that it was with reluctance I turned to prose composition. And in that field I strove for some time before succeeding, if one may use the word success. Nor is there any form of poetry which I did not attempt. The things that have fortunately perished or are unknown I shall leave in obscurity and, as the Greek proverb has it, not rouse the ill that's safely hid. It was in Paris that my indiscretions first began to be made known to the public, for it was there that my friends published a heroic poem, with an admixture of tetrameters in the same style, addressed to Fausto Andrelini,[3] ... And many years before I had written a poem in sapphics on the archangel Michael, not of my own choice, but driven to it by the appeals of a certain great man who presided over a church dedicated to St Michael.[4] I pitched this in such a low key that it might have been taken for prose; but he did not dare post it up, on the ground that it was so poetical that, as he said himself, it might be thought written in Greek. Such were the standards of those unhappy days! And though I had spent so much labour on it, when I delivered my poem, my generous patron gave me money to buy a pint of wine – which was about what the poem was worth. I thanked him for his generosity, and refused the gift on that ground, saying it was too much for a humble person like myself. In no kind of verse have I had less practice than in epigrams; yet sometimes while out walking, or even over the wine, I have at different times thrown off a certain number, some of which have been put together by friends over-zealous for my reputation, and published in Basel; and to make them even more ridiculous, they appended them to the epigrams of Thomas More, who is a master of the art.[5] A poem addressed to Guillaume Cop[6] on old age I wrote in the Alps, when I first visited Italy. A bitter dispute had arisen between a herald of the English king, who accompanied us as far as Bologna to give us more safety on the journey, and the tutor of the young men[7] whom I was then taking to Italy under the terms of an agreement in which I was caught like a rat in a trap, not as their governor (for I had ruled out any responsibility for their behaviour) nor to give them lessons, but to keep an eye on them and steer them on a suitable course of study – my destiny must needs be replete with every form of disaster, for it was the most unpleasant year I ever spent. These two it was, then, between whom a quarrel had broken out, so fierce that after violent insults swords were drawn. At that stage I was angry with one of the two only; but when, after such a tempest, I saw them reconciled of their own accord after downing a stoup of wine, I was disgusted equally with both. Not only do I think men must be mad to get so angry unless they have suffered some serious injury; even more do I regard as quite untrustworthy those who make it up so suddenly after being at each other's throats. And so, to relieve the tedium while riding, I avoided any conversation with the two parties and finished this poem, scribbling it down from time to time on a piece of paper on my saddle-bow, so that I might not forget part of it while pursuing the rest; when we reached an inn, I copied out from my notes what had come into existence. Such is my equestrian, my nag-born and crag-born poem; and yet, born as it was, good judges do not find it altogether a failure.

I have written at various times a number of epitaphs at the request of friends, which it is needless to recount. But some years before my visit to Italy, in order to practise my Greek (for teachers were not to be had), I had made a version of the *Hecuba* of Euripides. Then, when letters and promises from my friends of the proverbial mountains of gold had persuaded me to return to England, I added a preface and a poem in iambics, very much on the spur of the moment, to fill a chance space in my paper, and on the advice of learned friends, and particularly of William Grocyn,[8] who was at that time the most distinguished of the many scholars in England, I offered the book with a dedication to William, archbishop of Canterbury, primate of all

England and chancellor of the realm,[9] which means the supreme judge. This was then the happy opening of my acquaintance with him. Having greeted me briefly before dinner (for I am a man of few words, and do not push myself forward), he spoke with me again after dinner at no great length, being himself a man of most congenial manners, and sent me away with a handsome present, which passed, as the custom is with him, in private between the two of us, so as to spare the recipient any embarrassment or jealousy. This happened at Lambeth; and while we were returning thence by boat, as the custom is there, Grocyn asked me as we sailed along how big a present he had given me. I named a very large sum, by way of a joke. He laughed, and I asked him why: Did he not think the archbishop was the sort of man who would be ready to give so much? Was he too poor to bear the expense of such generosity? Did my work not deserve some very handsome present? At length I confessed the amount of the gift; and when I asked him jokingly why he had given me so little, he replied under pressure that it was nothing to do with any of my reasons; but the suspicion had told against me that I might perhaps have dedicated the same work elsewhere to someone else. This took me aback; and when I asked him what on earth could have put that idea into his head, he laughed (and a mirthless laugh it was) and said 'It is the sort of thing you people do,' suggesting that men like myself make a habit of it. This barbed shaft remained fixed in my mind, which was not used to such two-edged remarks. So as soon as I reached Paris, intending to go on from there to Italy, I gave the book to Bade[10] to be printed, adding the *Iphigeneia in Aulis*, which I had translated more fully and freely while I was in England; and though I had offered the archbishop only one play, I dedicated both to him. Thus I took the sting out of that remark of Grocyn's, though at the time I had no intention to revisit England and no thoughts of another approach to the archbishop; such was my pride in those days, however empty my pocket. This work underwent two or three revisions; and I have revised it finally this year.

As a young man not yet eighteen, being weaker in elegiacs, I began to write rhetorical pieces in that form against the vices – lechery, avarice, and ambition. These frivolous things were put out in print by my friends when I was far away, not without some damage to my reputation, and they would have published more had I not returned. A poem written entirely on the spur of the moment to greet Philip on his first return from Spain was published on my own responsibility, some three and twenty years ago if I mistake not.[11] A long time before that, I had published some verses in a mixture of heroic hexameters and iambic trimeters in praise of King Henry VII and his children,[12] and also of Britain itself. This was three days' work; but work it really was, for it was now some years since I had either read or written anything in verse. It was extracted from me partly by embarrassment, partly by irritation. I had been carried off by Thomas More, who had come to pay me a visit on an estate of Mountjoy's,[13] where I was then staying, to take a walk by way of diversion as far as the nearest town; for that was where all the royal children were being brought up, except only Arthur, who at that time was the eldest. When we reached the court, there was a solemn gathering not only of that household but of Mountjoy's as well. In the middle stood Henry, who was then nine years old and already looked somehow like a natural king, displaying a noble spirit combined with peculiar courtesy. On his right was Margaret, then perhaps eleven, who afterwards married James, king of Scots. On the left was Mary, a playful child of four; Edmund was still a babe in arms. More and his friend Arnold greeted the boy Henry, under whose rule England now flourishes, and gave him something he had written. I was expecting nothing of the kind and, having nothing to produce, I promised that some day I would prove my devotion to him somehow. At the time I was slightly indignant with More for not having warned me, all the more so as during dinner the boy sent me a note, calling on me to write something. I went home, and even in despite of the Muses, from whom I had lived apart so long, I finished a poem within three days. Thus I got the better of my annoyance and cured my embarrassment. There was published also a poem comprising elementary instruction for the individual Christian. This was written in a very simple style; for those were my instructions from John Colet, who just then had founded a new school at great expense, in which he meant the children to be educated and brought up in religion as well as book-learning.[14] As a man of exceptional wisdom, faced with the lamentable state of the times, he chose out the younger generation, that he might pour Christ's new wine into new bottles.

I had begun to translate *Podagra*, the first of Lucian's two pieces on the gout, a most amusing work, but gave it up, deterred mainly by the epithets in which the choruses are so rich; for in them there was no hope of reproducing in Latin the happy formation of compound words so noticeable in the Greek vocabulary, while had I expressed each Greek word in several Latin ones, the point of the whole poem would be lost. For religious hymns often consist of such compound epithets of the gods put together in a traditional way, especially in Greece. Of this kind are Homer's

> Ares all-power-surpassing, chariot-burdening, golden-helmed,
> Mighty-spirited, shield-uprearing, city-guardian, brazen-armed,

or Lucian's

> Bandage-fancier bedward-sender
> Gait-obstructer joint-tormentor
> Ankle-burner tender-stepper
> Pestle-fearer knee-lamenting-sleep-destroyer
> Knuckle-chalkstone-devotee
> Knee-excruciator.

These words and others like them are most attractive in Greek because of the scope they give for humorous imitation, but the Latin language could not produce a pale reflection of them. Of Greek I had a taste as a boy, and returned to it when I was already grown up, thirty years old in fact more or less, but at a time when we had no supply of Greek books and no less a shortage of teachers. In Paris there was only one man, Georgius Hermonymus,[15] who had a smattering of Greek, and he was the sort of man who would not have known how to teach had he wanted to, nor wished to had he known how. Finding myself obliged therefore to be my own teacher, I translated many of Lucian's essays to make myself at least read the Greek with attention: *Saturnalia, Cronosolon, Epistolae Saturnales, De luctu*, the *Declamatio de abdicato, Icaromenippus, Toxaris, Pseudomantis, Gallus, Timon*, the *Declamatio pro tyrannicida, De his qui mercede vivunt in aulis principum*; besides these, a selection of eighteen from his shorter dialogues, and in addition the *Hercules Gallicus, Eunuchus, De sacrificiis, Convivium* and *De astrologia*. Pieces of this kind I used at different times as a sort of modest new-year's present to greet my friends, as the English custom is. I had also translated his *Longaevi*, only dictating a draft; but my amanuensis purloined it and published it at Paris with a dedication to Mountjoy as his own work. These trifles were snapped up at first by those who wished to learn, and warmly welcomed; but when the knowledge of Greek began to be widely shared, as happened most successfully in our part of the world, they began to fall into neglect, which I knew of course would happen, and am very glad it has happened. I attempted the same thing in the *Moralia* of Plutarch, whose style is somewhat more difficult, and there is more obscurity in this matter, owing to his out-of-the-way learning. These exercises I enjoyed all the more because they contributed substantially to the building of character no less than to the learning of Greek; for I have read nothing outside Scripture with such a high moral tone. There was this one inconvenience, that Aldus printed Plutarch's work from a copy which was corrupt in many places,[16] nor was there any supply of ancient copies within my reach. I made a version of one declamation by Libanius, put in the mouth of Menelaus, who is asking the Trojans to return his wife, and this was my first experiment in translation. I also rendered some other short declamations of uncertain authorship.

I have written several things designed to be of use in education, among which are two books, *Copia: Foundations of the Abundant Style*,[17] which I sketched long ago as a pastime rather than started, to please John Colet, who with great importunity forced rather than persuaded me to dedicate a new work to his new school.[18] At his request I also corrected a small book by Lily,[19] whom he had made high master of his school, on syntax; but I made so many changes that Lily was unwilling to take responsibility for the work, nor could I do so. To please Pierre Vitré, a friend out of the common albeit of lower degree, I wrote the little book *On the Method of Study*,[20] he having the task of educating several well-born boys of great promise. To this class perhaps belong the first two books of the grammar of Theodorus Gaza,[21] which I turned into Latin in hopes of attracting more people to the study of Greek, baiting the hook as it were by making it so easy; and the work I put into it, such as it was, was so successful that it already seems unnecessary. I had also made some notes, for the benefit of a certain Englishman, on the theory of letter-writing,[22] but with no thought of publication. After his death, I saw the work, mutilated as it was and full of mistakes, published in England, and so was obliged to waste a few days on trifles of that kind, which I really wished might be suppressed, had that been possible. There had also appeared a small book of *Colloquies*,[23] pieced together partly from familiar conversation and partly from my notes, but with a certain amount of nonsense thrown in which was not only foolish but bad Latin and simply packed with blunders; and this worthless piece was given a surprisingly warm welcome – such a game does fortune play, here as everywhere. So here was more nonsense to which I was obliged to devote some labour. At length, by taking more than ordinary pains, I added a good deal, to bring it up to the right size for a book and make it at least seem to deserve the honour of a dedication to Johann Froben's son, Johannes Erasmius, who was then a boy of six and astonishingly gifted. That was in the year 1522. However, a book of this kind is naturally open to receive additions as often as one pleases. So, for the benefit of those who wish to learn and of Johann Froben, I have frequently supplied further matter already, always so managing my subjects that, besides agreeable reading and the advantage of improving the reader's style, there might be some contribution to the formation of character as well.

And to be sure, as long as there was nothing in that book but the merest trifles, it found surprising favour on all sides. When it began to be useful in many ways, it could not escape the poison-fangs of slander. A certain divine in Louvain,[24] who is physically purblind and mentally even more so, detected in it four passages that were heretical. This book had another experience worthy of record. It was printed lately in Paris after the correction, which means of course the disfigurement, of several passages which were thought to glance at monks, vows, pilgrimages, indulgences, and other things of the kind which, if they were to have the greatest influence with the public, would mean larger profits for that party.[25] Even in this he displayed such folly and such ignorance that you would swear it was the work of some itinerant buffoon, though the author of this tedious comedy is reported to be a theologian of the Dominican order, Saxon by birth. There is little point in adding his name and designation, which he himself makes no attempt to conceal. Such a monster does not know what it is to be ashamed; he is more likely to expect credit for his misdemeanours. ...

I perceived that many authors were either entirely neglected or read with very little profit because they were full of errors everywhere, and further, that some of them were in addition more defaced than expounded by the most witless commentaries. And so there too I set myself to do what I could for the studies of the young and, following the Greek proverb, did not try my prentice hand on potting a great jar but started with the school-book they call the *Cato*.[26] To this I added the *Mimi Publiani*, which are witty enough, to be sure, but were lying concealed among Seneca's works under a false title,[27] and not only teeming with corruptions but defiled by the admixture of many maxims which did not belong to the author. All these I provided with notes. I also added certain other pieces, after revising them, too small to deserve record here if judged by the labour I spent on them. In this class one should perhaps also place Ovid's *Nux*, which I emended and explained in a brief commentary for the benefit of a young man of great promise, John More,[28] and to that I added two hymns of Prudentius, one celebrating the birth and the other the epiphany of the child Jesus. These too I cleaned up and expounded in brief notes to oblige an honourable young lady by name Margaret Roper.[29] This was in 1524. I attempted something similar with Aldus, after the appearance of my *Proverbia*, on all the comedies of Terence and Plautus; but here my avowed purpose was no more than the rearrangement of the lines, which were in great confusion, wherever it might have been possible. Then the same on Seneca's tragedies, in which I felt I had made a few successful corrections, but not without the help of ancient codices.

After these preliminary exercises, I addressed myself to the New Testament, in which I had made up my mind to be so sparing of words that my plan was to write notes in two or three words on every passage, especially as I had already issued Lorenzo's critical work,[30] which seemed to me more long-winded than the subject requires. None the less, when Froben was already set to print my work, scholarly friends, to whom I sometimes defer more than I should, moved me actually to alter the Vulgate text, and to be rather fuller in my annotations. This work of mine provoked a great many men to the study either of Greek or of a purer form of theology; but at the same time the reputation it earned me was leavened with much ill will. Here too I soon paid penalties that were by no means light, either for my audacity or for my undue readiness to follow my friends' wishes rather than my own judgment. With incredible labour I remade the whole work and sent it again to the printer. Once again I have taken it in hand, for the third time, and supplemented it most carefully, in the year 1522, and this is the latest edition I have yet published. But I have a fourth ready, having discovered while writing the paraphrases many things that had previously escaped me.

Then again, I took Jerome's letters, which stand so high in both scholarship and style but were current in a most corrupt text, and corrected them with explanatory notes, separating what is spurious with critical comment. This work I went over a second time in the year 1522, with corrections or additions in not a few places where something had escaped me in the earlier edition. This was printed a second time in the year 1524. In this labour I acquitted myself so well that an attentive reader will easily see that in undertaking this revision my time was not wasted. In this I did not lack ancient codices, but they could not protect me in a number of places from the need to conjecture. These conjectures however I put forward with such moderation in my notes that no one could easily be led astray by them, but that the reader's interest might merely be aroused to pursue the trail. And I hope to see someone with the help of more correct copies restoring other passages which eluded me; I shall gladly pay their industry the tribute it deserves, and at the same time they will have no call to criticize my attempts for, though I made many successful restorations, I was obliged in certain passages to make my own the old Greek proverb, 'As best I could, not as I would.'

For some men are disposed by nature, if they can add to the efforts of their predecessors, to claim the whole credit for themselves; and they pursue the other man with a torrent of abuse if they find him nodding or if in any place he has not achieved what he was trying to do. In such people I for my part know not which to think more abominable, their unkindness or their ingratitude. No one has stood in their way if they wish to produce something nearer perfection.

But I perceive, my dear Botzheim, that you have been recalling me for some time now to my catalogue. Suetonius Tranquillus[31] – I collated with a codex of astonishing antiquity, and restored with some success a number of passages which no one had previously noticed. I have done the same with the works of Cyprian.[32] I have also revised the commentary of Arnobius on the Psalms, a work which I dedicated to Adrian VI,[33] who had then been lately elected pope. I did the same for Hilary, who set me some surprising problems; and these efforts I offered to Jean Carondelet, archbishop of Palermo and chancellor of the emperor Charles in Brabant.[34] Besides these, when I considered the important contribution made to elegance and richness of style by brilliant aphorisms, apt metaphors, proverbs, and similar figures of speech, I made up my mind to collect the largest possible supply of such things from approved authors of every sort and arrange them each in its appropriate class, to make them more accessible to those who wish to practise composition with a view to securing a rich and ready diction. In this field I made an experiment, if I mistake not, twenty-seven years ago.[35] The occasion was this. On the beach at Dover, before going on board ship, all my supply of money suffered shipwreck; this was in those days small enough, but it meant a great deal to me, for it was all I had. The agent in this was the officer (I almost said the pirate) in charge of the coast in the king's name, though More and Mountjoy convinced me that there was no risk unless I were exporting English coin; and I had no English currency and no money either earned or given me in England. On the beach, however, I learned that it was illegal to export any coin whatever, even iron coin, to a higher value than six angels.[36] Such was the price I paid for my first and last lesson in English law. When I had returned to Paris with an empty purse, I did not doubt that many people expected me to avenge this misfortune with my pen, as men of letters normally do, by writing something to arouse feeling either against the king or against England; and I feared at the same time that William Mountjoy, having brought about the situation in which I lost my money, might suspect that my feelings towards him were changing. I had to disappoint them, or rather, I had to show, clearly that I was not so prejudiced as to blame my private mishap on a whole country or so thoughtless as for so small a loss to call down either on myself or on the friends I had left in England the resentment of so great a prince; at the same time I had to prove to my friend Mountjoy that my feelings of friendship towards him had not changed in the least. And so I decided to publish something forthwith. Having nothing ready at hand, I accumulated at random from a few days' reading some sort of a collection of adages, guessing that this book, such as it was, might find a welcome among those who wish to learn, at least for its utility. This I used as evidence that my friendship had not grown cold. Then I added the poem I have already mentioned, to show that I bore no ill will against either the king or the country for the confiscation of my money; and this plan of mine was not unsuccessful, for such a moderate and fair-minded attitude won me many friends at the time in England, good scholars and men of high character and position. This slight work was printed a few years later by my friend Bade[37] with a few additions and revisions by me mainly from Greek sources, and later in Strasbourg by Matthias Schürer,[38] although I had meanwhile put together a more abundant supply for a Venice edition, which was published by the house of Aldus. Moreover, as I saw that this work was so popular with keen students that it was clearly destined for a long life and was being published in competition by many printers, I enriched it repeatedly as either leisure or a larger supply of books became available. The latest revision was published by Johann Froben[39] in the year of our Lord 1523. Besides which, in rereading a number of authors in order to enrich my *Adages*, I noted down many parallels on the side, more pointing the way and setting others an example of a work to come than finishing a book with the necessary care. This makes one book of *Parallels*, addressed to Pieter Gillis, lawyer and citizen of Antwerp, who was once the companion of my studies.[40]

Perhaps it will not be out of place if I subjoin to this class of work my correspondence, although in all my output there is nothing I like less. In this department I have been over-responsive to the wishes of my friends, particularly as with changing circumstances they often turn into their opposites; but on this point I have already gone on record fully enough in the first letter of the latest edition, which appeared from Froben's press in 1521. What I then conjectured, I learned afterwards from actual experience only too well. The facts themselves testify that some men who were once my sworn friends – as true, I might have said, as any Pylades[41] – have become my bitterest enemies, combining deepest ingratitude with deepest perfidy, for no other reason except that I would not lend my name to a perilous enterprise, which I always foresaw would end in disastrous discord. Yet I have never broken off a friendship with anyone because he was either more inclined towards Luther or more against Luther than I was. My disposition is naturally such that I could love even a Jew,[42] provided he were in other respects an agreeable person to live with and friendly, and provided he did not vomit blasphemies against Christ in my hearing. And this courteous approach can, I believe, do more towards ending strife. I am, to be sure, only slightly moved when those who used to describe me in print as the sun of Germany, the prince of true theology and the champion of sound learning, now find me of less worth than seaweed; for those pompous titles, which I always disliked, I gladly hand back to them. But the ties of friendship I do not readily abandon to please anyone.

I also tried my hand at the art of declamation, for which I was by nature more fitted than for those collections of materials, although some inclination urged me strongly in that direction.

And so I amused myself in early days with a panegyric on marriage. This I did for the benefit of a distinguished young man, William Mountjoy, whom I was then grounding in rhetoric. I asked him whether he liked what I had written. 'Yes,' he merrily replied. 'I like it so much that you have quite persuaded me to get married.' ... But in early youth, when I was hardly twenty, I had written in the same style the *Praise of the Monastic Life* to please a friend who was laying traps for a nephew of his, whom he hoped to lure as a proselyte into his net. ... *The Complaint of Peace*[43] I wrote about seven years ago, when first invited to join the prince's court ...

I wrote my light-hearted *Praise of Folly* while staying with Thomas More, having at that time returned from Italy – a work of which I thought so little that I did not even reckon it worth publication (for I was myself in Paris when it was seen through the press by Richard Croke,[44] very badly printed and full of errors), in spite of which hardly anything of mine has had a more enthusiastic reception, especially among the great. A few monks only, and those the worst, together with some unusually squeamish theologians, took offence at its freedom; but more were offended when Listrius added notes,[45] for before that moment it had gained from not being understood. I had at that time conceived the idea of three simultaneous declamations, in praise of Folly, Nature, and Grace; but some people I could name proved so difficult that I changed my mind. It was as the merest youth that I began *The Antibarbarians*,[46] for this too belongs, I consider, to the class of declamations. And although even among the works I have listed there are several which relate to the theory of the good life, those I shall now mention were written by me as a serious contribution to orderly and godly living. Among these is the *Panegyricus* which I offered to Prince Philip[47] on his first return from Spain; for though I praised him, praise was combined with the reminder of the objects to be observed by a good prince, as I showed clearly enough in the letter to Jean Desmarez,[48] which I then added to the work. Then there was the short book *The Education of a Christian Prince*,[49] which I offered to the emperor Charles (as he now is) when I had recently been summoned to join the staff of the prince's court and serve as one of his councillors. So in this way I first entered on the duties of a trusty councillor. 'Right trusty' is a conventional epithet of councillors, though most princes like nothing less than those who are really trustworthy, and most councillors do nothing to live up to their description. And yet none of the great men took offence at the freedom of this book, small as it was. Good princes tolerate freedom in their advisers; it is facetious licence that they cannot stand.

*The Handbook of the Christian Soldier* I began about thirty years ago,[50] when I was lodging in the castle of Tournehem, to which I had been driven by the plague that was then raging in Paris. It started by accident. I had in the castle a friend, whom I shared with Batt.[51] He had a wife of a deeply religious turn of mind, while he himself was no man's enemy but his own – a spendthrift, plunged in fornication and adultery, but in other respects a pleasant companion in every way. For all theologians he had the greatest contempt, except for me. The wife was fearfully concerned for her husband's salvation, and she approached me through Batt to ask if I would write something that might get a little religion into the man; but on condition that he must not know that this was his wife's initiative, for he was cruel even to her, to the extent of beating her, as soldiers will. I did as she asked and jotted down something appropriate to the situation. This won the approval even of good scholars, particularly Jean Vitrier,[52] a Franciscan who was the great authority in those parts; and when the plague, which was raging everywhere, had again driven me from Paris, this time to Louvain, I finished it at leisure. For some time my piece attracted no notice. After that, it began to sell surprisingly well. And this year, in 1524 that is, I have published my *Exomologesis*, or On the principles of confessing offences to a priest.

I also attempted greater things: I made an explanation by way of paraphrase of Paul's Epistle to the Romans. After this, encouraged to go progressively further by the success of my rash attempt and the urging of my friends, I completed paraphrases on all the apostolic Epistles. This work not being a continuous effort but finished at intervals, in such a way that as each section was completed I determined to refrain from more of the kind, the result was that, contrary to my usual practice, the whole was not dedicated to any individual. Later, encouraged by Matthäus, the cardinal of Sion,[53] I attempted the same thing, not long ago, for Matthew. This piece of work I dedicated to the emperor Charles, who was, I know, much pleased with the result of my efforts. I had already ceased to think about making paraphrases when, being unexpectedly recalled to this field by many friends, I completed the paraphrase on John, for John more than anyone makes many difficulties which hold up the reader. Nor was I allowed to stop there: there began to be a demand for Luke, for there are many things in him which he shares with no other evangelist – so easy was it to find some excuse for asking. This work was dedicated to the English king, Henry VIII. The addition of Mark was then suggested to me by an eminent friend, that a gap in the middle of the work might not tempt someone to interrupt its uniformity by adding something of his own. This was dedicated to Francis I, king of France. There remained the Acts of the Apostles, part of St Luke's Gospel, and those I dedicated to Pope Clement VII.[54] The Apocalypse on no account admits of paraphrase. And so at this point my paraphrases reached a fairly successful conclusion; nor has any other work of mine earned me less unpopularity than they have. I have also written a commentary on two psalms, being invited to undertake this by urgent demands from certain quarters. Here, however, I am deterred not only by the size and difficulty of the work but by the multitude of commentators, such that there is a risk of their burying the message rather than explaining it. The third psalm at any rate I expounded in paraphrase, to please a learned friend, Melchior Vianden.[55] I also wrote a paraphrase on the Lord's Prayer, at the request of Jost or Justus Weissenburg,[56] secretary of the king of Poland. I have lately finished the *Sermon on the Mercy of the Lord*, for which I was asked by that saintly prelate Christopher, bishop of Basel, who had dedicated a chapel under that name,[57] and at the same time the *Comparison between Virgin and Martyr*, asked for by a man of high character, Helias, warden of the College of Maccabeites in Cologne.[58] The *Homily on the Child Jesus* I had written long before at the request of John Colet.[59] My *Method of True Theology*, which had already gone through several editions, I revised and enlarged in the year 1522, and again in the following year.[60]

For my part, I had formed the habit of boasting that, although I had written so much, both light-hearted and serious, I had never yet attacked any mortal man in print by name; but some evil genius grudged me this enviable reputation. Not but what I have maintained my record of not writing to hurt to the extent of never drawing sword against anyone except under insufferable provocation; nor have I ever answered anyone without overcoming by forbearance an adversary who had the advantage of me in scurrility. This is, I think, so clear from my publications that I have the right to claim this much credit without being criticized for boasting. At first it was my whole ambition to be attacked by no one and attack no one myself, and so ply my pen with a light heart without ever drawing blood. But in this I was doubly disappointed: first because I was indeed attacked by many people most unpleasantly in published books, and even by those to whom I had never given any cause; and secondly, because they were men whom I could win no credit by defeating, while there was no honour – no profit, even – in being matched against such creatures. Whenever therefore I am driven to it, I remain laconic, I glance at the question in the fewest possible words. Nor have I ever dedicated any such piece of mine to any fellow creature: sometimes I neither expected nor wished them to survive, sometimes I was unwilling to burden anyone with unpopularity, for I have tried hard all my life to see that no trouble recoils from me onto my friends. Maarten van Dorp,[61] at the instigation of certain people I could name, opened the very first of these minor attacks on me; and I replied to him as one friend to another, defending my *Praise of Folly* and the New Testament together in a single letter. Nor did this cavalry skirmish cause any rift in our friendship, for I knew that he did not stoop to this from any dislike of me, but was young in those days and impressionable and was pushed into it by others. He was followed by Jacques Lefèvre d'Etaples,[62] an honest man, a good scholar, and an old friend of mine. In reply to him I took the line that I preferred to suppose this a necessity, for which fate and not the individual was responsible; and this incident, serious as it was, did not lead me to renounce my friendship with him – even today the mutual good will between us subsists unimpaired. Over this I lost twelve days' work. And not long after, up jumped Edward Lee,[63] a friend turned suddenly into an enemy, whose attack on me showed by its form that he was not interested in taking prisoners but wished to see Erasmus annihilated; and him I answered in three pamphlets, though in the second edition I left out the first of these because it merely answered his poisonous, quarrelsome tirades, worthy of any fishwife, from which the reader could derive neither profit nor pleasure. On this, with the writing and the printing (for I corrected every page myself), I wasted fifty days, as I have witnesses to prove. Then out crawled Jacobus Latomus,[64] who was at the time a candidate for the highest honours in theology, which I know not how have for some years now been awarded to hardly anyone in Louvain unless he has first published a sample of his powers of malignant invention. To his book, since in its twists and turns it reflected its author's mind, I issued a more than laconic reply, refraining for the time being even from any expression of feeling, for in those days I hoped that he would sometime adopt more straightforward behaviour. This meant a loss of three days, not counting the time taken to read his pamphlets while I was travelling by carriage. They had also pressed Atensis[65] to their cause; he was at that time vice-chancellor of the university there, an honourable man and in theology the best person they have, a not uncivilized person and a fairly good friend of mine, but irascible by nature. And there were experts there who, although capable of driving the mildest nature into a frenzy, urged him at least on to his death; for his age and state of health were not equal to the burden of such sorry business. They had put him up, as I say, in a public lecture-room, on a solemn university occasion, to reflect on me with the most extraordinary innuendo and indirect attacks, actually labelling me a heretic because (so he said) I had spoken too highly of the estate of matrimony. On this point he had already given me satisfaction, first by sending Maarten van Dorp and Gillis van Delft to talk to me on the subject,[66] and then in friendly conversation with himself. Later on therefore, when I published a reply, it was addressed not to Atensis but to the suspicions of men in general, and more in his interest than my own. And because there was a plot behind all this, one disturbance succeeded another; for they thought that if they could thus drive me out of the university, all the ancient languages and the humanities would be off too and never be heard of again. About the same time a clamour was raised against me by monks at London in England, at Paris in France, and at Brussels in Brabant, and raised in sermons before crowded audiences, because I had put *In principio erat sermo* in my version instead of *In principio erat verbum*.[67] This disturbance too I suppressed with a pamphlet, making it clear that the authors of the uproar were simply insane, though that was clear enough to educated people even before I uttered a word. The very first person to attack my version of the New Testament had been an obscure man[68] whom I thought sufficiently answered in a letter which did not mention his name.

And now it seemed that we should hear no more of this trouble, when lo and behold in Spain, all of a sudden, up jumps Diego López Zúñiga[69] – what sort of a man is clear from what he writes: boastful, shameless, stupid, a great admirer of his own perfections, and a bitter controversialist, born, one might think, for just such sorry business. Rumour of something frightful had preceded, and the book itself was full of extraordinary delusions. I answered him briefly, and never so much disliked answering anyone. He proceeded to Rome to enjoy the triumphs of his exquisite performance, and again put out an attack on me, which he entitled *Erasmus' Blasphemies and Impieties* – the maddest thing that ever appeared. As a result, the order of cardinals had forbidden its printing; and when none the less it was printed secretly by certain monks, who regard the pope's authority as sacrosanct when it happens to suit them, they again forbade the sale. Scarcely had I answered him, briefly and with the contempt that he deserved, when another pamphlet took the air, a forerunner of those three in which, like a leading actor, he left no doubt of his prowess in scurrility. So I answered that one too, by the oil of the same lamp, as the saying goes. A brother stood at his right hand, one Sancho Carranza, a theologian of Alcalá,[70] to defend Zúñiga at least in the three passages which he had chosen and, in the process of trying to make me out a heretic, to advertise his own effrontery as a traducer. His pamphlet too I answered. And Rome finds readers for such trash as this! Some people must read it, for some buy it, though there is hardly anywhere there where you can find on sale the works of the Fathers, which make for true religion. In fact, plenty of people believe it right for the standing of the church to be defended by such support as this; and though the chief point in their program is that the constitutions of the Roman pontiff should carry weight everywhere, he shows in fact what respect they deserve from other nations by so often making game of the edicts of popes and cardinals in Rome itself with impunity. They tell you ... that Zúñiga is tolerated in Rome as Pasquil is.[71] Pasquil is not so mad as that, and he performs only once a year. This man neglects everything else and makes this his sole business; and this he thinks a piece of rare good fortune. Of Carranza I hear nothing, but Zúñiga is hard at work even now. He ranges up and down, collecting support, and is pressing the pope for leave to publish those three famous pamphlets with official approval. Personally I am astonished at some men's abandoned impudence: they take it upon themselves to attack with great virulence those who are working for the benefit of others, they are so often detected in barefaced errors, and yet, as though they had won the day, they take the field again and deliberately challenge their opponents. They offer no excuses in the meantime; they continue to throw mud at other people. I myself at least, if anything of the sort had happened to me, should hide my head in solitude, and be ashamed to take the stage again before a learned audience. The man who errs while trying to be helpful secures our forgiveness; but who can pardon those who make the most disgraceful errors in the course of an attack on a fellow creature? Zúñiga had published the first fruits of his malevolence at Alcalá; but when such a book found few buyers, he carried off his wares to Rome like any bagman. When Pope Leo refused him leave to publish the rest of his trumped-up accusations, he put out some things after the pope's death during the interregnum,[72] as I said, and would have published more, had not an edict of the cardinals restricted him more than once; for Adrian hung about for several months in Spain before proceeding to Rome. Then, after a vain attempt to get leave, from Adrian this time, to publish what he had written, as soon as the pope was dead[73] he returned to his tricks and, while the cardinals were behind closed doors and fighting over the choice of a new pope, he issued a number of conclusions which he had extracted from the whole range of my work, and was meanwhile getting ready to bring the rest before the public. And so he would have done, had not the authority of Clement VII suppressed the man, who by this time was clearly raving mad. To this book likewise I wrote a brief reply, although I had already answered before.

There is in Louvain in the theological faculty a certain Carmelite[74] who has a habit of boasting that he uses his tongue rather than his pen; and a tongue he most certainly has, though it is only fit for the purpose suggested by Catullus.[75] This man's pastime, over his wine, in the theology lecture-room and even in public sermons, is to call me a heretic; and he makes such good progress that all sane men now despair of his sanity. His example is followed by several others, who think it is quite enough to give them the air of eminent divines if they call anyone they please a heretic, a schismatic, or a forger, as though any cart-driver could not do the same. This man publicly, in his ordinary lectures, accused me of two trifling misdemeanours, heresy and falsification of the Scriptures. ... This sort of rubbish is unloaded every day by a man advanced in years who is the leading spirit of the Louvain theologians; and then they wonder that the pope's policy makes so little progress, when such are the men and methods used to carry it out! Men worthy indeed to be supported by the world in idleness! A theologian of great authority, who well deserves that intelligent citizens should entrust their children to him! For he has taken upon himself the additional office of protecting the multitudes from the humanities. He has here a boon companion, another man who has spent sleepless nights composing an attack on me,[76] which he means to publish, if he could find a vicar-general of his order as mad as he is. Nothing has done more to make Luther acceptable to the world than the characters of such men as this.

And it seemed already that controversy was over, had not Ulrich von Hutten arisen, suddenly and quite unexpectedly, a friend turned all at once into an enemy;[77] such is the power of malignant gossip over men who have no ballast. No one ever attacked me with more hostility than he; and yet I intended not to answer, had not influential friends judged that my reputation was at stake. And so I published my *Sponge*, the title of which already promised that I would write with moderation, though some people think I did nothing of the kind; while I can say with a clear conscience that I strove really hard to reflect on no one in passing while defending myself, and did my best to spare Hutten himself so far as the subject permitted. Those who wish Hutten's reputation to be universally watertight should reserve their indignation for the men whose falsehoods drove him into this position, and still more for those (but really they are the same people) who use all their endeavours to make me take pen in hand against a man even when he is dead. This however they shall never force me to; to be raving mad is not to my taste, and I perceive that this business has now issued in mere madness. And so I have no mind henceforward to take issue with prizefighting pamphlets of this kind. My first effort shall be to keep my conscience clear in the sight of Christit, and I trust that the reasons behind my policy will be endorsed by all men of good will. As for those noisy ruffians who seem quite unaware of the difference between writing and raving, I for my part would rather do them a mischief in deeds than in words, if a Christian could wish to hurt anyone at all. Those who represent my *Sponge* as vindictive and insolent will please remember one thing: the special affection I had for Hutten's gifts, the generosity with which I recommended him to the public in so many of my publications when he was not yet well known, and all the letters in which I praised him to my friends, and specially to the cardinal of Mainz.[78] In one particular letter I compare him with Thomas More, the most upright, fair-minded, friendly, intelligent man on whom the sun has shone for many generations. How emphatically unlike him Hutten has shown himself, and falsified my praise of him! In my work on the New Testament, which is now in its third edition, I sing his praises with no ordinary warmth. Will they please remember something else: I never gave him any cause to withdraw from our friendship (and friendship ought not to be severed without very grave cause), and furthermore it was he who not only breached the laws of friendship but delivered the most bitter attacks out of a kind of ambush on the reputation and life of his friend. The facts absolutely speak for themselves: Hutten had no other purpose in writing against me as he did except to assassinate with his pen one whom his sword could not reach. Regarding himself as a man of valour, 'He is a poor old man,' he thought, 'he is an invalid, he is frightened and feeble; he will not be long for this world when he reads such a savage attack.' That those were his thoughts was shown by the vaunting words he used.

I will now appeal to the honest opinion of those who knew Hutten at close quarters, though even men who were acquainted with him are aware that he always lived a soldier's life, to use no harsher term; and yet all through my *Sponge* I never cast in his teeth that lascivious living which not even his pitiful disease could teach him to abandon, nor the gaming and the wenching, the bankruptcy brought on by his extravagance, the massive debts, the disappointed creditors. And then the outrages he planned – the extortion of money from the Carthusians, the mutilation of several monks, the assaults on the public highway on three abbots (a crime for which one of his servants was seized and beheaded by the Count Palatine)[79] – these, I say, and very many others of the sort are public knowledge everywhere; but I revive none of these old sores in the *Sponge*, nor do I answer an enemy's fire by charging him with true and notorious crimes though he has brazenly poured such a cesspit of utterly false accusations on a friend, and one moreover who has done him service. In my whole *Sponge* no one is reviled as a robber or a ravisher, a highwayman or a bankrupt. What I say there in general terms aims not at the denigration of any single man but at the good of all. And some people find me savage in the *Sponge*! ... It has not escaped me that this was the strategy of some men I could name who falsely boast themselves to be champions of the gospel – to overwhelm me with frenzied pamphlets to stop me from making any move against Luther. Let them suppose that I have been stoned to death: will they at once be more successful? They do not stop to consider how much harm I could have done, and still can do, to their cause if I had as great a passion for vengeance as they have for violence. Who would not recognize in this that spirit of the gospel which the world has not seen for a thousand years? Very well: let it be gospel teaching that we should pour frenzied scurrilities upon the guilty. When it comes to discharging barefaced lies on those who are quite innocent, does this too follow the gospel pattern? The physician in the gospel pours wine into the wounds, but he pours in oil as well, and it is wine not vinegar. Some of these men pour in not wine but deadly poison. They kill no man with the sword, but more villainously with tongue and pen.

And yet they have nothing they can bring against me except that I am reluctant to risk my own neck by professing beliefs which I do not hold, or regard as doubtful, or reject, and which would do no good if I did profess them. Apart from that, has anyone been a more active opponent in print of putting one's trust in ceremonies; of superstition concerning food and liturgy and prayer; of those who give more weight to human inventions than to Holy Scripture, who value the decrees of man more than the commandments of God, who put more trust in the saints than in Christ himself; of academic theology, corrupted as it is by philosophic and scholastic quibbling; of the rash practice of laying down rules for every mortal thing; of the topsy-turvy judgments of the multitude? How far I am from flattery of princes, even the greatest of them, my books are enough to show. This, and very much else, which I have taught according to the measure of grace accorded me, I have taught steadfastly, but never standing in the way of any man who had something better to teach. And they say Erasmus has taught nothing but rhetoric! I wish they would persuade my friends of that, the foolish babblers, who steadfastly maintain that all Luther's teaching has been drawn from what I have written. Not that I grudge Luther any credit on that score; he is welcome to the whole of it, provided the gospel is glorified. My misdeeds amount to this: I am all for moderation, and the reason why I have a bad name with both sides is that I exhort both parties to adopt a more peaceable policy. Freedom I have no objection to, if it is seasoned with charity. But this mad-dog scurrility can produce nothing but sedition and bloodshed. If we speak ill of the Roman church, and Rome in turn advertises what we have done wrong, this will surely provide an agreeable spectacle for the enemies of our religion. Clement professes himself ready to heal the corruption of the church; he dispatches a legate who is as fair-minded and civilized as one could wish – and all they do is to abuse him, as though what they really enjoyed was universal chaos. On their head be it, if the princes at length lose all patience and start venting their fury without distinction on the livelihood and lives of most of us. If that happens, I fear some people will approve my moderate policy, and it will be too late. Who can endure certain men on that side whom I could name who, using the gospel as a pretext, obey neither princes nor popes, and do not listen to Luther himself except when it suits them? On all other occasions they regard even Luther as a mere man led by no inspiration, or consider that he did not mean what he said. My offence is rank indeed if I merely wish to see what is now done in a subversive spirit done without subversion and with the consent of princes. But if the princes seem unlikely to act for the best, what crime have I committed if I warn them? I do not restrain those who wish to put out the fire; but I do condemn those who pour oil on the flames and are in a great hurry to remove by violent drugs a disease which has by now grown chronic over a thousand years and more, to the very great peril of the whole body. The apostles showed toleration to the Jews, who could not be weaned away from their ingrained taste for the Law;[80] and the same, I believe, they would rightly show to these men who for so many centuries have accepted the authority of all those councils and popes and distinguished teachers, and find some difficulty in swallowing the new wine of this modern teaching. And for the time being I assume that one party is wrong and the other entirely right in what they maintain. Let both sides pursue Christ's business on Christian principles, and they will see what I have to contribute as my own humble share.

I know what you will be saying already: What has this to do with the play? You are quite right; and I return to my catalogue. In the class of defences may be included the letter which I lately wrote to that paragon of all the gifts proper to a prelate, Christopher, bishop of Basel,[81] on the eating of meat; which nevertheless I had not written with a view to publication. But when I found that it was in circulation and would infallibly be published by someone else, I preferred to revise it and publish it myself, especially since I was recommended to do so by some of the leading men in this university.

I will now indicate what has appeared in a mutilated state, and what is still in my hands and is not yet finished. My small work on abundance of style[82] lacks the example of a subject sketched with the greatest brevity and then treated a second time at full length. I had chosen a topic, the need to teach children their letters from the start, and I still have it by me, but two pages in the middle written in a very minute hand went astray in Rome through the carelessness of those who had copied out the text. Of *The Antibarbarians* I had revised and enlarged two books in Bologna, and had a mass of material collected long ago for the remainder. This, and some other things with it, went astray through dishonesty, not on the part of Richard Pace,[83] my most honourable friend, with whom I had left it in Ferrara on my departure for Rome, but thanks to another man, who had too much of an eye to his own interests to be true to those of any of his friends; though later, as luck would have it, I secured from England the beginning of the second book and in Bruges the end of it, with the loss of many pages in between. If only I could find the second book, I could easily finish the rest; and I have no doubt it is lurking in some thieves' kitchen or other, for I put two copies into safe keeping.

I still have by me several things which I started long ago; among them is a commentary on Paul's Epistle to the Romans, of which I had finished four books, if I mistake not, twenty-two years ago.[84] For a work on the theory of preaching[85] I had only jotted down some divisions of the subject-matter. And yet, if Christ grants me life and tranquillity, I have a mind to finish a work on preaching, which may do some good, especially as I am urged to do so by men whose opinion carries great weight. Some time I also made an attempt to publish the entire works of St Augustine, corrected by means of ancient copies and with added notes, identifying and separating out those which pass falsely under his name. The whole corpus of his writings was divided into seven parts or volumes.

As for correspondence, I have written so much, and even today I write so much, that in future two wagons will scarcely suffice for the load. I myself acquired many by chance and burnt them, for I observed that they were preserved by many people. In Bologna I had written a brief declamation of the hortatory kind, in which I discouraged a man from adopting the religious life and then again urged him to adopt it. In my view it was worth printing, if anything of mine ever is; but the outside pages have been lost at either end, and what remains is still among my papers. When I was living in Rome, to please Raffaele, cardinal of San Giorgio, I wrote a speech against the proposal to declare war on Venice, for which he asked me in Julius' name,[86] for the question was then under discussion in the sacred college. I then put the opposite case; and the second speech won the day, although I had spent more effort on the first and written it more from the heart; through the treachery of a man I could name, the original text was lost. I have begun again to jot down some of the heads of the argument from memory, and I suppose that it is lurking somewhere among my papers. Very many things have fallen by the way which I do not regret; but I could wish that some speeches in sermon form still survived which I delivered long ago in Paris, when I was living in the Collège de Montaigu.

Such, my excellent Botzheim, is the list of my trifling productions, and I hope it may arouse you acquisitive instinct. Now, when you complain that your purse is empty because you have to buy the same book so often, I should like you to look at it like this. Suppose that my *Proverbs* [*Adages*] had just appeared for the first time, and that the moment the book was published I had died: would you have regretted your expenditure? I doubt it. Now suppose something else, that after several years I came to life again and that at the same time the book revived with me, better and fuller, would you regret what you had spent, or would you be delighted to see again both your friend and his immortal work? Now I know what you will say: 'I should be delighted to see you alive again; but none of this has really happened.'

Which then do you suppose to be the more blessed state, to rise again from the dead, or not to die? If you would be pleased to see me risen, you must be much more pleased to see me still alive. Last but not least, if the later edition contains nothing worth the extra money, you are free not to buy it; but if it does, you are making a gain and not a loss. If that earlier edition brought you good value for that small outlay, and if the later edition does the same, surely you have made two good bargains, not suffered a loss. 'You might,' you will say, 'have given us a book that was perfect in the first edition.' But it is like life: as long as we live, we are always devoted to self-improvement, and we shall not cease to make our writings more polished and more complete until we cease to breathe. No one is so good a man that he could not be made better; and no book has had so much work put into it that it cannot be made more perfect. Not but what I did myself openly admit long ago that on this point I take less trouble than I ought to; yet all the time other people make in my opinion a worse mistake who are far better scholars than I and yet, through some sort of religious scruple either publish nothing or leave it till very late. Do not hope therefore that I of all people shall relieve you of this inconvenience, until I leave the stage and once and for all utter my 'So farewell and clap your hands' to the whole lot of you (and this, believe me, would have happened shortly, had not the wine of Burgundy come to my rescue like some god from the machine); so you must make up your mind whether you would rather wish for that moment, or from time to time buy a book that has been enlarged and revised. In fact, if you recall what a lot of money you had spent on trash in the old days, you will not, I think, regret this expense quite so much. ...

Of the financial return you shall now have some account. With friends in more modest situations you know yourself how far I am from being mercenary, for after trying every means you have never been able to make me accept anything. In this context sincerity of feeling is of more value to me than any gift. In fact, while it is a question of skill either to accept gracefully or to give a courteous refusal, my friends know that it comes far more easily to me to express refusal than acceptance. And if they ever offer me anything in such a way that I cannot refuse it, I always recompense them to the utmost of my power, and go further if I can. And so from the by no means scanty offerings I have made to my more modest friends I derive the most ample satisfaction of having given them pleasure, and having joined their memory with my own in a way that may perhaps survive to posterity. As for princes, let me say at the outset that to some who have not rewarded me my debt is no less than to those who have, and to those who have rewarded me I owe the more because they did so unasked. ...

Now suppose a man surveyed the stately row of names and titles, and believed me to resemble most other men, would he not suspect that my dedications must have made me as rich as Midas?[87] I do not recall this because I have any complaints of the generosity of princes. I reckon any profit that accrues to humane studies as though it were money in my own purse; it is for their sake that I have wooed the favour of princes. And indeed, that there was nothing sordid in the way I wooed their generosity is clear from this if nothing else, that so often it has been quite hard work to be able to refuse their generosity towards me personally without hurting their feelings. My annual income is fixed at a little more than four hundred gold florins.[88] This fortune is unequal, I confess, to the expenses demanded by my age and state of health, by the assistance which my work must have in the way of servants and transcribers, by my keeping a horse, by my constant journeys, and by a spirit (to give it no other name) that will not tolerate meanness and squalor, that abhors bills unpaid, services unrequited, and friends neglected in their distress. And so I have friends who make good the shortfall in my income by their generosity, not so much giving me presents as forcing me to take them.

So much for the treasures I have accumulated by flying high in my dedications. The topic suggests that I should also throw a sop to certain trade rivals who get me a bad name among those who know no better for having reaped a generous harvest out of the munificence of Johann Froben[89] – a man of whom I think most highly, and for nothing more so than the zeal for promoting humane studies, in which he surpasses almost all other printers, and gets more reputation than profit for his pains. And I should at any rate have made no small gain out of him, had I accepted whatever he offered me; for he is most generous. As it is, he will himself bear me witness how small is the total I have let myself be forced to accept; nor would he have had even that much success, had he not explained that the money was put up by the partnership, so that the share which fell on him personally would be a very light burden. And yet, had he wished to do no more than pay for the work of my servants, he would have had to give me more than I received. Nor did I allow my meals at his table to cost me nothing. I lived in his house nearly ten months, and for this I forced him to accept 150 gold florins,[90] against great reluctance; for he would rather have paid me as much again, but I forced him. And that no one may suppose me dependent on Froben's generosity, Froben himself can bear witness – for he received a good part of it in his own hands on my behalf in Frankfurt – that the sum of money, part of which I brought here with me two years ago and part I received by way of remittance from Brabant, exceeded 1,900 florins.[91] Of which sum not much is now left. And yet all the time my annuity from the emperor is postponed: but postponed on terms that it will be ready for me at once on my return. This is promised in a letter to me by the Lady Margaret,[92] illustrious aunt of the emperor Charles, to whom the emperor himself had lately written from Spain, giving instructions for my annuity to be paid out of due turn, the annuities due in respect of all other offices being suspended on account of the burdens of the war. And so anyone who is jealous of Froben had better challenge him in a contest of generosity, and I shall be on the winning side. At least there is no reason why anyone should grudge me his friendship. If thanks to him I can do learning some service, it is without harming anyone else or standing in his way as he races to be rich; nor have I any agreement with Froben, only good will mutual and unfettered, in which I shall never endure to come second, challenge me who will. I have presented my true account; it is reasonable that their criticisms should now cease. But this is the wretched constraint upon those of us who publish books and begin to act our play before the public: we must satisfy everyone, even the dregs.

# *ERASMUS AS EDUCATOR* 2

## The Antibarbarians / *Antibarbarorum liber*

This satiric dialogue is among the earliest of Erasmus' compositions. He tells us that he wrote the first draft before he was twenty years old, that is, in the 1480s. The subsequent history of the work is remarkable. Erasmus took the manuscript with him on a journey to Italy in 1506. On receiving an invitation to come to England, he departed hurriedly, leaving the manuscript in the care of a friend, Richard Pace. When Pace had to leave himself, he in turn entrusted the manuscript to a countryman who apparently sold or gave it away. For many years Erasmus tried to recover this work, but without success. Finally he managed to obtain the first section and, after some revision, published it in 1520.

In the following selection Erasmus is the narrator. The main speaker is 'Batt,' that is, Jacob Batt (c 1465–1502), who studied in Paris and returned to his native Bergen to become master of the public school and, later on, secretary of the town council. The interlocutor ('the doctor') is Joost van Schoonhoven (d c 1502), town physician of Bergen. This extract is taken from CWE 23 41–59, translated and annotated by Margaret Mann Phillips.

[Batt begins his speech in defence of the New Learning]:
'If I did not know that I was to speak before most cultivated judges,

and was not largely assisted by the very soundness of my cause, I should be afraid that, in the face of such hatred on the part of the stupidest people, literature was not going to have a very good advocate today. But, as it is, I am so far from any apprehension of not being able to refute all the objections that the anti-rhetoricians can ever raise that I do not think it necessary in such an easily won cause even to use an introduction. It is not only in front of you, my good friends, with all your learning, you who have begged me for this speech and who cannot, I know, be anything but kind, willing, attentive hearers, but even among the Sauromates[1] or whatever may be more barbarous, provided they are human beings, I can promise myself certain victory; human beings, I say, who follow the lead of reason and not the dictates of passion. For as to these brawlers who go on obstinately defending their obvious idiocy, I look on them as Diogenes looked on his public assembly.[2] When several thousand men had come together there, he still declared he had not yet seen a man. They say that learning is deadly to mortals, and the thing to wish for is ignorance,

> Olive no stone shall have nor nut no shell.[3]

Sure as I am already of making my point, this one thing I ask: do not expect magnificent oratory on such a thorny and intractable subject; even on the most favourable topics you should not require this of a Batt. You will not even demand to be amused, except when the crass stupidity of the barbarians' reasoning makes you laugh.'

Beginning with an apology, I said, 'Is it permissible to interrupt you sometimes as you speak?'

'Certainly,' replied Batt, 'interrupt me as often as you like; we are not speaking by the clock, and the cause will not be lost if a little time is spent on the way.'

'You seem to me,' I said, 'to have dispensed with an introduction in such a way that not to have one is in itself an introduction. But go on, I beg, do not let us hold you up in your first stage any longer.'

'That's just like you,' retorted Batt; 'it isn't my way; you have got by heart all those subtleties and rhetorical tricks, but it is enough for me, I think, to set forth the thing as it is in the fewest possible words. And so I shall not go back further to inquire how it happened that the learning of antiquity fell from such a pinnacle of honour into this pit of darkness, or try to find out what fate caused this, when it came about, by what stages, as you were trying to do just now. That could be better done at another time perhaps. It is not really important to decide how someone fell into a well; the main thing is how to get him out. We shall therefore plead the cause of the old learning against its new opponents, and I see that the trouble comes mainly from three types of enemy.

'There are those who want the Republic of Letters to be destroyed root and branch. Others are doing their best to get its power not exactly extinguished, but restricted within narrower limits. Lastly there are those who want to see the republic preserved but utterly ruined, by themselves becoming tyrants, abrogating the laws of our fathers, and introducing foreign magistrates and behaviour.

'The first-named of these, as I see it, are those quite uncouth people who detest the whole of literature (which they call poetry) on some vague religious pretext, whether from jealousy or stupidity I cannot say. The second lot I understand to be the educated who are really uneducated, the people who somehow find other studies acceptable (that is, their own), but as for the humanities, without which all learning is blind, they hate them worse than a snake. Then there are the last, and who else are they but the people who admire and approve of every kind of literature, especially poetry and rhetoric, but on condition that they themselves are considered the finest poets and orators – which is far from the case.

'It would not be easy to say which of these enemies does the most grievous and dreadful harm to the Republic of Letters, or which of them is to be credited with the largest share of its disasters. For the first (do not let us underestimate them) may have nothing in the way of weapons and knowledge of warfare, but, as a savage horde massed together from the fields and hills, I wonder whether any kind of enemy could be more dangerous. They do not march into battle; they throw themselves into it like ravening wild beasts, mistaking fury for fortitude. They have four strong points: fury (like the Andabatae), noise (like Stentor in Homer), numbers (in which they exceed even the army of Xerxes),[4] and lastly a kind of shield which is the pretence of religion; and under that they are always sheltering – it is all they can put up against all kinds of missiles. These people are entirely outside the world of literature, and have a burning hatred of the glory attached to men of letters; they think it proper and pious to carp at the finest studies of others, and it is amazing how cunningly they mask their sluggishness, their envy, and their pride under the attractive names of simplicity and religion.

'The second lot are rather better educated than these, and they attack us from far and near: from a distance with missiles, but quite laughable ones (they hurl at us tow,[5] smoke, and dung); in hand-to-hand fighting they go for us with daggers, but leaden ones. They offer peace, but on obviously arrogant terms, on condition that we should get our learning without the humanities – though without these no literature can exist. They ban all culture, and whatever they themselves have not learnt. They are difficult to get hold of, and most troublesome on this account. They never make a stand; they are more elusive than the Parthians, now saying yes and then no; they are always shuffling, getting away with a quibble, and like Proteus,

> Into all kinds of wondrous shapes they change.[6]

'The last group might perhaps be judged not very bitter enemies, because their offence comes from zeal, not hatred; but I find them far and away the most harmful. The others attack under hostile banners and can be driven from the ramparts, but these are living inside the walls, in our very strongholds, and by their weapons and badges look like our friends, but all the time they are planning for the eternal ruin of the republic under a deceptive appearance of devotion, and the more they strive to deliver their country, the more they entangle it in shameful slavery. One might also warm to the first group of opponents, because their hatred of letters means that they never touched them. The second group are the less harmful for having kept away from the best writers, that is, the poets and orators, being content with their own state. The last want to know everything. It is said, and how truly, that there is nothing less kind than a mistimed kindness. Just so, these people have tried to come to the rescue of literature in distress, and they have entirely wiped it out by their disastrous zeal. The thing to do was to measure their powers, to determine the range of their intellect, before taking up so strenuous a task. What they did was to prefer to imitate Phaethon, the inexperienced driver who tried to manage his father's chariot, and upset it to his own downfall.[7] And as they are like Phaethon in their folly, they deserve a similar calamity or even worse. It is by their rashness that philosophy, the great, old, and true, has been reduced to sheer nonsense, mere fantasy. Through them we have lost innumerable works of the early writers; the fact that corrupt textual readings abound, and abound the more the more learned the author, is something we owe to them; if the fine theology of the old days has so much degenerated, this is their doing and no one else's; if the grammarians write and teach nothing but sheer barbarism, we have them to thank. And to bring this to a close: it is their doing that in both verse and prose mute and inarticulate authors are prized above the most learned; one among them writes on grammar, another on rhetoric, another on dialectic, another on natural philosophy, another on theology; while this one writes commentaries on the best authors, shedding darkness on them, not light, not adorning but corrupting, and another one tries to emend what he does not understand, and a third turns into bad Latin what was in good Greek, though he knows practically nothing of either language; and so, I say, while they are vying with each other to make an uproar, they have managed to confuse, corrupt, and overturn everything with their futile efforts; and the more industriously each of them tries to do his part, the more ruin he causes. It is like someone trying to wipe a speck of dust off a purple robe with hands smeared with ordure – the harder he tries to help the more harm he does.

'But, leaving them aside (for to discuss the subject one would have to go on forever), I shall fall on the other two lines in two separate offensives; and here I shall acquit myself so that you will swear I am more expert than Pyrrhus.[8]

'As to the army of yokels, I shall be content to have dispersed them with a hastily raised force, and put them to flight stripped of their shields of religious pretence; this will not need much doing. For they are an unwarlike crowd made up of old men, who, realizing that their time has been passed in self-indulgence and run out, are futilely jealous of the young who are advancing to better things. I shall first force them to turn tail, using the most cogent arguments as javelins, and then, when they turn again to fight, I shall stab them with swords – the testimony of Holy Writ. When they are stunned by this barrage of instances, I shall drive them from their strongholds, and once these have been reduced I shall drive on in the same flush of battle to attack the stragglers, and, stripping them of all their arms, carry off the victory in every kind of warfare.

'But now the first lot are to be challenged ... Tell me, I say, you loutish fellows, race of Midas,[9] senseless blocks of marble, what have letters done ("profane" letters as you call anything you have not learnt) to deserve that you should attack them with such obstinate virulence, as if men were born for one thing only, to hate learning? It annoys you that you learnt nothing, and cannot learn now, but must you choose to hate? If you have sunk into hopeless sloth, do you think it a fine thing to look on others with envy? Why not rather set vigorously to work, and wrest from us this glory which you envy? But you are afraid we shall poke the ancient jests at you, "a donkey learning the fiddle, a bull in the wrestling ring; what has a jackdaw to do with a harp, or a pig with amaranth?"[10] But there is nothing remarkable in your hating – the wonder would be if you were to love. What the greatest of Peripatetic philosophers[11] wrote is true, as usual – "only the ignorant is an enemy to knowledge." "A cock does not appreciate a bit of jasper,[12] nor do pigs delight in roses; no picture pleases an ape, no light the purblind; for Midas there is no pleasure in the song of Apollo." Why do you foolishly show off the asses' ears; you are even sillier than your father Midas who did try to keep them hidden. Why not rather bury the shame of your ignorance in the ground? Why not imitate the artfulness of some people who praise letters, to give themselves the air of knowing? Why not at least keep your mouths shut and look like philosophers? Now you are caught in your own accusation like squeaking mice. But maybe you are so far advanced in your madness as to think it a clever thing to do to hate and envy and carp at the best things of all, which the wisest men think worth obtaining with many labours. That bit of glory, in case you don't know, you share with porters, cobblers, sailors, and grave-diggers; they hate cultivated studies too, and despise and curse them, but they are better than you for two reasons; their hate is less violent, and they despise our studies for love of their own skills. You detest the refined arts and have none of your own. They prefer one skill to another, one kind of study to another; you put ignorance before knowledge, madness before a sane mind, animals before men. You slavish herd of sneerers, even the asses laugh at you!

'Now just look and see how unfair it is to hate without knowing what you hate or why you hate it. You condemn rhetoric, but what that might be you have not the foggiest idea. You hate poetry, without understanding what it is or what kind of thing. You hate antiquity, but the ancients mean nothing to you. In short, you pour scorn on the whole of what learned scholars toil for far into the night, and the whole of its greatness is unknown to you. For if you ever did learn these things yourselves why rebuke those who want to learn, and if you never learnt them (and this you not only admit but glory in) why pronounce judgment so ponderously on matters you know nothing about? You have heard, I think, that there is something bad in these studies. Of course you have, but from people like yourselves, envious, ignorant, and hostile; it is like pig teaching pig, or the blind leading the blind. But show me, if you can, one person who has found fault with this literature when he has thoroughly understood it, one person who has said that he regretted the time spent on it. Why should a dolt be believed, jabbering about things he does not understand, and a learned man disbelieved when he talks about what he knows? Do you think your jealousy is concealed from anybody? Do you think you are deceiving us with your pretences? Or that we cannot see what disease is eating you up? Suppose we now give things their proper names: stop posing as devout and religious men instead of the jealous, sluggish creatures you are!'

The doctor said then: 'As you have given leave, I will make use of it and interrupt you. You have shown yourself a valiant skirmisher, and I think you are rightly called Batt!'

When the other asked him why he thought so, he went on: 'These are no riddles to you who know the fables so well. You have shown up the tricks of the barbarians so well that I could almost believe that a second metamorphosis had transformed you back from that legendary stone into Batt again,[13] and then your challenge to these fellows provoking them to fight was clever too. There is nothing which can so rouse their rage as to charge them as you do with stupidity, ignorance, envy – in fact, hearing some truths about themselves.'

'You are right,' said Batt, 'and it really is no wonder if scabby fellows jump when you touch their sore places. You may see the arrogant men giving proof of their soul's rage by their flashing eyes and the savagery written all over their faces; even though in the midst of this they do not yield a step in their fake religious fervour – like characters in a play they act out their tragic parts. For religion, while it is the best of all things, is also, the famous historian tells us,[14] the most convenient cloak for any vice you like to name, because if anyone tries to draw attention to the vices themselves he appears to many people to be attacking religion, by which they are masked; and so it often happens that "evil oft lurks, masked by its neighbour, good."

'These people are soaked in vice – in much worse vices than any other mortals, whom they, demigods as they are, regard as the common herd; yet they make attacks on others' lives with their impudent tongues and spare nobody, neither age nor sex nor nationality nor order, neither a man's person nor his good fame. But whenever anyone finds them drunk, or whoring, or committing some deed even worse than these, they put up excuses, they cover up, they will have it hushed up for the honour of their order, as they say – as if other mortals were outside all orders. When they bawl about the vices of the secular clergy, and preach revolt, and incite the ignorant mob to stone them, they think of the risk of rousing the anger of Christ, the Founder of *that* order – for he was a priest, but not a Dominican. If anyone dares to divulge any of their secrets and disturb the Augean stable,[15] they announce that he is in danger of destruction from an irate Francis, or Dominic, or Elijah, so help me! One of his flock recently gave high praise to a colleague of his order, because he shouted all manner of things in a public sermon against priests with concubines, and tried to persuade the people and the magistrates that priests' concubines should be compelled to wear a red cross on the left shoulder. As he was enjoying himself mightily over this story, someone asked him – with compliments about the other man's speech – what colour would he wish the cross to be for the Dominicans, the Carmelites, and the rest. Would he like the concubines of the Friars Minor to wear grey crosses, those of the Carmelites white, of the Dominicans black? At this the pious man crossed himself vigorously against the evil omen. The second man continued, "You will never succeed, however big a sign of the cross you make, in hiding from many people what shameful things are sometimes perpetrated by your colleagues. It could not possibly be otherwise, given such a heap of offscourings of men and races. But perhaps it is not right to make all this public, for the sake of the order." The first speaker agreed heartily with this. Then the other asked, "And the priesthood, is not that an order?" As he could not deny it, the second man asked why he should think the wrongdoings of priests ought to be howled out in front of the people with such inflammatory uproar. Not to digress further from our subject, we may say that they use the same cloak for their crass ignorance as for the other shameful things in their lives.

'They hold out false piety everywhere as their shield, and they do it with such art and cunning that they manage to deceive not only other people, but themselves as well, clever fellows that they are! Not that they are moved by any real religious fervour – they have no wish to appear religious in anything but this one particular – but, as Quintilian puts it, they want to "skulk in the shadow of a great name."[16] This is the religion of evildoers, of robbers and murderers, who have a habit of flying to the altar and the temple as soon as they have perpetrated any crime, like the wicked slave in Plautus. Why do they do this? Because they are charmed with the religious feeling of the place? Not in the least – they do it to escape the cross, to go unpunished for their evil deeds. In the same way our severe critics – who may be Dionysius or Clodius in other things – want to appear like Numa whenever it comes to discussing good studies;[17] it is then that they remember they are Christians; it is then that they begin to chant the bits out of the Gospel, and wrap up ugly things in attractive words, and say they are inspired by zeal, not envy, and do not hate our studies but despise them – that being the special duty and honour of a Christian. They hold up before us the rustic simplicity of the apostles. They say that there is a high reward among the blessed which awaits those who for religion's sake can despise these heathen teachings, invented for ostentation and pride. Ignorant piety, they say, is most pleasing to heaven; as if heaven were in any way gratified by our being boorish – in that case why do we not cherish stupidity more than anything? – or as if ignorance were useful to any aspect of the management of life. When the truth is that to despise in others the splendid thing which you have not got and never hope to have is utterly absurd and a mark of insanity. They are wildly wrong if they think a contempt for any kind of thing will redound to their own credit. Take Thersites, the least of the Greeks: supposing that he in his utter cowardice were to declare that he despised the glory of Achilles, and the arms by which it was won (those arms which Ajax and Ulysses quarrelled about), would he not provoke a universal shout of laughter?[18] Who would not smile if a snail despised the speed of the horse? Or an owl mocked at the eagle's eyes, or a mole at a roebuck's? If a raven scorned the colours of a parrot? Or a donkey belittled the intelligence of an elephant? Or if a doltish fool despised the prudence of a wise man? That will never win him praise. And so I shall be doing the barbarians a good turn if I explain the rational basis of scorn, and thus prevent their using scorn as a means of self-glorification.

'In human affairs there are certain things which attract the minds of mortal men with a special ingrafted longing, whether because they look honourable and beautiful, or sweet, or useful, and in this category are wealth, fame, rank, pleasure; if you possess these, or if they are easily within your reach, to hold them lightly is an act worthy of a strong and upright man – at least in so far as they turn him away from virtue. It is equally praiseworthy to disdain the sad things and the sweet; that is, to be able to renounce the latter and go to meet the former. Plato does not altogether approve of the Spartan way of life, because while they made nothing of the hardest toil they seemed less practised in the contempt of pleasure. But these Catos[19] of ours are weaker than any woman on both counts; they only show themselves men when it comes to the contempt of literature. To make it even funnier, they pour scorn not only on the most admirable things, but on things entirely outside their knowledge. They scorn Ciceronian eloquence being themselves as dumb as fish; they scorn the acuteness of Chrysippus,[20] and they themselves are as dull as a pounded pestle. They scorn poetry, being uninitiated and, as Plato says, foreign to the Muses. They scorn the refined literary style of the old theologians, which they cannot hope to follow, and if they were to hope for this they would be all the crazier. What a doltish herd of scorners! Just tell me, what new greatness of soul is this? What is this extraordinary type of contemptuousness? You cannot despise money, but you bask in the glory of despising erudition? For kissing and cuddling a whore you beat Hercules, silly childish lust is your master, any kind of adulation ravishes you, the least opposition dismays you, and you think you will cut the figure of a strong man if you manage to pour scorn on things more important than you could possibly understand? To take pride in a well-turned speech is not permitted, but you sell yourself to the womenkind with your well-cut gown; you prefer your speech to be empty and squalid but your skin is well filled and shining. You turn away in disgust from the mention of girls in the stories of the poets, but meanwhile you have no disgust at all about forcing other men's wives, even Vestal virgins.[21] The pen must not be sleek and shining, but the purse can. Listen, proud scorner, you must get learning first and then despise it; if you want to play the strong man, first acquire the object of your scorn; unless perhaps your boast is that you are imitating the apostles in this also, that your reputation of virtue rests on the relinquishment of desire, and not on the kind of thing relinquished. Come now, suppose there were no difference between wealth and learning: the apostles were indifferent to poverty or to the hope of greater wealth, and that without envy; stripped bare themselves, they did not envy the riches of others. You have not even a little learning, which you could claim to despise, but a great hopelessness, because learning is a matter of great difficulty and needs infinite toil, and your brains are heavier than lead.

'Finally, supposing you were right to despise learning, why should you envy others? If you envy, that means you wish for something; and if you wish, why do you not come down with us into the arena, and try to be happy with us instead of being wretched because of us? Strive, win, triumph. But lazy men see how our learning is hedged in on all sides by hard labour and nightly vigils; if they were equal to making light of it, they would not talk so boastfully and stupidly about despising erudition. When I have mastered the whole of literature, that will be the time when I shall be right in despising it, not that I shall lose interest in it, but so as to avoid arrogance; and I will see to it that, though I excel all others in learning, I shall not put myself before anyone, not even the stupidest. I shall frankly encourage modest efforts; I shall congratulate the victor and not envy him. The greater I am, the greater will be my humility – the more I know, the more gently I shall tolerate the ignorance of others, and bearing with all I shall take care that no one has anything to bear from me. I shall vie with the studious in learning, and with all men in gentleness, courtesy, modesty; I shall conduct myself so that it is clear that I am better for being wiser. The more others look up to me, the more I shall look down on myself. Finally, when I have tried my best to learn everything, I shall not seem to myself to know anything.

'This is the way in which our scorn may be praiseworthy, if we are scorning not others' learning but our own. Looking at it this way, not erudition only but virtue itself is to be despised, and the thing above all to be scorned is scorn. Augustine "despised" heathen culture in this way, but only after becoming a prince of learning in this field. Jerome's "contempt" for the writings of Cicero and Plato did not debar him from an excellent mastery of them, and he used them continuously. Basil and Chrysostom[22] were so neglectful of the orators' and philosophers' talents that you have only to look at the documents to see that they knew all about them!

'To sum up, why on earth should these fellows glory in their scorn? Is it because, like the fox in the fable, they have vain longings? The fox began to be disgusted by the ass's testicles only when it had stopped hoping; "what vile food," it said, "I could never have eaten that!" But if we are to call things by their right names, this is sheer envy, not scorn. Or perhaps the reason is that they are weaklings, frightened by the difficulty of work, without which there is no approach either to virtue or to learning. Anyone can see that this is the attitude of a lazy man, and a spiteful one too. Or perhaps they have an innate uncouthness which makes them hate the elegance of literary studies? This seems to me not the attitude of a pious Christian (as they say), but of a clodhopping and actually brutish mind. Now let us have a little modesty, please; let them give way to those who are trying for better things. Let it be enough for them to acknowledge their own ignorance to themselves, and not go on making unnecessary trouble for us, and looking down on people they should respect and admire; and if they find nothing better or sweeter than sleep and idleness, let them show more justice as regards others; they can just leave the gloomy night-watchings and crazy toil to us, seeing that we have not the slightest envy of their delights. It is a worse kind of envy to be galled by other people's hard work.

'If we are to be forbidden to use the inventions of the pagan world, what shall we have left I ask you, in the fields, in the towns, in churches and houses and workshops, at home, at war, in private and in public? To such an extent is it true that we Christians have nothing we have not inherited from the pagans. The fact that we write in Latin, speak it in one way or another, comes to us from the pagans; they discovered writing, they invented the use of speech.

'These people say, "Am I to carry books by damned men in my hand

and in my bosom, and read them over again and reverence them? Virgil is burning in hell, and is a Christian to sing his poems?" As if many a Christian were not burning there too, whose writing – if any good ones survive – would not be shunned for that reason by anybody. Really, who can bear this capricious way of sitting in judgment, waving a Mercurial wand[23] and sending off whoever they wish to hell, and calling up whom they wish to heaven? I will not enter here on that quarrelsome discussion about the pagans, which is unworthy even of women; it is not for us to discuss the damnation of the heathen, those, I mean, who lived before our faith. If we wished to indulge in guesswork, I could easily prove that the great men among the pagans are saved, or else no one is; let us concern ourselves with the fineness of their teaching, rather than ask ourselves how well they lived. The judge orders stage-actors to be heard as witnesses, even though anyone who knows their manner of life condemns it. The books of Origen,[24] censured as heretical in many passages, are read by the Christian church with profit to scholarship; and yet we shun the divine writings of men on whose moral character we cannot pass judgment without the greatest impertinence. Or, to put it better, one may judge them favourably with credit, but one could not criticize them without great fault.

'"Be off!" they say. "Am I to let myself be called a Ciceronian or a Platonist, when I have once and for all chosen to be called a Christian?" Why not call yourself a monster of a man? If you can truly be called a Sardanapalus when you copy his abandoned luxury, or a Gnatho because you are a flatterer, or a Thraso when you are a stupid boaster,[25] why should not someone who imitates Cicero's language be called a Ciceronian, or why, if I try to emulate something of Virgil's should I not be called Virgilian? You arrogate to yourself those barbarous titles and love to be called Albertist, Thomist, Scotist, Occamist, Durandist[26] as long as you take these names from Christians. For my part, I will allow myself to be called after any pagan so long as he was deeply learned or supremely eloquent; nor shall I go back on this declaration, if only the pagan teaches me more excellent things than a Christian.

'To bring this discussion to an end at last: if our opponents were not made blinder than moles by their own envy, they would see what is clear even to the blind – they would see that among the inventions of the pagans there are distinctions to be made; some of them are useless, doubtful, unwholesome, while others are extremely useful, health-giving, and even necessary. Let us leave the bad things to them; why should we not take over the good for ourselves? This is what a Christian man should do, a prudent and studious man. But what we do, heaven help us, is just the opposite: we imitate the vices of the heathen all the time, in fact we beat them at lust, avarice, ambition, superstition: but the one thing it would be right to imitate, their learning, is the one thing we reject, whether from stupidity or pride I cannot yet tell. For if we have inherited from them, without doing wrong, things which were to be of general usefulness to us, what is there to hinder us from doing the same in the case of their arts? Nothing more useful or more excellent than these exists in the affairs of men, if we are to believe Jerome.

# On Education for Children / *De pueris instituendis*

One of Erasmus' most important works on education, *On Education for Children*, was originally intended to serve a rhetorical as much as a pedagogical purpose. Erasmus composed it as a practical demonstration of the rhetorical precepts given in *Copia: Foundations of the Abundant Style*, his manual of style. Today the tract is of course more interesting as a statement of educational principles than as a rhetorical showpiece. Composed during Erasmus' travels in Italy (1506–9), it was published in 1529 with a dedication to William, the thirteen-year-old son of the Duke of Cleves. From the dedicatory letter it is clear that the decision to publish the treatise was motivated by an awareness of its moral and intellectual significance. In essence, *On Education for Children* is a Christian-humanist reformulation of the classical ideal of education and, more specifically, of the recommendations made in the pedagogical works of Plutarch and Quintilian. It reflects Erasmus' own priorities in its firm depreciation of mechanical rote-learning, its lively insistence on the educative power of play in the instruction of the young, and in the emphatic rejection of corporal punishment. Erasmus' keen social and psychological insights give *On Education for Children* a vitality and an imaginative grasp that goes beyond its antecedents and accords the treatise a special place among the educational tracts of the Renaissance and Reformation period.

This extract is taken from CWE 26 298–346, translated and annotated by Beert C. Verstraete. The complete title is: *A Declamation on the Subject of Early Liberal Education for Children / De pueris statim ac liberaliter instituendis declamatio.*

For a long time there was despair whether your wife would ever bear children, but now I have learned that you have become a father and have been blessed with a son who bears the stamp of his distinguished parentage and who, as far as one may judge from early signs, shows excellent promise of nobility of character. It is your intention, therefore, that your son, as the object of so much hope, should begin a liberal education and be instructed in the most valuable subjects and moulded by the beneficial teachings of philosophy as soon as he has grown a little older. You want to be a complete father and want your child to be your true son, reflecting you not only in facial feature and physical detail but resembling you also in gifts of mind and character. I am overjoyed at my very dear friend's happiness, but even more, I express my firm approval of his wise resolution.

I must offer you one piece of advice; on this point my words may be bold, but they also bear a deep affection for you. Do not follow common fashion and opinion by allowing your son's first years to pass by without the benefits of instruction and by deferring his first steps in learning to an age when his mind will already be less receptive and more subject to grave temptations (which by that time, in fact, may have entangled him completely in their brambles). Instead, you should straightway begin to search for a man of good character and respectable learning to whose care you may safely entrust your son to receive the proper nourishment for his mind and to imbibe, as it were, with the milk that he suckles, the nectar of education. Responsibility for your child should be divided equally between nurse and teacher, the former to nurture him in body, the latter in mind and character.

With your insight and understanding, you ought not to pay attention to those silly women, or to men very much like women save only for their beards, who maintain out of a false spirit of tenderness and compassion that children should be left alone until early adolescence, to be pampered in the meantime by their dear mothers and spoiled by nurses, while providing the servants with a convenient outlet for indecent fun and horseplay. They actually think that children should be kept from education as though it were poison, contending that at this young age they are not as yet capable of absorbing instruction and are too weak to bear the rigours of studying; and their final argument is that the benefits derived from study at this stage are too slight to justify either the expenditures required of the parents or the disturbances created in the lives of these fragile creatures.

I shall refute each of these objections, so I ask you to grant me your close attention for a while. Remember that I am writing these words as one of you closest friends, and that my subject is one that precedes all your other interests, namely your own son. Is there anything more precious than a son, especially an only son, into whom we would pour, not only all our riches but also, if it were possible, our very life? It would be absurd and grotesque for someone to lavish his utmost care on his estates, buildings, and horses and to consult knowledgeable and expert people for this purpose, and yet at the same time to attach so little importance to the upbringing and education of his children – for whose sake he is acquiring all this wealth – that he would not follow even his own judgment, let alone listen to the experts, but would instead, as though only a trifling issue were at stake, lend an ear to any ignorant woman or common nobody. It would be no less ridiculous than to expend great care on shoes but to neglect the feet or to be meticulous about clothing but to disregard one's health.

I need not waste your time, my esteemed friend, with commonplaces. We are all aware of the obligations towards children that natural instinct, parental love, divine law, and custom impose upon parents. It is through their children that parents escape, in so far as this is humanly possible, their mortal condition and attain to some kind of immortality. Yet there are persons who believe they have fulfilled their parental obligations through the simple act of procreation. This, however, represents only the least aspect of parental love, which is the prerequisite for the name of father. To be a true father, you must take absolute control of your son's entire being; and your primary concern must be for that part of his character which distinguishes him from the animals and comes closest to reflecting the divine.

An expectant mother is apprehensive that her child will be born deformed – squint-eyed, cast-eyed, wry-necked, disfigured by hanging jowls, protruding shoulder-blades, twisted legs or feet, or completely lacking in physical proportion. Mothers swaddle their children and bandage their heads, and keep a watchful eye on their eating and drinking, bathing, and exercising. The medical authors, especially Galen,[1] have explained in many volumes how a fine constitution may be secured by these methods, and mothers do not postpone this attention until the sixth or seventh year, but put the child into this regime as soon as it has dropped from the protection of the womb. These mothers are indeed right: neglected childhood means a sick and afflicted old age, if this final stage is ever reached. Even before her child is born a mother exercises constant care, avoiding inappropriate movements as well as certain types of food. If something by chance marks her face, she immediately plucks it away and transfers it to a hidden part of her body; long experience has shown that this is an effective means to conceal a deformity in the child which would otherwise be exposed to view.

No one would call this care premature although it is expended on man's lower nature. Why then should we neglect during all these years that part of our being which marks our true humanity? Would it not be ridiculous if someone sported a fine hat, yet allowed his hair to be uncombed and encrusted with filth? Yet it is much more absurd to devote all necessary care to the mortal body but to ignore the immortal soul. When a pup or a foal showing qualities of superior breeding is born on an estate it is subjected, as a matter of course, to immediate training, for at that age the animal is more responsive to the master's will and therefore more likely to fulfil his expectations. Parrots are taught to mimic the human voice when they are still young; for it is known that the older a bird grows, the less tractable it becomes; as the saying goes, 'An old parrot does not heed the rod.' But why should a bird receive all this attention, and your own son suffer neglect?

Efficient farmers train seedlings when they are still tender to lose their wild nature before the process of hardening sets in. They watch that their saplings do not grow crooked or suffer any other kind of harm; in fact, even if something has already gone wrong, they act quickly to rectify the damage while the trees are still pliant and responsive to a guiding hand. Can any animal or plant serve our will and convenience unless our own efforts come to the aid of nature? The sooner this is done, the more successful will be the results.

Nature, the mother of all things, has equipped brute animals with more means to fulfil the functions of their species; but to man alone she has given the faculty of reason, and so she has thrown the burden of human growth upon education. Therefore it is right to say that the beginning and the end, indeed the total sum of man's happiness, are founded upon a good upbringing and education. Demosthenes[2] used these terms in speaking about correct pronunciation. He is right of course, but a sound education contributes much more to human wisdom than mere pronunciation can enrich eloquence. A proper and conscientious instruction is the well-spring of all moral goodness. By contrast, the doors are flung wide open to folly and evil when education becomes corrupted and careless. Education is that special task which has been entrusted to us. This is why to other creatures nature has given swiftness of foot or wing, keenness of sight, strength or massiveness of body, coverings of wool or fur, or the protection of scales, plates, horns, claws, or poisons, and has so enabled them to protect themselves, hunt for food, and rear their young. Man alone she has created weak, naked, and defenceless. But as compensation, she has given him a mind equipped for knowledge, for this one capacity, if properly exploited, embraces all others. Animals are less easily taught than humans, but their instincts are more highly developed. Bees, for example, do not have to be taught how to construct cells, gather nectar, or make honey. Ants are not trained to store up their winter supplies during the summer in a hole in the ground, because they are guided by instinct. But man cannot even eat, walk, or speak without instruction. Trees, as you well know, do not grow any fruit, or only inferior fruit, unless they are properly grafted, and animals are of no use to man if they are left to their own capacities. A hound is not prepared by nature for the hunt, nor a horse for the saddle, nor an ox for the plough, unless we apply our efforts to their training. So what then are we to expect of man? He will most certainly turn out to be an unproductive brute unless at once and without delay he is subjected to a process of intensive instruction. Here I do not need to remind you of the well-known anecdote told of Lycurgus,[3] who produced two dogs, the first pure-bred, the other a mongrel. The pure-bred dog, however, had been poorly trained and so went straight for the food placed in front of him, whereas the mongrel, who had been well drilled, abandoned his meal and rushed after game. This story demonstrates that while nature is strong, education is more powerful still.

Men will do everything to have dogs that will serve them well in the hunt or to have horses that are full of stamina for travel, and any care they devote to these ends seems to be perfectly in order. But they neglect altogether or postpone until it is too late any thought of raising a son who will be a source of pride and well-being to his parents, to whom they can safely entrust a good share of responsibility in the administration of the family estate, and whose affection will comfort and sustain them under the growing burden of old age, a son who will be a faithful protector of his family, a good husband to his wife, and a solid and useful citizen of his country.

For whom do men plough, sow, and build? For whom do they ransack land and sea for wealth? Do they not do it all for their children? But what advantage or honour lies in these things if the beneficiaries are unable to make proper use of them? It is strange that so much energy should be expended on amassing property, while the owner as such receive no attention at all. Who would buy a lyre for an unmusical person or present an illiterate with a library? Why then all this accumulation of wealth for the benefit of someone who has not been taught how to make use of it? If you give wealth to a person who has been properly educated, you are handing him the tools for doing good; if you give the same to a person whose nature is savage and uncultivated, however, you are only providing him with the resources for living a wicked and irresponsible life. Can anything represent greater heights of madness than a father who acts in this manner? Such a father may ensure that his son suffers no physical harm and can perform his ordinary functions; yet at the same time he neglects the spirit, which is the driving force of all moral action.

I hardly need to add that nothing is more conducive to wealth, social status, and even good health, all blessings which parents earnestly desire their children to enjoy, than moral and intellectual excellence. Parents wish for their children to be successful in the hunt yet give them no hunting-spear to make the catch possible. You cannot bestow upon your son the supreme good, but at least you can equip him with the means to win its sublime treasures. You have surely fallen to the depths of absurdity when you possess a dog that has been carefully trained or a horse that has been painstakingly broken and schooled, but at the same time have a son who lacks moral and intellectual instruction. So it is possible that you may own land that is beautifully cultivated but a son whose culture has been shamefully neglected, or a mansion filled with exquisite works of art but a son whose soul has no beauty at all.

And then there are parents, parents often widely praised for their practical wisdom, who postpone any thought of educating their child until he is already at an age when results are less easily obtained; or indeed they never entertain the thought at all. All their concern is for his material and external well-being, even before the heir to their wealth is born. So the parents take every precaution. While the woman is still with child, a reader of horoscopes is summoned to determine whether the infant will be male or female. He is also asked what the child's career will be; and so he may predict, 'He will be as a soldier,' and the parents will say, 'We will enter him for service at court'; or he may predict, 'He will occupy a high position in the church,' and they will say, 'We must find him a prosperous diocese or abbey somewhere and make him a provost or a dean.' If this kind of foresight, which extends even into the period before birth, is not considered premature, is it too early to take thought for a child's education? Why all this early concern that your son should be a general or a magistrate, but no reflection at all on the fact that he should serve the state well in these positions? Well in advance you arrange for your son to become a bishop or abbot, but you fail to give him an upbringing that would enable him to discharge these offices well. You set him, as it were, on a chariot, but fail to teach him the art of driving; or you post him at a ship's tiller, but neglect to teach him what every captain ought to know. Thus the most precious of all your possessions, for whose sake all the rest is gathered, is the most neglected. Your lands, mansions, utensils, clothing, and furnishings gleam with prosperity; your horses have been splendidly schooled and your servants superbly trained; your son's mind alone presents a bleak picture of waste and neglect. Suppose you buy a slave, 'just off the block,' as the saying goes, a rough and uncivilized creature. If he is still young, however, you will determine what occupation would be suitable for him and you will soon begin to train him in a particular skill such as cooking, medicine, farming, or household administration. Yet you would neglect your son as though he were born for a life of idleness. You may object that your son has the necessary means to live his life. True, but he does not have the means to live a good life.

It seems to be customary that the wealthier a person is, the less he cares for the education of his children. 'What need,' our magnate says, 'do my children have of philosophy? They will have plenty of everything.' Yes, but the greater your wealth the more you need the guidance of philosophy. The larger a ship and the bulkier its cargo, the more it needs a skilful steersman. What single-mindedness marks the actions of princes, who strive to bequeath such huge domains to their sons! Yet these same persons could not care less to have their children educated in the skills which are so essential for good government.

How much more does he give who gives the means for living well than he who merely gives life. Children owe little gratitude to parents who are their parents only in the physical sense of the word, but have failed to provide them with the proper upbringing. There is a well-known saying attributed to Alexander the Great: 'Were I not Alexander,

I should want to be Diogenes.' Plutarch is right to criticize Alexander for this remark: the more he expanded his empire the more Alexander should also have wished for the wisdom of Diogenes.[4]

But it is even more disgraceful if parents not only neglect their children's education but also corrupt them into following evil habits. The famous philosopher Crates[5] of Thebes saw this perversity in human character, and was fully justified in threatening that he would climb to the highest point in the city and there cry out at the top of his voice, denouncing the folly of mankind, 'What kind of insanity has beset you, wretched people? Why all this anxious care to gather wealth and possessions, while you give no attention to your children, for whom you are accumulating all these things?' Women who only give birth to their children but are not concerned to raise them are hardly even half-mothers; so also fathers who supply all their children's physical wants to the point of spoiling them but totally neglect their upbringing are not even father in half the sense of the word. Trees perhaps come into existence as trees once and for all, even if they turn out wild and barren; and horses are born as horses, even if they prove to be useless. But man certainly is not born, but made man. Primitive man, living a lawless, unschooled, promiscuous life in the woods, was not human, but rather a wild animal. It is reason which defines our humanity; and where everything is done at the whim of physical desire, reason does not hold its rightful place. If physical shape constituted man's true nature, then statues would have to be included among the human race.

Aristippus[6] once gave a witty answer to a wealthy but dull-witted citizen who had asked what benefits a young man would derive from education: 'Well, he will at least have this advantage, that in the theatre he won't sit down as one lump of stone upon another.' Another philosopher, Diogenes[7] if I am not mistaken, showed an equally delightful sense of humour. In full daylight he used to make his way through the crowded market-place, carrying a lamp; when asked what he was looking for, he replied, 'I am looking for a man.' He was aware, of course, of the crowd around him, but to him it was nothing more than a herd of animals, not a gathering of human beings. Another day the same philosopher stationed himself in a prominent place and summoned a throng of people, shouting, 'Let all men come here.' A large number of people assembled but he kept on shouting, 'Let all men come here,' so that some became rather annoyed and shouted back, 'Here we are, the men you are looking for; tell us what you have to say.' To which he replied, 'I want men, not you; you are not human,' and he drove them away with his stick.

It is beyond argument that a man who has never been instructed in philosophy or in any branch of learning is a creature quite inferior to the brute animals. Animals only follow their natural instincts; but man, unless he has experienced the influence of learning and philosophy, is at the mercy of impulses that are worse than those of a wild beast. There is no beast more savage and dangerous than a human being who is swept along by the passions of ambition, greed, anger, envy, extravagance, and sensuality. Therefore a father who does not arrange for his son to receive the best education at the earliest age is neither a man himself nor has any fellowship with human nature. ...

Although this is a duty which you owe to God and nature, you should also consider, even if you expect no gain, what a great source of comfort, support, and pride to their parents children are who from their earliest years have been soundly educated; whereas children who have received an indifferent education bring nothing but disgrace and disaster upon them. I do not need to offer illustrations from ancient history; merely let your mind range at will through all the families in your city and you will be confronted with numerous examples from everywhere. I am sure you often hear parents saying, 'Oh how happy I should be if I had no children,' or 'Oh how fortunate I should be if I had never borne children.' The education of one's children is certainly a heavy responsibility; but no one is born simply to look after himself or to live a life of idleness. You wanted to be a father; so now you must be a good father. You became a father, not only for your own benefit, but also for that of the community; or to speak in Christian terms, it was for God's sake and not just for yourself.

St Paul[8] writes that women shall find salvation only through child-bearing and raising their children to walk in the ways of holiness. God will punish the parents for the sins of their children. Therefore if you fail to give your son an education founded on moral principles, you are above all wronging yourself; for through your own negligence you are preparing for yourself a fate which is more grim and terrible than anyone could wish upon his enemy. Dionysius,[9] the story goes, lured the youthful son of the exiled Dion to his court and corrupted him with degrading pleasures, knowing full well that this would cause the father more grief than outright murder. Later when Dion returned and tried to persuade his son to go back to his former innocence, the latter committed suicide by jumping from one of the upper storeys. How true are the words of the Hebrew sage,[10] 'A wise son maketh a glad father; but a foolish son is the heaviness of his mother.' Indeed a wise son is not only his father's delight, but also his glory, his strength, and his whole life. On the other hand, a foolish and wicked son inflicts not only grief, but also dishonour, poverty, and a premature old age upon his parents, and makes death welcome to those to whom he owes his existence. Do I need to elaborate? Every day we have examples before our eyes of citizens who, because of their dissolute children, have been reduced from wealth to indigence, who are tormented and crushed by unbearable shame because their son has been led to the gallows or their daughter has turned to prostitution. I know eminent citizens of whose numerous children scarcely one has escaped unscathed: one child, for instance, is being consumed by that horrible affliction euphemistically called the 'French pox,' and drags himself about as a living corpse; another burst his bowels during a drinking bout; and a third, while on a nocturnal prowl for prostitutes, his face hidden by a mask, was ignominiously stabbed to death.

How could all this have happened? Well, these parents thought it was enough to bring their children into the world and to shower them with riches, but had no interest in their education. There are severe laws against people who expose their children and abandon them in some forest to be devoured by wild animals. But is there any form of exposure more cruel than to abandon to bestial impulses children whom nature intended to be raised according to upright principles to live a good life? If there existed a Thessalian witch who had the power and the desire to transform your son into a swine or a wolf, would you not think that no punishment could be too severe for her? But what you find revolting in her, you eagerly practise yourself. Lust is a hideous brute; extravagance is a devouring and insatiable monster; drunkenness is a savage beast; anger is a fearful creature; and ambition is a ghastly animal. Anyone who fails to instil into his child, from his earliest years onwards, a love of good and a hatred of evil is, in fact, exposing him to these cruel monsters; and what is even worse, not only does he abandon his child to these bestial forces, which is the cruelest form of exposure imaginable, he also nurtures a grim, destructive monster within his own home and to his own ruin.

Abominable is that tribe of men who would destroy young bodies by witchcraft. What, then, are we to think of parents who, as it were, bewitch their children's souls through negligence and perverse upbringing? We call those who slay new-born children infanticides. But these destroy only the body. How much greater a crime is it to kill the spirit; for foolishness, ignorance, and wickedness signify the death of the spirit. Parents also cause harm to society when they, in so far at least as it lies within their power, present the community with a citizen who constitutes a real threat. They also sin against God, for God gave them children to be raised in the ways of religion. All these considerations make it abundantly clear that neglect of the first years of a child's education is more than simply a venial sin.

It is an even greater crime, as I have already said in passing, not only to neglect a child's upbringing, but to go so far as to poison his young mind with evil principles, so that children are taught evil before they actually understand what in fact it is. How can a youngster who crawls around in fine purple grow up to practise modesty and humility? Before he can even pronounce his letters, he already knows what purple or scarlet cloth is and insists on getting it, and spoiled by such delicacies as wrasse and mullet[11] he disdainfully pushes away more common fare. Can a child who is brought up to behave impudently be expected to turn out to be a respectful young man? Can we look for generosity in a person who as a child was constantly reminded of the importance of gold and money? Can a young man refrain from extravagant ways if during his childhood he was already quite spoiled long before any beginning had been made with his moral upbringing? The art of making clothes is continually producing new marvels nowadays, as formerly Africa was said to do, and we foist any novel design in clothing upon a child, who is thereby taught to be vain, and who gets angry if it is taken from him. How can anyone when he has grown older dislike drunken behaviour when as a child he had already acquired a disposition for drink? Youngsters are also exposed to filthy language that would have been scarcely permitted even to Alexandrian pleasure-boys, if I may use Quintilian's expression. If they repeat any of this language, they are rewarded with kisses. Of course, since their own lives have served as the model, the parents will not recognize any signs of moral corruption in their children. A child readily responds to the shameless caresses of his nursemaids and is thus handmoulded by their indecent fondling, as the saying goes. A youngster who continually sees his father intoxicated and uttering streams of profanities, who repeatedly witnesses banquets highlighted by extravagance and sensuality, and who constantly hears the house ringing with the din of mime-actors, flautists, lyre-players, and dances, will be so accustomed to this way of life that habit will gradually pass into second nature.

Among some peoples it is a practice that children who are still fresh from their mother's womb are reared in the arts of cruel warfare. They are trained to put on a savage face, to love weapons, and to deal blows. After these preliminaries, they are assigned to a teacher. We should not be surprised that these children, who have imbibed evil along with their mother's milk, are completely insensitive to good. I have heard some defend their folly by claiming that the pleasure they derive from the playful mischief of their children is a pleasant compensation for the irksome chore of bringing them up. Really, what kind of an excuse is this? Can a true father take greater pleasure in seeing his child pick up gross words and mimic shameful acts than to watch him repeat, with childish lisp, edifying sayings and imitate good deeds? Nature has given small children as a special gift the ability to imitate – but the urge to imitate evil is considerably stronger than the urge to imitate the good. Can an upright person find greater delight in evil than in good, especially when displayed in children? Would you wash off any dirt that might tough a child's skin, and yet pollute his mind with disgusting filth? After all, nothing clings more tenaciously than something that is poured into empty minds.

What kind of maternal feeling is it that induces some women to keep their children clinging to their skirts until they are six years old and to treat them as imbeciles? If their love of play goes this far, why do they not procure for themselves a monkey or a Maltese puppy? 'They are only children,' they argue. Quite true, but even so, one cannot emphasize too strongly the importance of those first years for the course that a child will follow throughout his entire life. Hard and unbending before his teacher is a child that is the product of such a soft and permissive upbringing – gentleness is their word for it, but its effects are totally corruptive. Should mothers of this type not be prosecuted for maltreatment of their children? In a sense they are indeed guilty of poisoning and infanticide. It is punishable by law to bewitch children and to poison young bodies. Then what penalty should not be meted out to men who destroy with deadly poisons the most precious part of a child's being? To kill the body is a crime less serious than to kill the spirit. If a youngster is raised among stutterers or cross-eyed persons or cripples, this contact will hurt him physically; but any harmful influence upon the soul, although it may act in a less obtrusive manner, will strike more swiftly and penetrate more deeply. It was with good reason, therefore, that St Paul[12] was so fond of Menander's saying, 'Bad company ruins good morals,' a moral that applies especially to young children. When asked once what the methods and principles were for raising first-class horses, Aristotle answered, 'Raise your horses among the pure-bred.' ...

As a general principle, human happiness depends on three prerequisites: nature, method, and practice. By nature I mean man's innate capacity and inclination for the good. By method, I understand learning, which consists of advice and instruction. Finally, by practice I mean the exercise of a disposition which has been implanted by nature and moulded by method. Nature is realized only through method, and practice, unless it is guided by the principles of method, is open to numerous errors and pitfalls.

It is a serious mistake, therefore, to think that the character we are born with is all-determining. And it is an equally serious mistake to believe that we can become wise through practical experience without the benefit of education. Can anyone be a good runner who practises strenuously but in darkness and without any direction? Or can we expect anyone to be a good swordsman if he merely brandishes his weapon with his eyes closed? The teachings of philosophy are, as it were, the eyes of the soul, casting light on the road ahead, revealing what is the right and what is the wrong path to follow. Varied experience over a long period of time is, of course, quite useful, but only to the wise man who has been thoroughly imbued with the precepts of philosophy. Think of all the hardships and sufferings that have befallen people who have indeed, through practical experience, gained some measure of understanding, but only at the cost of great misery in their lives. You might then ask yourself whether you would have your son suffer such an unhappy experience. You might also ponder the fact that philosophy can teach more within the compass of a single year than the most diverse range of experience stretched over a period of thirty years. Moreover, the guidance of philosophy is safe, whereas the path of experience leads more often to disaster than to wisdom. The ancients were right to describe someone who was trying out something by way of test as setting a trial for himself or being tried. Suppose that someone wishes his son to become a competent physician. What would he prefer him to do? Study all the available literature, or learn by trial and error what is dangerous poison and what is good medicine? If a captain has to learn the art of navigation from repeated shipwrecks, or if a ruler has to learn the proper exercise of authority from continual wars, uprisings, and public disturbances, what an unfortunate way this is to become wise! It is fools' wisdom, bought at too high a price, to gain a belated wisdom after being struck by the blows of misfortune. Philip[13] gravely admonished his son Alexander to show himself a willing pupil of Aristotle and to acquire from his tutor a thorough mastery of philosophy in order that he might avoid the many mistakes which his father was already regretting. And yet Philip has been credited with a keen intellect; we know what to expect of the common masses. Method is the quickest means of determining what is the right or wrong course of action to follow. It does not tell us belatedly after the harm has been done, 'This turned out badly for you; watch out from now on.' No, before we take even the first step it cries out, 'If you do this, you will bring ruin and disgrace upon yourself.' Three strands must be intertwined to make a complete cord: nature must be developed by method and method must find its completion in practice.

Even in animal life we can observe the great ease with which each creature learns everything that is natural to its own species and is especially conducive to its well-being. To ensure this well-being, it must avoid anything that would cause harm and suffering. This instinct is found not only in animals but even in plants. Trees, for instance, when exposed to the salt sea-gales and icy blasts of the north wind contract their leaves and branches but spread their foliage luxuriantly when placed in a gentler environment.

But what is man's real nature? Is it not to live according to reason? This is why he is called a rational being, and this is what sets him apart from the animals. And what is the most harmful influence upon man? Surely it is ignorance. Nothing will the child learn more readily than goodness, nothing will it learn to reject more than stupidity, if only parents have worked to fill the natural void from the start. Of course, we often hear extravagant complaints that children are inclined by nature to evil, and that it is very difficult to instil in them a love of the good. But these accusations against nature are unfair. The evil is largely due to ourselves; for it is we who corrupt young minds with evil before we expose them to the good. It is not surprising, therefore, that children who have already been schooled in the ways of evil should exhibit so little promise for being trained in the ways of the good; for it is universally recognized that the unteaching of bad habits not only has to precede the teaching of good habits, but is also far more difficult.

Parents generally make three mistakes. First of all, they may neglect the education of their children entirely. Secondly, they may begin to turn their children's minds to learning when it is already too late. Or finally, they may entrust their children to unworthy teachers whose instruction leaves bad effects that later have to be overcome. The first category of parents I have already discussed, and I have shown that they do not deserve the name of parents and are indeed no different from people who abandon and expose their children; they therefore deserve to be punished by the existing laws that provide for the education of children and young people. The second class of parents is found everywhere, and my quarrel has so far been mainly with them. Parents of the third type act partially out of ignorance and partly out of carelessness. It would be unusual and disgraceful if you did not know the person to whom you were going to entrust your horse or your estate. How much more disgraceful it is not to know the man into whose care you have committed the most precious of your possessions. Would you, in the one instance, be eager to learn and make up for your lack of knowledge by consulting the very best experts, and yet in the other, consider it of no importance into whose hands you should entrust your own son? Each of your servants has his duties carefully assigned. You watch closely to whom you should give the responsibility of looking after your farm or kitchen or whom you should make your steward. But let there be one person who is quite incapable of doing anything, a lazy scoundrel and an ignorant brute, and to him you entrust the education of your child. A task that requires a craftsman, so to speak, you assign to the meanest of your servants. Is it possible to think of a more perverse frame of mind?

Some parents are deterred by sheer meanness from hiring a qualified instructor. They are willing to pay their groom better than their son's teacher, while at the same time they indulge themselves with luxurious feasting, spend days and nights on ruinous gambling, and squander money on hunting parties and entertainers. Their meanness and parsimony applies only to one activity, education, although expenditure for this purpose would be a legitimate excuse for economy in everything else. I wish there were fewer fathers who would spend more money on a stinking whore than on the upbringing of their son. As the satirist[14] puts it, nothing costs a father less than his own son. It is, I suppose, not out of place to cite here from the diary which used to be attributed to Crates.[15] It has the following entries: 'Allot ten minae for the cook, one drachma for the physician, five talents for the flatterer, a thank-you for the adviser, a talent for the courtesan, and three pennies for the philosopher-in-residence.' Only one thing is missing from this absurd account, namely the allotment of a penny for the teacher – although I believe he may be mentioned here under the title of philosopher. One day a citizen with a full purse but an empty head approached the philosopher Aristippus,[16] asking him how high a fee he would charge to undertake the education of his son. When Aristippus asked for five hundred drachmas, he exclaimed, 'That is a large sum of money you are asking for; one could buy a slave with that.' To which the other wittily replied, 'Yes, but you will have two servants at your disposal instead of one: a son who can perform his duties, and a philosopher to teach him.' Again, if someone were asked if he would want to have a hundred horses at the cost of the life of his only son, he would surely reply, if he had any grain of feeling, 'Never.' Why, then, do you value your horse more than your own son and lavish more care on the animal? Why do you lay out more money to engage an entertainer than to have your son educated? Economy has its place everywhere except in education, where it would not be thrift but sheer madness.

There are also parents who are willing to exercise some judgment in their selection of a teacher for their children, but who nevertheless allow themselves to be influenced by the canvassing of their friends. So it happens that a teacher who is qualified to instruct the young is passed over, while an incompetent person is hired, for no other reason but that he bears the recommendation of a friend. Why should you be so foolish? When you wish to sail your ship, you would not let yourself be swayed by the opinions of others, but would set at the helm the man who is the most expert steersman. However, when your son's well-being is at stake – indeed the well-being of his parents, his whole family, and all of society – would you not use your judgment at all? If your horse is sick, would you hire a doctor solely on the basis of a friend's recommendation rather than on the basis of his medical skill? Is your son worth less to you than your horse? Or rather let me say, are you worth less to yourself than your horse? It would be disgraceful enough if people of modest means should act so unthinkingly; it is all the more so for persons of high rank in society. At a single banquet some may shipwreck, as it were, their entire wealth upon that most perilous reef of all, gambling, and so lose as much as thirty thousand; yet these same count it a burden to spend a thousand for the education of their children.

No one can bestow natural ability, either upon himself or upon others. But even here wise parents can exert some influence. First of all, it is important that the future father choose as his wife a woman who comes from a good family, who is well educated and in good health. Body and soul are so closely joined together that it is inevitable that the one must influence the other, either for better or for worse. Furthermore, the husband should not have intercourse with his wife if he is inebriated or in a state of emotional upheaval, for any such disturbance will be passed on by a mysterious kind of contagion to the embryo. A remark once made by a sage[17] illustrates this. Seeing a young man act in a rather intoxicated fashion, he made the pointed comment, 'I should be surprised if your father did not beget you in a drunken fit.' I also believe that at all times, but especially during the period of conception and pregnancy, both father and mother should have a good conscience and be unburdened by any feelings of guilt. To possess such a state of mind is the very height of joy and tranquillity. It is at this stage that parents should begin to think seriously of their child's education rather than wait until he is nine or even, as many do, until he is sixteen years old.

It is also best for a child to be nursed by his own mother. However, if this is impossible, it should be done by a wet-nurse who is of sound constitution and whose milk is untainted. She must be a woman of good morals, not given to quarrelling, drinking, or indecent behaviour, for any physical or mental harm that is inflicted on a child during the earliest stages of his life will continue to affect him well into his adult years. For this reason it is said that it makes a difference with whom a child shares the breast or with whom he plays. Finally, the child should be entrusted to a teacher who has been carefully selected, has been recommended from all directions, and has been well tested by a rich variety of experience. The choice should be made carefully, and it should be permanent. 'A multitude of masters' was already condemned by Homer; and as the ancient saying of the Greeks has it, 'Caria was brought to ruin because of the large number of its leaders.' A frequent change of doctors has often proved fatal; similarly, nothing is more harmful than a constant succession of different instructors, which calls to mind Penelope's weaving and unravelling of her web. I have actually known youngsters who, before they were twelve years old, had already gone through more than fourteen teachers simply because of the carelessness of their parents.

But responsibility does not end once the choice of teacher has been made. Parents should keep a close watch on both pupil and instructor; they cannot relinquish responsibility as they do when they present their daughter in marriage. Rather, the father should pay frequent visits to the classroom in order to see what progress is being made, being mindful of the sober wisdom of the ancient saying: 'A watchful gaze never turns its back. Nothing sleeks a horse faster than the eye of his master, and no manure is richer than the owner's footsteps in the field.' I am speaking here of small children. Older children should be kept out of sight now and then; such a separation is the equivalent of grafting and the best method for imparting vigour to young minds. Among the outstanding qualities recorded of Aemilius Paulus[18] was his habit of visiting, as often as the affairs of state permitted, the classes which his sons attended. Pliny the Younger[19] took upon himself the responsibility of inspecting the school where his protégé, the son of one of his friends, was receiving his education.

What I have said so far concerning human nature does not exhaust the subject. Each species of living creature possesses a common nature; so, for example, the nature of man consists in living according to the dictates of reason. There is also, however, a nature unique to each individual being. Thus one child may have an aptitude for mathematics, another for theology, a third for poetry and rhetoric, and again another for military life. Each individual is so strongly drawn to his own unique pursuit that he cannot be separated from it. By contrast, he may be so averse to a certain course of study that he would rather go through fire than apply himself to the hated discipline. At one time I knew very well a young man who was a distinguished Greek and Latin scholar and excelled also in the other liberal arts. But he had been advanced to this level by his protector, the archbishop, in order that he might begin to attend the lectures of the law professors, and against this his whole spirit rebelled. We shared a room at the time and so it was to me that he voiced his unhappiness. I urged him that since what was difficult at first would become easier later one, he should comply with his patron's wishes and devote at least some part of his time to these studies. He cited me some examples of the gross ignorance which those demigods, the professors, were passing on, with an air of vast authority, to their students. But I told him to ignore all this and simply pick out what was sound in their lectures. As I continued to press a number of arguments upon him, he exclaimed, 'I feel so strongly about this that whenever I turn to my studies it is as if a sword is driven through my heart.' If such is a person's nature, then I do not think he should be compelled against the will of Minerva;[20] as the common saying has it, one should not drag an ox to the wrestling-pit or an ass to the lyre.

It is possible that this kind of inclination in young children can be recognized even at an early stage. Some parents try to obtain predictions by means of horoscopes; I leave it to anyone's free judgment, however, to determine the value of these. Still, it would be advantageous to be able to detect these special signs, because we take in most easily the work for which nature has designed us. I do not believe it is merely idle speculation to define a person's character on the basis of his facial appearance and expression and of his physical bearing and presence. The great philosopher Aristotle did not hesitate to write a study of physiognomy, an outstanding work supported by a wealth of learning. As it is easier to sail a ship when the sea is calm and wind and tide are favourable, so it is also easier to be taught in a discipline that agrees with our personal inclinations. Virgil[21] point out the marks by which one can recognize an ox good for the plough or detect a cow suitable for breeding: 'A good heifer,' he says, 'will glare aggressively.' The same author also tells how to pick out a foal that will make a good showing in the Olympic games: 'A foal of noble breed steps forthwith in the fields,'[22] and so forth – you know the poem. It is a mistake to think that the distinguishing marks that reveal a person's basic character have not been given to us by nature; but it is a moral failing to ignore these signs once they have become clear to us.

All the same, I still hold that human nature is amenable to almost any form of learning provided we subject it to instruction and practice. We can teach elephants to walk a rope, bears to dance, and donkeys to perform amusing tricks. So is there anything we could not teach a human being? Man cannot create or change his natural aptitudes, but, as I have shown, we can reinforce to some extent what nature has given us.

As for method and practice, these are entirely within our control. We see every day how engineering skill and machinery can raise weights which otherwise could not have been moved by any force; this feat demonstrates the power of method. Practice also is indispensable, as is emphasized by the well-known saying of an ancient sage[23] that ascribes all progress to care and forethought. Method, of course, presupposes a capacity for learning, and practice a readiness for work. Some people may object that exertion is not natural for a youngster; and they may also ask how we can expect a genuine capacity for learning in a child who is scarcely aware as yet of his own humanity. I can give a summary reply to these objections. How can anyone think children cannot learn their letters at an age when they can already be taught good behaviour? There are elementary principles in acquiring knowledge just as there are in developing virtue; and the process of education, too, goes through the phases of childhood, adolescence, and adulthood.

Let me illustrate. A foal that bears all the signs of pure-bred lineage is not bridled immediately and so transformed into a calvary horse, but rather with gentle practice is taught to anticipate combat. A bullock marked for the plough is not yoked straightway and driven onwards with a sharp goad. No, rather, as Virgil so charmingly describes it, 'a loose halter of light osier is first tied around it neck; then, when necks that were once free have been accustomed to bondage, matched pairs of bullocks are yoked with the same halters and made to walk step by step. And now they draw empty carts time and time again over the ground, pressing a light track in the dust. Then, finally, the beechen axle strains and groans with a heavy load, while the linked wheels are drawn by the brass-studded shaft.'[24] Peasants take the age of their cattle into consideration and regulate the work according to their strength. We should apply the same consideration even more carefully to the education of our children. A young child, I agree, is not ready for Cicero's *De officiis*, Aristotle's *Ethics*, or Seneca's or Plutarch's moral treatises, or St Paul's Epistles. Nevertheless, a child who misbehaves at the dinner-table is corrected, and expected from then on to behave properly. When he is taken to church, he is told to kneel, fold his hands, uncover his head – in short, assume a pose of complete reverence; and when mass is being celebrated, he must be silent and raise his eyes to the altar. Children are taught these first beginnings of good behaviour and proper devotion before they can even speak; these principles remain with them into adulthood and thus contribute in no small way to the growth of true spirituality. Moreover a child does not at first distinguish between his parents and strangers. But he learns to recognize first his mother and then his father, and gradually learns to respect, obey, and love them. He is told by his parents to kiss another child who has stirred up his rage and is taught to free himself from angry and vindictive outbursts. He is also taught to refrain from chattering at inappropriate moments. And finally, he learns to stand up in the presence of his elders and to bare his head before a crucifix.

To think that these first intimations of goodness, whatever their nature may be, are of no avail towards the child's moral progress is in my view a serious mistake. Plato[25] once reprimanded a young man for playing dice. When the latter complained because he was being so severely scolded for such a minor transgression, the other replied, 'Gambling may be only a minor sin, but once it grows into a habit, it becomes a major vice.' Therefore, just as small acts of wrongdoing habitually repeated amount to a great sin, so also, small acts of goodness, habitually repeated, amount to a great virtue. It is the young who most easily acquire the good, since they possess that natural flexibility which enables them to bend in any direction, are not as yet enslaved by bad habits, and are readily inclined to imitate whatever is suggested to them. Just as children generally learn wrong before they really know what it is, they can also learn good with almost equal ease. Goodness, then, is best instilled at an early stage, for once a certain pattern of behaviour has been imprinted upon a young and receptive mind, that pattern will remain. Horace writes, 'You may drive out nature with a pitchfork, but she will inevitably rush back.'[26] The poet is, of course, right, although he is referring here to fully grown trees. The shrewd farmer sets his seedlings from the beginning to take on the growth he wants to see established in the tree. What is implanted into our being at the very beginning becomes an integral part of us. Clay may sometimes be too moist to retain any impression, and wax may be too soft for moulding; but no human being is ever too young for learning.

Seneca says that no age to too old for learning. I do not know whether this is true or not; but it is certainly much more difficult to learn certain skills in old age, whereas it is indisputable that no one is ever too young to learn, especially to learn those skills that are natural to mankind. As I have already pointed out, nature has equipped children with a unique urge to imitate whatever they hear or see; they do this with great enthusiasm, as though they were monkeys, and are overjoyed if they think they have been successful. This is how we are able to form our first impressions regarding our children's talents and aptitudes. As soon as a child is born, he is ready for instruction in right conduct and, as soon as he is able to speak, he is ready for learning his letters. Anything that carries the more decisive claim will be learned without delay. Learning certainly bestows innumerable benefits, but it will do more harm than good unless it is put in the service of moral conduct. ...

Nurses, teachers, and playmates all make a significant contribution to the development of correct speech. Children have such a marked ability to pick up a foreign language that, for instance, a German boy could learn French in a few months quite unconsciously while absorbed in other activities. In fact, it is the youngest who are always most successful. If one can learn with such ease a language as barbarous and irregular as French, in which spelling does not agree with pronunciation, and which has harsh sounds and accents that hardly fall within the realm of human speech, them how much more easily should one be able to learn Greek and Latin? We know that king Mithridates[27] was able to speak twenty-two languages and thus could administer justice to each of his subject peoples without the use of an interpreter. Themistocles[28] learned Persian within a period of one year in order that he might converse more easily with the king of Persia. If this can be accomplished by an adult, then what can we not expect of a child?

The learning of a language depends mainly on two mental faculties, memory and imitation. We have already shown that children have a natural impulse to imitate. Scholars have also credited the young with an extremely powerful memory; even if we put no trust in their authority, our own experience will abundantly bear out this fact. The visual impressions we absorbed in our childhood have been so firmly imprinted on our minds that it seems as if we received them only yesterday. On the other hand, anything that we read as adults seems unfamiliar if we read it again after two days. Moreover, we see very few grown persons who have successfully mastered a new language; even if some succeed, there are few, if any, who also master the native accent and pronunciation. That there are a few people who have accomplished this feat should not be invoked as a general rule. Cato the Elder,[29] for instance, applied himself to literary studies in his own language when he was already in his later years and began his study of Greek when he was almost seventy; but this is not a valid reason for deferring our children's instruction in Greek and Latin until they are at least sixteen years old. After all, Cato the Younger,[30] who was a much greater scholar and orator than his great-grandfather, was placed under the tutelage of Sarpedon when he was still a very young boy.

Formerly the moral and intellectual upbringing of each member of the family was considered the most important responsibility loving parents owed to their children. But now the only concern of parents is to provide their sons with well-dowered wives; having accomplished this, they think they have fulfilled their obligations. Civilization again took a turn for the worse when parents, indulging their own selfishness, started to appoint domestic servants as tutors and thus began to entrust free-born children to the charge of slaves. Yet if discrimination was used in the selection, there was less hazard, not only because the teacher lived under the watchful eye of the parents, but also because he was subject to their authority if he should do any wrong. Also, the more intelligent parents in the past would either buy slaves who were already well trained and educated or would give their own slaves suitable training so that they might put them in charge of their children's education. Still, these parents would have acted more wisely if they had themselves acquired that culture and education and so passed it on to their children. Such a policy, which one might compare to that of a bishop who leads a spiritual life in order to inspire religious devotion in as many people as possible, would have benefited both parents and children.

You may object that not everyone has the leisure to do this and that it is a burdensome task. But really, my dearest friend, consider all the time we waste on gambling, drinking, theatre, and jesters; we should be ashamed to pretend that we have no time to devote ourselves to an undertaking which ought to have priority over everything else. If we employ our time carefully and sensibly, we will have enough to meet all our obligations. A day seems short only when it is mostly frittered away. Think of all the time we spend attending to our friends' interests, which are often of a frivolous nature. We cannot please everyone, and this is why our children should have the first claim to our attention. Are we not willing to endure any discomfort to ensure that our children will have a rich and well-established inheritance? Why, then, should we shun the effort of providing them with a far nobler possession, when our natural affection and the progress of our dear ones will sweeten any inconvenience? If this were not so why would mothers endure long periods of pregnancy and breast-feeding? Any father who finds it a burden to raise his son loves his son only superficially.

It is also argued that the conditions of education were more favourable among the ancients, since both the educated upper classes and the ignorant masses spoke in the same language, except that the former spoke it with greater correctness and refinement as well as with more discrimination and fluency. I agree, and the intellectual gain of our society would be immense if the same situation still prevailed today. Yet even at present there are people who emulate the example of the ancients. Among the Dutch I might single out the Canter family,[31] and among the Spanish I might mention Isabella,[32] the wife of King Ferdinand, who comes, in fact, from a family which has produced several women who deserve our admiration both for their learning and for their spirituality. In England there is the illustrious Thomas More,[33] who despite his commitments to the affairs of state did not hesitate to serve as a tutor to his wife, son, and daughters, beginning with their religious education and then advancing to their Greek and Latin studies. We no less ought to display such an active concern towards our children, whom we have marked out for an education.

There is no danger that our children will not learn the vernacular, for this they will acquire even involuntarily through their daily association with other people.

If no one in the family possesses the necessary education, then we should obtain the services of an instructor whose learning and character have been subjected to a thorough scrutiny. It would be madness to play hazard with your son (as though with a Carian,[34] as the saying goes) in order that you may discover whether the teacher you are hiring has all the moral and intellectual qualifications. In other areas, perhaps, negligence would be excusable; but here you must watch with the eyes of an Argus.[35] There is a saying that no second mistake is permitted in war; in this matter you are not even allowed one. I repeat, therefore, that the sooner a child is entrusted to a teacher, the more fruit education will bear. ...

A teacher can expect success in the classroom if he displays the qualities of gentleness and kindness and also possesses the skill and ingenuity to devise various means of making the studies pleasant and keeping the child from feeling any strain. Nothing is more harmful than an instructor whose conduct causes his students to take an intense dislike to their studies before they are sufficiently mature to appreciate them for their own sake. A prerequisite for learning is that the teacher must be liked. Gradually, after first enjoying learning because of their instructor, children will come to like their teacher for the sake of learning. Just as we cherish many gifts because they were given to us by those whom we consider our dearest friends, so also children who are still too young for any intellectual appreciation take pleasure in school because of their fondness for their teacher. There is a good deal of truth in Isocrates' saying[36] we learn best when we have the desire to learn; and it is from those whom we like and respect that we learn most eagerly.

There are teachers whose manners are so uncouth that even their wives cannot have any affection for them. Their expression is always forbidding, their speech is invariably morose, even when they are in a good humour they seem ill-tempered, they are unable to say anything in a pleasant manner, and they can hardly manage to return a smile – one might truly say that the Graces frowned upon the hour of their birth. I should scarcely think such men fit to look after my horses, let alone to see to the upbringing of helpless children who have just been weaned from their mother's breast. There are people, however, who equate a forbidding exterior with a saintly character and think these types are ideal as instructors of children. But in fact it is not safe to trust in appearances: often behind an austere mask lurks a depraved mind. One would blush to mention some of the indignities to which these monsters have subjected their students through playing on terror and fear. Even parents cannot give their children a sound upbringing which is based on fear alone. The first duty of the teacher is to inspire affection in his pupils, so that gradually, instead of fear, a spontaneous feeling of respect may grow for him, which is much more effective than any feeling of dread.

It shows marvellous foresight, indeed, when boys who are scarcely four years old are sent to schools presided over by a master who is a complete unknown, a boor, a man of dubious morals, often mentally deranged and subject to spells of madness, or afflicted with the falling sickness or that horrible disease commonly known by us as the 'French pox.'[37] No useless, disreputable scoundrel nowadays is disqualified by general opinion from running a school. A teacher of this sort fancies he has gained for himself a private little empire, and it is shocking to see how this illusion of absolute power will lead him to inflict acts of savagery, no, not upon wild beasts, as the author of the comic stage has it, but upon a young generation that should be raised with gentleness. So schools have become torture-chambers; you hear nothing but the thudding of the stick, the swishing of the rod, howling and moaning, and shouts of brutal abuse. Is it any wonder, then, that children come to hate learning? And once this hatred has been implanted in young minds, the disgust with education will remain through the years of adulthood.

It is even more ridiculous that some people send their sons to an incompetent, drunken female in order to learn their reading and writing. Indeed, it is contrary to nature that a woman should rule over men. Nothing is more cruel than the opposite sex once its anger has been aroused; its passions are easily kindled and quietened only when the lust for revenge has been satisfied.

Nowadays even monasteries and houses of the Brethren,[38] as they call themselves, chase after income by providing inside their hidden recesses schooling for the young. However, these people lack sufficient learning, or rather, their learning is not sound, even though in other respects one might allow them to be decent, intelligent persons. So, while others may recommend instruction of this type, I should personally advise anyone who wishes a liberal education for his son to look elsewhere.

We must choose, therefore, between a private tutor and a public school. A public school, of course, is the more common as well as the more economical solution; it is much easier for one schoolmaster to frighten a whole class into submission than to instruct one pupil according to liberal principles. However, while there is no great accomplishment in giving orders to cattle and donkeys, imparting a liberal education to children is a challenge that is both difficult and glorious. A tyrant controls his subjects through fear, but a true prince makes it his task to rule with benevolence, moderation, and wisdom. When Diogenes[39] was put up for sale after he had been taken captive by the Aeginetans, he was asked by the auctioneer how he wished to be advertised to his prospective buyers. He told the man to shout, 'Who wants to buy a slave who can rule children of free men?' Many laughed at this incongruous claim. But one man, who had small children at home, approached the philosopher and asked whether his advertisement was really true. Diogenes replied that it was and after a brief conversation the other person realized that this was not an ordinary sort of fellow but that underneath the shabby cloak was concealed a sage of great distinction. So he bought him and took him home, where he placed him in charge of his children's education.

Next to the Scots, French schoolmasters are the most inveterate floggers in the world. But if you tax them with it, they argue that only beatings will make their people mend their ways – the same thing that used to be said of the Phrygians.[40] I leave it to others to decide whether this is true or not. Although I admit that each nation has its own distinctive traits, still this quality is more typically an individual characteristic. There are people you could not mend by flogging even though you beat them to death; yet, if you used kindness and persuasion, you might lead them in any direction you pleased. I must confess that this was my nature when I was a boy. My teacher had more affection for me than for any other pupil, and on the pretext that he had conceived the greatest hopes for me, he kept a closer watch on me than on anyone else. Finally, wishing to ascertain for himself how well I could stand up to the rod, he charged me with an offence I had never even dreamed of committing and then he flogged me. This incident destroyed all love of study within me and flung my young mind into such a deep depression that I nearly wasted away with heart-break; the result was, at any rate, that I was presently seized with the quartan fever. When my teacher at last realized the mistake he had made, he expressed his regrets to his friends, saying 'I almost destroyed his character before I had learned to understand it.' He was certainly not an insensitive, ignorant or, as far as I can imagine, a malicious person; he did recover his senses, but too late as far as I was concerned. Just think, my noble friend, how many promising minds are destroyed by these brutes, these ignorant creatures inflated with pride in their imaginary learning, these ill-tempered, brutal drunkards who flog their pupils only in order to gratify their own instincts and who obviously possess that monstrous mentality which finds pleasure in the pain of another person. Men of this sort should be butchers or executioners, not teachers of the young. ...

To instructors of this sort parents entrust their children, their most precious possession! And these are the teachers who complain that their labours are not sufficiently rewarded! The brutal scoundrel I was speaking of realized his mistake, but preferred to persist in his madness rather than acknowledge his own guilt. Yet men of this type are never prosecuted for maltreatment, nor are the strict penalties of the law any deterrent against their barbarities. A great many customs have crept into the lives of Christians that would have been too horrible even for Scythians or Phrygians.[41] Without digressing too far from my argument, I may single out one of these, namely 'hazing,' a practice inflicted upon students at the beginning of their studies at a public school. It is an ugly custom matched with an ugly name. Young men of good families sent to school to learn the liberal arts are subjected as part of their initiation to outrages that are unfit for human beings. First, their chins are doused as though to be shaved – and urine, or something even more disgusting, is the liquid used. This is then forced into their mouths, and they have no chance to spit it out. They are also painfully beaten, so that they may lose, as the pretence would have it, their novice's horns. Sometimes large quantities of salt or vinegar – or anything else that will satisfy the savage instincts of youth – are thrust into their mouths. Of course, before the foolery starts, victims are ordered to swear an oath of unconditional obedience. Then, finally, they are grabbed and lifted up from the ground, and their backs are used as battering-rams as often as it pleases their tormentors. These barbaric indignities often lead to fevers and irreparable injuries to the spine. It goes without saying that these senseless pranks are concluded with a drunken feast. Such are the opening ceremonies that mark the beginning of a liberal education! ...

Returning to my main theme, I maintain that nothing is more damaging to young children than constant exposure to beatings. When corporal punishment is applied too harshly the more spirited children are driven to rebellion while the more apathetic ones are numbed into despair. If it is too frequently used, the body will gradually grow inured to beatings and the mind will become unresponsive to what it hears. Nor should sharp words of admonition be used too often. Any medicine wrongly administered aggravates rather than relieves the disease; or if it is taken too often it gradually loses its force and has the effect only of an unpalatable and unwholesome substance which has to be swallowed.

I will stop quarrelling with flogging schoolmasters, but I wish to add one more point: laws and governments which only rely on punishment as a deterrent but do not hold out any possibilities of reward, and which only punish crimes that have been committed but do not provide for anything to prevent these crimes, have always been condemned by wise men. In the same way, we must also condemn the large majority of teachers who will beat their pupils for any misbehaviour but do not foster within them a moral sense as a check against wrongdoing. Suppose a child is ordered to recite a lesson: if he makes a mistake, he is flogged; when this is repeated day after day, the child grows used to this punishment and the teacher thinks he has done his duty well. Surely, other methods should be used. Children should be induced to grow fond of their studies and to refrain from hurting the teacher's feelings. I may seem to have expatiated more than enough on this subject; true, perhaps, if it were not for the fact that this abuse is so widespread that no one can ever speak out sufficiently against it.

It is also beneficial if the prospective teacher deliberately adopts a fatherly attitude towards his pupils; in this way his students will undertake their studies with great enthusiasm, while he himself finds less tedium in his work. Love will overcome almost any difficult challenge. The old saying has it that like rejoices in like; so the teacher must, as it were, become a child again and thus win the affection of his students. Of course it is foolish to entrust one's children to old, nearly decrepit men for their first education. Such men are truly children; their stammering speech is real and not pretended. I prefer a teacher who is of an age when his vigour is in its prime, an age which does not repel his pupils and allows him to assume any role. In guiding the intellectual development of his students, the instructor should abide by the same principles that are followed by parents and nurses in promoting physical growth. For example, when an infant is taught how to articulate words, his instructor relies on imitation and prattles baby-talk. Also, when a child is taught how to eat, he is fed porridge which consists largely of milk and which has already been chewed beforehand; only when the food has been well softened is it slowly put into his mouth. And again, when a child is being taught to walk, his instructor bends his body and accommodates his own pace to that of the other. At first, an infant is given only limited quantities of selected foods, and by gradual steps is permitted to advance to more solid nourishment as he grows older. So a very natural kind of food, not very different from milk, is what a child requires at the beginning; even this, when it is introduced in too large a quantity, will choke the infant or cause him to vomit and stain his clothes – only when it is slowly and gradually introduced will it please the child. We observe the same thing happening when a liquid is poured into a vessel that has a narrow opening: if too much is poured in, the jar will overflow; but if the liquid is introduced only very gradually, step by step, so to speak, the vessel will become filled – slowly, of course, but filled all the same. Just as food and drink introduced slowly in small quantities will give the right nourishment for young bodies, so also young minds exposed to a congenial programme of studies that is assimilated in gradual stages and intermingled with play will soon adapt themselves to a more substantial course of learning. This can be done without any weariness since the slow process of accumulation is free from any sense of fatigue and thus can produce the most impressive results. We know the story, for instance, of an athlete[42] who would carry a young calf for several miles every day and was still able to do it without any strain even when the animal had grown into a bull; it was because the daily small increase in weight was imperceptible that he could accomplish this feat. There are those, however, who expect boys to grow into old men within the shortest period of time, not taking into consideration the limitations to which the early years of life are subject, and without measuring the intellectual capacities of the young against their own. So they exert relentless pressure on students, demand a full load of work, and wrinkle their foreheads when a pupil does not meet their expectations; they act as if they were dealing with adults, forgetting that they too were once children. How much more understanding is the advice given by Pliny the Younger to a rather strict schoolmaster: 'Remember that your pupil is still only a youth and that you were once young yourself.'[43] Indeed, many act so cruelly towards their students that one would think that they had forgotten that both they themselves and their pupils were human beings.

You will now ask me to explain what type of learning is suitable for a young mind and can be instilled into small children. First of all, there must be training in the use of the classical languages; this is a skill which children will acquire without any effort, whereas adults will scarcely accomplish it even with the greatest application. As I have already pointed out, children are attracted to this study because of their natural urge to imitate, an instinct of which we discover traces in starlings and parrots also. Can you imagine anything more appealing than the fables of the ancient authors? Their charm casts such an enticing spell upon children's ears that even adults will derive a great deal of benefit from these stories, not only for the study of language, but also as a guide to practical thinking and as a source of good vocabulary. ... Or is there anything that gives greater pleasure than comedy? The essence of comedy is portrayal of character, but it leaves an impression even on children and the uneducated; here, too, an immense amount of moral teaching is imparted by means of humour. Children should also learn the names of objects of every variety; it is incredible how many people, even those who have a reputation for learning, are completely in the dark as far as the correct names of all sorts of things are concerned. Finally, young children should be taught brief, pointed aphorisms, which include almost all proverbs and sayings of famous men, and which used to be the only means whereby moral truths were passed on to the common people.

Sometimes signs of a special inclination towards certain branches of study, such as music, arithmetic, and geography, appear in very young children. I have myself known young pupils who, though decidedly backward in learning grammatical and rhetorical rules, were found to have a great propensity for other, more recondite disciplines. Each individual talent, therefore, should be helped to follow its own spontaneous inclinations. Going downhill is no effort at all, but 'nothing can be said or done against the will of Minerva.'[44] I once knew a boy who could not yet speak but who would pretend he was reading while sitting before an open volume; he would spend many hours in this way and never grow bored; and no matter how bitterly he wept you could always calm him by putting a book in front of him. His parents naturally saw in this a promise that their son would one day be a great scholar, and the boy's name, Jerome, seemed to confirm this. I do not know how he is doing at present, I have not laid eyes on him since he has grown up.

Children make good progress in learning a language if they are raised among adults who are well spoken. They also learn their stories and fables with greater enthusiasm and remember them more easily if the contents are displayed before their eyes by means of skilful illustration, and if every story is presented through pictures. This works equally well when you are teaching children about trees, plants, and animals and their names and characteristics, especially when you are speaking about animals that are very rare, like the rhinoceros, the horse-stag, the pelican, the Indian ass, or the elephant. ...

Most children enjoy pictures of hunting scenes, and these provide the teacher with an excellent opportunity for introducing his students quite casually to a large variety of trees, plants, birds, and animals. But I shall not detain you with any further examples since in this case it is easy to form some general idea from one example.

The teacher must, of course, be careful in his choice of subject-matter and put before his students only what he finds to be especially agreeable, relevant, and attractive material, which flowers, so to speak, with promise. For youth is the springtime of life, abounding with sweetly smiling flowers and brightly verdant fields, followed by the harvest time of full manhood when the ripened crops are gathered in. As it is foolish to search for a ripe grape in spring or a rose in autumn, so also the instructor must observe what is appropriate for each stage of life. Gaiety and charm – these are the qualities that belong to youth. In fact, dullness and harshness ought to be entirely banished from all study. The ancients, if I am not mistaken, expressed the same idea when they attributed to the Muses radiant beauty, song, and dance enjoyed amid pleasant groves, and furthermore gave them the Graces as companions; for they believed that success in study depended basically on a relationship of good will between student and master; this is why they applied the term 'humanities' to literary studies.

Yet there is nothing which prevents usefulness from going hand in hand with pleasure, and integrity with enjoyment. When these qualities are combined, children acquire a whole range of beneficial learning without experiencing any boredom. What is there to hinder them from learning delightful tales, witty aphorisms, memorable incidents from history, or intelligent fables with no greater effort than that with which they pick up and absorb stupid, often vulgar ballads, ridiculous old wives' tales, and all sorts of tedious womanish gossip? Think of all the rubbish we can still remember now as grown men – dreams, inane riddles, silly nursery rhymes about phantoms, spectres, ghosts, screech-owls, vampires, bogeymen, fairies and demons; all those unedifying falsehoods taken from popular story-books, and all those crazy tales and fantasies of a risqué sort – all those things we learned as children, sitting with our grandfathers or grandmothers, or with nurses and girls at their spinning, while they caressed us and played with us.

I have now come to the stage of my argument where I shall briefly explain how love of study may be instilled in children – a subject which I have already touched upon in part. As I have said, through practice we acquire painlessly the ability to speak. The art of reading and writing comes next; this involves some tedium, which can be relieved, however, by an expert teacher who spices his instruction with pleasant inducements. One encounters children who toil and sweat endlessly before they can recognize and combine into words the letters of the alphabet and learn even the bare rudiments of grammar, yet who can readily grasp the higher forms of knowledge. As the ancients have demonstrated, there are artful means to overcome this slowness. Teachers of antiquity, for instance, would bake cookies of the sort that children like into the shape of letters, so that their pupils might, so to speak, hungrily eat their letters; for any student who could correctly identify a letter would be rewarded with it. Other teachers would carve ivory in the shape of letters as toys for their pupils, or would resort to any other devices which would readily capture the attention of the young. The English are very partial to archery, which is the first thing they teach their children. One clever father, therefore, seeing how fond his son was of the game, had a beautiful set of bow and arrows made, decorated all over with the letters of the alphabet. As targets he used the shapes of letters of the Greek and Latin alphabets (starting with the Greek); when the boy hit a target and pronounced the letter correctly he would be applauded and be rewarded in addition with a cherry or something else that children like. I might add that even better results are obtained with this game if there are two or three well-matched contestants competing with each other, the reason being that hope of victory and fear of disgrace will make each of them more alert and enthusiastic. It was by means of this stratagem that the boy in question learned in a few days of fun and play to identify and pronounce his letters – something which the majority of teachers, with all their beatings, threatenings, and insults, could scarcely have accomplished in three years.

I disapprove, however, of certain teachers, whose zeal in applying these methods goes too far and who add spurious colour to these methods by introducing games of chess or dice. Such games are beyond the capacity of children; so how can they be used to teach them? Rather than relieving the burden placed on our children's intellects, they pile up more strain. I am also critical of the use of techniques that are so complicated they actually delay the results that are to be achieved. Here I am thinking of certain mnemonic devices which seem to have been dreamed up only to serve personal gain or fame rather than for any useful purpose; in fact, their effect on the faculty of memory is quite harmful. The best technique for remembering anything is as follows: have a thorough grasp of your subject and arrange in order everything you have grasped, and then go over repeatedly everything you wish to recall.

The motives of victory and competition are deeply embedded in our children, and the fear of disgrace and desire for praise are also deeply rooted, especially in children who have outstanding intellectual abilities and energetic personalities. The teacher should exploit these motives to advance their education. If he cannot make headway with a certain pupil by using entreaties, flattery, or praise or by promising small rewards, he should organize a mock contest between him and his fellow-students. A lazy student should hear his comrades being praised; and a boy who is deaf to his teacher's exhortations will be stirred to action by the desire to emulate his fellows. The palm of victory should not be conferred for good and all, but hope should be held out to the loser that with concentrated effort he may make good his disgrace – this is how commanders exhort their soldiers in war. Sometimes it is right to leave a pupil in the illusion that he can win even though he does not have the capacity. In short, by alternating praise and blame, the instructor will awaken in his pupils a useful spirit of rivalry, to use Hesiod's expression.[45]

There remains one final objection to be answered. It is frequently argued by some that the benefits obtained by a pupil over three or four years are not worth all the effort that goes into the teaching and all the expenses that are incurred. It appears to me, however, that the primary concern of these people is not to think of their children's interests but to spare the instructor and their own purse. I would deny anyone to be a true father who is so anxiously concerned about expense when the education of his son is at stake. It would be foolish indulgence on our part to let several years in a child's life go to waste in order that the teacher may spare himself some effort. It may be true, as is not denied by Quintilian, that more may be accomplished in a single year at a later stage than in these first three or four years; but even so, why should we slight these results, small though they may be, when we are concerned with something of supreme value? Even though the results may be trifling, still it is better for children to be engaged in learning than to learn nothing at all, or to learn something that they have to unlearn later. Is there any better way to keep children occupied once they are able to speak? We know that they must always have something to do. Even though the gains made during these early years may be quite modest, still a child who has made them his own will be able to advance to higher grades of learning at a time when otherwise he would have to cover the preliminary stages. As Quintilian says, 'Knowledge accumulated year after year will add up to a great total, and time already gained during childhood will be a gain for the years of adolescence.'[46]

I need not repeat the fact that certain things that would later require much effort may be easily learned during the first years. We learn best when the time is right. Granted that the first steps may be trifling, they are nevertheless of critical importance. In fact, I would say that to have acquired, if not complete proficiency in, at least a taste of Greek and

Latin, and to have made a good start in acquiring a wide vocabulary and the skills of reading and writing, represents no mean step in one's intellectual development.

But what is our practice now? We keep our children at home past their years of puberty. Then, having corrupted them with habits of idleness, luxury, and sensuality, we finally send them off belatedly to a public school. ...

The best years of our lives are wasted in idleness and bad habits; infected by these, we give only a small portion of our time to study, but squander the greater part on whoring, feasting, and gambling. And over this wretched material presides a master-craftsman who is no better, who teaches either worthless nonsense or things which have to be unlearned later. Yet, faced with these conditions, we still offer excuses: that young children are frail creatures whose minds are not ready as yet for instruction, that the gains are only meagre, and many other excuses, whereas only a misdirected education ought to be blamed for any harm that is done.

I shall not weary you by prolonging my discussion. I appeal to that practical wisdom which you have always displayed in other things. I ask you to consider how dear a possession your son is; how many-sided and exacting, and yet also how glorious, is the pursuit of knowledge; consider the agility of a child's mind for absorbing every kind of teaching, and the flexibility of the human mind in general. Remember how easily anything that is good and congenial to nature may be learned, especially when the subject is taught in the guise of play by a wise and sympathetic instructor. Remember also how easily young and receptive minds take in and retain knowledge that at a more advanced age must be acquired with greater difficulty and is also lost with much greater ease. Finally, reflect how precious time is; once spent it can never be restored. It is of the utmost importance, therefore, to make an early beginning and to do everything in season. The power of persistence is great; you will recall Hesiod's proverbial heap, rising higher and higher as more and more tiny grains are added. Above all, remember that time is fleeting, youth is always busy, and old age is beyond instruction. If you reflect upon all this, you will not allow your new-born son to lose, no, not seven years, but even three days, during which he might receive to some advantage his first grounding or instruction in knowledge.

# On Good Manners / *De civilitate*

*On Good Manners*, published in 1530, was the last of Erasmus' educational treatises. It was dedicated to the eleven-year-old Henry of Veere, with whose family Erasmus had long-standing connections. The treatise is written in the tradition of medieval manuals offering instruction in courtly manners, but is characterized throughout by the purpose of instilling piety and seeing it realized in everyday conduct. Another characteristic feature of *On Good Manners* is the absence of dogmatic pronouncements. Erasmus' own travels throughout Europe are reflected in the variety of social customs on which he draws to illustrate his theme.

The work was an immediate success and saw more than a dozen editions in 1530 alone. Its pervasive influence can be gauged by its translation into the vernacular: English in 1532, German in 1536, French and Czech in 1537.

This extract is taken from CWE 25 273–89, translated and annotated by Brian McGregor. The complete title is *On Good Manners for Boys / De civilitate morum puerilium.*

## ON GOOD MANNERS FOR BOYS

TO THE MOST NOBLE HENRY OF BURGUNDY, YOUTH OF OUTSTANDING PROMISE AND SON OF ADOLPH, PRINCE OF VEERE

### 1 On the body

If on three separate occasions that illustrious man St Paul[1] was not averse to becoming all things to all men so that he might benefit all, how much less ought I be irked at repeatedly resuming the role of youth through a desire to help the young. And so, just as in the past I adapted myself to the early youth of your brother, Maximilian of Burgundy,[2] while I was shaping the speech of the very young, so now, my dearest Henry, I adapt myself to your boyhood so that I may give instruction in manners appropriate to boys. You, of course, are not in any great need of these rules, having been, in the first place, brought up from infancy at court, and then having obtained in Johannes Crucius[3] an outstanding teacher of the very young. Nor is everything that we shall set forth apposite to you who are born into, and destined for, the purple. My purpose is rather to encourage all boys to learn these rules more willingly because they have been dedicated to a boy of such momentous destiny and of such outstanding promise. For it will be a considerable additional spur to all the young to observe that children of illustrious descent are dedicated to learning right from their earliest years, and are competing in the same race as themselves.

The task of fashioning the young is made up of many parts, the first and consequently the most important of which consists of implanting the seeds of piety in the tender heart; the second in instilling a love for, and thorough knowledge of, the liberal arts; the third in giving instruction in the duties of life; the fourth in training in good manners right from the very earliest years. This last I have now taken up as my special task. For others as well as I have written at great length on the other aspects I have mentioned. Now although external decorum of the body proceeds from a well-ordered mind, yet we observe that sometimes even upright and learned men lack social grace because they have not been taught properly. I do not deny that external decorum is a very crude part of philosophy, but in the present climate of opinion it is very conducive to winning good will and to commending those illustrious gifts of the intellect to the eyes of men. It is seemly for the whole man to be well ordered in mind, body, gesture, and clothing. But above all, propriety becomes all boys, and in particular those of noble birth. Now everyone who cultivates the mind in liberal studies must be taken to be noble. Let others paint lions, eagles, bulls, and leopards on their escutcheons; those who can display 'devices' of the intellect commensurate with their grasp of the liberal arts have a truer nobility.

Thus, for the well-ordered mind of a boy to be universally manifested – and it is most strongly manifested in the face – the eyes should be calm, respectful, and steady: not grim, which is a mark of truculence; not shameless, the hallmark of insolence; not darting and rolling, a feature of insanity; nor furtive, like those of suspects and plotters of treachery; nor gaping like those idiots; nor should the eyes be constantly blinking, a mark of the fickle; nor gaping as in astonishment – a characteristic observed in Socrates; not too narrowed, a sign of bad temper; nor bold and inquisitive, which indicates impertinence; but such as reflects a mind composed, respectful, and friendly. For it is no chance saying of the ancient sages that the seat of the soul is in the eyes. Old pictures tell us that it was once a mark of singular modesty to observe with eyes half-closed, just as among certain Spaniards to avoid looking at people is taken as a sign of politeness and friendship. In the same we learn from pictures that it was once the case that tightly closed lips were taken as evidence of honesty. But the naturally decorous is recognized as such by everyone. Nevertheless in these matters too it is occasionally appropriate for us to play the polypus and adapt ourselves to the customs of the region. There are certain manners of the eyes which nature bestows differently upon different men and which do not fall within our purview, save that ill-composed gesture often destroys the character and appearance not only of the eyes but of the whole body as well. On the other hand, well-composed gestures render what is naturally decorous even more attractive: if they do not remove defects, at least they disguise and minimize them. It is bad manners to look at someone with one eye open and one shut. For what else is this than to deprive oneself of an eye? Let us leave that gesture to tunnies and smiths.[4]

The eyebrows should be smooth: not contracted; which denotes fierceness; not arched, a sign of arrogance; not pressed down over the eyes, like those of an evil schemer. The brow also should be cheerful and smooth, indicating a good conscience and an open mind: not lined with wrinkles, a sign of old age; not irresolute like a hedgehog's; not menacing like a bull's.

The nostrils should be free from any filthy collection of mucus, as this is disgusting (the philosopher Socrates was reproached for that failing too). It is boorish to wipe one's nose on one's cap or clothing; to do so on one's sleeve or forearm is for fishmongers, and it is not much better to wipe it with one's hand, if you then smear the discharge on your clothing. The polite way is to catch the matter from the nose in a handkerchief, and this should be done by turning away slightly if decent people are present. If, in clearing your nose with two fingers, some matter falls on the ground, it should be immediately ground under foot. It is bad manners to breathe noisily all the time, which is the sign of furious anger. It is even worse to make a habit of snorting like one possessed, although we must make allowance for heavy breathers who are afflicted with asthma. It is ridiculous to trumpet with one's nose; this is for horn-blowers and elephants. Twitching the nose is for scoffers and buffoons. If you must sneeze while others are present, it is polite to turn away. When the attack has subsided you should cross your face, then, raising your cap and acknowledging the blessings of those who have (or you assume to have) blessed you (for sneezing, like yawning, completely mocks one's sense of hearing), beg pardon or give thanks. One should be scrupulous in blessing another when he sneezes. If older people are present and bless a high-ranking man or woman, the polite thing for a boy to do is to raise his cap. Again, to imitate or consciously repeat a sneeze – in effect to show off one's strength – is the sign of a fool. To suppress a sound which is brought on by nature is characteristic of silly people who set more store by 'good manners' than good health.

A natural and wholesome modesty, not false or artificial colouring, should give the cheeks their glow. Although even that modesty should be so moderated that it is not construed as insolence and does not connote embarrassment or stupidity and the fourth degree of insanity, as the proverb puts it. For this condition is so uncontrolled in some people that it seems very close to madness. This defect can be mitigated if a boy is accustomed to living among older people and if he is given an outlet in play-acting. Puffing out the cheeks is a sign of arrogance, while deflating them is a sign of mental despair: the former is the characteristic of Cain, the latter of Judas the betrayer.

The mouth should be neither tight-set, which denotes someone afraid of inhaling someone else's breath, nor gaping open like an idiot's, but formed with lips lightly touching one another. Nor is it very polite to be repeatedly pursing the lips as if making a clucking sound, although that gesture is excusable in grown-ups of high rank as they pass through the midst of a throng; for in the case of such people all things are becoming, while we are concerned in moulding a boy.

If you should feel the urge to yawn and are unable to turn aside or withdraw, you should cover your mouth with a handkerchief or with the palm of the hand and then make the sign of the cross. To laugh at every word or deed is the sign of a fool; to laugh at none the sign of a blockhead. It is quite wrong to laugh at improper words or actions. Loud laughter and the immoderate mirth that shakes the whole body are unbecoming to any age but much more so to youth. The neighing sound that some people make when they laugh is also unseemly. And the person who opens his mouth wide in a rictus, with wrinkled cheeks and exposed teeth, is also impolite. This is a canine habit. The face should express mirth in such a way that it neither distorts the appearance of the mouth nor evinces a dissolute mind. Only fools use expressions like: 'I am dissolving with laughter,' 'I am bursting with laughter,' 'I am dying with laughter.' If something so funny should occur that it produces uncontrolled laughter of this sort, the face should be covered with a napkin or with the hand. To laugh when alone or for no obvious reason is put down to either stupidity or insanity. If, however, something of that sort happens, it is good manners to explain the reason for your laughter to others, or if you do not believe that a true reason should be offered, fabricate something lest someone suspect that he is being laughed at. It is not polite to grip the lower lip with the upper teeth, for this is a threatening gesture, as is biting the upper lip with the lower teeth. But it is simply silly to be repeatedly licking round the edges of the lips. Their pictures tell us that it was once a sign of politeness among the Germans to pucker the lips slightly and form them as for a kiss. It is foolish to poke the tongue out to mock someone. Turn away when spitting to avoid spitting on or spraying someone. If any disgusting matter is spat onto the ground, it should, as I have said, be ground under foot lest it nauseate someone. If that is impermissible, catch up the spittle with a cloth. Reswallowing spittle is uncouth as is the practice we observe in some people of spitting after every third word, not through need but through force of habit. Some have the distressing habit of coughing slightly while speaking, again, not through need but through habit. That is a gesture of liars and of those who deceitfully contrive their words when they speak. Some have the even more disagreeable habit of belching after every third word, a practice which if developed from the earliest years stays with one even in later life. The terms in which Terence's Clitipho[5] is censured by his slave are equally applicable to hawking. If you feel the need to cough see that you do not cough into someone's face and avoid the absurdity of coughing more loudly than necessity requires. Withdraw when you are going to vomit; vomiting is not shameful, but to have vomited through gluttony is disgusting.

Attention must be paid to the care of the teeth, but to whiten them with fine powder is for girls, while brushing with salt or alum harms the gums. To brush them with urine is a custom of the Spaniards. Food particles should be removed from the teeth, not with a knife or with the nails, in the manner of dogs or cats, and not with a napkin, but with a toothpick of mastic wood, or with a feather, or with small bones taken from the drumsticks of cocks or hens. To rinse the mouth in the morning with clean water is both polite and healthy, but it is foolish to do so again and again. We shall talk about the exercise of the tongue at the appropriate point.

It is boorish to go about with one's hair uncombed: it should be neat, but not as elaborate as a girl's coiffure. It should be free from infections of nits and vermin. It is not polite to be continually scratching one's head in front of others just as it is unsightly to scratch the rest of the body, especially if it is done through habit rather than necessity. The hair should neither cover the brow nor flow down over the shoulders. To be constantly tossing the hair with a flick of the head is for frolicsome horses. It is not very elegant to brush back the hair from the forehead with the left hand; it is more discreet to part it with the hand. Letting the neck droop forward and hunching one's shoulders betokens laziness, while tossing the head back from the body is a sign of haughtiness. It should be held gently erect, and the neck should incline neither to left or right (for that is the gesture of mimes) unless conversation or some such thing requires it. The shoulders should be held evenly balanced, not like sailyards, with one raised and the other lowered. If neglected in boyhood, bodily habits of this sort become ingrained and deform the natural posture of the body. Accordingly, those who through laziness have acquired the habit of hunching their bodies are ensuring for themselves a humpback which nature has not bestowed, and those who have become used to holding their heads to one side grow fixed in that habit, with the result that their efforts to alter it in later life are to no avail. Young bodies resemble young shoots, which come to maturity and acquire the fixed characteristics of whatever you determine for them with a pole or trellis. Twisting both arms behind your back makes you look like an idler and a thief; nor is it much more seemly to stand or sit with one hand resting on the groin, although to some people such a posture seems elegant and to give a soldierly bearing. But what accords with nature and reason is a ready guide to decency; the taste of fools is not. I shall deal with what remains when I come to the sections on discourse and feasts.

To expose, save for natural reasons, the parts of the body which nature has invested with modesty ought to be far removed from the conduct of a gentleman. I will go further: when necessity compels such action, it should none the less be done with decency and modesty even if there is no observer present. For the angels, from whom derives that most welcome sense of shame that accompanies and protects the chastity of boys, are always near. Modesty requires such things be hidden from sight, much less exposed to contact with somebody else. To repress the need to urinate is injurious to health; but propriety requires it to be done in private. There are some who lay down the rule that a boy should refrain from breaking wind by constricting his buttocks. But it is no part of good manners to bring illness upon yourself while striving to appear 'polite.' If you may withdraw, do so in private. But if not, then in the words of the old adage, let him cover the sound with a cough. Besides, why do they not rule in the same way that boys should not purge their bowels, since it is more dangerous to refrain from breaking wind than it is to constrict the bowels?

Sitting with knees apart or standing with legs wide apart or crossed is the hallmark of a braggart. The knees should be together when sitting, the feet together, or only slightly apart, when standing. Some people adopt the posture of crossing one leg over the other when sitting, while others stand with their legs crossed; the former is a sign of uneasiness, the latter of ineptness. It used to be customary for kings to sit with the right foot resting on the left thigh, but this has gone out of fashion. Among the Italians, some people out of respect press one foot on the other and almost take the weight on one leg in the manner of storks. Whether this is becoming in boys I cannot say. Likewise in bowing, standards of propriety and impropriety vary from people to people. Some bend each knee equally, and there again, some do so while keeping the body erect, others while bowing slightly. There are those who, considering this to be somewhat effeminate, maintain the erect posture of the body but bend first the right knee and then the left, a gesture which is favoured among the English for the young. The French accompany a measured turn of the body with a bow of the right knee only. In such matters, where the various techniques do not conflict with basic good taste, it will be permissible either to follow one's native fashion or comply with foreign practice (since some are much enamoured of foreign ways). The gait should be neither mincing nor headlong, the former being a sign of effeminacy, the latter of rage. Nor should it be reeling – a gait which Quintilian disapproves of.[6] We should leave the foolish semihalting gait to Swiss soldiers and to those who consider it a great decoration to sport feathers in their caps. And yet we see that bishops pride themselves in such a bearing. Shuffling the feet while sitting is the mark of fools just as gesticulating with the hands is the sign of an unsound mind.

## 2 On dress

We have dealt in general terms with the body, and now we should say a few words about dress, because clothing is in a way the body's body, and from this too one may infer the state of a man's character. And yet, no fixed rule can be laid down on this matter, because everyone does not have the same fortune or rank, and standards of what is becoming and what is not differ among nations. Finally, what pleases or displeases varies from age to age. Consequently here too, as in many other things, some allowance must be made, as the proverb has it, for custom and place and also for time, which the wise bid us take into account. Nevertheless, allowing for these variables, naturally good or bad taste does exist. Things which are useless to the function of an article of dress, for example, are in bad taste. To drag long trains after one is ridiculous in women, reprehensible in men; whether becoming in cardinals and bishops I leave for others to judge. Transparent clothing has always been strongly disapproved of both for men and for women, since the second function of clothing is to cover what gives offence to men's sight. It was once held to be somewhat effeminate not to wear a belt, but nowadays nobody is faulted for this, because with the invention of underwear, shirts, and hose, the private parts are concealed even if the tunic fly open. Furthermore, clothing too short to conceal, when one is bending over, those parts that modesty requires to be hidden is distasteful in every society. Slashed garments are for fools; embroidered and multicoloured ones for idiots and apes.

Consequently, style of dress should be in accordance with one's means and station, one's locality and its standards, neither conspicuous by its shabbiness nor indicative of opulence, loose living, or arrogance. A degree of negligence in dress suits young men provided it does not lapse into slovenliness. Disgustingly, some people decorate the hems of their shirts and tunics with drops of urine or encrust their shirt-fronts and sleeves with a repulsive plastering, not unfortunately of plaster, but of snot and phlegm. Some wear their clothing lopsided, while others have it hitched up in back as far as the kidneys – some people even think this is elegant! Just as the entire dress of the body should be tasteful and well-ordered, so too should it harmonize with the lines of the body. If your parents have given you clothing of a superior elegance, do not swivel about to admire yourself or leap for joy and preen yourself in front of other people, for the former behaviour is for apes, the latter for peacocks. Let others admire while you yourself appear unaware that you are well turned out. The greater a man's wealth, the more agreeable is his modesty. To those of lesser means one should allow the consolation of modest self-pride. But a rich man, by flaunting the magnificence of his dress, brings home to others their own wretchedness and incites envy against himself.

### 3 On behaviour in church

Whenever you pass the doors of a church, bare your head and kneel modestly, facing the host, and invoke Christ and the saints. A similar pattern should also be followed at any time when the image of the cross appears, whether in the city or in the countryside. Do not pass the threshold of a church without addressing Christ in at least a short prayer with a similar degree of reverence, that is, with bared head and on both knees. When mass is being celebrated the entire bearing of the body should accord with the nature of the rite. Reflect on the presence there of Christ together with countless thousands of angels. If someone intended to address a king – a mortal surrounded by a throng of courtiers – without uncovering his head and bowing, he would be taken by all to be not merely uncivilized but completely mad. If this is so, what kind of behaviour would it be to have one's head covered during mass and to remain standing in the presence of the King of Kings, immortal and giver of immortality, surrounded by the venerable host of heavenly spirits? It does not matter that you do not see them; they see you, and their presence is no less certain than if you were to see them with the eyes of the body. For the eyes of the spirit perceive more clearly than those of the flesh. It is also somewhat lacking in decorum to walk up and down in church and play the peripatetic[7] as some people do. Promenading is appropriate to the portico and the market-place, but not to church, which is dedicated to sermons, the sacred mysteries, and prayer. The eyes should be fixed upon the preacher, the ears should be attentive to him, the mind should be concentrated on him in total reverence, as if you were listening not to a man, but to God speaking to you through the mouth of a man. When the Gospel is being recited, rise up and try to listen reverently. During the singing of the Creed, when they come to the passage 'and was made man' fall down on your knees, even in this way lowering yourself in honour of him who for your salvation, although lord of all the heavens, came down to earth; who, although God, deigned to become a man to make you one with God. While the sacred mysteries are being enacted, with every fibre in your body striving towards the state of reverence, let your face be turned towards the altar, your mind towards Christ. Touching the ground with one knee while the other is upright supporting the left elbow is the gesture of the impious soldiers who addressed the Lord Jesus in mockery, 'Hail, King of the Jews!'[8] You should kneel on both knees with the rest of the body slightly bowed in veneration. For the rest of the time either read something from the missal, whether on prayer or on the doctrine of salvation, or let the mind meditate on some aspect of the divine. At such a time, to murmur nonsense in the ear of your neighbour is for people who do not believe that Christ is present there, while to let the eyes roam hither and yon is a sign of foolishness. Consider in effect that you have entered the church to no purpose unless you leave it a better and purer man.

## 4 On banquets

At banquets there should be joviality but no wantonness. Never sit down without having washed and without first trimming your nails lest any dirt stick to them; before sitting down you should have urinated in private, or defecated if need be; and if your belt happens to be too tight it is prudent to slacken the buckle a little – an action that would be inelegant at table. When wiping your hands, wipe away at the same time whatever troubles your mind, for it is bad manners to be sad at a banquet or to sadden anyone else. If bidden to say grace, compose your expression and hands as befits the solemn office, looking towards either the one first in order of precedence at the banquet or the image of Christ, if one should be there, genuflecting at the name of Jesus and the Virgin Mary. If this duty has been delegated to someone else, listen and make your responses with no less reverence. Gladly yield precedence in seating in another, and decline courteously when invited to a place of great honour. If, however, someone in authority should make repeated and pressing demands for this, comply modestly, so that you do not, through courtesy, appear intransigent. When sitting down have both hands on the table, not clasped together, nor on the plate. It is permissible for the elderly and convalescent to lean one or both elbows on the table; but this, as practised by some affected courtiers who consider their every action elegant, is something to be avoided, not imitated. Meanwhile, be careful not to be a nuisance by nudging the person beside you with your elbow or kicking the person opposite you. Fidgeting in one's seat, shifting from side to side, gives the appearance of repeatedly breaking wind or of trying to do so. The body should, therefore, be upright and evenly balanced. If given a napkin, put it over either the left shoulder or the left forearm. When you are at table with persons of note, comb your hair and take off your cap, unless the custom of the area decrees otherwise, or one whose rank it would be impolite not to accede to requests it. It is the custom among some peoples for boys to stand bareheaded and take their food at the end of the table of their elders. In such societies a boy should not approach the table unless bidden nor should he remain until the end of the banquet, but having satisfied his hunger and removed his plate, he should bow and salute the guests, especially the most distinguished among them. The cup and small eating knife, duly cleaned, should be on the right-hand side, the bread on the left. Grasping the bread in the palm of the hand and breaking it with the fingertips is an affected practice which should be left to certain courtiers. You should cut if properly with your knife, not tearing off the crust or cutting it away from both sides as this smacks of affectation. The ancients were in the habit at every banquet of piously treating bread as something sacred and it is from this that the present custom has derived of kissing the bread if it happens to fall on the ground.

To begin a meal with drinking is the hallmark of a drunkard who drinks not from need but from habit. Such a practice is not only morally degrading but also injurious to bodily health. One should not start drinking as soon as one has a spoonful of soup, much less so after taking some milk. For a boy to drink more than twice or at most three times in the course of a banquet is neither seemly nor healthful. He should have his first drink at some time during the second course of the meal, especially if it is a dry one; his second, towards the close of the banquet. He should take it in moderate sips, and not gurgle it down sounding like a horse. Both wine and beer (which is no less intoxicating than wine) are as injurious to a boy's health as they are harmful to his character. Water is suitable for the vigour of youth, or if the nature of the region or some other reason prevents his drinking water a boy should drink a light beer, or nonpotent wine diluted with water. Otherwise the wages of addiction to undiluted wine are decaying teeth, bloated cheeks, impaired eyesight, mental dulness – in short, premature old age. Chew your food before you drink and do not raise the cup to your lips without first wiping them with a napkin or cloth, especially if someone offers you his cup or when drinking from the common cup. It is discourteous to look askance at others while you are drinking, just as it is impolite to turn your neck round like a stork lest a drop remain at the bottom of the cup. You should courteously acknowledge someone toasting you with his cup, and touching your own cup with your lips sip a little and pretend to drink: this will satisfy a polite man simply playing the buffoon. When someone boorishly presses you to drink, promise to reply when you have grown up.

Some people have scarcely seated themselves comfortably before they thrust their hands into the dishes. That is the behaviour of wolves. Do not be the first to touch food set on the table, not only because that convicts you of greed, but because it does, on occasion, involve danger, since someone who takes a mouthful of burning hot food without first testing it is forced either to spit it out, or, if he swallows it, to scald his gullet – in either event appearing both foolish and pitiful. Some degree of delay is necessary so that a boy becomes accustomed to controlling his appetite. With such an end view, Socrates never let himself drink from the first wine bowl of the evening even when he was an old man. If seated with his elders, a boy should be the last to reach for his plate – and only when he has been invited to do so. It is boorish to plunge your hands into sauced dishes. You should take what you want with a knife or fork; nor should you select from the entire dish as epicures do but should take whatever portion is in front of you – as you may learn from Homer who frequently employs this line: 'They put forth their hands to the dishes lying ready before them.'[9] But if that portion also is extremely choice, then you should leave it for someone else and take the next piece. Just as it is, therefore, a sign of intemperance to thrust your hand into every part of the dish, so it is equally impolite to turn the dish so that the choicer morsels come to you. If someone else offers you a choicer portion of food, you should demur a little before accepting, but after cutting off a small portion for yourself you should offer the remainder to the giver or share it with your neighbour. What cannot be taken with the fingers should be taken on your plate. If someone offers you a piece of cake or pie take it on a spoon or plate, or take what is offered on a spoon and, placing the food on your plate, return the spoon. If what is given is rather fluid, take it on a spoon for tasting and return the spoon after wiping it on a napkin. It is equally impolite to lick greasy fingers or to wipe them on one's tunic: you should wipe them with a napkin or cloth. To consume whole pieces of food at a gulp is for storks and buffoons. If a portion is cut by someone else, it is impolite to hold out your hand or plate before the carver has offered the portion, lest you appear to be snatching what has been prepared for someone else. What is offered should be taken in three fingers or by holding out your plate. If what is offered does not agree with you be careful not to use the comic character Clitophon's words: 'I cannot, sir!'[10] but rather thank him courteously. For this is the most polite form of refusal. If the person persists in urging it on you, say respectfully either that it does not agree with you or that you want nothing more.

The technique of carving should be learned from the earliest years, and not performed overelaborately as some do, but politely and properly. For the shoulder is carved in one way, the haunch in another, the neck in another, the ribs in another; a capon in one way, a pheasant in another, a partridge in another, and a duck in another; so that to teach them one by one would be time-consuming and not worth the trouble. The following can be given as a general guide: it is excessively fastidious to carve off from every portion what is pleasing to your palate. It is rude to offer someone what you have half eaten yourself; it is boorish to redip half-eaten bread into the soup; just as it is disgusting to spit out chewed food and put it on your plate: if you happen to have eaten something that cannot be swallowed, you should discreetly turn away and toss it somewhere. It is discourteous to pick up again half-eaten food or bones once these have been deposited on the plate. Do not throw bones or similar left-overs under the table to litter the floor, or toss them onto the table cloth, or replace them in the serving dish, but put them at the side of your plate or in the dish which some people provide as a receptacle for left-overs. To offer food from the table to other people's dogs is put down to a lack of tact; it is even more tactless to stroke them at the banquet. It is ridiculous to pick an eggshell clean with finger-nails or thumb; to do so by inserting one's tongue is even more ridiculous; the polite way is to use a small knife. To gnaw bones is for a dog; good manners requires them to be picked with a small knife. Three fingers thrust into the salt-cellar is, by common jest, said to be the sign of the boor. The salt you require should be taken on a small knife. If the salt-cellar is some distance away, the plate should be held out to obtain some. To lick a plate or dish to which some sugar or other sweet substance has adhered is for cats, not for people. One should first cut one's meat into small portions on the plate and then add some bread and chew them for some time before swallowing. That is conducive not only to good manners but also to good health. Some rend rather than eat their food, just like those who, as the saying goes, are shortly to be marched off to prison. Such gorging should be left to brigands. Some stuff so much at one time into their mouth that their cheeks swell like a pair of bellows. Others open their jaws so widely in chewing that they produce a noise like pigs. Some in their voracity, breathe heavily through the nose as if they were being strangled. It is neither polite nor safe to drink or speak with one's mouth full. Continuous eating should be interrupted now and again with stories. Some people eat or drink without stopping not because they are hungry or thirsty but because they cannot otherwise moderate their gestures, unless they scratch their head, or pick their teeth, or gesticulate with their hands, or play with their dinner knife, or cough, or clear their throat, or spit. Such habits, even if originating in a sort of rustic shyness, have the appearance of insanity about them. When you have to listen to the conversations of others and you are not given an opportunity to speak, you should conceal any sign of boredom. It is impolite to sit at table rapt in thought. You may, however, observe some people so withdrawn into their private thoughts that they neither hear what others are saying nor are aware that they are eating, and if you call them by name they give the appearance of being roused from sleep – so completely absorbed are they in the dishes. It is bad manners to let your eyes roam around observing what each person is eating, and it is impolite to stare intently at one of the guests. It is even worse to look shiftily out of the corner of your eye at those on the same side of the table; and it is the worst possible form to turn your head right round to see what is happening at another table. It is bad taste for anyone, but much more so for a boy, to gossip about an indiscretion of word or deed someone has committed when in his cups. When seated with his elders a boy should never speak unless the occasion demands it or someone invites him to do so. He should laugh moderately at wittiness but never at improprieties; he should not frown, however, if the person who has uttered them is of superior rank, but so control his expression that he appears either not to have heard them or at least not to have understood them. Silence is becoming in women but even more so in boys.

Some people reply before the speaker has finished what he has to say, so that their unrelated response makes them a laughing-stock and gives rise to the old proverb, 'I was looking for sickles but they said they did not have any spades.' This is taught by the wisest of kings who makes it a sign of stupidity to answer before you hear: he who has not understood does not listen. If he has not fully grasped what a person is saying he should keep silent for a time until the speaker offers to repeat what he has said. Should he fail to do so and presses for a reply, the boy should politely beg his pardon and ask him to repeat what he has said. When a question has been understood he should pause for a moment and then answer briefly and agreeably. Nothing should be blurted out at a banquet that might cloud the spirit of merriment. It is wrong to defame the character of those not present; nor should one's personal sorrow be unburdened to another on such an occasion. It is impolite and shows ingratitude toward your host to find fault with what is set before you. If the banquet is being given at your expense, while it is polite to apologize for the humble quality of the fare, to praise or recall the cost of each item takes the edge off the guests' appetite at once. Finally, if someone through inexperience commit some *faux pas* at a banquet, it should be politely passed over rather than mocked. One should feel at ease during a party. It is a base act, as Horace says,[11] to expose to the light of day something that someone lets slip at dinner without thinking. Pay no heed to what is done or said there, putting it down to the wine: 'I detest a drinking companion who remembers all.'[12] If the banquet goes on later than is suitable for a boy and seems to be slipping into debauchery, as soon as you fully satisfy your needs, take yourself off either surreptitiously or after begging to be excused. Those who compel boys to fast are, in my opinion, no better than those who stuff them with too much food. For fasting undermines the growth of a young body, while too much food destroys the vigour of the mind. Moderation, however, must be learned right from the start. A boy's body should be replenished without being filled to satiety, through frequent rather than heavy meals. Some do not realize that they are full unless their belly is so distended that they are in danger of bursting or unless they discharge their burden by vomiting. Those who habitually allow the very young to sit at banquets that last far into the night show a complete disregard for the well-being of children. If, therefore, you have to rise from a banquet that has gone on for too long, take up your plate with its left-overs and bow to the man who seems to be the most distinguished of the guests, then to the others as a group, and take your leave, but promise to return shortly lest you appear to have left frivolously or out of impoliteness. On your return, wait to see if anything is required or sit respectfully at the table waiting to see if someone asks for something. If you place anything on the table or remove it make sure you do not soak someone's clothing with sauce. When you are going to snuff out a candle, first remove it from the table and immediately dip the wick in sand or stamp it with your shoe to prevent any distasteful smell assailing the nostrils. If offering or pouring something see that you do not do it with your left hand. When called to give a vote of thanks compose your expression showing that you are ready until the guests finally fall silent and the chance to speak presents itself. Meanwhile your gaze should be respectfully and firmly directed towards the master of ceremonies.

## 5 On meeting people

If someone comes along the road who should be respected because of his age, or revered because of his calling, or is heavy with honours, or is worthy of respect for any other reason, a boy should remember to step out of the way, respectfully bare his head, and even make a bow.

By no means should he think along these lines: what have I to do with a stranger; with someone who has never done me a good turn? This mark of respect is being bestowed not on a mere man, not upon the worthy, but on God. Even so did God transmit his command through Solomon who decreed that one should stand up out of respect for the elderly; likewise, through Paul, he bade us show double respect towards our elders; in short, to show respect to everyone to whom respect is due, including even the heathen magistrate. Even if the Turk (heaven forbid!) should rule over us, we would be committing a sin if we were to deny to him the respect due to Caesar. I say nothing for the moment about one's parents to whom, next to God, the highest respect is due. No less respect is owing to teachers who, in forming men's minds, are in a sense their intellectual parents. Even among equals Paul's dictum[13] that they should defer to one another in point of honour holds good. He who defers to an equal or inferior in point of honour does not thereby lower himself but becomes more polite and therefore more worthy of respect. With superiors one should converse respectfully and succinctly; with equals, affectionately and affably. While speaking one should hold one's cap in the left hand while the right hand rests lightly across the belly; to be even more polite, the cap held in both hands with thumbs extended should cover the private parts. It is held to be rather impolite to carry a book or cap under the arm. Modesty should be displayed, but modesty of the becoming sort, not that which attracts attention. The eyes should be directed at the person to whom you are speaking, but should be calm and frank, with no trace of boldness or insolence. Looking down at the ground as the catoblepas[14] does gives the impression of a bad conscience. Looking sideways at someone gives the appearance of being an embezzler. Turning the face this way and that is a sign of inconstancy. It is unseemly to be constantly changing your expression so that at one moment you wrinkle your nose, at another scowl, at another raise an eyebrow, at another twist temperament like that of Proteus.[15] It is also unseemly to toss your head and shake your hair, to cough unnecessarily, to clear your throat, likewise also to scratch your head, to pick your ears, to wipe your nose, to stroke your face as if wiping away your shame, to rub the back of your head, to shrug your shoulders (a characteristic of some Italians). To deny by shaking the head or summon by nodding and, to cut the matter short, 'to converse' by gestures and nods, while appropriate on occasion for a man, is less fitting for a boy. It is ungentlemanly to toss the arms about, to gesticulate with the fingers, to reel about, in short, to converse not with the tongue but with the entire body, which is said to be like turtle-doves or wagtails, and almost as incongruous as the behaviour of magpies.

The voice should be soft and calm, neither raucous like a farmer's nor so subdued that it does not carry to the person you are addressing. Speech should not be precipitate and outstrip its meaning, but slow and distinct. Such a practice too, if it does not completely remove a natural stutter or stammer, certainly reduces it to a large extent, since an overquick delivery creates in many a handicap which nature has not bestowed. When conversing it is polite regularly to employ the correct mode of address of the person to whom you are speaking. Nothing is more honourable or more pleasant than the name of father and mother; nothing more endearing than that of brother or sister. If particular titles escape you, then all learned people should be addressed by you as 'esteemed teachers,' all priests and monks, 'reverend fathers,' all equals, 'brothers and friends,' briefly, all men you do not know should be 'sir,' all women 'madam.' An oath whether made in jest or in earnest comes ill from a boy's lips. For what is more distasteful than that custom among certain peoples where even the girls make every third word an oath: 'by the bread,' 'by the wine,' 'by the candle,' 'by anything at all'? An upright boy should not employ uncouth words in his speech nor lend his ears to them. Finally, whatever causes offence when revealed to men's sight likewise offends when forced upon their hearing. If the conversation requires one to mention some private part of the body, it should be referred to by the way of polite circumlocution. Again if something should come up that might physically upset a listener, for example, if someone should mention vomiting or a latrine or a stench, he should preface it by saying, 'by your leave.'

If something calls for refutation, one should be careful not to say, 'you are not telling the truth,' especially if he is talking to someone of more advanced years, but should beg pardon and say: 'so-and-so gave me a different version of that.' A polite boy should not provoke a quarrel with anyone, not even with his equals, but if a disagreement arises he should concede victory or appeal to arbitration. He should not set himself above anyone, or boast of his possessions, or undermine someone's resolution, or mock the character and customs of any people, or divulge a secret entrusted to him, or spread fresh rumours, or damage anyone's reputation, or hold a natural disability as a matter of reproach to anyone. For such behaviour is not only outrageous and uncivil but also foolish, tantamount to someone calling a one-eyed man one-eyed, or a bandy-legged man bandy-legged, or a cross-eyed man cross-eyed, or a bastard a bastard. By following the principles I have outlined one should win praise without envy and gain friends. It is tactless to interrupt a speaker before he has finished his story. Although a boy should not pick a quarrel with anyone and should be courteous to all, he should, nevertheless, carefully choose a handful of people for the inner circle of his friends. He should not, however, entrust to anyone's confidence what he wishes to keep quiet. It is ridiculous to expect in someone else the bond of silence you cannot fulfil in yourself, for no one is so tight-lipped as not to have someone to whom he would impart a secret. The safest course is not to confide anything that you would be ashamed to have put about. Do not be inquisitive about other people's affairs and if you happen to notice or overhear something, see to it that you appear ignorant of the knowledge you possess. It is impolite to glance sideways at a letter which has not been offered for your perusal. If perchance someone opens his correspondence in your presence, move away. While it is improper to glance at something, it is more so to scrutinize it. Likewise, if you sense that others' conversation is becoming rather private, withdraw unobtrusively and do not intrude upon such a conversation without being asked.

## 6 On play

Even proper games ought to be fun, although obstinacy, the source of quarrels, should have no place in them, and neither should trickery and dishonesty, for these lead on to more injurious faults. He who yields in a contest achieves a nobler victory than he who grasps victory at any cost. Do not protest against the judges. If you are competing against less experienced players and you can win time after time, occasionally allow yourself to be defeated in order to make the game more exciting. When playing against poorer competitors you should appear unaware of your superiority to them. It is for the spirit of the thing that one should play, not for any reward. They say that boys' characters are nowhere more readily apparent than in a game. If a person is prone to deceit, dishonesty, quarrelling, anger, violence, or arrogance, it is here that such flaws in his nature come to light. Consequently the boy of high principle should be true to himself in sport no less than at a banquet.

### 7 On the bedroom

Silence and modesty are laudable qualities in the bedroom. Certainly noise and chatter are unbecoming there, and much more so in bed. Whether undressing or rising remember to be modest and see that you do not unveil to another's sight what custom and nature require to be covered. If you are sharing a bed with a companion, lie quietly and do not toss about and uncover yourself or be a nuisance by pulling the blankets off your companion. Before you rest your head on the pillow make the sign of the cross over your brow and chest, entrusting yourself to Christ in a short prayer. Do the same when you first get up in the morning, making a favourable start to the day with a brief prayer, for there is no more auspicious beginning to a day than this. After going to the toilet, immediately wash your face and hands and rinse your mouth before doing anything else. It is degrading for people of good family not to observe the manners of their position. Those for whom destiny has decreed an ordinary, humble, or even rustic lot should strive all the more keenly to compensate for the malignity of fate with the elegance of good manners. No one can choose his own parents or nationality, but each can mould his own talents and character for himself.

I shall add by way of a postscript what seems to me a point of cardinal importance. The essence of good manners consists in freely pardoning the shortcomings of others although nowhere falling short of yourself: in holding a companion no less dear because his standards are less exacting. For there are some who compensate with other gifts for their roughness of manner. Nor should what I have said be taken to imply that no one can be a good person without good manners. But if a companion makes a mistake through ignorance in a matter that seems of some consequence, then the polite thing to do is to advise him courteously of it in private.

Whatever benefit can be derived from all this, my dearest Henry, I wish to be imparted through you to the entire fellowship of boys, so that by this donation you may win the hearts of your fellow troops and commend to them the pursuit of good letters and morals. May the grace of Jesus honour and preserve your illustrious nature and carry you always from strength to strength.

Erasmus of Rotterdam, Freiburg, March 1530

# ERASMUS THE CHRISTIAN HUMANIST

# 3

## The Ciceronian / *Dialogus Ciceronianus*

*The Ciceronian: A Dialogue on the Ideal Latin Style* represents Erasmus' challenge to purists who accepted none but Cicero as their model of correct speech and disdained any author who did not employ phrases and constructions actually used by their hero. Ciceronianism was primarily an Italian phenomenon. Extremists claimed that only Italians had the true gift of the Latin tongue; other nations, they thought, were automatically precluded from writing Latin of a quality fit to be called Ciceronian. Even Erasmus, who was considered the most eloquent of the northern humanists, was held in contempt and called a 'barbarian' by these extremists. He reacted by lampooning the Ciceronians in a dialogue that exemplifies his dramatic skill and power of expression. The characters in the dialogue are Nosoponus ('Workmad'), whose dream is to be recognized as a true Ciceronian, Bulephorus ('Counsellor'), and his supporter Hypologus ('Back-up'), who endeavour by their arguments to cure Nosoponus of his obsession and point him to the Christian ideal of speech.

The dialogue begins with a caricature of the principles and methods of the Ciceronians, as set forth by Nosoponus. A survey of writers in Latin from classical times down to Erasmus' own day fails to produce a single author whom Nosoponus is prepared to accept as a true Ciceronian. His ideal is thus shown to be unrealistic. This recognition leads to a wide-ranging discussion about the nature of *imitatio*. Erasmus proposes a sort of Christian Ciceronianism, that is, a classical style adapted to Christian needs.

The dialogue, first published by Froben (Basel 1528), aroused a storm of controversy. Erasmus no doubt intended to offend Italian purists, but his list of 'failed Ciceronians' caused a greater furore than he had anticipated. The literary criticism put into Nosoponus' mouth was thought to be an expression of Erasmus' own views. Those whose names were not included in the list were equally offended, thinking that Erasmus had not considered them worthy of mention. Of course the list was not meant to be taken all that seriously, but in subsequent editions (1529, 1530) Erasmus bowed to criticism and modified it. In his dialogue Erasmus had made the point that no sensible person would want to be hailed as a Ciceronian by Nosoponus, but not everyone was capable of understanding Erasmus' irony or of accepting his criticism. Erasmus soon grew weary of the continuing controversy. His last word on the Ciceronians was to describe them as 'limbs of Satan,' and to declare that Satan would prefer to have everyone Ciceronian rather than Christian.

This extract is taken from CWE 28 384–448, translated and annotated by Betty I. Knott.

**Bulephorus** I'll tell you a story – not a bit of hearsay, but something I saw with my own eyes, heard with my own ears. In Rome at the time the two men with the most distinguished reputation as speakers were Pietro Fedra and Camillo.[1] Camillo was younger and in actuality the more powerful speaker, but the older man had occupied the citadel first. Neither of them though, unless I'm mistaken, was actually Roman by birth. Now a certain person had been appointed to speak on the death of Christ, on the holy day known as the Day of Parasceve,[2] in the presence of the pontiff himself. A few days before the event I received an invitation from the literary community to go and hear the speech. 'Be sure to be there,' they said. 'Now you will really hear how the language of Rome sounds in the mouth of a Roman.' I was there, full of expectation. I stood as close to the platform as I could, so as to miss nothing. Julius II[3] was present himself, and that doesn't happen very often, because of his health, I think. There were rows of cardinals and bishops and, besides the common crowd, quite a number of scholars who were staying in Rome. I won't tell you the name of the speaker, then no one will think it my intention to damage the reputation of an honest scholar. He held the same views as you do, Nosoponus, that is, he was an aspirant after Ciceronian eloquence. His preface and his peroration – which was almost longer than the entire speech – were taken up with singing the praises of Julius II, whom he called Jupiter Optimus Maximus, describing him as grasping and hurling with his omnipotent right hand the three-forked unerring thunderbolt and with a mere nod performing whatever is his will. All that had been done in the preceding years in France, Germany, and Spain, in Portugal, Africa, and Greece had come about, he maintained, by the nod of his will and his alone. In all of which to be sure, he spoke as a Roman in Rome, using Roman speech and a Roman accent. But what had all this to do with Julius as the high priest of the Christian religion, the vicar of Christ and successor of Peter and Paul? What had it to do with the cardinals and bishops who act in the stead of the other apostles? As for the subject he had undertaken to treat, what could be more sacred, more real, more wonderful, more sublime, more fitted to stir the feelings? What speaker, even one endowed with quite ordinary gifts of expression, could fail to wring tears even from men of stone on such a theme? The general plan of his speech was first to represent the death of Christ as piteous, and then, swinging his oratory onto the other tack, to show it as glorious and triumphant, no doubt in order to give us a demonstration of that Ciceronian power of impassioned presentation which enabled him to swing the emotions of his audience in any direction he chose.

**Hypologus** Well did he succeed?

**Bulephorus** To tell you the truth, when we were in the thick of his tragic emotions I wanted to laugh. Nor did I see anyone in all that assembly showing the slightest sign of sorrow when he deployed his every oratorical gift in a harrowing description of the unjust sufferings of the entirely innocent Christ; nor for that matter did anyone look one jot gladder when he was straining every nerve to present that death to us as triumphant, admirable, and glorious. He spoke of the Decii and Quintus Curtius who dedicated themselves to the spirits of the dead to save the republic, and of Cecrops, Menoeceus, Iphigenia, and several others who had set the safety and honour of the fatherland above their own lives.[4] With a sob in his throat he bemoaned the fact that the heroes who came to the aid of the republic of Rome by putting themselves in peril received the thanks of the nation by official proclamation: some were awarded a gold statue in the forum, others became the recipients of divine honours; but Christ, in return for his benefits, received from the thankless Jewish race not a reward but the cross, horrible sufferings, and utter degradation. And there he was, rousing our pity for that good, innocent man, who deserved nothing but gratitude from his people, as if deploring the deaths of Socrates and Phocion,[5] who were sentenced by their ungrateful fellow-citizens to drink hemlock, though innocent of all crime; or Epaminondas,[6] who, in return for his distinguished public career, was made to stand trial for his life by his own countrymen; or Scipio,[7] who went into exile after all he had done for the Roman republic; or Aristides,[8] whom the Athenian people voted into exile by the procedure of ostracism because they could not stand his nickname 'the Just,' given him because of his outstanding integrity of character. I ask you, could anything be more tedious and irrevelant? And yet he emulated Cicero to the best of his ability. But never a word about the hidden plan of the supreme Godhead, who willed by this incredible means to redeem the human race from the tyranny of the devil through the death of his only Son, not a word of those mysteries, of what it means to die with Christ, to be buried with him, to rise with him again. He wept for his innocence, trounced the ingratitude of the Jews; but never a tear for our wickedness, our ingratitude – ours who have thus been redeemed, granted so many blessings, summoned by unheard-of generosity to partake of such bliss, and who, as far as in us lies, crucify him again, turning back of our own choice to the tyranny of Satan, slaves of avarice, indulgence, pleasure, ambition, more in thrall to this world than even the pagans were, to whom God had not yet revealed this heavenly philosophy.

In the other part of his speech, where he was making great efforts to fill us with exultation, I felt more like crying, when I heard the triumphs of Scipio, Aemilius Paulus, and Julius Caesar[9] and the apotheosis of Roman emperors compared with the triumph of the cross. Anyone who wanted to do justice to the glory of the cross ought to have taken the Apostle Paul as his model rather than Cicero. How Paul exults on this theme, how he gets carried away, how he glories, lords it, triumphs, looks down on all earthly things with contempt as if from the heights of heaven, once he starts preaching the cross. In short, this Roman spoke so Romanly that I heard nothing about the death of Christ. Yet this eager aspirant after the Ciceronian idiom was judged by the Ciceronians to have spoken marvellously; though he said practically nothing on the subject, which he seemed neither to understand nor care for, said not a thing that was appropriate, and stirred no feelings. The only thing he could be praised for was for speaking in Roman fashion and recalling something of Cicero. One could approve of a speech like this as being a demonstration of ability and intelligence if it were delivered by a schoolboy before his fellow pupils in class, but what connection, I ask you, did it have with such a day, such an audience, such a theme?

**Nosoponus** And is this man without a name?

**Bulephorus** As I said, I prefer to leave the name to be inferred, as it is not my present purpose to cast aspersions on anyone's name. What I am doing is to point out an error that should be avoided, one that under the shadow of a mighty name leads a good many people astray these days. This is what concerns us, Nosoponus; the name of the man in my story does not matter. But the story has its implications also for the fame of Cicero, for which I see you are so very concerned, for which every scholar anywhere in the world is rightly concerned. The fact is that those apes not only create obstacles for the young in their studies and in their moral development, but also darken Cicero's name by putting themselves forward under the title of Ciceronian when that is the last thing they are. ... So the first concern of the Ciceronians should have been to understand the mysteries of the Christian religion, and to turn the pages of the sacred books with as much enthusiasm as Cicero devoted to the writings of philosophers, poets, experts in law and religion, and historians. With all this did the great Cicero equip himself. So how shall we ever be Ciceronians when we never touch – when we positively despise and recoil from – the laws, prophets, histories, and commentators that belong to what we profess?

Well then, a speech has to be made before a Christian audience, but on a non-religious subject, say on an election, or a marriage, or the signing of a treaty, or the declaration of war. Shall we as Christians, before other Christians, discuss these topics in exactly the same way as the pagan Cicero did before pagans? Shouldn't every action of our lives be referred to the standard of Christ? If your speech departs from that you will prove neither a good orator nor a good man.

But suppose our speaker is one who utters no word unless it is recorded in his lists. The complete change that has occurred in the lives of men has introduced words that are new, so what will the Ciceronian do, faced with these, when he won't be able to find them either in Cicero's works or in his own word list? Any word which can't be pin-pointed in Cicero's writings is to be rejected; but since so many of his writings have not survived, just think how many things we shall avoid as barbarisms which Cicero did in fact write; and how many we shall avoid which he would have used if he had had to talk about our sort of subject. Nowhere in Cicero do we find the expressions 'Jesus Christ,' 'word of God,' 'Holy Spirit,' 'Trinity,' or 'evangel,' ... What is our aspirant after the Ciceronian turn of phrase going to do here? Is he going to say nothing, or is he going to make the kind of substitution I've suggested for established Christian vocabulary?

**Nosoponus** And why shouldn't he? ...

**Bulephorus** The person who studies Christian philosophy with as much application as Cicero did pagan philosophy; who drinks in the psalms and prophets with as much enthusiasm as he did the poets; who works as hard and as long to understand the commands of the apostles, the rites of the church, the origins, progress, and decline of the Christian world as he laboured to grasp the rights and laws governing the provinces, municipalities, and allied states associated with the city of Rome; who, finally, adapts all he has learnt by such studies to suit his present situation. He will have some right to claim the title of Ciceronian.

**Nosoponus** The only effect all that will have, it seems to me, is to make us speak in a Christian way, not a Ciceronian one.

**Bulephorus** But surely you won't consider anybody a Ciceronian if he doesn't speak in a way that fits his subject, and doesn't understand what he's talking about?

**Nosoponus** Of course not.

**Bulephorus** But this is what does result from the endeavours of our present day would-be Ciceronians. The purpose of our inquiry is to prevent it happening to us. There is nothing to stop a person speaking in a manner that is both Christian and Ciceronian, if you allow a person to be Ciceronian when he speaks clearly, richly, forcefully, and appropriately, in keeping with the nature of his subject and with the circumstances of the times and of the persons involved. Some people have indeed suggested that the ability to speak well is not a question of skill but of judgment. Cicero himself neatly defines eloquence in his

*Partitiones*[10] as 'sense expressing itself with fluency,' nor is there any doubt that this is the type of eloquence that he himself practised. But good God! how far short of this definition those people fall who endeavour to speak in Ciceronian fashion on subjects which are totally and in every respect alien from Cicero, which moreover they neither understand nor care for. This idea that everything that diverges from Cicero is a disgusting example of bad Latin is a pernicious hallucination which we must banish from our minds if we are to win among Christians the reputation that Cicero won among his contemporaries. 'Good sense is of writing well the source and starting point,' as that most acute of critics[11] said. So what then is the proper source of an eloquence worthy of Cicero? An understanding richly supplied with a thorough knowledge of all kinds of subjects, especially the ones you have decided to talk about, an understanding prepared by theory, by much practical experience in writing and speaking, and by long thinking on the subject; and, the fountain-head of the whole activity, a heart that genuinely loves what it proclaims and genuinely hates what it attacks. Combined with these there must be capacity for judgment, common sense, and discernment, which as gifts of nature cannot be part of any instruction in the art. I ask you, from what source will those people acquire all this, who read nothing but Cicero, who desire no author but Cicero to 'thumb by night and thumb by day'?

**Nosoponus** All the same, that was a neat observation about people who have been out in the sun for some time going brown, and those who have sat for any length of time in a perfumer's shop carry the scent of the place away with them when they go.

**Bulephorus** I find that a very good comparison. All they carry away is a colouring of the skin and a faint aroma that soon vanishes. Anyone who is satisfied with that kind of achievement may sit as much as he likes among Cicero's perfume jars and rose beds or bask in his sunshine. I would prefer to take internally any fine aromatic substances that are going and get them into my system, so that I don't just scatter a whiff of perfume over the people near me, but am myself thoroughly heated and invigorated, and then, whenever the occasion demands, a voice will issue forth which can be recognized as the product of a sound, well-nourished personality. A speech that holds the hearer's attention, that moves him, that sweeps him away on some tide of emotion, is born out of the depths of the speaker's person, not out of his skin. I don't mean to suggest that the material available to Cicero is either unremarkable or in any way unsatisfactory, but that he alone will not prove an adequate source for a rich treatment of any and every subject. In short, we must learn how to imitate Cicero from Cicero himself. Let us imitate him as he imitated others. If he settled down to reading a single author, if he submitted himself to one single guide and mentor, if he thought concern for words more important than concern for matter, if he never wrote except at bedtime, if he tortured himself for a whole month over one letter, if he thought anything eloquent that did not fit with his subject, then let us do the same in order that we may become Ciceronians. But if this is all very different from what Cicero did, let us instead follow his real practice: let us make sure our minds are thoroughly equipped with the necessary knowledge; let us first take care of what to say and only then of how to say it, and let us fit words to matter, not the other way round; and while we are speaking let us never lose sight of what is appropriate to the subject. A speech comes alive only if it rises from the heart, not if it floats on the lips. Let us be acquainted with the theory of our art, for it has much to contribute to invention, arrangement, treatment of arguments, and the avoidance of whatever is irrelevant or indeed damaging to our case. If a genuine case has to be argued, let us give first place to sound judgment, though even in fictitious cases handled for practice, it is a good thing if what is said sticks to the realms of probability. ...

All Christian speech should have the savour of Christ, without whom nothing is pleasing or impressive, useful or creditable, stylish or eloquent or learned. Of course, schoolboys may participate in games by way of preparation for serious things later on, but can anyone really endure those pagan training exercises when the subject is real, serious, and, what is more important, spiritual?

**Nosoponus** What do you advise me to do then? Throw Cicero away?

**Bulephorus** No, no. Any young candidate for eloquence must always have Cicero in his pocket – and in his heart. But we must certainly throw away the captious, fault-finding attitude displayed by certain persons who are always rejecting works, in every other respect learned and well expressed, and decreeing them not fit to read simply because they were not worked up with an eye to the imitation of Cicero. In the first place, the Ciceronian idiom does not suit every cast of mind, so that the attempt to imitate it is bound to fail; second, if you do not have the natural gifts which will enable you to reproduce that inimitable flair for the perfect expression, what is more stupid than torturing yourself over the unattainable? Besides, the Tullian idiom does not suit every topic or person to be treated, and even if it did, it is better to let some things go than pay too dear for them. If his eloquence had cost Marcus Tullius as much as ours does us, he would, I am sure, have neglected the finer points of oratory to some extent. It costs too much when the price is such an outlay in years, health, and life itself. It costs too much when to achieve it we neglect areas of learning which are far more essential to us. It costs too much when the price is our devotion to God.

If we learn how to speak effectively in order to delight a leisured audience, is it worth toiling such long hours merely to achieve good theatre? If our aim is to persuade people to honourable conduct, remember that Phocion the Athenian was a more effective speaker than Demosthenes. Cato of Utica won his point more often than Marcus Tullius.[12] Or perhaps our purpose is to write books that people will constantly be thumbing. Well, even if a style just like Cicero's could be ours for the asking, we would still need to apply our rhetorical expertise to achieving a variety of style that would save the reader from being sickened by sameness. Variety is of such importance in life that it is not a good thing to use even the best all the time. Variety is the spice of life; that's what the Greek proverb says, and it's true whatever you are talking about. The main reason why Homer and Horace are so highly thought of is that their impressive variety of subject and style prevent their readers getting bored. Nature shaped us for variety, giving each man his own characteristics, so that it would be difficult to find two people sharing the same abilities or passions. There is nothing more fastidious and difficult to please than individual taste, and we have to devour such a huge quantity of books in our pursuit of learning; so who could endure being constantly engaged in reading, if all the writers employed the same style and a similar idiom? It is better therefore in the case of books, as in a banquet, to have some things of a lower standard, rather than have everything absolutely identical. What kind of a host would he be who invited a crowd of guests, hardly two of whom agree in questions of palate, and served up all the dishes seasoned in the same way, even if the individual dishes were delicacies fit for Apicius?[13] As it is, different people are taken by different styles, so nothing fails to find a reader. Not to reiterate that your ambition conflicts with nature herself, who intended speech to be the mirror of the mind. Minds differ far more than voices and physical features do, and the mirror will lie unless it reflects the true born image of the mind. The very thing which the reader enjoys is getting to know the writer's feelings, character, disposition, and type of mind from the way he writes, just as he would by living on familiar terms with him for several years. This is why different people display such different attitudes towards the various writers, according to whether the moving spirit proves congenial or antipathetic, attracts or repels, just as a person's physical appearance pleases some and gives offence to others. I'll illustrate this from my own experience. When I was young I adored all the poets, but as soon as I became better acquainted with Horace, the others by comparison began to stink in my nostrils, though marvellous enough in absolute terms. What do you think was the reason, if not a certain secret affinity of spirit sensed through the silent letters? This genuine, true born reality cannot breathe through the utterances of those who express nothing but Cicero.

Besides, decent men, even if not particularly blessed with fine features, don't wish to wear a mask in order to make themselves look handsome, and wouldn't even agree to be painted with features other than those nature gave them. It's dishonest to impose on others by disguising oneself, and the idea of a lying mirror or a portrait that represents a man not as he is but as he would like to be is ludicrous. And it would be an even more shocking deception, if I, Bulephorus, set out to be taken for Nosoponus or anybody else. So men of letters are surely right to ridicule those presumptuous fellows who send packing authors characterized by learning and eloquence, authors worthy of an immortal name, and more or less banish them from their libraries, simply because they preferred, in their writing, to express themselves rather than Cicero. It is after all a form of imposture not to express yourself but to perform a kind of conjuring trick and appear as somebody else. I do in fact doubt whether we would find many people who would want to change their whole physical appearance for somebody else's, even if God gave them the chance, and I think there would be even fewer who would exchange their whole mind and character for another's. For one thing, nobody wants to be different from what he is; for another, nature has seen to it that each of us is endowed with a mixture of characteristics which ensures that even if there is some fault in our make-up it is balanced by accompanying virtues. Speech reveals the features of the mind much as a mirror reflects the face, and to change the natural image into something different is surely the same as appearing in public wearing a mask.

**Nosoponus** Mind your speech doesn't jump the barrier, as they say. It seems to me to have been so carried away as to condemn the whole idea of imitation – yet instruction, imitation, and experience are the three chief components of the art of speaking – unless of course those who imitate Cicero put on someone else's face, while those who imitate any other writer keep their own!

**Bulephorus** I welcome imitation with open arms – but imitation which assists nature and does not violate it, which turns its gifts in the right direction and does not destroy them. I approve of imitation – but imitation of a model that is in accord with, or at least not contrary to, your own native genius, so that you do not embark on a hopeless enterprise, like the giants fighting against the gods. Again, I approve of imitation – but imitation not enslaved to one set of rules, from the guidelines of which it dare not depart, but imitation which gathers from all authors, or at least from the most outstanding, the thing which is the chief virtue of each and which suits your own cast of mind; imitation which does not immediately incorporate into its own speech any nice little feature it comes across, but transmits it to the mind for inward digestion, so that becoming part of your own system, it gives the impression not of something begged from someone else, but of something that springs from your own mental processes, something that exudes the characteristics and force of your own mind and personality. Your reader will see it not as a piece of decoration filched from Cicero, but a child sprung from your own brain, the living image of its father, like Pallas from the brain of Jove.[14] Your speech will not be a patchwork or a mosaic, but a lifelike portrait of the person you really are, a river welling out from your inmost being.

Above all, you must make sure you thoroughly understand the matter you undertake to treat. That will supply you with a flood of things to say, with genuine unassumed emotions. That will make your speech live, breathe, move, influence, carry away; it will make it express you wholly ...

**Bulephorus** All that remains to do, I think, is to draw together and sum up our rather disconnected discussion.
**Nosoponus** What do you really think of Marcus Tullius?
**Bulephorus** I consider him the supreme master of the art of speaking and, for a pagan, a good man. If he had studied the philosophy of Christ, he would, I think, have been numbered with those who are now honoured as saints for their blameless and spiritual lives. Technique and experience contributed much to his oratory, of course; but far the greatest part he owed to natural endowment, which no one has it in his power to give himself. In my opinion there is no single Latin author who should be more read and esteemed by schoolboys and students who are being educated to the glories of eloquence – though I would support the reading of the Latin poets before starting on Cicero, in so far as this form of literature is more suited to those of tender years.

Nor would I have anyone called to the serious imitation of Cicero unless he has first grasped the principles of rhetoric. Next I wish him to have someone available who can draw his attention to the speaker's technique, as painters take some famous picture and point out to their pupils its technical felicities and failures. Again, it is my wish that Marcus Tullius should occupy the first and foremost place in the scheme of study, but that there should be others as well; and my view is that he should not be blindly followed, but taken as a pattern and even challenged. Anyone who merely follows treads in someone else's footsteps and obeys rules. It's a true saying that one cannot walk properly if one is always placing one's foot in someone else's footprints, and no one will ever learn to swim if he hasn't the courage to throw away his float. The true imitator tries not so much to say identical things as similar things, sometimes not even similar things but equivalent things. The challenger endeavours to speak even better if he can. No artist has ever been so perfect that one cannot discover something in his work that could be bettered.

Furthermore I would not have this imitation carried out anxiously and meticulously, as this very thing prevents us achieving what we are after. Nor do I think our passion for Cicero should turn us against all other writers: I think we should first read all the best writers and extract from the best the best that each has to offer – it isn't necessary to imitate anyone in every feature. We shouldn't scorn even writers like Aristotle, Theophrastus, and Pliny,[15] who don't help to improve our style, to be sure, but do supply us with material.

Then I wouldn't have anyone so dedicated to the imitation of Cicero that he abandons his own essential nature and expends health and life in the pursuit of something he will never achieve because his native genius is against it or which will cost him far too dear if he does eventually achieve it. Nor would I have this as a man's only activity: pursuing the renown of a Ciceronian style should not mean that you neglect the essential disciplines of a liberal education.

You must avoid like the plague men who are always declaring that it is a sin to use a word which doesn't occur in the works of Cicero. Now that common usage is no longer the arbiter in determining what is correct in Latin, we have every right to employ any word found in a good author when need for it arises, and if it seems rather strained or far gone in obsolescence because few writers use it, we shall bring it out into the light and smooth the way to its acceptance by employing it frequently in appropriate contexts. What harm is there in this, considering that the ancients borrowed from Greek whenever the Latin term was either missing or less expressive? So why should we abstain from using words, when occasion demands, which we have found in respectable authors?

We should shun with equal determination those persons who are always loudly proclaiming that anything that fails to conform to Cicero's pattern in vocabulary, phraseology, and rhythm should be rejected as quite unfit to be read; for it is possible, with different stylistic virtues, to be, if not like Cicero, at least comparable to him. Let us have nothing to do with this fault-picking censoriousness. Rather let us, in reading our authors, display in all seriousness the attitude of mind which Ovid jestingly tells us he found himself displaying in his various affairs with girls.[16] He found a tall girl attractive because of her heroic stature, a short one attractive because she was easy to handle; youthful bloom commended a young one, experience one who was a bit older, the naivety of an uneducated girl was delightful, in an educated one the attraction was wit, in a fairskinned girl he adored the loveliness of her colouring, in a dusky one he imagined I know not what lurking charm. If we show the same generosity of spirit and extract from each writer whatever deserves commendation, we shall disdain none of them, but channel off something from each to give a flavour to our own speech.

Above all we must be on our guard lest an age as yet innocent and unformed be led astray by the outward show of the title 'Ciceronian' and turn out not Ciceronian but pagan. This kind of plague is not yet extinct but constantly threatens to break out afresh – under one showy front lurk the old heresies, under another Judaism, under another paganism. A good many years ago, for example, those factions of Platonists and Aristotelians sprang up among the Italians. Away with these labels which mark opposed attitudes; let us rather inculcate ideas that encourage and nourish mutual benevolence in study, in religion, in the whole life. Where sacred things are concerned, one must right at the start absorb convictions that are truly worthy of a Christian. If that happens, we shall find nothing that offers more scope than the heavenly philosophy, nothing more delightful than the name of Jesus Christ, nothing more pleasing than the words used by the luminaries of the church to deal with matters of the faith. Nor will pleasure be taken in any speech that does not fit the speaker's personality and accord with his subject; and a person who treats matters of the faith in the phrases of unbelievers and contaminates his Christian subject-matter with pagan follies will be thought a positive monstrosity. Even if a certain leniency is here accorded to youth, those of more advanced years are not to assume the same prerogative.

Anyone who can be Ciceronian only by being unchristian is not even Ciceronian. He does not speak in a manner befitting his subject, he has no intimate understanding of what he is talking about, he has no genuine feelings roused by what he is discussing. Finally, he doesn't elaborate and embellish themes provided by the faith he professes, as Cicero embellished topics provided by his own day and age. This is the purpose of studying the basic disciplines, of studying philosophy, of studying eloquence, to know Christ, to celebrate the glory of Christ. This is the goal of all learning and all eloquence.

Another thing to remember is that we must imitate the most distinctive thing that Cicero offers us, and that lies not in mere words nor in the outer layer of verbal expression but in substance and sentiments, in intellectual ability, in right judgment. What is the good of a son being like his father in physical feature if he is unlike him in mind and character?

Finally, if we never have the happiness of being voted Ciceronians by that clique, we must bear with equanimity something we have in common with all those distinguished men whose names we have listed. It is foolish to pursue something you cannot achieve. It is self-indulgent to make yourself miserable over something which so many outstanding writers have endured without a qualm. It shows no sense of what is fitting to aspire to things that are not suited to us. It shows lack of judgment to adopt a style that conflicts with what the situation demands. It is madness to pay so dearly in effort and lost sleep for something which is hardly ever going to be of use.

This is the kind of medicine that doctor used to cure me of my sickness, and if you are prepared to swallow it down, I have every hope, Nosoponus, that the fever will leave you, and you too, Hypologus.

**Hypologus** Oh, I got better long ago.

**Nosoponus** And I'm nearly cured, except that I've had the disease so long I'm still conscious of a few remaining symptoms.

**Bulephorus** Those will gradually fade away, and if necessary, we will fetch in Dr Word again.

# The Handbook of the Christian Soldier / *Enchiridion militis christiani*

*The Handbook of the Christian Soldier* was written in 1501 on request of an unnamed woman who hoped that the tract would improve her husband's morals (see above 35). In December 1504 Erasmus sent a copy to his friend John Colet, with a description of his broader aims; 'I composed it not in order to show off my cleverness or my style, but solely in order to counteract the error of those who make religion in general consist in rituals and observances of an almost more than Jewish formality,[1] but who are astonishingly indifferent to matters that have to do with true goodness. What I have tried to do, in fact, is to teach a method of morals, as it were, in the manner of those who have originated fixed procedures in the branches of learning' (Ep 181:53–9). *The Handbook of the Christian Soldier* was a moral 'how-to' book. We are not told whether it changed the life habits of the man for whose benefit it was written, but it proved an immense success with the general reader of the time. By the end of the century there were more than seventy editions of the Latin text and an extraordinary number of translations into all major European languages.

In 1518 Erasmus added to the book a lengthy prefatory letter addressed to the abbot of Hugshofen, Paul Volz, in which he set out the essence of his *philosophia Christi*. The core passage bears quoting in full:

I could see that the common body of Christians was corrupt not only in its affections but in its ideas. I pondered on the fact that those who profess themselves pastors and doctors for the most part misuse these titles, which belong to Christ, for their own advantage; to say nothing for the moment of those whose fiat, yes or no, keeps all human affairs in perpetual flux, and at whose faults however obvious it is scarcely permitted to let fall a sigh. When all is dark, when the world is in tumult and men's opinions differ so widely, where can we take refuge, if not upon the sheet-anchor of the Gospel teaching? Is there any religious man who does not see with sorrow that this generation is far the most corrupt there has ever been? When did tyranny and greed lord it thus widely or go thus unpunished? When was so much importance ever attached to ceremonies? When did iniquity abound with so little to restrain it? When did charity wax colder? All we appeal to, all we read, all we hear, all our decisions – what do they taste of except of ambition and greed? Our plight would be sorry indeed, had not Christ left us some live coals of his teaching, some living unfailing rivulets from the spring of his mind. What we must do is this: abandon the cinders offered us by men and blow up those coals of his into flame (I gladly use Paul's word); follow up those rivulets until we find the living water that springs up to life eternal. We explore the bowels of this earth of ours to get the ores which feed our vices; are we never to mine the rich lodes of Christ, to win thence the salvation of souls? The winter of our wickedness never brings so low the fire of charity that it cannot be rekindled from the flint. Christ is our Rock; and this rock has in it the seeds of heavenly fire and veins of living water. Abraham long ago dug wells in every country, seeking veins of living water; and when the Philistines filled them with earth they were dug anew by Isaac and his sons, who, not content with restoring the old wells, dug new ones besides. Again the Philistines stir up strife and opposition; but he does not cease to dig.

Nor are we quite free of Philistines nowadays, who get more pleasure from earth than from fountains of living water – those people, I mean, who reek of earthly things and twist the Gospel teaching to serve earthly appetites, compelling it to be the slave of human ambition and to enhance their own discreditable gains and their despotic rule. And if some Isaac or one of his household should dig and find a pure source, at once they are all protests and objections because they know this source will be an obstacle to their gains and block their ambitions, even though it makes for Christ's glory. It is not long before they throw earth into it and stop up the source by some corrupt interpretation, driving away the man with the spade, or at the least so befoul the water with mud and filth that he who drinks from it gets more dirt and filth than liquid. They do not wish those who thirst after righteousness to drink from the crystal spring but take them to their trampled cisterns, which are full of rubble and contain no water. But the real sons of Isaac – Christ's true worshippers, that is – must not grow weary of this labour. For those who tip earth into the Gospel springs wish to be thought to be of their number, so that now it is by no means safe to teach the pure faith of Christ among Christians. So much have the Philistines grown in strength, fighting for earth, preaching earthly things and not the things of heaven, human things and not divine – those things, in fact, which tend not to Christ's glory but to the profit of those who traffic in indulgences, in compositions, in dispensations, and suchlike merchandise. And this traffic is all the more perilous because they give their greed a façade of great names, eminent princes, the supreme pontiff, even Christ himself. And yet no man more truly forwards the business of the pontiff than he who publishes in its pure form the heavenly philosophy of Christ, of which the pope is the principal teacher.

If only we have the single eye filled with light of which the Gospel speaks, if our minds are like a house with the lamp of true faith set on a lampstand, these minor points will easily be scattered like a mist. If we have Christian charity like a carpenter's rule, everything will easily be set straight by that. But what will you do if this rule disagrees with the accepted tradition of centuries and the conduct laid down by princes in their laws? For even that not seldom happens. Do not condemn what is done by princes in the execution of their duty; but conversely do not sully that heavenly philosophy of Christ by confusing it with the decrees of man. Let Christ remain what he is, the centre, with several circles running round him. Do not move that central mark from its place. ... Ecclesiastics form the first circle around Christ, secular princes the second, and the common people the third, but there is no reason to excuse any walk of life from pursuing the highest goal. The perfection of Christ lies in our desires, not in our walk of life; it is to be found in the spirit, not in clothing or in choice of food' (Ep 858:167–245, 352–4).

In *The Handbook of the Christian Soldier* itself Erasmus sets out the foundations of a Christian life in a series of rules of which the fifth rule – the text selected here – is the most crucial. Here Erasmus encourages the reader to pass through the visible things of this world to the higher, invisible things of heaven. This section more than any other in the book expresses Erasmus' theology, that is, his emphasis on the internal and spiritual nature of faith.

This extract is taken from CWE 66 65–84, translated and annotated by Charles Fantazzi.

## Fifth rule

Let us add a fifth rule, as a kind of reinforcement to the previous one, that you establish firmly in your mind that perfect piety is the attempt to progress always from visible things, which are usually imperfect or indifferent, to invisible, according to the division of man discussed earlier.[2] This precept is most pertinent to our discussion since it is through neglect or ignorance of it that most Christians are superstitious rather than pious, and except for the name of Christ differ hardly at all from superstitious pagans. Let us imagine, therefore, two worlds, the one merely intelligible, the other visible. The intelligible, which may also be called the angelic, is the one in which God dwells with the blessed spirits, while the visible world comprises the celestial spheres and all that is contained therein. Then there is man, who constitutes, as it were, a third world, participating in the other two, in the visible world through the body, and in the invisible through the soul. Since we are but pilgrims in the visible world, we should never make it our fixed abode, but should relate by a fitting comparison everything that occurs to the senses either to the angelic world or, in more practical terms, to morals and to that part of man that corresponds to the angelic. What the visible sun is here in the visible world the divine mind is in the intelligible world and in that part of you related to it, namely, the spirit. What the moon is here is in that world the assembly of angels and blessed spirits, which they call the church triumphant, and in you it is the spirit. Whatever influence the upper world has over the earth, which lies beneath it, God exercises this same influence over your soul. The sun sets, rises, scorches, becomes temperate, quickens, produces, ripens, attracts, debilitates, cleanses, hardens, softens, illumines, brightens, gladdens. Therefore whatever you observe in it, or rather, whatever you observe in this material world, which is made up of elements, and which some have distinguished from the rest of the universe, and, lastly, whatever you see in the more material part of yourself, learn to refer to God and to the invisible part of yourself. In that way, whatever offers itself to the senses will become for you an occasion for the practice of piety.

As it delights the bodily eye each time this visible sun spreads new light upon the earth, consider for a moment what must be the pleasure of the heavenly spirits, for whom that eternal sun ever rises and never sets; consider what great joy it is for a pure spirit, illumined by divine light. And in response to the promptings of visible creation pray in the words of Paul that 'he who commanded light to shine forth from darkness will begin to shine in your heart to illumine the knowledge of the glory of God in the face of Christ Jesus.'[3] Search out similar passages from the sacred books in which the grace of the divine Spirit is frequently compared to light. Night seems sad and gloomy to you;

think of the soul deprived of divine light and shrouded in vice. And if you discern signs of night within yourself, pray that the sun of justice may rise upon you.

Be so convinced of the existence of invisible things that those things that are seen become but mere shadows, which present to the eye only a faint image of invisible realities. Moreover, whatever attracts or repels the senses in material things must be all the more intensely loved or hated by the spirit in the realm of the spirit. A handsome physical appearance is appealing to the eye. Imagine how fair must be the beauty of the soul! A misshapen face is unpleasant to look upon. Consider how odious is a mind defiled by vice. And similarly for the rest. For just as the soul has its own comeliness or deformity according as it pleases God or the devil, like rejoicing in like, so it also has a youth of its own, old age, sickness, health, death, life, poverty, riches, pleasure, sorrow, war, peace, cold, heat, thirst, drink, hunger, and food. In a word, whatever we perceive in the body must be understood to exist also in the soul. Therefore the road to the spiritual and perfect life consists in gradually accustoming ourselves to be weaned from those things that do not really exist but appear partly to be what they are not, such as base pleasure or worldly honour, and are partly in a state of flux, hastening to return to nothing, and let ourselves be carried away to things that are real, eternal, unchangeable, and authentic. Socrates, a philosopher not so much in his words as in his life, was aware of this.[4] He said that the soul would migrate happily from the body only if it had previously meditated seriously upon death with the help of philosophy and had long become accustomed to be absent, as it were, from the body through contempt for material things and love and contemplation of spiritual things. The cross to which Christ has called us and the death that Paul wishes us to die together with our Head – echoing the words of the prophet: 'Since for your sake we are slain all the day long and account as sheep for the slaughter,'[5] and expressed by the Apostle in yet other terms: 'Seek the things that are above, not the things that are on earth, have taste for the things that are above'[6] – all of this simply means that we should become numb to material things and render ourselves insensitive to them so that we may have more taste for things that pertain to the spirit as we have less taste for material things. Let us begin to live the interior life all the more sincerely as we live less exteriorly. To sum it all up in simple language, we should be less influenced by transitory things as we come to know more fully the things that are eternal, and we should have less esteem for insubstantial things as we begin to raise our thoughts to those that are real.

Therefore let this rule be ever in readiness, that we do not linger over temporal matters at any time, but move on, rising up to the love of spiritual things, which are incomparably better, despising visible things in comparison to those that are invisible. Illness of the body will be easier to bear if you consider it as a physic of the soul. You will be less solicitous about the health of the body if you concentrate your attention on guarding the health of the soul. Death of the body frightens you, but much more to be dreaded is the death of the soul. You shudder at visible poison, which is deadly to the body, but far more dreadful is the venom that destroys the soul. Hemlock is a poison for the body, but much more deadly is the venom of the soul, sensual pleasures. You are terrified and pale with fear that a lightning bolt, flashing out of the clouds, may strike you, yet how much more to be feared is the invisible lightning bolt of divine wrath: 'Go, ye cursed, into everlasting fire'? You are ravished by physical beauty; why do you show no passion for that beauty which does not manifest itself to the senses? Transfer your love to that beauty which is everlasting, heavenly, and incorruptible, and you will be more moderate in your love of the fleeting and fading beauty of the body. You pray that your field will receive rain, so that it will not dry up; pray rather that God will water your mind so that it will not become unproductive of virtue. With greatest care must you repair the bankruptcy of the soul. You make provisions for your old age so that nothing will be lacking to your body, and should you not take thought that nothing be lacking to the soul?

This is how we should act in the face of all those things that daily present themselves to our senses and variously influence them according to the diversity of their appearance, producing hope, fear, love, hatred, sorrow, and pleasure. ...

Let what is represented there to the eyes be enacted within you. The death of the Head is represented. Examine yourself in your inmost heart, as they say, to see how close you are to being dead to the world. If you are still subject to anger, ambition, greed, pleasure, and envy, even if you touch the altar, you are still far from the sacrifice. Christ was slain for you; offer these animals to him as sacrificial victims. Sacrifice yourself to him who once immolated himself for you to the Father. If you confide in him without reflecting on these things, God will hate your flabby and gross religion. You were baptized, but do not think that *ipso facto* you became a Christian. Your whole mentality still smacks exclusively of the world; outwardly you are a Christian, but in private you are more pagan than the pagans. Why is that so? Because you possess the body of the sacrament, but you are devoid of its spirit. What does it matter if the body has been washed when the soul remains defiled? What good is it that a few grains of salt have been put on your tongue if the soul remains unsalted? The body has been annointed, but the soul remains unannointed. But if you have been buried with Christ inwardly and are already to walk with him in newness of life, then I recognize you as a Christian. What is the use of being sprinkled with a few drops of holy water as long as you do not wipe clean the inner defilement of the soul? You venerate the saints, and you take pleasure in touching their relics. But you disregard their greatest legacy, the example of a blameless life. No devotion is more pleasing to Mary than the imitation of Mary's humility. No devotion is more acceptable and proper to the saints than striving to imitate their virtues. Would you like to win the favour of Peter and Paul? Imitate the faith of the one and the charity of the other, and you will accomplish more than if you were to dash off to Rome ten times. Would you like to pay the greatest homage to Francis? You are arrogant, you are a worshipper of money, you are quarrelsome. Make this gift to the saint: control your feelings and be more modest after the example of Francis; despise sordid gain and covet the goods of the mind. Abandon you contentiousness and conquer evil with good. That saint will value this honour more than if you were to light a hundred candles before his shrine. Do you think it is important if you are transported to the grave with your head wrapped in the cowl of Francis? Likeness of habit will be of no profit to you when you are dead if your morals were unlike his in life. And although the model of all piety is readily found in Christ, nevertheless, if you take great delight in worshipping Christ in his saints, then make sure you imitate Christ in his saints and in honour of each saint eradicate one vice or strive to attain a particular virtue. If this is the fruit of your devotion, I shall not be averse to these external manifestations.

With great veneration you revere the ashes of Paul, which I do not condemn, if your religion is consistent with your devotion. If you venerate mute and dead ashes and ignore his living image still speaking and breathing, as it were, in his writings, is not your religion utterly absurd? You worship the bones of Paul preserved in a relic casket, but do not worship the mind of Paul hidden away in his writings? You make much of a piece of his body visible through a glass covering, and you do not marvel at the whole mind of Paul shining through his writings? You worship ashes, which are sometimes of some efficacy in removing bodily imperfections; why do you not honour the written word more, by which vices of the soul are healed? Let those without faith to whom these miracles have been accorded express their wonder, but you as a man of faith embrace his writings, so that with the firm belief that God can do all things you may learn to love him above all else. You give homage to an image of Christ's countenance represented in stone or wood or depicted in colour. With how much more religious feeling should you render homage to the image of his mind, which has been reproduced in the Gospels through the artistry of the Holy Spirit. No Apelles[7] has ever portrayed with his brush the shape and features of the body in the way that speech reveals each person's mind and thought. This is especially so with Christ, for as he was the essence of simplicity and truth, there could be no dissimilarity between the archetype of the divine mind and the form of speech that issued from it. Just as nothing is more like the Father than the Son, the Word of the Father emanating from the innermost recesses of his spirit, so nothing is more like Christ than the word of Christ uttered in the innermost sanctuary of his most holy mind. And you do not gaze with wonder upon this image, do not worship it, scan it with reverent eyes, treasure it in your mind? With such holy and efficacious relics of the Lord at your disposal, do you disregard them and seek out much more extraneous ones? You gaze with awe at what is purported to be the tunic or shroud of Christ, and you read the oracles of Christ apathetically? You think it an immense privilege to have a tiny particle of the cross in your home. But that is nothing compared to carrying about in your heart the mystery of the cross. If such things constitute religion, who could be more religious than the Jews? Even the most impious among them saw Jesus living in the flesh with their own eyes, heard him with their own ears and touched him with their own hands. Who is more fortunate than Judas, who pressed his lips upon the divine mouth? So true is it that the flesh is useless without the spirit that it would have been of no use even to the Virgin Mary to have borne Christ of her own flesh if she had not also conceived his spirit through the Holy Spirit. This is a very great proof, but here is greater still.

As long as the apostles enjoyed the physical company of Christ, do you not read how weak they were and how crass was their understanding? Who could desire anything more to assure his complete salvation than this continuous familiarity between God and man? And yet after the performance of so many miracles, after they had been exposed for so many years to the teaching that proceeded from the mouth of God, after so many proofs of his resurrection, did he not upbraid them for their incredulity at the very last hour as he was about to be received into heaven? What reason can be adduced for this? It was the flesh of Christ that stood in the way, and that is what prompted him to say: 'If I do not go away, the Paraclete will not come. It is expedient for you that I go.' If the physical presence of Christ is of no profit for salvation, shall we dare to place our hopes for the attainment of perfect piety in any material thing? Paul had seen Christ in the flesh. What greater thing can be imagined? But he makes little of that, saying: 'Even if we knew Christ in human terms, we no longer know him in that way.' Why did he not know him? Because he had advanced to a higher state of grace.

Perhaps this discussion is becoming more verbose than is fitting for one who is merely passing on rules. But I am taking great pains for very good reason, because I have found out from experience that this error is the common plague of all Christianity and is all the more insidious because in appearance it bears a great resemblance to piety. There are no vices more dangerous than those which simulate virtue. For aside from the fact that it is easy even for the good to slip into these excesses, they are among the most difficult to correct because the untutored masses think it is a profanation of religion to criticize such things.

Immediately the world will protest and certain blustering preachers will emit their barkings, since they gladly sing their own tunes, that is, they look to their own profit, not to Christ. In response to their ignorant superstition or feigned piety I must insist once more that I do not disapprove in any way of the external ceremonies of Christians and the devotions of the simple-minded, especially those that have been approved by the authority of the church, for they are often signs or supports of piety. Since they are almost a necessity for infants in Christ until they grow up and arrive at complete manhood, they should not be scorned by those who have achieved manhood, lest the weak suffer hurt from bad example. I approve of what you do as long as your purpose is not vitiated and you do not consider as a fixed goal a stage from which you must make further progress towards salvation. But to worship Christ through visible things for the sake of visible things and to think of this as the summit of religious perfection; to be complacent with oneself and to condemn others on this basis; to become transfixed by them and die there and, to put it succinctly, to be alienated from Christ by those very things that should be employed to lead us to him – this would be to desert the law of the gospel, which is spiritual, and to sink into a kind of Judaism, which perhaps is no less grave a peril than if, free of these superstitions, one struggled against great and overt vices of the soul. This disease may be more deadly. Granted, but the other is more uncurable.

How hard Paul, that incomparable defender of the spirit, had to toil in all his travels to woo the Jews away from their faith in works and spur them on to spiritual things! And yet I see that the common run of Christianity has reverted to this again. Did I say common run? That would be tolerable, if this aberration had not taken hold of a good part of priests and theologians and practically all of their followers, who in name and manner of living profess the spiritual life. If the salt has lost its savour, what will the others be salted with? I am ashamed to mention with what superstition so many of them observe silly little ceremonies, instituted by mere men, but certainly not with this purpose in mind. With what spite they exact these same ceremonies of others, with what a sense of security they trust in them, with what temerity they judge others, with what jealous rivalry they defend them! They think heaven is owed to them because of these actions of theirs, and once they become hardened in these practices they fancy themselves Paul or Antony[8] returned to life. They begin to censure the lives of others with great superciliousness in accordance with that rule of the unwise, as the comic poet said, 'esteeming nothing right save what they do themselves.[9] But when they have grown old in their way of life, you will see that they still have not acquired any of the qualities of Christ.

Rather, they are like animals, steeped in certain repulsive vices, difficult to get along with in their communal life and barely putting up with themselves, frigid in charity, ardent in their anger, unrelenting in their hatred, venomous in their speech, invincible in kindling animosity. They are ready to fight to the death for matters of the least importance and so removed are they from the perfection of Christ that they do not even possess the common virtues that the pagans acquire either through natural reason or the experiences of life or the precepts of philosophers. They are unruly, intractable, quarrelsome, avid for pleasure, nauseated by the divine word, agreeable to no one, suspicious of others, and indulgent to themselves.

Is this the result of so many years of toil, that you are the worst element of mankind and think you are the best? Instead of being a Christian you are a Jew, slave to empty observances,[10] so that you may receive praise not in secret with God, but in public before men? But if you walked in the spirit, not in the flesh, where are the fruits of the Spirit? Where is charity, where is that joy of the mind? Where is peace toward all men? Where is patience, long-suffering, goodness, kindness, gentleness, faithfulness, modesty, self-control, chastity? Where is the image of Christ in your morals? You say: 'I am not a whore-monger, not a thief, not guilty of sacrilege, and I observe what I have professed.' What does this recall but those words: 'I am not like other men, robbers, and adulterers, and I fast twice a week'?[11] I prefer, yes, I prefer the humble publican who implored mercy to this kind of just man enumerating his own good deeds. What did you profess, that you would *not* do what you swore to in baptism, namely, to be a Christian, that is spiritual, and not a Jew? Thus it would seem, since for the sake of petty traditions invented by men you transgress the commandments of God. Or is Christianity not the spiritual life? Listen to Paul speaking to the Romans: 'There is therefore no condemnation for those in Christ Jesus who do not walk according to the flesh. For the law of the spirit of life in Christ Jesus has liberated me from the law of sin and death. God has done what the law, which was weak because of the flesh, could not do: by sending his own Son in the likeness of sinful flesh and as an offering for sin he condemned sin in the flesh, so that the justification of the law might be fulfilled in us, who do not walk according to the flesh but according to the spirit. For those who live according to the flesh are wise in the things of the flesh, but those in the spirit sense the things of the spirit. For the wisdom of the flesh is death, whereas the wisdom of the spirit is life and peace. For the wisdom of the flesh is inimical to God; it is not subject to the law of God, nor can it be. Those who are in the flesh cannot please God.'[12] What could be said more fully or more plainly?

But men who are skilful at indulging their own vices and quick to criticize the vices of others do not think that this has anything to do with them. What Paul said about walking in the flesh they apply only to adulterers and whore-mongers and they contort his words about the wisdom of the flesh, which is inimical to God, applying them against those who have learned 'secular' literature as they call it. They congratulate themselves on both counts, that they are not adulterers and that they are egregiously ignorant of all literature. ...

A tree is known by its fruit.[13] It does not matter to me that you do not neglect vigils, fasts, silence, little prayers, and all other such observances. I shall not believe that you are in the spirit until I see the fruits of the spirit. Why should I not insist that you are still in the flesh when after you have practised these observances almost all your life, I still detect in you the works of the flesh: jealousy worse than you would find in a woman, a military proneness to anger and violence, an insatiable passion for quarrelling, unbridled invective, a malicious tongue as venomous as a viper's, pompous haughtiness, inflexible obstinacy, slippery loyalty, vanity, pretence, and flattery? You judge your brother in meat or drink or dress. But Paul judges you from your deeds.

Or perhaps what distinguishes you from worldly men dedicated to the flesh is the fact that you are subject to the same vices but in less grave circumstances. Which is worse, that a man give in to feelings of anger, enmity, and jealousy because of a stolen birthright, the rape of his daughter, an injury done to his parents, or to obtain public office or the prince's favour, or that you (I am ashamed to say it) do all these things with much more brutality for no reason at all? A lesser reason for committing sin does not diminish guilt, but aggravates it. The magnitude of the sin does not matter so much as the degree of passion involved. On the contrary the lesser the reason for deviating from correct conduct the more criminal is the wrong-doer. I am not talking now about those monks whose morals even the world detests, but of those whom the common peoples admire not as men but as angels.

But those same monks should not be offended by my words, which are directed at vices, not men. If they are good-living men, they should be glad to be reminded by anyone, whoever he may be, of things that pertain to salvation. It is no secret to me that there are many among them who, aided by their literary studies and gifts of intelligence, have had some experience of the mysteries of the spirit. But, as Livy said, 'it is often the case that the greater part overcomes the better.' But if we be allowed to admit the truth, do we not see that those monks who live the strictest lives place the highest religious perfection in ceremonies or a fixed recitation of the psalms or manual labour? But if anyone were to examine and question them about spiritual things, he would find very few who do not walk in the flesh. And from this derives this great weakness of souls, which tremble with fear where there is nothing to be afraid of and yawn with weariness where the danger is greatest. This is the reason, too, for that perpetual infancy in Christ, not to use stronger language, by which, giving reverse values to things, we ascribe great importance to that which is worthless and disregard the only thing that is important. ...

Do not tell me now that charity consists in being an assiduous churchgoer, prostrating yourself before the statues of the saints, lighting candles, and repeating a certain number of prayers. God has no need of this. This is what Paul calls charity: to edify our neighbour, to consider everyone as members of the same body, to regard everyone as one in Christ, to rejoice in the Lord at your brother's prosperity as if it were your own and to heal his misfortunes as if they were your own. It is to correct the erring gently, teach the ignorant, lift up the fallen, console the downhearted, aid the struggler, support the needy, in a word, devote all your resources, all your zeal, all your care to this one end, that you benefit as many as you can in Christ. Just as he was not born for himself and did not live for himself or die for himself, but dedicated himself entirely to our needs, so let us also devote ourselves to the interests of our brethren, not to our own. If this were to be done, there would be nothing happier or more effortless than the religious life, which now on the contrary we observe to be joyless and toilsome, full of Jewish superstitions, and not free of any of the vices of the laity, while in some it is even more contaminated. If Augustine, whom most of them vaunt as the founder of their way of life, were now to come back to life, he would not even recognize this breed of men. He would cry out that nothing could have been further from his mind than this type of life, and that he had instituted a rule of life not modelled after the superstition of the Jews but after the example of the apostles.

But for some time now I have heard this rejoinder from certain more sensible individuals: 'One must be vigilant in the smallest things lest he sink little by little into greater vices.' I agree, but you must be no less vigilant that you do not become so stuck in small things that you isolate yourself altogether from things of great importance. In the first instance the peril is more evident, in the second it is more serious. Flee Scylla in such a way that you do not fall victim to Charybdis.[14] It is salutary to be faithful in small things, but it is fatal to put your trust in them. Paul does not forbid you to use the elements of this world, but does not wish that one who is free in Christ should be a slave of these elements. He does not condemn the law of works if one puts them to legitimate use. Without these, perhaps, you will not be a pious Christian, but they do not make you pious. They will lead to piety if you use them to this extent, but if you begin to derive pleasure from them, they extinguish piety once and for all. ...

What, then, will the Christian do? Shall he neglect the precepts of the church? Shall he despise the honourable traditions of his ancestors? Shall he condemn pious customs? On the contrary, if he is weak, he will preserve them as necessary to him, but if he is strong and mature, he will observe them all the more lest through his superior knowledge he offend his weak brother and bring about the spiritual ruin of one for whom Christ died.

It is right not to omit these observances, but it is necessary to perform those others. Corporal works are not condemned, but those that are invisible are preferred. Visible worship is not condemned, but God is appeased only by invisible piety. It would be shameful that Christians do not know what a certain pagan poet did not fail to recognize: 'If God is spirit, as poets say / With purest mind must he be worshipped.'[15] Let us not belittle the author because he is a pagan or a rather unimportant writer. This saying is worthy of a great theologian, and, as I have discovered, as little understood as it is read. The meaning is that like is affected by like. You believe that God is greatly moved by the slaying of a bull or by the odour of incense, as if he were a body. He is mind, the purest and the simplest of minds. Therefore he must be worshipped above all with a pure mind. You think that the burning of wax is a sacrifice. But David said: 'A contrite spirit is a sacrifice to God.'[16] And if he despised the blood of goats or of bullocks, he will not despise a contrite and humbled heart. If you do what is valued in the eyes of men, apply yourself even more to do what the eyes of God require. The body may be covered with a monk's cowl, but what good is that if the mind wears a worldly garb? If the outer man is clad in a white tunic, let the garments of the inner man be as white as snow. You observe exterior silence; take much more care that your mind is free within. In a visible place of worship you kneel on bodily knees; but nothing is accomplished thereby if in the shrine of the heart you stand erect in defiance of God. You venerate the wood of the cross; better to follow the mystery of the cross. You observe fasts and abstain from things that do not defile a man, and you do not refrain from obscene speech which defiles both your own and another's conscience. Food is denied to the body, and the soul is gorged with swine's husks. You adorn a stone building, and you have places sacred to religion; of what use is it if the temple of the heart, whose wall Ezekiel's vision penetrated,[17] has been profaned by the abominations of Egypt? You keep the sabbath externally, and within everything resounds with the tumult of vice. The body does not commit adultery, but by your cupidity your mind is adulterous. You sing psalms with the bodily tongue, but listen to what your mind says within. You bless with the mouth and curse with the heart. Physically you are confined to a narrow cell, but in your thoughts you wander over the whole world. You hear the word of God with your bodily ears; listen rather within. What does the prophet say? 'Unless you hear within, your soul will weep.'[18] What do you read in the gospel? 'So that seeing they may not see, and hearing they may not hear.'[19] And again the prophet: 'You will hear with your ears, but you will not understand.'[20] Blessed, therefore, are they who hear the word of God within. Happy those to whom the Lord speaks inwardly, and their souls will be saved. It is this inward ear that David bids the daughter of the king to incline, she who was bedecked within her chamber with gold-embroidered robes.[21]

In a word, what good is it not to do the evils that you lust after in your desires? What good is it to do good exteriorly if interiorly one's thoughts are quite the opposite? Is it any great feat to visit Jerusalem bodily when within you there is Sodom, Egypt, and Babylon? There is no great merit in treading where Christ trod with human footsteps, but it is a great thing to follow in the steps of Christ in the affections of the mind. If it is a great achievement to have touched the Lord's sepulchre, will it not be just as meritorious to have reproduced the mystery of his burial? You confess your sins to a priest, who is a mere man; take care how you confess them to God. For to confess them inwardly to him is to have hatred for them. Perhaps you believe that your imperfections are washed away once and for all by wax seals[22] or a paltry sum of money or some brief pilgrimage. You are all wrong. The wound was inflicted within you, and it is within that the remedy must be applied. Your affections have been corrupted; you loved what was worthy of hate, you hated what should have been loved. The sweet was bitter to you, and the bitter sweet. I am not concerned with what you manifest externally. But if by a complete reversal you begin to hate what you once loved, to flee from it and shudder at it, if what once tasted like gall becomes sweet to your affections, then I regard this as proof of your return to good health. Mary Magdalene loved much; hence many sins were forgiven her. The more you love Christ, the more you will hate your vices; for hatred of sin follows upon the love of piety as the shadow follows the body. I prefer that you hate your vicious habits once and for all, truly and from within, than that you detest them ten times verbally before a priest.

Therefore, as I have illustrated in a few examples, in the whole theatre of this visible world, in the old law, in the new, in all the teaching of the church, and finally in yourself and in every human activity there is externally something we can call the flesh, and internally there is the spirit. In all of which, if we do not reverse the order of things, if we put only such confidence in visible things as they contribute to things of more importance, and look only to the spirit and to those things that pertain to charity, we will end up not gloomy and weak, like those who remain always children (as the proverb has it), brutish, dry bones, as the prophet says,[23] lifeless, lethargic, stupid, quarrelsome, envious, and maligners. Rather we shall be high-minded in Christ, of abundant charity, strong and constant in good or bad fortune, closing our eyes to petty things, striving towards higher things, full of enthusiasm, full of knowledge, that knowledge the repudiators of which are in turn repudiated by the Master of all learning. For it is ignorance, usually accompanied by indocility and self-love which alone brings it about, as the prophet says, that 'we rely on things of no value and speak falsities, conceive trouble and bring forth iniquity,'[24] and submit ourselves with fear and abjection to Jewish ceremonies. Of such people Paul says: 'I bear witness to them that they have a zeal for God, but it is without wisdom.'[25] What were they ignorant of? Obviously that the end of the law is Christ. Christ is spirit; he is love. Isaiah describes more openly the wretched and futile slavery of those who live in the flesh: 'For this reason my people were led away captive, that they had no wisdom. And their noblemen perished of hunger, and their multitude was parched with thirst.[26] It is no wonder that the people are the slaves of the elements of this world, that is to say, the untutored masses, who know nothing save what they learn from others. More astonishing is the fact that those among the highest ranks of the Christian religion perish of hunger and are parched with thirst in the same captivity. Why do they perish of hunger? Because they did not learn from Christ to break barley loaves. They lick only the rough husk without extracting the kernel. Why are they parched with thirst? Because they did not learn from Moses to make the water spring from the spiritual rock. Nor did they drink of 'the streams of living water that flow from the belly of Christ. This was said of the spirit,'[27] not of the flesh.

Therefore, my brother, do not progress slowly by dint of reluctant effort, but by moderate exercise arrive at quick and vigorous adulthood in Christ. Embrace zealously this rule, not to be willing to crawl along the ground with unclean animals, but supported on those wings whose growth Plato thinks are induced in our minds by the heat of love and shoot out anew,[28] raise yourself as on the steps of Jacob's ladder[29] from the body to the spirit, from the visible to the invisible, from the letter to the mystery, from sensible things to intelligible things, from composite things to simple things. In this way, the Lord will draw nigh in his turn to the one who draws nigh to him, and if you will attempt to the limit of your powers to rise out of your moral darkness and the tumult of the senses, he will obligingly come forth to meet you from his inaccessible light and that unimagined silence, in which not only all the tumult of the senses, but also the forms of all intelligible things fall silent.

# *ERASMUS AS REFORMER AND CRITIC OF THE CHURCH*

# 4

## Praise of Folly / *Moriae encomium*

In his dedicatory letter to Thomas More (Ep 222, CWE 2 161–4), Erasmus relates the circumstances in which the *Praise of Folly* was conceived. On the long journey from Italy to England in 1509, he decided to amuse himself with meditations on human folly rather than waste his time on idle gossip and small talk. Upon his arrival he committed his reflections to paper and gave his *jeu d'esprit* the title *Moriae encomium*, punning on the similarity of Thomas More's name with the Greek word for 'Folly,' *Moria*. Thus the title might be taken to mean either *Praise of/by Folly* or *Praise of More.*

The essay was immensely popular with humanists but evoked sharp criticism in clerical circles. Erasmus wrote 'in a Lucianic spirit of irreverent burlesque,' as Betty Radice put it in her introduction to the text (CWE 27 80). Critics immediately cried 'Heresy!' and the book ended up on the *Index of Prohibited Books*. But Erasmus protested his good intentions: 'You can find a good many people whose religious sense is so distorted that they find the most serious blasphemies against Christ more bearable than the slightest joke on pope or prince, especially if it touches their daily bread. And to criticize men's lives without mentioning any names – I ask you, does this look like sarcasm, or rather warning and advice? ... and so anyone who protests that he is injured betrays his own guilty conscience, or at any rate his apprehensions' (CWE 27 84).

The *Praise of Folly* was first published in 1511. By Erasmus' death in 1536, there were thirty-six Latin editions and translations into Czech, French, and German. Italian and English versions followed in short order. The book remains Erasmus' most popular work today.

This extract is taken from CWE 27 86–153, translated and annotated by Betty Radice. We are grateful to Penguin Books Ltd for permission to reproduce Betty Radice's translation in this reader.

Folly speaks: Whatever is generally said of me by mortal men, and I'm quite well aware that Folly is in poor repute even amongst the greatest fools, still, I am the one – and indeed, the only one – whose divine powers can gladden the hearts of gods and men. Proof enough of this is in the fact that as soon as I stepped forward to address this crowded assembly, every face immediately brightened up with a new, unwonted gaiety and all your frowns were smoothed away ...

In short, no association or alliance can be happy or stable without me. People can't tolerate a ruler, nor can a master his servant, a maid her mistress, a teacher his pupil, a friend his friend nor a wife her husband, a landlord his tenant, a soldier his comrade nor a party-goer his companion, unless they sometimes have illusions about each other, make use of flattery, and have the sense to turn a blind eye and sweeten life for themselves with the honey of folly. I dare say you think this is the last word on the subject, but there are more important things to come.

Now tell me: can a man love anyone who hates himself? Can he be in harmony with someone else if he's divided in himself, or bring anyone pleasure if he's only a disagreeable nuisance to himself? No one, I fancy, would say he can unless there's someone more foolish than Folly. Remove me, and no one could put up with his neighbour, indeed, he'd stink in his own nostrils and find everything about himself loathsome and disgusting. The reason is that Nature, more of a stepmother than a mother in several ways, has sown a seed of evil in the hearts of mortals, especially in the more thoughtful men, which makes them dissatisfied with their own lot and envious of another's. Consequently, all the blessings of life, which should give it grace and charm, are damaged and destroyed. What good is beauty, the greatest gift of the gods, if it is tainted by the canker of decay? Or youth, if it is soured and spoiled by the misery of advancing age? And finally, is there any duty throughout life which you can perform gracefully as regards yourself or others (for the importance of decorum extends beyond mere skill and covers every action) unless you have Self-love at hand to help you, Self-love who is so prompt to take my place on all occasions that she is rightly called my sister? What is so foolish as self-satisfaction and self-admiration? But then what agreeable, pleasant, or graceful act can you perform if you aren't self-satisfied? Take away this salt of life and immediately the orator and his gestures will be a bore, the musician will please no one with his tunes, the actor and his posturings will be hissed off the stage, the poet be a laughing-stock along with his Muses, the painter and his works deemed valueless, and the doctor starve amidst his remedies. Finally, you'll look like Thersites and Nestor instead of Nireus and Phaon, a pig rather than Minerva,[1] and a speechless child and a boor instead of an eloquent and civilized man; which shows how necessary it is for a man to have a good opinion of himself, give himself a bit of a boost to win his own self-esteem before he can win that of others. And since for the most part happiness consists in being willing to be what you are, my Self-love has provided a short cut to it by ensuring that no one is dissatisfied with his own looks, character, race, position, country, and way of life. And so no Irishman would want to change places with an Italian, nor Thracian with an Athenian, nor Scythian with an inhabitant of the Islands of the Blest.[2] What remarkable foresight of Nature it was, to level out all these variations and make all alike! Where she has withheld some of her gifts she generally adds a tiny bit more Self-love – but it's silly of me to say this, seeing that Self-love is her greatest gift. ...

There are the theologians, a remarkably supercilious and touchy lot. I might perhaps do better to pass over them in silence without stirring the mud of Camarina[3] or grasping that noxious plant, lest they marshal their forces for an attack with innumerable conclusions and force me to eat my words. If I refuse they'll denounce me as a heretic on the spot, for this is the bolt they always loose on anyone to whom they take a dislike. Now there are none so unwilling to recognize my good services to them, and yet they're under obligation to me on several important counts, notably for their happiness in their self-love, which enables them to dwell in a sort of third heaven, looking down from aloft, almost with pity, on all the rest of mankind as so many cattle crawling on the face of the earth. They are fortified meanwhile with an army of schoolmen's definitions, conclusions, and corollaries, and propositions both explicit and implicit. They boast of so many bolt holes that the meshes of Vulcan's net[4] couldn't stop them from slipping out by means of the distinctions they draw, with which they can easily cut any knot (a double axe from Tenedos[5] wouldn't do better), for they abound in newly coined expressions and strange-sounding words.

In addition, they interpret hidden mysteries to suit themselves: how the world was created and designed; through what channels the stain of sin filtered down to posterity; by what means, in what measure, and how long Christ was formed in the Virgin's womb; how, in the Eucharist, accidents can subsist without a domicile. But this sort of question has been discussed threadbare. There are others more worthy of great and enlightened theologians (as they call themselves) which can really rouse them to action if they come their way. What was the exact moment of divine generation? Are there several filiations in Christ? Is it a possible proposition that God the Father could hate his Son? Could God have taken on the form of a woman, a devil, a donkey, a gourd, or a flintstone? If so, how could a gourd have preached sermons, performed miracles, and been nailed to the cross? And what would Peter have consecrated if he had consecrated when the body of Christ still hung on the cross? Furthermore, at that same time could Christ have been called a man? Shall we be permitted to eat and drink after the resurrection? We're taking due precaution against hunger and thirst while there's time.

There are any amount of quibbles even more refined than these, about concepts, relations, instants, formalities, quiddities, and ecceities, which no one could possibly perceive unless like Lynceus[6] he could see through blackest darkness things which don't exist. Then add those maxims of theirs, which are so paradoxical that in comparison the pronouncements of the Stoics, which were actually known as paradoxes, seem positively commonplace and banal; for example, that it is a lesser crime to butcher a thousand men than to cobble a poor man's shoe on a single occasion on the Lord's day, and better to let the whole world perish down to the last crumb and stitch, as they say, than to tell a single tiny insignificant lie. These subtle refinements of subtleties are made still more subtle by all the different lines of scholastic argument, so that you'd extricate yourself faster from a labyrinth than from the tortuous obscurities of realists, nominalists, Thomists, Albertists, Ockhamists, and Scotists[7] – and I've not mentioned all the sects, only the main ones.

Such is the erudition and complexity they all display that I fancy the apostles themselves would need the help of another Holy Spirit if they were obliged to join issue on these topics with our new breed of new theologian. Paul could provide a living example of faith, but when he says 'Faith is the substance of things hoped for, the evidence of things not seen,'[8] his definition is quite unscholastic. And though he provides the finest example of charity, in his first letter to the Corinthians, chapter 13, he neither divides nor defines it according to the rules of dialectic. The apostles consecrated the Eucharist with due piety, but had they been questioned about the *terminus a quo* and the *terminus ad quem*, about transubstantiation, and how the same body can be in different places, about the difference between the body of Christ in heaven, on the cross, and at the sacrament of the Eucharist, about the exact moment when transubstantiation takes place, seeing that the prayer which effects it is a distinct quantity extended in time, they wouldn't, in my opinion, have shown the same subtlety in their reply as the Scotists do in their dissertations and definitions. The apostles knew personally the mother of Jesus, but which of them proved how she had been kept immaculate from Adam's sin with the logic our theologians display? Peter received the keys, and received them from one who would not have entrusted them to an unworthy recipient, yet I doubt whether Peter understood (nowhere does he show signs of subtle reasoning power) how a man who has not knowledge can still hold the key to it. The apostles baptized wherever they went, yet nowhere did they teach the formal, material, efficient, and final cause of baptism, nor did they ever mention the delible and indelible marks of the sacraments. They worshipped, that is true, but in spirit, in accordance only with the words of the Gospel, 'God is a spirit: and they that worship him must worship in spirit and in truth.'[9] Apparently it had never been revealed to them that a mediocre drawing sketched in charcoal on a wall should be worshipped in the same manner as Christ himself, provided that it had two fingers outstretched, long hair, and three rays sticking out from the halo fastened to the back of its head. Who *could* understand all this unless he has frittered away thirty-six whole years over the physics and metaphysics of Aristotle and Scotus? ...

Nothing will make me believe that Paul, from whose learning we may judge all the other apostles, would so often have condemned questions, arguments, genealogies, and what he himself called 'battles of words'[10] if he had been well up in those niceties, especially when all the controversies and disagreements of that time would have been clumsy and unsophisticated affairs in comparison with the more than Chrysippean subtleties[11] of the schoolmen of today. Not but what these are extremely moderate men. If anything written by the apostles lacks polish and the master's touch, they don't damn it outright but suggest a suitable interpretation, and this, I suppose, is intended as a tribute in deference to its antiquity and apostolic authorship. It would of course hardly be fair to expect such a standard from the apostles when they never heard so much as a word on these matters from their own teacher. If the same sort of thing turned up in Chrysostom, Basil,[12] or Jerome, then they'd have good reason to mark it 'not accepted.'

Those apostles certainly refuted pagan philosophers and the Jews (who are by nature the most obstinate of men),[13] but did so more by the example of their way of life and their miracles than by syllogisms, especially in the case of those who would have been intellectually quite incapable of grasping a single *quodlibet* of Scotus.[14] Today there's no heathen or heretic who doesn't give way at once when confronted by these ultra-subtle refinements, unless he's so thick-headed that he can't follow them, or so imprudent that he shouts them down, or so well trained in the same wiles that the battle's evenly matched – as if you set magician against magician or a man with a lucky sword fights another who has one too. This would just be reweaving Penelope's web.[15] And in my opinion Christians would show sense if they dispatched these argumentative Scotists and pigheaded Ockhamists and undefeated Albertists along with the whole regiment of sophists to fight the Turks and Saracens instead of sending those armies of dull-witted soldiers with whom they've long been carrying on war with no result. Then, I think, they'd witness a really keen battle and a victory such as never before. For who is too cold-blooded to be fired by their ingenuities, too stupid to be stung into action by their attacks? And is there anyone so keen-sighted that they can't leave him groping in the dark?

You may suppose that I'm saying all this by way of a joke, and that's not surprising, seeing that amongst the theologians themselves there are some with superior education who are sickened by these theological minutiae, which they look upon as frivolous. Others too think it a damnable form of sacrilege and the worst sort of impiety for anyone to speak of matters so holy, which call for reverence rather than explanation, with a profane tongue, or to argue with the pagan subtlety of the heathen, presume to offer definitions, and pollute the majesty of divine theology with words and sentiments which are so trivial and even squalid.

Yet those who do so are so happy in their self-satisfaction and self-congratulation, and so busy night and day with these enjoyable tomfooleries, that they haven't even a spare moment in which to read the Gospel or the letters of Paul even once through. And while they're wasting their time in the schools with this nonsense, they believe that just as in the poets Atlas[16] holds up the sky on his shoulders, they support the entire church on the props of their syllogisms and without them it would collapse. Then you can imagine their happiness when they fashion and refashion the Holy Scriptures at will, as if these were made of wax, and when they insist that their conclusions, to which a mere handful of scholastics have subscribed, should carry more weight than the laws of Solon[17] and be preferred to papal decrees. They also set up as the world's censors, and demand recantation of anything which doesn't exactly square with their conclusions, explicit and implicit, and make their oracular pronouncements: 'This proposition is scandalous; this is irreverent; this smells of heresy; this doesn't ring true.' As a result, neither baptism nor the gospel, neither Paul, Peter, St Jerome, Augustine, or even Thomas, the greatest of Aristotelians, can make a man Christian unless these learned bachelors have given their approval, such is the refinement of their judgment. For who could have imagined, if the savants hadn't told him, that anyone who said that the two phrases 'chamber-pot you stink' and 'the chamber-pot stinks,' or 'the pots boil' and 'that the pot boils' are equally correct can't possibly be a Christian? Who could have freed the church from the dark error of its ways when no one would ever have read about these if they hadn't been published under the great seals of the schools? And aren't they perfectly happy doing all this?

They are happy too while they're depicting everything in hell down to the last detail, as if they'd spent several years there, or giving free rein to their fancy in fabricating new spheres and adding the most extensive and beautiful of all in case the blessed spirits lack space to take a walk in comfort or give a dinner-party or even play a game of ball. Their heads are so stuffed and swollen with these absurdities, and thousands more like them, that I don't believe even Jupiter's brain felt so burdened when he begged for Vulcan's axe to help him give birth to Athene.[18] And so you mustn't be surprised if you see them at public disputations with their heads carefully bound up in all those fillets[19] – it's to keep them from bursting apart.

For myself, I often have a good laugh when they particularly fancy themselves as theologians if they speak in a specially uncouth and slovenly style, and while they mumble so haltingly as to be unintelligible except to a fellow-stammerer, they refer to their powers of perception, which can't be attained by the common man. They insist that it detracts from the grandeur of sacred writing if they're obliged to obey the rules of grammar. It seems a most peculiar prerogative of theologians, to be the only people permitted to speak ungrammatically; however, they share this privilege with a lot of working men. Finally, they think themselves nearest to the gods whenever they are reverently addressed as 'our masters,' a title which holds as much meaning for them as the tetragram[20] does for the Jews. Consequently, they say it's unlawful to write MAGISTER NOSTER[21] except in capital letters, and if anyone inverts the order and say *noster magister*, he destroys the entire majesty of the theologians' title at a single blow.

The happiness of these people is most nearly approached by those who are popularly called 'religious' or 'monks.' Both names are false, since most of them are a long way removed from religion, and wherever you go these so-called solitaires[22] are the people you're likely to meet. I don't believe any life would be more wretched than theirs if I didn't come to their aid in many ways. The whole tribe is so universally loathed that even a chance meeting is thought to be ill-omened – and yet they are gloriously self-satisfied. In the first place, they believe it's the highest form of piety to be so uneducated that they can't even read. Then when they bray like donkeys in church, repeating by rote the psalms they haven't understood, they imagine they are charming the ears of their heavenly audience with infinite delight. Many of them too make a good living out of their squalor and beggary, bellowing for bread from door to door, and indeed making a nuisance of themselves in every inn, carriage, or boat, to the great loss of all the other beggars. This is the way in which these smooth individuals, in all their filth and ignorance, their boorish and shameless behaviour, claim to bring back the apostles into our midst!

But nothing could be more amusing than their practice of doing everything to rule, as if they were following mathematical calculations which it would be a sin to ignore. They work out the number of knots for a shoe-string, the colour and number of variations of a single habit, the material and width to a hair's breadth of a girdle, the shape and capacity (in sacksful) of a cowl, the length (in fingers) of a haircut, the number of hours prescribed for sleep. But this equality applied to such a diversity of persons and temperaments will only result in inequality, as anyone can see. Even so, these trivialities not only make them feel superior to other men but also contemptuous of each other, and these professors of apostolic charity will create extraordinary scenes and disturbances on account of a habit with a different girdle or one which is rather too dark in colour. Some you'll see are so strict in their observances that they will wear an outer garment which has to be made of Cilician goat's hair and one of Milesian wool[23] next to the skin, while others have linen on top and wool underneath. There are others again who shrink from the touch of money as if it were deadly poison, but are less restrained when it comes to wine or contact with women. In short, they all take remarkable pains to be different in their rules of life. They aren't interested in being like Christ but in being unlike each other.

Consequently, a great deal of their happiness depends on their name. Some, for instance, delight in calling themselves Cordeliers, and they are subdivided into the Colletines, the Minors, the Minims and the Bullists. Then there are the Benedictines and the Bernardines; the Brigittines, Augustinians, Williamites and Jacobins; as if it weren't enough to be called Christians. Most of them rely so much on their ceremonies and petty man-made traditions that they suppose heaven alone will hardly be enough to reward merit such as theirs. They never think of the time to come when Christ will scorn all this and enforce his own rule, that of charity. One monk will display his wretched belly, swollen with every kind of fish. Another will pour out a hundred sacksful of psalms, while another adds up his myriads of fasts and accounts for his stomach near to bursting by the single midday meal, which is all he usually has. Yet another will produce such a pile of church ceremonies that seven ships could scarcely carry them. One will boast that for sixty years he has never touched money without protecting his fingers with two pairs of gloves, while another wears a cowl so thick with dirt that not even a sailor would want it near his person. Then one will relate how for over fifty years he has led the life of a sponge, always stuck in the same place; others will show off a voice made hoarse by incessant chanting, or the inertia brought on by living alone, or a tongue stiff with disuse under the rule of silence. But Christ would interrupt the unending flow of these self-glorifications to ask: 'Where has this new race of Jews sprung from? I recognize only one commandment as truly as mine, but it is the only one not mentioned. Long ago in the sight of all, without wrapping up my words in parables, I promised my father's kingdom, not for wearing a cowl or chanting petty prayers or practising abstinence, but for performing the duties of faith and charity. I do not acknowledge men who acknowledge their own deeds so noisily. Those who also want to appear holier than I am can go off and live in the heavens of the Abraxasians,[24] if they like, or give orders for a new heaven to be built for them by the men whose foolish teaching they have set above my own commands.' When they hear these words and see common sailors and waggoners preferred to themselves, what sort of looks do you think they'll give each other? But for the moment they're happy in their expectations, not without help from me. ... But now that I have donned the lion-skin,[25] let me tell you another thing. The happiness which Christians seek with so many labours is nothing other than a certain kind of madness and folly. Don't be put off by the words, but consider the reality. In the first place, Christians come very near to agreeing with the Platonists[26] that the soul is stifled and bound down by the fetters of the body, which by its gross matter prevents the soul from being able to contemplate and enjoy things as they truly are. Next, Plato defines philosophy as a preparation for death because it leads the mind from visible and bodily things, just as death does. And so as long as the mind makes proper use of the organs of the body it is called sane and healthy, but once it begins to break its bonds and tries to win freedom, as if it were planning an escape from prison, men call it insane. If this happens through disease or some organic defect, by general consent it is called insanity. Even so, we see this type of person foretelling the future, showing a knowledge of languages and literature they had never previously learned, and giving clear indication of something divine. Undoubtedly this happens because the mind is beginning to free itself from contamination by the body and exercise its true natural power. I think this also explains why those who are struggling at the hour of death often have a somewhat similar experience, so that they speak wonders as if inspired.

Again, if this happens through pious fervour, it may not be quite the same kind of insanity, but is so like it that most people make no distinction, especially as the number of folk who differ in their whole way of life from the general run of mankind is very small. And so we have a situation which I think is not unlike the one in the myth in Plato,[27] where those who were chained in a cave marvelled at shadows, whereas the man who had escaped and then returned to the cavern told them that he had seen real things, and they were much mistaken in their belief that nothing existed but their wretched shadows. This man who has gained understanding pities his companions and deplores their insanity, which confines them to such an illusion, but they in their turn laugh at him as if he were crazy and turn him out. In the same way, the common herd of men feels admiration only for the things of the body and believes that these alone exist, whereas the pious scorn whatever concerns the body and are wholly uplifted towards the contemplation of invisible things. The ordinary man gives first place to wealth, the second to bodily comforts, and leaves the last to the soul – which anyway most people believe doesn't exist because it is invisible to the eye. By contrast, the pious direct their entire endeavour towards God, who is absolute purity, and after him towards what is closest to him, the soul. They have no thought for the body, despise wealth and avoid it like trash, and if they are obliged to deal with such matters they do so with reluctance and distaste, having as if they did not have, possessing as if they did not possess.

There are moreover in each of these things widely differing degrees. To begin with, though all the senses have some kinship with the body, some of them are grosser, such as touch, hearing, sight, smell, and taste, while other faculties are less physical, for instance, memory, intellect, and will. The power of the soul depends on its inclinations. Since, then, all the power of the pious soul is directed towards what is furthest removed from the grosser senses, these become blunted and benumbed. The vulgar crowd of course does the opposite, develops them very much and more spiritual faculties very little. That explains what we have heard happened to several saints, who drank oil by mistake for wine.[28] Again, take the affections of the soul. Some have more traffic with the grossness of the body, such as lust, desire for food and sleep, anger, pride, and envy, and on these the pious wage unceasing war, while the crowd thinks life impossible without them. Then there are what we could call intermediate affections, which are quasi-natural to all, like love for one's country, and affection for children, parents, and friends. The crowd sets great store by these, yet the pious strive to root them too from their soul, or at least to sublimate them to the highest region of the soul. They wish to love their father not as a father, for he begot nothing but the body, and this too is owed to God the Father, but as a good man and one in whom is reflected the image of the supreme mind, which alone they call the *summum bonum*[29] and beyond which they declare nothing is to be loved or sought.

This is the rule whereby they regulate all the remainder of life's duties, so that anything visible, if it is not wholly to be despised, is still valued far less than what cannot be seen. They also say that even in the sacraments and the actual observances of their religion, both body and spirit are involved. For example, they think little of fasting if it means no more than abstaining from meat and a meal – which for the common man is the essential of a fast. It must at the same time reduce the passions, permitting less anger or pride than usual, so that the spirit can feel less burdened by the matter of the body and can aim at tasting and enjoying the blessings of heaven. It is the same with the Eucharist: the ritual with which it is celebrated should not be rejected, they say, but in itself it serves no useful purpose or can be positively harmful if it lacks the spiritual element represented by those visible symbols. It represents the death of Christ, which men must express through the mastery and extinction of their bodily passions, laying them in the tomb, as it were, in order to rise again to a new life wherein they can be united with him and with each other. This then is how the pious man acts, and this is his purpose. The crowd, on the other hand, thinks the sacrifice of the mass means no more than crowding as close as possible to the altars, hearing the sound of the words, and watching other small details of such ritual. I quote this only as one example; in fact the pious man throughout his whole life withdraws from the things of the body and is drawn towards what is eternal, invisible, and spiritual. Consequently, there is total disagreement between the two parties on every point, and each thinks the other mad; though in my view, the epithet is more properly applied to the pious, not the common man.

This will be clearer if I do as I promised, and show briefly how the supreme reward for man is no other than a kind of madness. First consider how Plato[30] imagined something of this sort when he wrote that the madness of lovers is the highest form of happiness. For anyone who loves intensely lives not in himself but in the object of his love, and the further he can move out of himself into his love, the happier he is. Now, when the soul is planning to leave the body and ceases to make proper use of its organs, it is thought to be mad, and doubtless with good reason. This, surely, is what is meant by the popular expressions 'he is beside himself,' 'he has come to,' and 'he is himself again.' Moreover, the more perfect the love, the greater the madness – and the happier. What, then, will life in heaven be like, to which all pious minds so eagerly aspire? The spirit will be the stronger, and will conquer and absorb the body, and this it will do the more easily partly because it is, as it were, in its own kingdom, partly for having previously in life purged and weakened the body in preparation for this transformation. Then the spirit will itself be absorbed by the supreme Mind, which is more powerful than its infinite parts. And so when the whole man will be outside himself, and happy for no reason except that he is so outside himself, he will enjoy some ineffable share in the supreme good which draws everything into itself. Although this perfect happiness can only be experienced when the soul has recovered its former body and been granted immortality, since the life of the pious is no more than a contemplation and foreshadowing of that other life, at times they are able to feel some foretaste and savour of the reward to come. It is only the tiniest drop in comparison with the fount of eternal bliss, yet it far exceeds all pleasures of the body, even if all mortal delights were rolled into one, so much does the spiritual surpass the physical, the invisible the visible. This is surely what the prophet[31] promises: 'Eye has not seen nor ear heard, nor have there entered into the heart of man the things which God has prepared for those that love him.' And this is the part of folly which is not taken away by the transformation of life but is made perfect.

So those who are granted a foretaste of this – and very few have the good fortune – experience something which is very like madness. They speak incoherently and unnaturally, utter sound without sense, and their faces suddenly change expression. One moment they are excited, the next depressed, they weep and laugh and sigh by turns; in fact they truly are quite beside themselves. Then when they come to, they say they don't know where they have been, in the body or outside it, awake or asleep. They cannot remember what they have heard or seen or said or done, except in a mist, like a dream. All they know is that they were happiest when they were out of their senses in this way, and they lament their return to reason, for all they want is to be mad for ever with this kind of madness. And this is only the merest taste of the happiness to come.

But I've long been forgetting who I am, and I've overshot the mark. If anything I've said seems rather impudent or garrulous, you must remember it's Folly and a woman who's been speaking. At the same time, don't forget the Greek proverb 'Often a foolish man speaks a word in season,' though of course you may think this doesn't apply to women. I can see you're all waiting for a peroration, but it's silly of you to suppose I can remember what I've said when I've been spouting such a hotchpotch of words. There's an old saying, 'I hate a fellow-drinker with a memory,' and here's a new one to put alongside it: 'I hate an audience which won't forget.'

And so I'll say goodbye. Clap your hands,[32] live well, and drink, distinguished initiates of Folly.

The End

# Letter to Dorp

This lengthy epistle, Ep 337, is a reply to a letter (Ep 304) from the Louvain theologian Maarten van Dorp reproaching Erasmus for his hostility toward professional theologians and warning him against pursuing a philological approach to biblical studies.

Dorp had served as the mouthpiece of the faculty of theology at Louvain, and Erasmus' reply is an apologia effectively addressed to all conservative theologians. It was first published in 1515 and reprinted numerous times, often together with the *Praise of Folly*, and finally placed among the controversies in Erasmus' *Opera omnia* of 1540.

Dorp had attacked Erasmus' *Praise of Folly* and questioned the value of his current undertaking, an edition of the New Testament. The *Praise of Folly*, which first appeared in 1511, lampooned the folly and self-love of mankind, but in particular that of the quibbling scholastic theologians. It promoted a Christian folly, that is, a turning away from the things of this world.

At the time of writing his letter to Dorp, Erasmus was engaged in preparing an edition of the Greek New Testament with a Latin translation and notes. He had collated a number of Greek and Latin manuscripts and consulted numerous patristic and medieval exegetes in an effort to establish a critically sound text and idiomatically correct translation. Erasmus' insistence on language studies as an essential prerequisite for understanding Holy Writ and his seeming audacity in correcting the Vulgate – then thought to be Jerome's version – greatly exercised traditional theologians. Numerous controversies resulted, of which the exchange with Dorp is the first. Thomas More entered the fray on Erasmus' behalf, addressing a long admonitory letter to Dorp. The combined efforts of the two humanists brought about Dorp's conversion to the Erasmian position. Cordial relations prevailed between the two men until Dorp's death in 1525. Indeed, Erasmus honoured his former adversary with an epitaph.

This extract is taken from CWE 3 111–38, translated by R.A.B. Mynors and D.F.S. Thompson, annotated by James K. McConica.

ERASMUS OF ROTTERDAM TO MAARTEN VAN DORP, THE DISTINGUISHED THEOLOGIAN

Your letter never reached me, but a copy of it – secured I know not how – was shown me by a friend in Antwerp. You say you regret the somewhat unfortunate publication of my *Folly*, you heartily approve my zeal in restoring the text of Jerome, and you discourage me from publishing the New Testament.[1] This letter of yours, my dear Dorp, gave me no offence – far from it. It has made you much more dear to me, though you were dear enough before; your advice is so sincere, your counsel so friendly, your rebuke so affectionate. This is, to be sure, the mark of Christian charity that, even when it gives rein to its indignation, it retains its natural sweetness none the less. Every day I receive many letters from learned men which set me up as the glory of Germany and call me its sun and moon and suchlike grand descriptions as are more onerous than honorific. My life upon it, none ever gave me so much pleasure as my dear Dorp's letter, written to reproach me. How right St Paul was![2] Charity is never wrong; if she flatters, she flatters in order to do good, and if she is indignant, it is with the same end in view. I wish I could reply at leisure to your letter, and give satisfaction to so dear a friend. For I am truly anxious that whatever I do should be done with your approval, for I have so high an opinion of your almost divine intelligence, your exceptional knowledge, and your keen judgment, that I should value Dorp's single vote in my favour more than a thousand votes of other men. But I still feel the upset of my sea-voyage and the weariness of the riding that followed, and am, besides that, very busy packing; and so I thought it better to write what I could than to leave a friend thinking as you do, whether these thoughts are your own or were slipped into your head by others, who put you up to write that letter that they might use you as a stalking-horse for their own designs.

First then, to be perfectly frank, I am almost sorry myself that I published my *Folly*. That small book has earned me not a little reputation, or notoriety if your prefer; but I have no use for reputation coupled with ill will. Although, in heaven's name, what is all this that men call reputation, except a perfectly empty name left over from paganism? Not a few things of the kind have survived entrenched among Christians, when for instance they use 'immortality' for leaving a name to posterity, or call a man interested in any form of literature a 'virtuoso.' In all the books I have published my sole object has always been to do something useful by my exertions or, if that should not be possible, at least to do no harm. We see even great writers misusing their gifts to discharge their own personal feelings – one singing of his foolish loves, another flattering those he has set his cap at, another using his pen as a weapon to avenge some injury, another blowing his own trumpet and in the art of singing his own praises outdoing any Thraso or Pyrgopolinices.[3] So be it; for myself, in spite of my small wit and most exiguous learning, I have always had one end in view, to do good if I can; but if not, to hurt no one. ...

It is a long standing habit of learned men to confide their griefs or their joys to paper as though to a bosom friend, and to pour out all their emotions into that sympathetic ear. Indeed, you will find that some men have taken to authorship with no other purpose in mind than to stuff their books full of their own current feelings and in this way to transmit them to posterity.

But I, who in all the volumes I have published have spoken very sincerely of so many men, whose fair name have I ever blackened? On whose reputation have I cast the smallest slur? What people, class, or individual have I criticized by name? If you only knew, my dear Dorp, how often I have been provoked to do so by falsehoods no man could endure! But I have always fought down my resentment, moved more by the thought of what posterity will make of me than by the wish to treat their malignity as it deserves. If the facts had been as well known to others as they were to me, I should have been thought not satirical but fair-minded and even humble and moderate. No, I said to myself, my private feelings are no other man's concern. How can these affairs of mine be within the knowledge either of people at a distance or of posterity? I will maintain my own standard and not sink to theirs. Besides which, no man is so much my enemy that I would not rather, if I could, be on friendly terms with him again. Why should I bar the way to this, why should I now use language of an enemy which I may wish in vain that I had never used when he has become my friend? Why should I award a black mark to a man from whose record it can never be erased, however much he may deserve that it should be? If I must make a mistake, let me praise those who have done little to earn it rather than criticize those who deserve criticism; for if you praise the undeserving, this is ascribed to your open and generous character, while if you paint in his true colours a man who richly deserves to be exposed, this is sometimes thought to be due not to his deserts but to your vicious disposition. I need not mention in passing that the reciprocal exchange of injuries is not seldom the source of some dangerous conflagration, no less surely than reprisals for wrongs suffered on either side sometimes give rise to some enormous war; or that, just as it is unworthy of a Christian to return evil for evil, so it is unworthy of a generous heart to void its resentment in slander as women do.

Reasons like these have convinced me that whatever I write should hurt no one and draw no blood, and that I should never deface it by mentioning any wrongdoer by name. Nor was the end I had in view in my *Folly* different in any way from the purpose of my other works, though the means differed. In *The Handbook of the Christian Soldier*[4] I laid down quite simply the pattern of a Christian life. In my book on the education of a prince[5] I openly expound the subjects in which a prince should be brought up. In my *Panegyric for Archduke Philip of Austria*,[6] though under cover of praising a prince, I pursue indirectly the same subject that I pursued openly in the earlier work. And the *Folly* is concerned in a playful spirit with the same subject as *The Handbook of the Christian Soldier*. My purpose was guidance and not satire; to help, not to hurt; to show men how to become better and not to stand in their way. Plato, serious sage that he was, approves the habit of taking wine with a man at drinking-parties on a generous scale, because he thinks some faults can be dissolved under the cheerful influence of wine which severity could not correct. Horace too thinks good advice even when given in jest no less effective than when serious. 'To tell truth with a smile,' he asks, 'does aught forbid?'[7] And long ago some very wise men perceived this, and thought fit to set out the principles of a good life in fables which are humorous and at first sight childish, because truth by itself is a trifle astringent, and when thus made palatable finds an easier entrance into the minds of mortal men. This surely is the honey which physicians ... when they have to give medicine to children, smear on the cup of wormwood. And the purpose for which those princes of old brought fools into their courts was simply this, that their freedom of speech might point out some lighter faults and put them right without offending anyone. Perhaps it may seem inappropriate to mention Christ in such a context. But if it is ever permissible to compare things heavenly and earthly, surely his parables have something in common with the fables of antiquity? The Gospel truth slips into our minds more agreeably, and takes root there more decisively, when it has charms of this kind to commend it than if it were produced naked – a theme pursued at length by St Augustine in his *On Christian Instruction*. I saw how the common throng of mortals was corrupted by the most foolish opinions, and that too in every department of life, and it was easier to pray than to hope for a cure. And so I thought I had found a way to insinuate myself in this fashion into minds which are hard to please, and not only cure them but amuse them too. I had often observed that this cheerful and humorous style of putting people right is with many of them most successful.

If you reply that my assumed character is too trivial to provide an excuse for the discussion of serious subjects, this is a criticism I shall perhaps admit. Ill-judged I do not much object to its being called; ill-natured I do object to. Though the first of these charges I could successfully rebut, if in no other way, at least by the precedents of all the eminent authors whom I have listed in my modest preface. What was I to do? I was staying at the time with More[8] on returning from Italy, and was detained indoors for several days by pain in the kidneys. My books had not yet arrived, and if they had, my illness prevented anything more ambitious in the way of serious study. I began to amuse my idle moments with an encomium on Folly, with no thought of publishing it, but to take my mind off my physical discomfort. I showed a specimen of what I had begun to several ordinary friends, in order to enjoy the joke all the more by sharing it. They were highly delighted, and urged me to continue. I did as they said, and spent a week on it more or less which, considering how trivial the subject was, already seemed to me too much. After that the same people who had encouraged me to write it carried it off to France where it was printed, but from an imperfect as well as corrupt copy. What a poor reception it met with is shown, if by nothing else, by the fact that over seven editions were printed in a few months, and those too in different places. I wondered very much myself what anyone could see in it. So if all this, my dear Dorp, is ill-judged, your culprit owns up, or at least puts up no defence. Within these limits and in an idle moment and to please my friends I judged ill, and only once in my whole life. Who can be wise all the time? You yourself admit that my other things are of a kind that all religious and educated people highly approve of. Who are these stern critics, these grave and reverend Areopagites,[9] who will not forgive a man for doing something ill-judged even once?

What peevish pedantry is this, to take offence at one single humorous piece and instantly deprive the author of the credit won by nightly toil on his earlier works? What ill-judged things far worse than this I could produce by other men, even by eminent theologians, who think up the most frigid and contentious questions and do battle among themselves over the most worthless trifles as though they fought for hearth and altar! And they act their absurd parts, more farcical than the original Atellanes,[10] without a mask. I was at least more modest, for when I wanted to show how ill-judged I could be, I wore the mask of Folly and, like Socrates in Plato, who covers his face before reciting an encomium on love, I myself acted my part in disguise.[11]

You say that the self-same people who disapprove of my subject think well of wit, the wide reading, and style, but are offended by the freedom of my satire. These critics actually think more highly of me than I could wish. Not that I give a pittance for their kind words, especially as I believe them to have no wit, wide reading, or style themselves; and if they were well supplied with these, believe me, my dear Dorp, they would not be so ready to take offence at humour which aspires to be useful rather than either witty or well read. I ask you: in the name of all the Muses, what can they have in the way of eyes and ears and taste who take offence at the biting satire in that small book? To begin with, what satire can there be in something which criticizes no one by name except myself? Why do they not remember what Jerome so often maintains, that the discussion of faults in general carries no criticism of any individual in particular? If anyone does take offence, he has no cause of action against the author; he may, if he pleases, bring an action for slander against himself as his own betrayer, for having made it plain that that criticism applies to him in particular, which was levelled against everyone in such a way that it was levelled at no individual except such as deliberately made the cap fit. Do you not see how all through the work I have refrained from mentioning people's names so carefully that I have been reluctant even to name a whole country in any critical spirit? For where I list the form of self-love peculiar to each nation, I call the Spaniards proud of their military prowess, the Italians of their literary culture, the English of their good dinners and good looks, and allot to each of the rest in the same way faults of such a kind as anyone, hearing them laid at his door, might not be reluctant to accept them, or at least would greet them with a laugh. Besides which, though the subject I had chosen takes me through every class of men and I spend my time criticizing the faults of individuals, where have I ever said anything scurrilous or bitter? Do I ever uncover a sink of iniquity or stir the mud of Camarina[12] that lurks, as we know, beneath the life of man? Everyone knows how much may be said against evil popes, selfish bishops and priests, vicious princes, and, in a word, against any rank of society, if ... I had not been ashamed to record in writing what many men practise without shame. I have merely surveyed the humorous and comic, rather than the scurrilous, aspect of things, but have done this in such a way as sometimes to touch on major topics, and point out things in passing which it is very important they should know.

I know you have no time to spare for the descent into these details, but yet if you ever have the leisure, do look rather more carefully into the ridiculous jests that Folly makes; and you will find them a good deal closer to the teaching of the evangelists and apostles than some men's disputations which their authors think so splendid, so worthy of their professorial eminence. You yourself in your letter do not deny that much of what is there reported is the truth; only you think it inexpedient to 'let rough truths grate on tender ears.' If you think one should on no account speak one's mind and never tell the truth except when it does not hurt, why do physicians use bitter drugs, and reckon their *hiera picra*[13] among their most highly recommended remedies? If they do so when treating the ailments of the body, how much more reasonable for me to do the same when seeking to cure distempers of the mind? 'Rebuke, reprove, exhort,' says St Paul,[14] 'in season, out of season.' The apostle thinks faults should be attacked in every possible way; and do you think no sore place should be touched, and that, too, when this is so gently done that no one could even feel hurt unless he deliberately hurts himself? Why, if there does exist a way of curing men's faults without giving offence to anyone, that is, if I mistake not, the most appropriate way of all; to name no one by name, to refrain from things which good people cannot bear even to hear mentioned (for as some things in tragedy are too terrible to be displayed before the spectators and it is enough to tell the story, so in human behaviour some things are too disgusting to be described without embarrassment), and to recount what can be described in a lively and humorous fashion through the mouth of some ridiculous character, so that any grounds for offence are excluded by the light-hearted treatment. We all know what an effect a well-judged and well-timed pleasantry sometimes has even on the grimmest of tyrants. Could any supplication or any serious argument have mollified the heart of the king in the story so easily as the soldier's jest?[15] 'Not at all' says he; 'if the flagon had not gone dry on us, we should have said far worse things about you.' The king laughed, and forgave them. There was good reason for the careful discussions on wit and humour in those two great masters of rhetoric, Cicero and Quintilian. Such is the power of wit and liveliness that we can take pleasure in a witty remark even when it is aimed at us, as is reported of Julius Caesar. And so, if you admit that what I said is true, and if it is humorous rather than indecent, what better means can be devised for curing the defects that are common to men? For a start, pleasure alone is enough to attract the reader and hold his attention. For in every other department men's objectives differ; but pleasure attracts all alike, except those who are too stupid to feel any sense of pleasure from what they read.

Further, those who take offence where no names are mentioned seem to me to be swayed by the same sort of emotions as women who, if they hear anything said against loose members of their sex, are as indignant as if the criticism applied to them all individually; and conversely, if anyone praises virtuous women, they are as pleased with themselves as if what applies to two or three stood to the credit of the sex as a whole. Men should be above these ill-judged reactions, scholars still more, theologians most of all. If I find some accusation here of which I am not guilty, I take no offence, but think myself lucky to be free from failings which I see many people suffer from. If it touched on some sore place, and I see myself in the mirror, here too there is no call for me to be offended. If I have any sense, I shall conceal my feelings and not come forward to give myself away. If I am a virtuous man, I shall take the hint, and see to it that in the future no fault can be laid by name at my door like the one I see before me pilloried anonymously. Can we not allow this book at least the freedom conceded to those popular comedies even by the uneducated? Think of all the jibes discharged with such freedom against monarchs, priests, monks, wives, husbands, everybody! And yet, because nobody is attacked by name, everybody laughs; everyone either openly confesses his own fault or carefully covers it up. The most savage tyrants tolerate their zanies and court fools, though they are often criticized by them in public. The emperor Vespasian[16] took no steps against the person who said he had a face like a man straining at stool. Who then are these friends of yours whose ears are so delicate that they cannot endure to hear Folly herself cracking jests against the way men live in general without giving anyone a black mark by name? The Old Comedy would never have been driven off the stage if it had refrained from mentioning leading citizens by name.

But you, my excellent Dorp, almost write as though my *Folly* had made the whole theology faculty my enemies. 'Why need you make such a bitter attack,' you say, 'on the faculty of theology?' and you lament the position I find myself in. 'In the old days,' you say, 'what you write was read with enthusiasm by everybody and they all longed to see you here in person. Now your Folly, like Davus,[17] has upset everything.' I know you write nothing merely to find fault, and I shall not beat about the bush with you. I ask you, do you call it an attack on the faculty of theology if foolish and badly behaved theologians quite unworthy of the name come in for some criticism? If you think those ought to be the rules of the game, a man would make enemies of the whole human race who said anything against criminals. Was there ever a king so brazen as not to admit that there are a few wicked kings unworthy of a throne? Is any bishop too proud to admit the same about his own order? Is the faculty of theology the only one out of so many which offers us no stupid, uneducated, quarrelsome person, nothing but Paul and Basil and Jerome over again? Quite the contrary: the more distinguished a profession is, the fewer men in it who are good enough. You will find more good ship's captains than good princes, more good physicians than good bishops. In any case this casts no aspersions on the faculty; it tends to the credit of the few who in a most noble faculty have behaved nobly. Tell me, why are theologians more offended (if some have really taken offence) than kings, primates, magistrates, bishops, cardinals, popes? Or than merchants, husbands, wives, lawyers, poets – for no kind of mortal man has been spared by Folly, except that they are not so stupid as to think everything a direct attack on themselves which is said in general about bad men? Saint Jerome wrote to Eustochium on the subject of virginity; and in the process painted such a picture of the behaviour of lascivious women as Apelles himself could not have made more vivid. Was Eustochium hurt? Was she indignant with Jerome for casting aspersions on the good estate of virginity? Not in the slightest. And why so? Because, being a sensible woman, she did not think that, if any criticism was made of the bad members of her sex, it applied to her; on the contrary, she was glad to see virtuous women reminded that they must not sink to that level and equally glad to see bad women told to be different in future. He wrote to Nepotianus about the lives led by the clergy and to Rusticus on the monastic life, painting the faults of both classes in lively colours and taking them to task brilliantly. His correspondents took no offence, because they knew that none of it applied to them. Why was there no estrangement between me and William Mountjoy,[18] who is by no means least among noblemen at court, when Folly made all those humorous comments on eminent courtiers? Because, being himself a most excellent and most sensible man, he supposed (what is in fact true) that attacks on wicked and foolish grandees are nothing to do with him. Think of all the jests Folly aimed at wicked and worldly bishops! Why did the Archbishop of Canterbury[19] take no offence at all this? Because, being abundantly endowed with every virtue, he knows that none of this is meant for him.

Why need I go on to recount to you by name the eminent princes, the other bishops and abbots and cardinals and famous scholars, none of whom I have yet found estranged from me by one hair's breadth as a result of my *Folly*? Nor can I bring myself to believe that any theologians were irritated by it, except a few maybe who either do not understand it, or are jealous of it, or are so cantankerous by nature that they approve of nothing at all. Mixed in with that class of men, as everyone would agree, are certain persons so ill endowed with talents and with judgment that they have never been set to learn any subject, let alone theology. They get by heart a few rules from Alexander Gallus,[20] and strike up an acquaintance with a little idiotic formal logic, and then get hold of ten propositions out of Aristotle ... as though they were a sort of horn of plenty. Whereupon it is astonishing the airs they give themselves, for nothing is so arrogant as ignorance. These are the men who condemn St Jerome as a schoolmaster, because he is over their heads; who poke fun at Greek and Hebrew and even Latin, and, though as stupid as pigs and not equipped even with the common feelings of humanity, they suppose themselves to hold the citadel of all wisdom. They sit in judgment, they issue condemnations and pronouncements, they know no hesitations, are never at a loss – there is nothing they do not know. And yet these men, often only two or three of them, often rouse the greatest commotions. Nothing is so brazen, so pig-headed, as ignorance. These are the men who conspire with such zeal against the humanities. Their aim is to count for something in the councils of the theologians, and they fear that if there is a renaissance of the humanities, and if the world sees the error of its ways, it may become clear that they know nothing, although in the old days they were commonly supposed to know everything. These are the men who raise all this clamour and tumult; it is they who run this conspiracy against the devotees of liberal subjects. They do not like my *Folly*, because they have no understanding either in Greek or Latin. If these gentry – not theologians, but men dressed up to look like them – receive one or two shrewd hits, what has this to do with the infinitely respectable body of theologians who are real scholars? ...

And it is two or three worthless fellows dressed up to look like theologians who are trying to arouse feeling against me like this, as though I had attacked and antagonized the whole faculty. For my part I have such high regard for theological learning that it is the only learning to which I normally allow the name. For that faculty I have such respect and veneration that it is the only one in which I have entered my name and sought to be enrolled, though I am ashamed to claim so distinguished a title for myself, knowing as I do the gifts both of scholarship and of life required by one who would write himself theologian. The man who claims to be a theologian somehow claims something more than ordinary men. This is the proper dignity for bishops, not for men like me. Enough for me to have learned with Socrates that I know nothing at all and, where I can, to lend a helping hand to the studies of other people. For my part I do not know where they lurk, those two or three gods among the theologians who you say in your letter are not propitious towards me. Personally I have been many places since I published my *Folly*, and have lived in so many universities and great cities; and never have I felt that any theologian was annoyed at me, except one or two of the class that are enemies of all sound learning, and even they have never said a word of protest to me. What they may murmur behind my back I pay little attention to, relying on the verdict of so many of good will. If I were not afraid, my dear Dorp, that someone might think I was boasting rather than speaking the truth, how many theologians I could list for you, renowned for holiness of life, eminent for scholarship, and of the highest station, some of them even bishops, who have never given me such a warm welcome as since the publication of my *Folly*, and who think more highly of that small book than I do myself. I could give you them one by one here and now, by name and title, did I not fear that for Folly's sake even such eminent persons might incur the displeasure of your three theologians. One of them[21] at any rate I suppose to be the author of all this commotion in your midst, for I can guess pretty well what has happened. And if I were prepared to paint him in his true colours, no one would be surprised that such a man should disapprove of my *Folly*; in fact I would not approve it myself unless such people did disapprove. Not that I really like it; but it is a good reason for misliking it much less, that it is not liked by these great wits. The judgment of wise and learned theologians carries more weight with me; and they are so far from accusing me of bitterness that they even praise my moderation and fairness of mind for dealing with a naturally licentious subject without licence and, given a humorous theme, for having poked fun without hurting. For to answer only the theologians who are, I hear, the only men to have taken offence, everyone knows how much is said even in public against theologians who are immoral. Folly touches on nothing of the kind. She confines her jests to their useless discussions on minute points, and even these she does not disapprove of indiscriminately: she condemns the men who see in them alone the stem and stern, as they say, of theological science, and who are so fully occupied with battles of words, as St Paul called them,[22] that they have no time to read what was written by evangelists, prophets, and apostles.

I only wish, my dear Dorp, that fewer of them were exposed to this charge. I could produce for you men over eighty who have devoted their long lives to nonsense of this kind, and have never read the Gospels right through; I detected this, and at length they had to confess it themselves. Even under the mask of Folly I did not dare say what I have often heard deplored by many men who are themselves theologians, real theologians I mean, upright serious scholarly men who have drunk deep of Christ's teaching from the true springs. Whenever they are in company where it is permissible to say freely what they think, they regret the arrival in the world of this newer kind of theology and long for the return of the old sort. Never was anything so sacred, so noble, giving so much the true flavour and image of Christ's heavenly teaching. But the modern kind (to say nothing of the portentous filth of its barbarous and artificial style, its ignorance of all sound learning, and its lack of any knowledge of the tongues) is so much adulterated with Aristotle, with trivial human fantasies, and even with the laws of the Gentiles, that I doubt whether any trace remains, genuine and unmixed, of Christ. What happens is that it diverts its attention overmuch to consider the traditions of men, and is less faithful to its pattern. Hence the more intelligent theologians are often obliged to express before the public something different from what they feel in their own hearts or say when among friends. And sometimes they would be hard pressed for an answer to any earnest enquirer, for they see that what Christ taught and what mere human traditions ordain are not the same. What can Christ have in common with Aristotle? What have these quibbling sophistries to do with the mysteries of eternal wisdom? What is the purpose of these labyrinthine *quaestiones*, of which so many are pointless, so many really harmful, if for no other reason, as a source of strife and contention? But, you will say, there are things we must enquire into; on some points we must even have a decision. I do not dissent. But on the other hand there are a great many better let go than pursued (and it is part of knowledge to recognize that certain things are not for our knowing), a great many things on which to doubt is a more healthy state than to lay down the law. Finally, if laws must be laid down, let it be done reverently and not in arrogance and in accordance with Scripture, not with the so-called reasoning thought up by ordinary men. As it is, of these petty arguments there is no end; yet even in them what disagreements arise between parties and factions! And every day one pronouncement gives rise to another. In short, things have come to such a pass that the sum of the matter depends not so much upon what Christ laid down as upon the definitions of professors and the power of bishops, capable or otherwise; and in all this everything is now so much involved that there is no hope even of recalling the world to the old true Christianity.

All this, and a great deal else, is perceived and regretted by men of great piety and at the same time great learning, and they regard as the principal cause of it all this bold irreverent tribe of modern theologians. If only it were possible, my dear Dorp, for you to look silently into my thoughts – you would understand how much I deliberately leave unsaid at this point. But all this my *Folly* left untouched, or at least touched on very lightly, in order to hurt no one's feelings. And I took care to observe the same restraint throughout, to write nothing improper or corrupting or revolutionary, nothing that might seem to involve criticisms of any class of person. If anything is said there about the cult of the saints, you will always find something added to make it quite clear that criticism is confined to the superstition of those who do not venerate saints in the way they should. If any reflection is cast on princes or bishops or monks, I always go on to explain that no insult is intended to persons of that class, only to its corrupt and unworthy members, for I would not hurt a good man while pursuing the faults of bad ones. In so doing, furthermore, I have done what I could by suppressing names to give no offence even to bad men. Lastly, by conducting all the action in terms of wit and humour through an imaginary comic character, I have tried to arrange that even peevish folk who are hard to please may take it in good part.

One passage, you say, is criticized as not oversatirical but impious. How can the ears of a good Christian, you ask, endure to hear me call the felicity of the future life a form of lunacy? I ask you, my worthy Dorp, who taught an honest man like you this kind of innuendo, or (which I think more likely) what clever man took advantage of your simple heart to traduce me like this? This is just how those pestilent experts in calumny take a couple of words out of their context, sometimes a little altered in the process, leaving out everything that softens and explains what sounds harsh otherwise. Quintilian picks up this trick in his *Institutio* and shows us how to play it:[23] we recount our own story in the most flattering light, with supporting evidence and anything else that can mitigate or extenuate or help our case in any way; we should recite our opponent's case, on the other hand, shorn of all this assistance in the most invidious language it allows of. This art they have learned, not from the teaching of Quintilian, but from their own malevolence; and its outcome often is that things which would have been most acceptable if reported as they were written, give great offence when recounted differently. Pray reread the passage, and observe with care the stages, the gradual progress of the argument, which led me to describe that felicity as a species of lunacy, and then observe the language in which I unfold all this. So far from giving offence to really pious ears, you will find plenty there which might actually delight them. It is in the way you read it that a slight cause of offence arises, and not in what I wrote.

For, since the purpose of my *Folly* is to embrace the whole world of things under the name of foolishness and to show that the whole sum of human felicity depends on Folly, she ranged over the entire human race as high as kings and supreme pontiffs; thence she arrived at the apostles themselves and even Christ, all of whom we find credited in the Scriptures with some kind of foolishness. Nor is there any risk that someone at this point may suppose that the apostles or Christ were foolish in the ordinary sense, but that in them too there was an element of weakness, something attributable to our natural affections, which when compared with that pure eternal wisdom might seem less than wise. But this same folly of theirs overcomes all the wisdom of the world; just as the prophet compares all the righteousness of mortals to rags defiled with a woman's monthly discharge, not that the righteousness of good men is something foul, but because the things that are most pure among men are somehow impure when set against the inexpressible purity of God. Now I have set forth a kind of wise folly, and in the same way I produce a lunacy which is a sane and intelligent stupidity. And to soften what followed about the fruition of the saints, I begin by recalling the three kinds of madness in Plato,[24] of which the most blessed is the madness of lovers, which is nothing but a kind of ecstasy. But the ecstasy of godly men is nothing else than a foretaste of future blessedness, by which we are totally absorbed into God and shall live in future more in him than in ourselves. But this is what Plato calls madness, when a man, being rapt out of himself, exists in the object of his love and has the enjoyment of it. Do you not see how carefully I distinguish a little further on between the kinds of folly and insanity, so that no ingenuous reader could be misled by the words I used?

But I have no quarrel with the meaning, you say; it is the words themselves that revolt pious ears. But why are not those same ears offended when they hear Paul speak of the foolishness of God and the folly of the cross?[25] Why do they not pick a quarrel with St Thomas for using about Peter's ecstasy words like 'In his pious delusion he begins to speak of tabernacles.'[26] That sacred and blessed rapture he describes as delusions! And yet all this is recited in church. Why did they not bring me to court long ago for describing Christ in a certain prayer as a magician and enchanter? St Jerome calls Christ a Samaritan, although he was a Jew. Paul even calls him sin, as though that were more than to say a sinner; he calls him an accursed thing. What outrageous impiety, if one chose a malevolent interpretation! And what a pious tribute, if one accepts it as Paul meant it! In the same way, if one were to call Christ a robber, an adulterer, a drunkard, a heretic, would not all men of good will put their fingers in their ears? But suppose one expressed this in appropriate language; suppose one worked up to it, as though one were leading the reader by the hand up to this point gradually, until he saw how in his triumph through the cross he robbed Hell of its plunder which he restored to the Father; how he took unto himself the synagogue, like the wife of Moses (the wife of Uriah over again), that a peace-loving people might be born from her; how he was intoxicated with the new wine of charity when he gave himself for us; how he brought in a new kind of teaching, very different from all the current convictions of wise and foolish alike. Who could be offended then, especially as now and again we find some of these words used in Scripture in a good sense? I myself in my *Chiliades* (it occurs to me in passing) have called the apostles Silenus figures and even Christ himself a sort of Silenus.[27] Give me a prejudiced interpreter to put a brief and invidious explanation on this, and what could sound more intolerable? Let a pious and fair-minded man read what I wrote, and he will find the allegory acceptable.

It surprises me greatly that those friends of yours have never noticed another thing – how cautiously I put these things forward, and the care I take to soften them by adaptation. What I say is this: 'But now that I have donned the lion's skin, let me tell you another thing. The happiness which Christians seek with so many labours is nothing other than a certain kind of madness and folly. Do not be put off by the words, but consider the reality.' Do you see? To begin with, the fact that Folly holds forth on such a solemn subject is softened by a proverb, where I speak of her having donned the lion's skin. Nor do I speak just of folly or madness, but of 'a kind of folly and madness,' so that you have to understand a pious folly and a blessed madness, in accordance with a distinction which I go on to make. Not content with that, I say 'a certain kind' to make it clear that this is meant figuratively and is not literal. Still not content, I urge people not to take offence at the mere sound of my words, and tell them to watch more what is said than how I say it; and this I do right at the very beginning. Then in the actual treatment of the question, is there anything not said in a pious and thoughtful fashion – more reverently in fact than really suits Folly? But on that point I though it better to forget consistency for a moment than not to do justice to the importance of the theme; better to lose sight of the rules of composition than to offend against piety. ...

You see that I have never failed to cut short all excuse for the slightest offence. But this means nothing to men whose ears are closed to all but propositions and conclusions and corollaries. Should I mention that I provided my book with a preface in which I try to stop malicious criticism at the outset? Nor have I the slightest doubt that it is found satisfactory by all fair-minded readers. But what can you do for men who are too obstinate to accept satisfaction or too stupid to know when they are satisfied? Simonides said that the Thessalians were too slow-witted to be deceived by him;[28] and you can find some people like them too stupid to be placated. Nor is it surprising that a man should find matter for complaint who looks for nothing else. Anyone who should read St Jerome in that spirit will find a hundred places open to objection, and your friends will find no lack, in that most Christian of all the Fathers, of grounds for labelling him a heretic; to say nothing for the moment of Cyprian and Lactantius and others like them. Finally, who ever heard of a humorous subject being submitted for examination by theologians? If this is a good idea, why not by the same token apply these principles of examination to any frivolous stuff written by our modern poets? What a lot of impropriety they will find there, of things that reek of ancient paganism! But since no one regards these as serious works, none of the theologians supposes them to be any business of his.

Not that I would ask to be allowed to shelter behind the example set by your friends. I should not like to have written even in jest anything that in any way could weaken a Christian's faith; but I must be allowed a reader who understands what I have written and a fair and upright critic; one who is keen to learn the truth and not interested in making mischief. But suppose a man were to take into account the people you speak of, who in the first place have no brains and even less judgment; second, have never been in touch with liberal studies but are infected rather than educated by that mean and muddled schooling of theirs; and lastly, hate everyone who knows what they themselves do not know, bringing with them no object except to distort whatever it may be that perhaps they have half understood – such a man, if he wished to be free from calumny, would never put pen to paper. Need I add that some of them are led to make mischief by a desire for glory? Nothing is so vainglorious as ignorance combined with a delusion of knowledge. And so, if they have this thirst for fame and cannot satisfy it by honourable means, they would rather imitate that Ephesian youth[29] who made himself notorious by setting fire to the most famous temple in the whole world rather than live obscure. And since they themselves cannot produce anything worth reading, they devote themselves to picking to pieces the works of famous men.

Other men's works, I mean, not my own, for I am nobody. My *Folly* I myself think not worth a straw, so let no one suppose me concerned about that. Is it surprising if men of the sort I have described choose out a few statements from a long work and make some of them out to be scandalous, some irreverent, some wrongly expressed, some impious and smacking of heresy, not because they find these faults there, but because they bring them in themselves? How much more conducive to peace and suitable to a Christian's fairness of mind to be well disposed to scholars and promote their work; and then, if anything ill thought out should escape them, either to overlook it or to give it a friendly interpretation, instead of looking for holes to pick in a hostile spirit and behaving like an informer rather than a theologian. How much more promising to work together in order either to instruct or to be instructed and, to use Jerome's words, to take our exercise in the field of the Scriptures without hurting one another! But it is astonishing how those men know no middle course! Some authors they read in a spirit of being ready to defend the most blatant errors on any pretext however frivolous, and towards some they are so unjust that nothing is too carefully phrased for them to pick holes in it somehow. How much better it had been instead, while they rend in pieces and are rent in turn, wasting their own time and other people's, to learn Greek, or Hebrew, or Latin at least! A knowledge of these is so important for our understanding of Scripture that it really seems to me monstrous impudence for one who knows none of them to expect to be called a theologian.

And so, my excellent Maarten, devoted as I am to your welfare, I shall not cease to urge you, as I have often done before, to add to your equipment at least a knowledge of Greek. You are exceptionally gifted. You can write – solid, vigorous, easy, abundant stuff, evidence of a spirit as productive as it is wholesome. Your energy is not merely untouched by years but still fresh and green, and you have successfully completed the conventional course of study. Take my word for it, if you crown such a promising start with a knowledge of Greek, I dare promise myself and everyone else that you will do great things, such as none of our modern theologians has ever done before. If your view is that for love of true religion we should despise all human learning, and if you think that the shortest way to such wisdom is to be somehow transfigured through Christ, and that everything else worth knowing is perceived more fully by the light of faith than in the books of men, I shall subscribe without difficulty to your opinion. But if, in the present state of human affairs, you promise yourself a true understanding of the science of theology without a knowledge of the tongues, particularly of the language in which most of Scripture has been handed down, you are wholly at sea. ...

I now come to the second part of your letter. My work on the restoration of Jerome meets with your high approval, and you encourage me to take up other labours of the same sort. You spur a willing horse; though what I need is not so much people to spur me on to this task as helpers, such is its difficulty. But I hope you will never again believe anything I say if you do not find me speaking the truth in this: those friends of yours who take so much offence at my Folly will not approve my edition of Jerome either. Nor are they much better disposed towards Basil, Chrysostom, and Nazianzen[30] than they are to me, except that their assaults on me are more outspoken; though sometimes in moments of irritation they are not afraid to say some very foolish and improper things about those great luminaries. They are afraid of the humanities; they fear for their own dictatorship. I can show you that I am not making this up. When I had begun work and the news had already got around, up came certain reputedly influential men and distinguished theologians, by their own valuation, and adjured the printer by all that is holy not to allow any admixture of Greek or Hebrew; these two languages, they said, are fraught with peril and there is no good to be got out of them; they were designed solely to satisfy idle curiosity. Even before that, when I was in England,

I happened to find myself drinking wine with a certain Franciscan, a Scotist of the first rank, who in public estimation is a very clever man and in his own knows all there is to know. When I had explained to this man what I was trying to do in Jerome, he expressed astonishment that there should be anything in his works that theologians did not understand – and he such an ignorant man that I should be surprised if there are three lines in all the works of Jerome which he rightly understands. He added kindly that, if I had any problems in Jerome's prefaces, they had all been clearly expounded by LeBreton.[31]

I ask you, my dear Dorp, what can one do for these theologians of yours other than pray for them, except perhaps find a reliable physician to cure their brains? And yet it is sometimes men of this sort who talk loudest in any gathering of theologians, and these are the men who issue pronouncements about the Christian faith. They are terrified, as though it were something perilous and pestilential, of the very think that St Jerome, and Origen too even in his old age, tried so hard to secure for themselves, that they might truly be theologians. Moreover Augustine, when he was already a bishop and an old man, deplores in his *Confessions* that in his youth he had been disgusted by the study which might have been of such value to him in his exposition of Scripture. If there is any peril here, I shall not take fright at a risk which men of such wisdom have gone out to look for. If this is idle curiosity, I have no wish to be holier than Jerome – and how ill these men served Jerome in calling what he did idle curiosity is their own lookout. There exists a very ancient decree of a pontifical synod[32] providing for the appointment of professors to give public instruction in several tongues, while for the learning by heart of sophistics and Aristotle's philosophy no such steps have ever been taken, except that a question is raised in the *Decreta*[33] whether it is permitted to study these subjects or no. And the study of them is disapproved of by many eminent authorities. So what the authority of popes has instructed us to do we neglect, and what has been called in question and even disapproved of is the only thing we accept. Why? Not but what they are as badly off in Aristotle as they are in Scripture. They are dogged everywhere by the nemesis that waits for those who despise Greek; here too they are subject to delusions, half asleep, blear-eyed, blundering, producing more monstrosities. To these eminent divines we owe the loss of so many of the authors listed by Jerome in his catalogue; so few survive because they wrote over the heads of our *magistri*.[34] ...

Then again what you write in the third part about the New Testament makes me wonder what has happened to you, or what has beguiled for the moment your very clear-sighted mind. You would rather I made no changes, unless the Greek gives the meaning more fully, and you say there are no faults in the version we commonly use. You think it wrong to weaken in any way the hold of something accepted by the agreement of so many centuries and so many synods. I ask you, if what you say is true, my most learned Dorp, why do Jerome and Augustine and Ambrose so often cite a different text from the one we use? Why does Jerome find fault with many things, and correct them explicitly, which corrections are still found in our text? What will you do when there is so much agreement, when the Greek copies are different and Jerome cites the same text as theirs, when the very oldest Latin copies concur, and the sense itself runs much better? Do you intend to overlook all this and follow your own copy, though it was perhaps corrupted by a scribe? For no one asserts that there is any falsehood in Holy Scripture (which you also suggested), nor has the whole question on which Jerome came to grips with Augustine anything at all to do with the matter. But one thing the facts cry out, and it can be clear, as they say, even to a blind man, that often through the translator's clumsiness or inattention the Greek has been wrongly rendered; often the true and genuine reading has been corrupted by ignorant scribes, which we see happen every day, or altered by scribes who are half-taught and half-asleep. Which man encourages falsehood more, he who corrects and restores these passages, or he who would rather see an error added than removed? For it is of the nature of textual corruption that one error should generate another. And the changes I make are usually such as affect the overtones rather than the sense itself; though often the overtones convey a great part of the meaning. But not seldom the text has gone astray entirely. And whenever this happens, where, I ask you, do Augustine and Ambrose and Hilary and Jerome take refuge if not in the Greek original? This is approved also by decrees of the church; and yet you shuffle and try to reject it or rather to worm your way out of it by splitting hairs.

You say that in their day the Greek copies were more correct than the Latin ones, but that now it is the opposite, and we cannot trust the texts of men who have separated from the Roman church. I can hardly persuade myself to believe that you meant this seriously. What? We are not to read the books of renegades from the Christian faith; and how pray do they think Aristotle such an authority, who was a pagan and never had any contact with the faith? The whole Jewish nation turned away from Christ; are we to give no weight to the Psalms and the Prophets, which were written in their language? Now make me a list of all the heads under which the Greeks differ from the orthodox Latins; you will find nothing that arises from the words of the New Testament or has anything to do with this question. The whole controversy relates to the word *hypostasis*,[35] to the procession of the Holy Spirit, to the ceremonies of consecration, to the poverty of the priesthood, to the powers of the Roman pontiff. For none of these questions do they lean on falsified texts. But what will you say when you see their interpretation followed by Origen, Chrysostom, Basil, Jerome? Had somebody falsified the Greek texts as long ago as that? Who has ever detected falsification in the Greek texts even in one passage? And finally, what could be the motive, since they do not defend their particular tenets from this source? Besides which, that in every department of learning the Greek copies have always been more accurate than ours is admitted by no less than Cicero, who is elsewhere so unfair to the Greeks. For the difference between the letters, the accents, and the actual difficulty of writing all mean that they are less easily corrupted and that any corruption is more easily mended.

Again, when you say that one should not depart from a text that enjoys the approval of so many councils, you write like one of our ordinary divines, who habitually attribute anything that has slipped somehow into current usage to the authority of the church. Pray produce me one synod in which this version has been approved. How could it approve a text whose author is unknown? That it is not Jerome's is shown by Jerome's own prefaces. But suppose that some synod has approved it? Was it approved in such terms that it is absolutely forbidden to correct it by the Greek original? Were all the mistakes approved as well, which in various ways may have crept in? Was a decree drawn up by the fathers of the council in some such terms as this? 'This version is of unknown authorship, but none the less we approve it, nor do we wish it to be an objection that the Greek copies have something different, however accurate they may be, or if a different reading is found in Chrysostom or Basil or Anthanasius or Jerome, even though it may better suit the meaning of the Gospel, notwithstanding our high approval of these same authorities in other respects. Moreover, whatsoever in future may in any way, whether by men with a little education and rather more self-confidence or by scribes unskilled, drunken, or half-asleep, be corrupted, distorted, added, or omitted, we in virtue of the same authority approve, nor are we willing that any man should have licence to alter what has once been written.' A very comical decree, you say. But it must have been something like this, if you are to frighten me from this kind of work by the authority of a synod.

Finally, what are we to say when we see that even copies of our Vulgate version do not agree? Surely these discrepancies were not approved by a synod, which of course foresaw each change that would be made? I only wish, my dear Dorp, that the Roman pontiffs had sufficient leisure to issue salutary constitutions on these points, which would take care for the restoration of the works of good authors and the preparation and substitution of corrected copies. Yet I would not give any seats on that commission to those most falsely so-called theologians whose one idea is that what they learned themselves should be the only thing of current value. And what have they learned that is not utter nonsense and utter confusion? If they once become dictators, farewell to all the best authors! The world will be compelled to accept their brainless rubbish as oracles; and so little sound learning is there in it, that I would rather be a humble cobbler than the best of their tribe, if they can acquire nothing in the way of a liberal education. These are the men who do not like to see a text corrected, for it may look as though there were something they did not know. It is they who try not to stop me with the authority of imaginary synods; they who build up to this great threat to the Christian faith; they who cry 'the Church is in danger' (and no doubt support her with their own shoulders, which would be better employed in propping a dung-cart) and spread suchlike rumours among the ignorant and superstitious mob; for the said mob takes them for great divines, and they wish to lose none of this reputation. They are afraid that when they misquote Scripture, as they often do, the authority of the Greek or Hebrew text may be cast in their teeth, and it may soon become clear that what used to be quoted as an oracle is all a dream. St Augustine, that very great man and a bishop as well, had no objection to learning from a year-old child. But the kind of people we are dealing with would rather produce utter confusion than risk appearing to be ignorant of any detail that forms part of perfect knowledge, though I see nothing here that much affects the genuineness of our Christian faith. If it were essential to the faith, that would be all the more reason for working hard at it.

Nor can there be any danger that everybody will forthwith abandon Christ if the news happens to get out that some passage has been found in Scripture which an ignorant or sleepy scribe has miscopied or some unknown translator has rendered inadequately. There are other reasons to fear this, of which I prudently say nothing here. How much more truly Christian it would be to have done with quarreling and for each man cheerfully to offer what he can to the common stock and to accept with good will what is offered, so that at the same time you learn in humility what you do not know and teach others ungrudgingly what you do know! If some are so ignorant that they cannot rightly teach anything or so conceited that they are unwilling to learn, let us think no more of them (for they are very few) and concentrate on those who are intelligent or at any rate promising. I once showed my annotations, when they were still raw, still fire-new from the mint, as they say, to men of the highest integrity, eminent theologians and most scholarly bishops; and all admitted that those rudimentary pieces, such as they were had shed a flood of light for them on the understanding of Holy Scripture.

Furthermore, you tell me, but I knew already, that Lorenzo Valla[36] had been active in this field before me, for I was the first to publish his annotations; and Jacques Lefèvre[37] had his notes in hand already when I was getting this work under way, and it happened, a trifle unfortunately, that even in our most friendly conversations neither of us thought of mentioning his plans, nor did I learn what he had been at until his work appeared in print. His attempt also I heartily approve, although from him too I dissent in some places, reluctantly, for I should be happy to agree with such a good friend in everything, were it not necessary to consider truth more than friendship, especially where Scripture is concerned.

But it is not yet quite clear to me why you confront me with these two names. Is it to deter me from the project as though I were already anticipated? But it will be clear that even after such good men I had good reason to attack it. Or do you suggest that their efforts, like my own, were unpopular in theological circles? Personally I cannot see that Lorenzo added to his existing unpopularity; and Lefèvre I hear is universally approved. I might add that we do not attempt an exactly similar task. Lorenzo only annotated selected passages, and those, it is clear, in passing and with what they call a light touch. Lefèvre published notes on the Pauline Epistles only, and translated them in his own way; then added notes in passing if there was any disagreement. But I have translated the whole New Testament after comparison with the Greek copies, and have added the Greek on the facing pages, so that anyone may easily compare it. I have appended separate annotations in which, partly by argument and partly by the authority of the early Fathers, I show that my emendations are not haphazard alterations, for fear that my changes might not carry conviction and in the hope of preserving the corrected text from further damage. I only wish I had been man enough to perform what I so laboriously undertook! As far as the business of the church is concerned, I shall have no hesitation in presenting my labours, such as they are, to any bishop, any cardinal, any Roman pontiff even, provided it is such a one as we have at the moment. In the end I have no doubt that you too will be delighted with the book when it is published, although you now dissuade me from publishing it, once you have had even a brief taste of the studies without which no man can form a right judgment on these questions.

Observe, my dear Dorp, how by one kind deed you have made two parties grateful to you: one is your theologian friends, on whose behalf you have so diligently accomplished your mission, and the other is me, for your friendly advice is fresh evidence of your affection for me. You in your turn will take in good part the equally outspoken return I have made you, and if you are wise you will adopt my advice (for I have no one's interests at heart but yours) rather than theirs, whose sole object in trying to bring over to their party a gifted nature like yours that was meant for great things is to strengthen their own forces by the acquisition of such a leader as you. Let them follow better courses if they can; if not, you at least must follow only the best. If you cannot make them better men, as I hope you will try to do, at least mind that they do not make you a worse one. What is more, you must present my case to them with the same frankness with which you have put theirs to me. Make my peace with them as far as you can, and make them see that I follow this course not in order to discredit those who know nothing of these languages, but for the general good, which will be available to anyone who cares to use it and will not be a burden on the man who prefers to do without; also that my attitude is that, if anyone arises who can or will teach us something better, I shall be the first to tear up and abandon what I have written and subscribe to his opinion.

# The Luther Affair

Martin Luther (1483–1546) first approached Erasmus in March 1518 with a letter (Ep 933) that expressed his admiration for the Dutch scholar. At that time Luther was already the centre of a growing controversy, though he had not yet been condemned officially. Erasmus originally gave his qualified support to Luther although he objected to his tactics of confrontation. Luther's intransigence and Erasmus' need to defend himself against those who proclaimed that 'Erasmus laid the egg that Luther hatched' led to an open breach between the two men in 1524. The following three letters spanning the years 1518–1521 show the gradual change in their relationship.

Ep 980, dating from 1518, and addressed to Luther himself, is polite and well-meaning. Ep 1033 of October 1519 also expresses support for the reformer but contains a warning note. It is addressed to the archbishop of Mainz, Albert of Brandenburg (1490–1545), who was favourably disposed to the New Learning and to whom Erasmus had previously dedicated his *Ratio / Method of True Theology* outlining his approach to biblical studies. The letter, which was not intended for publication but found its way into the hands of a publisher through the indiscretion of a friend, contained some candid statements that pleased Luther's supporters but outraged conservative Catholics. Ep 1202 of May 1521 was written after Luther's appearance at the Diet of Worms and shows a shift in Erasmus' perception that foreshadows later developments. Whereas he had previously seen Luther as an instrument of God through which the church might be purged of its abuses, he now regarded him as a danger to the unity of the church. Ep 1202 is addressed to Justus Jonas (1498–1555), at the time professor at the University of Erfurt, a committed Lutheran and later to become one of Luther's closest associates in Wittenberg.

These extracts are from CWE 6 391–3, translated by R.A.B. Mynors and D.F.S. Thomson, annotated by Peter G. Bietenholz; CWE 7 110–16, translated by R.A.B. Mynors, annotated by Peter G. Bietenholz; and CWE 8 201–11, translated by R.A.B. Mynors, annotated by Peter G. Bietenholz.

**Ep 980**

ERASMUS OF ROTTERDAM TO MARTIN LUTHER

Greetings, dearest brother in Christ. Your letter gave me great pleasure: it displayed the brilliance of your mind and breathed the spirit of a Christian. No words of mine could describe the storm raised here by your books. Even now it is impossible to root out from men's minds the most groundless suspicion that your work is written with assistance from me and that I am, as they call it, a standard-bearer of this new movement. They supposed that this gave them an opening to suppress both humane studies – for which they have a burning hatred, as likely to stand in the way of her majesty Queen Theology, whom they value much more than they do Christ – and myself at the same time, under the impression that I contribute something of importance towards this outburst of zeal. In the whole business their weapons are clamour, audacity, subterfuge, misinterpretation, innuendo; if I had not seen it with my own eyes – felt it, rather – I would never have believed theologians could be such maniacs. One would think it was some disastrous infection. And yet this poisonous virus, starting in a small circle, spread to a larger number, so that a great part of this university[1] was carried away by the spreading contagion of this epidemic paranoia.

I assured them that you were quite unknown to me; that I had not yet read your books and could therefore neither disapprove nor approve anything. I merely told them not to make such an offensive uproar in public before they had even read what you have written, and that this was in their own interests, since their judgment ought to carry great weight. I also advised them to consider whether it was a good plan to produce before a casual audience of laymen a distorted account of views which it would be more proper to refute in print or discuss among specialists, especially since all with one voice speak highly of the author's manner of life. I did no good at all: they are so blinded by their own jaundiced, indeed slanderous disputations. When I think how often we have agreed terms of peace, and how often on some trifling and rash suspicion they have stirred up fresh trouble! And they regard themselves as theologians. Theologians in this part of the world are unpopular at court; and this too they think is my fault. All the bishops are cordially on my side. These men have no confidence in the printed word; their hope of victory lies entirely in malicious gossip. This I despise, for my conscience is clear. Their attitude to you has softened somewhat. They are afraid of my pen, knowing their own record; and, my word, I would paint them in their true colours, as they deserve, did not Christ's teaching and Christ's example point in quite another direction. Fierce wild beasts are tamed by kindness; these men are driven wild if you do anything for them.

You have people in England who think well of what you write, and they are in high place. There are some here too, the bishop of Liège[2] among them, who favour your views. As for me, I keep myself uncommitted, so far as I can, in hopes of being able to do more for the revival of good literature. And I think one gets further by courtesy and moderation than by clamour. That was how Christ brought the world under his sway; that was how Paul did away with the Jewish law, by reducing everything to allegory. It is more expedient to protest against those who misuse the authority of bishops than against the bishops themselves; and I think one should do the same with kings. The universities are not so much to be despised as recalled to more serious studies. Things which are of such wide acceptance that they cannot be torn out of men's minds all at once should be met with argument, close-reasoned forcible argument, rather than bare assertion. Some people's poisonous propaganda is better ignored than refuted. Everywhere we must take pains to do and say nothing out of arrogance or faction; for I think the spirit of Christ would have it so. Meanwhile we must keep our minds above the corruption of anger or hatred, or of ambition; for it is this that lies in wait for us when our religious zeal is in full course.

I am not instructing you to do this, only to do what you do always. I have dipped into your commentary on the Psalms; I like the look of it particularly and hope that it will be of great service. There is a man in Antwerp, the prior of the monastery there,[3] a genuine Christian, who is most devoted to you and was once your pupil, or so he says. He is almost the only one among them all who preaches Christ; the others as a rule preach the inventions of men or their own advantage. I have written to Melanchthon.[4] May the Lord Jesus ever more richly endue you with his spirit every day, for his own glory and the good of mankind. Your letter was not at hand when I wrote this.

Farewell, from Louvain, 30 May 1519

## Ep 1033

TO THE MOST REVEREND IN CHRIST ALBERT, CARDINAL ARCHBISHOP, MARGRAVE ETC, FROM ERASMUS OF ROTTERDAM, THEOLOGIAN, GREETING

... If the stormy seas of business have left your Eminence any leisure, there are several things which it is in my interest that you should know, and perhaps also it is in your own; certainly it is in the interest of humane letters, which should always receive the support of good men against bad. The first point I must make is this, that I have never had any connection either with Reuchlin's business[1] or with the case of Luther. Cabbala and Talmud,[2] whatever they may be, have never appealed to me. Those venomous conflicts between Reuchlin and the supporters of Jacob of Hoogstraten I have always found extremely offensive. Of Luther I know as little as I do of anyone; his books I have not yet found time to read, except for dipping into some of them here and there. If he has written well, none of the credit is due to me; if the reverse, there is nothing that can be laid at my door. One thing I do see: it is the best men who take least offence at what he writes, not because they approve of everything, I imagine, but because they read him in the spirit in which we read Cyprian and Jerome, or even Peter Lombard,[3] turning a blind eye to many things.

That Luther's books were published, distressed me; and when some short pieces, I forget which, began to be handed about, I did my best to prevent their publication, for this reason especially, that I was afraid they would give rise to disorders. Luther had written to me, in a very Christian spirit in my opinion, and in my answer I urged him in passing to publish no sedition, nothing derogatory to the Roman pontiff, nothing arrogant or vindictive, but to preach the gospel teaching in sincerity with all mildness. I did this courteously, in hopes it would have more effect. I added that there were some here who supported him, in order to persuade him more readily to adapt himself to their advice. These words have been read by some blockheads to mean that I supported Luther, though none of them have yet told him where he is wrong and I alone did tell him. I do not accuse Luther, I do not defend him, nor am I answerable for him. On the man's spirit I would not dare pass judgment; for this is a most difficult task, especially if the verdict is to be adverse. And yet, if I supported him as a man of high character, which even his enemies admit; as a man on trial, and even jurors on oath are allowed to pity without breaking the law; as a victim of persecution, which common humanity dictates – and persecution too by those who have found a trumped-up pretext to make a fanatical attack on the humanities – where in all this would there be grounds for suspicion, provided I did not meddle with the case? Last but not least, it is, I imagine, my Christian duty to support Luther to this extent: if he is innocent, I should be sorry to see him overwhelmed by some villainous faction; if he is wrong, I would rather he were set right than destroyed; for this agrees better with the example Christ has given us, who according to the prophet[4] quenched not the smoking flax and did not break the bruised reed.

I should like to see that heart of his, which does appear to house some glowing sparks of the gospel teaching, not overwhelmed but set right, and then invited to preach the glory of Christ. As it is, certain divines well known to me neither correct Luther nor instruct him; they merely traduce him with their crazy clamour before popular audiences and tear him to shreds with the most bitter and venomous denunciations, their mouths full of nothing but the words 'heresy' and 'heretics.' It cannot be denied that the most invidious attacks have been made on him here in public by men who have not yet set eyes on his books. It is a known fact that some have condemned specifically what they still did not understand. Here is an instance. Luther had put in writing that we are not bound to confess all our mortal sins but only those which are manifest, meaning by manifest those which were known to us when we made our confession. A certain Carmelite divine,[5] understanding this as though manifest meant openly committed, made a portentous uproar over something he had not understood. It is a known fact that these men have condemned as heretical in Luther's books things they read in the books of Bernard and Augustine as orthodox and even pious.

I told them at the beginning to refrain from this kind of public clamour and to proceed by preference in writing or by disputation. First, I said, a thing ought not to be condemned in public which has not been read or, rather, not considered – for I will not say not understood; secondly, that it was unseemly for theologians to use disorder as a weapon, for their decisions ought to be a serious matter; lastly, that it was not easy to rant and rail against a man whose life all know to be blameless. And then perhaps, I said, it was not safe to touch on such topics before a mixed crowd containing many people who much dislike confessing their secret sins. If they hear that there are divines who say we are not bound to confess all our sins, they will snatch eagerly at this excuse for a quite erroneous opinion.

Although this view of mine was shared by all the most intelligent people, yet my friendly warning gave rise to the suspicion that Luther's books were largely mine, and born in Louvain; while there is not a letter in them that belongs to me or was published with my knowledge or consent. And yet, relying on this utterly base suspicion, and being beyond the reach of any protest, they roused the most tragical scenes here, which were the most frenzied things I have yet seen in my whole life. Besides which, although a theologian's proper duty is to teach, I now seem many of them intent on nothing but compulsion or destruction and annihilation; though Augustine, even when confronted with the Donatists,[6] who were not only heretics but brutal ruffians as well, disapproves of coercion without instruction too. Men in whom gentleness was most to be expected seem to thirst for nothing but human blood, and are all agape for nothing so much as to seize Luther and destroy him. This is to play the butcher, not the theologian. If they wish to prove themselves eminent divines, let them convert the Jews, let them convert to Christ those who are now far from him, let them mend the standard of morality among Christians, which is as corrupt as anything even the Turks can show. How can it be right to hale off to punishment a man who, in the first place, put forward subjects for discussion which have always been discussed in all schools of theology, and have even given rise to doubts? Why should a man be tormented who wishes for instruction, who submits himself to the judgment of the Apostolic See, who entrusts himself to the judgment of the universities? If he does not put himself in the hands of certain people who would rather see him dead than right, we should not be surprised.

Above all, we must look clearly at the sources of this evil. The world is burdened with ordinances made by man. It is burdened with the opinions and the dogmas of the schools. It is burdened with the tyranny of the mendicant friars who, though they are servants of the Roman See, have risen to such influence and such numbers that the pope himself – yes, even kings themselves – find them formidable. To them, when the pope is on their side, he is more than God; in things which are not to their advantage, he has no more substance than a dream. I do not condemn them all; but there are very many of this description who, for gain and for despotic power, deliberately ensnare the consciences of men. With growing effrontery they now began to leave Christ out of it and preach nothing but their own new and increasingly impudent dogmas. Of indulgences they were speaking in such terms that even the unlettered could not stomach it. This and much like it little by little was sapping the vigour of the gospel teaching; and the result would have been, with things slipping always from bad to worse, that the spark of Christian piety, from which alone the spent fire of charity could be rekindled, would be finally put out. The centre of religion was tending to be a more than Jewish ceremonial.[7] Hence there is sorrow and sighing among men of good will. And all this is admitted in private conversation even by theologians if they are not monks, and by certain monks themselves.

It was these things, I think, that roused Luther's spirit to take the first bold step of opposing the intolerable impudence of some of them. What else am I to suppose of a man who does not seek high place and has no desire for money? Of the articles on which they base their charges against Luther I enter into no discussion for the moment, I discuss merely the manner and occasion. Luther made bold to doubt about indulgences; but this was a subject on which others previously had made brazen assertions. He made bold to speak, with some moderation, of the power of the Roman pontiff; but on this the other party had previously written with no moderation at all, the leaders of them being three Dominicans,[8] Alvarus, Silvester, and the cardinal of San Sisto. He made bold to condemn the pronouncements of Thomas [Aquinas]; but these the Dominicans set almost above the Gospels. He made bold to discuss some doubtful points on the subject of confession; but this is a subject on which the monks set endless traps for men's consciences. He made bold to neglect in part the pronouncements of the schools; but to these they themselves give too much weight, and on them they differ none the less among themselves, and finally they change them from time to time, tearing up the old to bring in new.

This was torment to religious minds, when they heard scarcely a word in the schools about the gospel teaching, and those sainted authors who had long ago been accepted by the church dismissed as out of date. Worse, in sermons they heard very little about Christ; almost everything concerned the powers of the papacy and the opinions of modern authorities, and all the preachers said now flaunted openly the money-grubber and the toady, the place-hunter and the charlatan. It is their fault, I think, even if Luther was rather too intemperate. Whoever is a supporter of the gospel teaching is a supporter of the Roman pontiff, who is its principal mouthpiece, while the other bishops are his mouthpieces in their turn. All bishops are Christ's vicegerents, but among them the Roman pontiff is the chief. Of him we must suppose that he supports nothing more than the glory of Christ, whose minister he boasts himself to be. Those men do him the greatest disservice who ascribe to him in adulation what he does not himself accept and what is not expedient for Christ's flock. And yet some of those who stir up these tragic commotions do it out of no zeal for the pope; they misuse his position to enhance their own interests and their own despotic power. We have, I should suppose, a pious pope. but in such a stormy sea of business there is much of which he is unaware; some things too which he cannot restrain even if he would, but, as Virgil[9] says, 'The driver's steeds now carry him away, / Nor will the chariot the reins obey.' And so the pope's pious duty can only be assisted by a man who encourages truly Christian behaviour. It is no secret that there are people who seek to arouse his holy fervour against Luther, or rather against anyone who dares open his mouth in opposition to their favourite ideas. But the greatest princes ought to consider the pope's abiding wishes, and not his acquiescence secured by force or fraud.

Indeed I could show you with perfect truth what sort of men are at the bottom of this tumult, did I not fear that while I try always to be truthful I may be thought merely spiteful. Many of them I know well; many have themselves displayed their true quality in the books they have published – nor does any mirror give a clearer image of a man's mind and life. If only those who assume for themselves the censorial staff, to purge the Christian body of whom they please, as the ancient censors purged the senate, had thoroughly absorbed Christ's teaching and Christ's spirit! This happy state is reserved for those hearts from which all the contamination of this world's desires has been cleared away. Whether the men we treat of are in this class will soon be discovered by anyone who does business with them on any point that touches their pockets, their ambition, or their love of revenge. I wish I could indicate to your Highness what I have both observed and been told upon this subject; for I must not forget the self-restraint proper to a Christian.

I say this all the more freely because I am in every way a stranger to both Reuchlin's case and Luther's. I should not be willing to write anything in that field myself, nor do I claim to possess sufficient learning to be ready to keep an eye on what other men write; but I cannot refrain from letting you into one secret – that those people have very different objects in view from those that their words profess. They have long resented the new blossoming of the humanities and the ancient tongues, and the revival of the authors of Antiquity, who up to now were wormeaten and deep in dust, so that the world is now recalled to the fountain-head. They are afraid for their own shortcomings, they do not wish it to be thought that there is anything they do not know, and they fear their own prestige may suffer. This is a sore place that they have long kept under, but pain proves too much for pretence, and it has lately burst. Before Luther's books appeared, they devoted great efforts to this, especially the Dominicans and the Carmelites, many of whom, I regret to say, are even more criminal than they are ignorant. When Luther's books had appeared, as though this gave them a handle they began to tie up the ancient tongues and the humanities and Reuchlin and Luther and even myself in the same parcel, their distinctions being as much at sea as their deductions. To begin with, what can liberal studies have in common with a question of religious faith? And then what have I in common with Reuchlin or with Luther? But they have cunningly confused all these things, to lay on all who follow the humanities a load of ill will which all share.

Further, that this campaign is dishonest, this alone is enough to show: they themselves admit that there is no author ancient or modern in whom mistakes may not be found, and would even make a man who defended those mistakes assiduously a heretic, and why, if so, do they probe so insidiously into two or three and ignore the rest? They do not deny that there are many errors in Alvarus, many in the cardinal of San Sisto, and many in Silvester Prierias.[10] These are not mentioned, because they are Dominicans. Reuchlin alone is the object of their clamour, because of his skill in languages, and Luther, whom they suppose to be equipped with the subjects that I study, although in fact his acquaintance with them is but slender. Luther has written much which is not so much irreligious as ill advised; and of this what hurts their feelings worst of all is that he does not attach much importance to Thomas [Aquinas], that he reduces the profit to be made from indulgences, that he does not think much of the orders of mendicants, that he does not pay to the decisions of the schools the same respect as he pays to the Gospels, and that he thinks the man-made subtleties of academic disputation can be ignored. These, we can all see, are insufferable heresies. Yet these they gloss over in the presence of the pope and produce charges loaded with prejudice; only the chance of hurting someone calls out all their unanimity and cunning.

In the old days a heretic was listened to almost with respect and was absolved if he did penance; if he remained obdurate after conviction, he was not admitted – that was the extreme penalty – to communion with catholics in the bosom of the church. Nowadays the accusation of heresy is a very different thing; and yet on the slightest pretext at once they are all crying, 'Heresy, heresy.' In the old days a heretic was one who dissented from the Gospels or the articles of the faith or things which carried equal authority with them. Nowadays if anyone disagrees with Thomas, he is called a heretic – indeed, if he disagrees with some newfangled reasoning thought up yesterday by some sophister in the schools. Anything they do not like, anything they do not understand is heresy. To know Greek is heresy; to speak like an educated man is heresy. Anything they do not do themselves is heresy. It is, I admit, a serious crime to violate the faith; but not everything should be forced into a question of faith. And those who mind the business of the faith ought to steer very clear of every kind of ambition for personal gain or hatred or revenge.

But anyone can see the goal they have set before them and the way they are heading. And if their greed is once allowed free rein, they will begin to show their resentment against all good men everywhere, and will end by threatening the very bishops, even the pope himself. I should not protest if this were to be thought untrue, except that we have seen some of them doing this already. How far the Order of Preachers can go, to produce no other example, we can learn from Girolamo Savaronella and that outrage at Bern.[11] I have no wish to refresh the memory of their disgrace; I issue a warning of what we must expect if all their rash attempts succeed.

All that I have said hitherto lies outside Luther's case; I discuss only their methods and the danger of them. Reuchlin's case has been reserved to himself by the pope. Luther's business has been delegated to the universities. Whatever they may pronounce will be free of all risk for me. I have always taken pains to write nothing indecent or seditious or at variance with the teaching of Christ. I shall never knowingly be either a teacher of error or a promoter of civil strife, for I will suffer anything rather than arouse sedition. But I had my reasons for wishing this to be known to your Eminence, not to give you good advice or show you the way, but so that, if the adversaries of the humanities attempt to misuse your great position, you may know more surely what the best decision in this field is. And in my opinion, the more your Eminence can keep clear of this case, the more you will honourably preserve your own tranquillity. The *Method*[12] which I dedicated to your Highness, I have revised, and enriched with considerable additions. May Christ the Almighty ever preserve your Eminence in health and wealth.

Louvain, 19 October 1519

Your Eminence's most obedient servant Erasmus of Rotterdam

**Ep 1202**

ERASMUS OF ROTTERDAM TO JUSTUS JONAS, GREETING

There has been a persistent rumour here for some time, dearest Jonas, that you gave Martin Luther steadfast support at Worms,[1] and I do not doubt that as a truly religious man you did as I should have done had I been there, in hopes of laying this tragic business to rest by moderate measures in a way that may prevent its breaking out again later with more disastrous results for the whole world. Personally, I am surprised that this did not happen; the best men had it very much at heart for, as befits truly Christian spirits, they wanted steps to be taken for the peace of the church, which if not held together in concord has ceased to deserve the name of church. For what is our religion, if not peace in the Holy Spirit? Moreover, the church of Christ, inasmuch as she still holds good and bad fish in the same net and is compelled to endure tares mixed with the wheat, suffered even in the old days from great faults, as orthodox Fathers testify, deploring from time to time the gross corruption of the ranks of society whence models of simple piety ought to proceed. And how far the church of Rome fell away even in the old days from its zeal for the purity of the Gospel, Jerome of himself is a sufficient witness when he calls her the Babylon of the Apocalypse, or St Bernard in his book *De consideratione*; not that there has been any lack even among the moderns of celebrated authors to demand the public restoration of church discipline.

But I doubt whether the princes of the church have ever displayed such a passionate and unconcealed appetite for the good things of this world, which Christ taught us ought to be despised, as we see today. The breakdown was no less in the study of Holy Scripture than in morality. The word of God was forced to become the slave of human appetites, and the simple faith of the multitude was distorted to the profit of the few. Well might religious souls lament all this, who set Christ's glory above all else. This was the reason why to start with Luther had such a favourable reception everywhere as has fallen to the lot of no other mortal, I suppose, for many centuries. We readily believe what we strongly wish to be true; and people thought a man had arisen who was unspotted by all this world's desires and would be able to apply some remedy to these great evils. Nor did I myself entirely despair of this, except that at the very first taste of the pamphlets which had begun to appear under Luther's name, I was full of fear that the thing might end in uproar and split the world openly in two. And so I sent warning letters both to Luther himself and to friends of his who might, I thought, carry some weight with him; what advice they gave him, I do not know; but at any rate the affair was handled in such a way that there is some danger of remedies wrongly applied making our troubles twice as great.

And I wonder very much, dear Jonas, what god has stirred up Luther's heart to make him write with such freedom of invective against the Roman pontiff, against all the universities, against philosophy, and against the mendicant orders. Had all he says been true – and those who examine what he has written declare that the case is quite otherwise – once he had challenged so many people, what other outcome was to be expect than what we see now? Luther's books I have not yet had the leisure to read; but to judge by the samples I have taken, and from what I have sometimes picked up in passing from the accounts of others, though it was perhaps beyond my meagre attainments to pronounce on the truth of the opinions he put forward, at any rate his method and the way he sets to work I could never approve. For seeing that truth of itself has a bitter taste for most people, and that it is of itself a subversive thing to uproot what has long been commonly accepted, it would have been wiser to soften a naturally painful subject by the courtesy of one's handling than to pile one cause of hatred on another.

What therefore was the point of dealing in paradoxes, and putting some things forward in language that was bound to give even more offence at first sign than when regarded steadily at close quarters? For some things are rendered offensive even by a kind of wilful obscurity. What was the point of a savage torrent of invective directed against men whom it was unwise to treat like that if he wished to make them better, and impious if he did it to provoke them and set the whole world by the ears? Furthermore, when a prudent steward will husband the truth – bring it out, I mean, when the business requires it and bring it out so much as is requisite and bring out for every man what is appropriate for him – Luther in this torrent of pamphlets has poured it all out at once, making everything public and giving even cobblers a share in what is normally handled by scholars as mysteries reserved for the initiated; and often a sort of immoderate energy has carried him, in my opinion at least, beyond the bounds of justice. To give an example: when it would have sufficed to point out to the theologians that they mix in too much Peripatetic,[2] or rather, sophistic philosophy, he calls the whole Aristotelian system the death of the soul.

That spirit of Christ in the Gospels has a wisdom of its own, and its own courtesy and meekness. That is how Christ attuned himself to the feelings of the Jews. He says one thing to the multitudes, who are somewhat thick-witted, and another to his disciples; and even so he has to bear with them for a long time while he gradually brings them to understand the celestial philosophy. With this in mind he bids his followers preach first repentance and the impending kingdom of God, and keep silence about Christ. So Peter in the Acts of the Apostles preaches without upbraiding but in a mild and affectionate style, when he adds that great multitude as first-fruits to the church. He does not declaim against those who had put Christ to death; he does not exaggerate their impious madness in savage language, although it is likely that in his audience there were men who had hounded Christ to his death. No: as though he wished to encourage them, he says that all this was done by the divine wisdom, and later even puts the responsibility for this impious crime on the world itself, urging them to save themselves from this untoward generation. He does not return insult for insult upon those who said that the apostles were drunk with new wine, but mildly finds reasons to excuse their mistake: it was the power not of new wine but of a new spirit. He produces the testimony of Joel,[3] because he knew that with them it would carry great weight. And he does not yet declare that Christ is both God and man; this mystery he reserves until its proper time. For the present he calls him a just man and declares him to be the Lord and the Messiah, and does this on the authority of God, whom they too scrupulously worshipped, so that the recognition of the Father might win acceptance for the Son. Besides which, when he demonstrated that what they understood of David was really said not of David but of Christ, he begins by softening a remark which will give offence with the words 'Men and brethren, let me freely speak unto you of the patriarch David.'[4]

Thus does Paul become all things to all men, that he may gain them all for Christ, training his disciples to teach with all gentleness, without estranging any man by harshness of behaviour and language, but by their gentleness winning over even those who are stubborn and hard to please. With what courtesy he preaches Christ to the Athenians, casting the responsibility for their sins on the age in which they lived! 'And the times of this ignorance,' he says 'God winked at,' addressing his audience with a respectful and acceptable opening as 'men of Athens.'[5] Nor does he use harsh words in rebuking their impious worship of demons, but in courteous language charges them with superstition, because they worshipped more than they ought. Having by chance observed the inscription on an altar,[6] he twists it into evidence for their faith, with the alteration and omission of several words; nor does he as yet call Christ anything but a man, by whom God had ordained that salvation should be conferred on the whole race of mortals. Nor does he produce before that audience the testimony of the prophets, which would have carried very little conviction, but uses the witness of Aratus[7] in his argument with them. Think of the courtesy with which he conducts his case before Festus and before Agrippa![8]

It is the same with Augustine. When he refutes the crazy Donatists, and the Manichaeans[9] who are worse than madmen, his indignation stops short of what the facts deserve, and everywhere there is an endearing admixture of charity, as though he thirsted for their salvation and not their destruction. It was this gentleness in teaching, this prudence in husbanding the word of God that conquered the world and made it pass under the yoke of Christ as no military force, no subtle philosophy, no eloquent rhetoric, no human violence or cunning could ever have done. All the more is it our duty, if we wish to do good, to refrain from all abusive language, especially if our target is men high in public authority. Paul would have honour paid to magistrates, even when they are gentiles, and offers as it were a recantation because he had used severe language of a Mosaic and openly criminal high priest. He wishes servants who are initiates of the mysteries of Christ to obey their gentile masters even more strictly than they did before. He would have wives, after they have made their profession to Christ, be still more obedient to their unbelieving husbands, solely in order that by their compliant behaviour they might win them all over to love the teaching of the Gospel. The man of a religious mind will in any case desire nothing but to do good to others, either holding his peace if there is hope of making progress, or bringing the truth out of his store and husbanding it, for fear lest instead of healing the evil it may make it more violent.

Brutus[10] is indignant with Cicero for infuriating in his speeches and writings men whose fury once roused he cannot put down. Plato[11] does not disapprove of pretence and concealment of the truth in a philosopher who has to govern the commonwealth, provided he uses these tricks for the good of the people. A Christian, I admit, ought to be free of all pretence; but even so an occasion sometimes offers when it is right for truth to remain unspoken, and everywhere the time, the manner and the recipients of its publication are of great importance. Reliable physicians do not take refuge at the outset in their ultimate remedies; first they prepare the patient's body with less powerful drugs, and they adjust the dose to cure and not to overwhelm. Nor will I listen to people who say that the distemper of our generation is too serious to be healed by the gentler remedies. It is better, as the Greek proverb has it, to let the evil lie that's well disposed, than by unskilful physic to arouse its full force.

I do not of course deny that sometimes God uses war, pestilence, and distress to correct his flock; but religious men have no call to introduce war or suffering contrary to their religion, although God sometimes turns the ills of other men to the good of his own people. The cross of Christ brought salvation to the world; and yet we abominate the men who crucified him. The deaths of the martyrs shed lustre on the church of God and strengthened it too; and yet we condemn the wickedness of those to whom we owe these advantages. Many bad men would be less bad if deprived of their wealth; but it is not a good man's business to rob anyone of his property in order to make him better. And furthermore, since every novelty causes an upheaval, even if it is a summons to better things, any proposal that diverges from what men are used to should be put forward in such a form as to make that divergence seem as small as possible.

But they say that sometimes, when Luther's teaching is no different from other people's, he tries, it seems, by his actual choice of words to make it seem very different. Now men are inclined by nature to go wrong, and their faults should be corrected in such a way as not to give others a handle to err with greater freedom. Paul preaches the liberty of the Gospel as against the baneful slavery of the Law, but adds this limitation, 'not to use liberty for an occasion to the flesh.[12] His discouragement from the cold works of the law goes closely with a ceaseless urging to works of charity. There were perhaps men who with no ulterior motive were in favour of summoning the orders and the princes of the church to mend their ways; but I rather think that some people are encouraged by this opportunity to covet the worldly wealth of churchman, and nothing, I think, can be more criminal or more dangerous to the public peace than that. For if they think it lawful to lay hands on the property of priests, just because some of them use their resources for a life of luxury or for purposes which are unworthy in other ways, many of our citizens and noblemen alike will find that their hold on their possessions is precarious. And it would be a pretty service to mankind to rob priests impiously of their property in order that military men may put it to worse uses; for the way in which they squander their own possessions, and sometimes other people's too, is of no benefit to any mortal man.

No more will I listen, my dear Jonas, to those who say that Luther has been provoked by the intolerable impudence of his opponents until he was unable to maintain the modesty of a true Christian. However others might behave, the man who had undertaken to play that part ought to have overlooked all else and stood by his principles.

And then he should have foreseen the outcome before he let himself fall into this pit, for fear of suffering the same fate as the he-goat in the fable.[13] Even in religious undertakings it is foolish to attempt what you cannot carry through, especially if an unsuccessful effort brings in its train not the benefits you hoped for, but infinite loss. We now behold things brought to such a pass that I for my part can see no happy issue, unless Christ uses his skill to turn certain men's rash folly to the public good.

Some people I could name make excuses for him because it was, they say, under compulsion from others that he first wrote so outrageously and then refused to trust himself to the judgment of that most merciful Pope Leo and to the honour of the emperor Charles, who is far the best and mildest of princes. But why did he choose to listen to those advisers rather than to his other friends, who are neither ignorant nor inexperienced, and who invited him to take a very different course? Look at the majority of his supporters: what sort of weapons had they with which to try and defend him? – ludicrous pamphlets, empty threats. As though their kind of nonsense could either frighten their opponents or satisfy the men of good will, to whose judgment the whole business should have been adapted, had they really wished their play to have a happy ending. As it is, the great army of evils unleashed by their temerity lays no mean burden of unpopularity on the study of good literature and on many good men who to start with were by no means hostile to Luther, either because they hoped he would handle things differently, or because they and he shared common enemies. For it happened by some accident that those who stirred up trouble for Luther in the beginning were enemies of good literature; and for this reason its devotees were less opposed to Luther, for fear that if they aided the party of his opponents, they would strengthen their own enemies against themselves. Although, whatever the state of affairs, religion should have come first in people's thoughts, before their favourite studies.

And on this point, my dear Jonas, I have sometimes been obliged to long for an example of the gospel spirit, on observing how Luther, and still more his supporters, use a kind of cunning to secure that others may be involved in this unpleasant and perilous affair. Why need they burden Reuchlin,[14] who already had enough to bear, with a still heavier load of ill will? Why need they so often mention me by name in a tendentious way, when this was quite uncalled-for? I had sent Luther warning in a private letter under seal; it was soon printed in Leipzig.[15] I had warned the cardinal of Mainz, in a letter under seal,[16] not to abandon Luther unadvisedly to the hostility of certain persons, when his case still had much to be said for it in the eyes of most men of good will; it was published in print even before it reached him. Willibald complains in a letter to me[17] that certain letters are circulating in printed form which no one has ever delivered to him. In these he is urged to continue on the course he has adopted, no doubt in order to drive him willy-nilly into membership of their own faction.

From my own books, written before I ever dreamt of Luther's appearing, they have made a selection of troublesome statements and published them in a German translation, that they might be thought to approximate to some of Luther's opinions. And the men who do this wish to be thought my friends, although an enemy set on one's destruction could do nothing more hostile. My worst enemies used not to have such a genius for making mischief. This weapon they have put into the hands of my opponents, so that now they can hold forth in their public sermons on the points of agreement between me and Luther. As though falsehood were not very close to truth on either side if you overstep the line. Somewhere maybe I point out that vows should not be undertaken unadvisedly, nor do I approve of those who leave at home the wife and children whose life and morals are their first concern, and go running off to Santiago[18] or Jerusalem, where they have no business. I point out that young men ought not to be inveigled into the shackles of the religious life before they know themselves and know what that life is; Luther, they say, entirely condemns all vows. Elsewhere I complain that the burden of confession has been made heavier by the traps laid by certain people; Luther, they say, teaches that all confession should be rejected as pernicious. Elsewhere I have laid it down that the best authors should be read first, adding that the books of Dionysius did not yield as much profit as their titles seem to promise;[19] Luther calls the man a fool, I hear, and entirely unworthy of a reader's attention.

A pretty form of agreement indeed, if given an opportunity I say something true and reasonable, and another man kicks over the traces and distorts it! How can I do business on such outrageously unfair terms, if I am expected to guarantee that no one shall misuse what I have written, even after my time? – a piece of good fortune that even the Apostle Paul never enjoyed, if we may believe his colleague Peter. Not but what (to be quite frank) had I known that a generation such as this would appear, I should either not have written at all some things that I have written, or should have written them differently. For I wish to be of use to all men, in such a way that if possible I hurt no one. Pamphlets are bandied about, the work of conspirators, in which I too am depicted, whereas there are no words I hate more than conspiracy and schism and faction.

The whole of this performance, whatever one thinks of it, was started against my advice, or at least I steadfastly disapproved the form it took. What I write has never been in the service of any party; I serve Christ, who belongs to us all. What my brains or my pen can achieve, I do not know; at least, all my efforts and my desires have been and are devoted to the good not only of Germans but of Frenchmen, Spaniards, Englishmen, Bohemians, Ruthenians, and even Turks and Saracens, if I can – so far am I from ever having wished to take a hand in a faction so fraught with peril. And all the time I find a lack of common sense in men who think that anyone can be attracted into their camp by tricks of this kind. If they wished to set an intelligent man against them, what better way could they find to do so? They make it clear enough what broken reeds they depend on, when in so perilous an enterprise they rely on resources such as these. And I am dreadfully afraid that this business will bring great discredit on our native Germany in the eyes of all other nations, seeing how prone the ordinary man is to attribute the folly of a few to a whole nation.

And so, with all these outrageous pamphlets, all this deception, all this formidable threatening and bombast, what I ask you has been achieved, except to take what has hitherto been discussed in the schools as an acceptable opinion and make it for the future into an article of faith? – to make it hardly safe to teach even the Gospel, now that everything is inflamed and everything is seized upon as material for calumny? Luther might have done wonders for Christ's flock by teaching the philosophy of the Gospel; he might have done great service to the world by publishing books, had he refrained from things that could not fail to end in strife. My own work has lost a great part of the good effect I hoped for, thanks to him. Even disputations in our universities are not free, which ought to be as free as air. If it were lawful to hate any man in return for wrongs suffered personally, no one has suffered more from Luther's party than myself. And yet I could wish to see him safe and sound and these our divisions ended, which are far the most dangerous we have suffered – ended in such a way that they may not break out again later in an even more dangerous form, like wounds not properly healed.

You ask me, dearest Jonas, why I spin this long complaint to you when it is already too late. For this reason first of all, that though things have gone farther than they ought to have, even now one should be on the watch, in case it may be possible to still this dreadful storm. We have a pope most merciful by nature, we have an emperor whose spirit is mild and placable. If it proves impossible, I would rather you had nothing to do with it. I have always admired the precious talents Christ has given you, and they make me wish all the more that you should be spared for the service of the Gospel. The more I admired the streak of genius in Hutten,[20] the more I regret that he has been torn from us by these tumults. Who would not suffer torment if Philippus Melanchthon,[21] a young man of such outstanding gifts, were carried off by this tempest, and the hopes of scholars everywhere frustrated? If there are things we do not like in the men whose judgment governs human affairs, my view is that we must leave them to their Lord and Master. If their commands are just, it is reasonable to obey; if unjust, it is a good man's duty to endure them, lest worse befall. If our generation cannot endure Christ in his fullness, it is something none the less to preach him so far as we may.

The points I put to you now, my dear Jonas, I should like you to put to Philippus [Melanchthon] and to others like him. Above everything I think we must avoid the discord which must be disastrous to every man of good will. We need a sort of holy cunning; we must be time-servers, but without betraying the treasure of gospel truth from which our lost standards of public morality can be restored. Someone may perhaps ask whether my attitude towards Luther is the same as it used to be. It has not changed. I have always wished that some things could be altered which I never liked and that he could then devote himself entirely to the gospel philosophy from which the standards of our generation have so lamentably fallen away. I have always wanted to see him put right rather than put down. I used to wish that he would treat Christ's business in such a way that leaders of the church might approve, or at least not disapprove. I wanted Luther to be loved in such a way that it might be safe to love him openly. Nor do I feel any differently about the wretches who attack me than I do about him. If they show the same energy in the virtuous preaching of Christ that they have in their vicious attacks on me, I shall forget what I have suffered from them and welcome their new zeal for Christ. The noisy fellow who becomes Christ's harbinger I shall no longer hate. Farewell.

Louvain, 10 May 1521

# Julius Excluded from Heaven / *Dialogus Julius exclusus e coelis*

The attribution of the *Julius exclusus* to Erasmus is problematic. The work first appeared in 1517/18 and was variously attributed to the poet Fausto Andrelini, to Ulrich von Hutten, and to the Italian adventurer Girolamo Balbi, but the majority of Erasmus' contemporaries and most modern scholars regard Erasmus as the author of the dialogue. Erasmus himself admitted that the style resembled his own. He never denied the authorship outright, but disavowed any connection with the publication of the piece. Significantly he maintained that those who brought such scandalous stuff before the public were more to blame than those who actually wrote it.

The subject of the dialogue, Julius II (pope 1503–13), was famous for his patronage of the arts and infamous for his immoral life and warmongering. The dialogue, which satirizes his wordly ambitions and his abuse of power, was immensely popular with readers. It saw thirteen editions within four years and was quickly translated into German, English, and French, thus becoming available to a large audience.

This extract is taken from CWE 27 168–97, translated and annotated by Michael J. Heath.

## JULIUS EXCLUDED FROM HEAVEN: *A DIALOGUE*

**Julius** What the devil is this? The doors won't open? Someone must have changed the lock, or at least tampered with it.
**Genius** Are you quite sure you haven't brought the wrong key? The key to your treasure-chest won't open this door – and anyway, why didn't you bring both of them with you? The one in your hand is the key of power, not of knowledge.
**Julius** This is the only one I've ever had and, as I've got it here, I don't see what use the other would be.
**Genius** Neither do I, except that we're shut out without it.
**Julius** I'm seething with anger. I'll bang on the doors. Hey! Hey!

Someone open this door at once! What's the matter? No one here? What's keeping the doorman? Snoring, I suppose, good and drunk.

**Genius** He judges everyone by his own standards.

**Peter** It's a good thing our gate is as solid as rock or he'd have broken the doors down, whoever he is. This must be some giant or paladin, some wrecker of cities. Immortal God! it smells like a sewer round here! I won't open the door directly, but I'll peep through the bars of this window and find out what kind of monster it is. Who are you? What do you want?

**Julius** I want you to open the doors, and quickly; if you did your job properly, you'd have come out to meet me – with a solemn procession of angels, too.

**Peter** He's domineering enough anyway! But first of all, tell me who you are.

**Julius** As if you can't see that for yourself.

**Peter** See for myself? Well, I can see a strange spectacle, or perhaps I should say monster, unlike anything I've ever seen before.

**Julius** But I imagine that unless you're quite blind you recognize this key, even if the golden oak[1] isn't familiar; and you can see my triple crown and my robe all glittering with gold and jewels.

**Peter** Yes, the silver key is vaguely familiar, but there's only one and it's very different from those which Christ, the true shepherd of the church, entrusted to me long ago. As for that sumptuous crown of yours, why on earth should I recognize it? No barbarian tyrant ever dared wear a thing like that, let alone anyone trying to get in here. I'm certainly not impressed by the robe, because I always scorned gold and jewels and trampled them like so much rubble. But what's this? I see that all your equipment, key, crown, and robe, bears the marks of that villainous huckster and imposter, who had my name but not my nature, Simon, whom I humbled long ago with the aid of Christ.

**Julius** Stop this nonsense, if you know what's good for you; for your information, I am Julius, the famous Ligurian;[2] and, unless you've completely forgotten your alphabet, I'm sure you recognize these two letters, P.M.

**Peter** I suppose they stand for Pestis Maxima.[3]

**Genius** Ha ha ha! Our soothsayer has hit the nail on the head!

**Julius** Of course not! Pontifex Maximus.[4]

**Peter** Well, you could be thrice Maximus but you can't come in here unless you're holy.
**Julius** Oh, if being called 'holy' has anything to do with it, it's most impertinent of you to take so long to open the doors; you may have been merely styled 'holy' or 'saint' for all these years, but everyone has always called me 'most holy.' There are thousands of bulls ...
**Genius** 'Cock-and-bulls,' you might say!
**Julius** ... in which I am many times called 'most holy lord'; in fact, I was always referred to as 'his Holiness,' not just 'holy,' so that whatever I fancied doing ...
**Genius** Even when he was drunk!
**Julius** ... people said that 'his Holiness, the most holy Lord Julius' had done it.
**Peter** Then ask your flatterer to let you into heaven, since they made you 'most holy,' and let those who gave you 'Holiness' grant you bliss as well. Do you really think there's no difference between being holy and being called holy?
**Julius** This is very annoying: if I'd only been allowed to go on living I wouldn't envy you your holiness or your bliss.
**Peter** How well your words reveal the holiness of your thoughts! But in any case, I've been watching you closely all this time, and I can see plenty of evidence of impiety, but none of saintliness. What, for instance, is the purpose of that strange escort of yours, so unlike a pope's? You've brought twenty thousand men with you, but not one of the whole mob even looks like a Christian to me. They seem to be the worst dregs of humanity, all stinking of brothels, booze, and gunpowder. I'd say they were a gang of hired thugs, or rather goblins of Tartarus plucked up from hell to wage war on heaven. And the more closely I look at you yourself the less I can see any trace of an apostle. First of all, what monstrous new fashion is this, to wear the dress of a priest on top, while underneath it you're all bristling and clanking with blood-stained armour? Then again, what fierce eyes and stubborn mouth, what a fearsome expression and haughty and arrogant brow you have! I'm ashamed to say, and sorry to see, that your whole body is disfigured by the marks of monstrous and abominable appetites, not to mention that even now you're all belches and that you stink of boozing and hangovers and look as if you've just thrown

up. Your whole body is in such a state that I should guess that it's been wasted, withered, and rotted less by old age and illness than by drink.

**Genius** A fine portrait: Julius to the life!

**Peter** Oh, I know you've been glowering at me for some time, but I can't help saying what I think. I suspect that you are that poisonous pagan Julius,[5] returned from hell in disguise to mock me, so closely do all your features resemble his.

**Julius** *Ma di si!*[6]

**Peter** What's that?

**Genius** He's in a temper: whenever he said that, all the cardinals would scurry away, for fear of feeling his Holiness's stick, especially after a banquet.

**Peter** You seem to understand his meaning very well: tell me, who are you?

**Genius** I am the mighty Genius of Julius.

**Peter** The evil genius, I should say.

**Genius** Whatever I am, I belong to Julius.

**Julius** Will you stop all this nonsense, and open the doors? Or would you rather they were broken down? Why all this chatter? You can see the kind of men I have under my command ...

**Peter** Yes indeed, I can see your gang of seasoned cutthroats, but, in case you don't know, you must storm these doors with very different arms.

**Julius** Enough talk, I say! If you don't obey me, and quickly, I'll hurl my thunderbolt of excommunication, even at you; I used to terrify the mightiest kings and even whole kingdoms with it. Do you see this bull already drawn up for the purpose?

**Peter** What on earth is all this about frightful thunderbolts and lightning and bulls and other fine talk? Christ never told us anything about these.

**Julius** Do as you're told, or you'll find out.

**Peter** You may have frightened men once with such fantasies, but they're no use in this place: only truth counts here. This citadel may be taken by good deeds, not foul words. But one question: you threaten *me* with your thunderbolt of excommunication; by what right?

**Julius** The best of rights, since you no longer hold office and are no more than a simple priest; no, not even a priest, as you haven't the power to consecrate.

**Peter** Because I'm dead, I suppose?

**Julius** Exactly.

**Peter** But by the same token you have no more power over me than a dead man.

**Julius** Ah, but as long as the cardinals are wrangling over electing a new pope, I'm still in charge.

**Genius** He's still dreaming the dreams of life.

**Julius** Now open up, I say.

**Peter** And *I* say that you won't get anywhere unless you give an account of your merits.

**Julius** What merits?

**Peter** I'll explain. Were you eminent in theology?

**Julius** Certainly not: I hadn't time, I was too busy with my wars. But there are plenty of monks occupied with it, if that's any good to you.

**Peter** Well, did you win many souls for Christ by the saintliness of your life?

**Genius** He sent a good many to Tartarus.[7]

**Peter** Were you famous for your miracles?

**Julius** This is all old-fashioned stuff.

**Peter** Did you pray simply and regularly?

**Julius** What's he jabbering about? Lot of nonsense!

**Peter** Did you mortify the flesh by fasting and vigils?

**Genius** I'd give up, if I were you; there's no point; you're wasting your time on him.

**Peter** I don't know what other qualities make an outstanding pope. If he has some more apostolic one, let him tell me.

**Julius** Although it's demeaning for the ever-invincible Julius to give in to Peter who was, to put it mildly, a mere fisherman and more or less a beggar, I'll tell you briefly so that you'll realize what a mighty prince you're sneering at. In the first place, I'm a Ligurian, not a Jew like you, although I'm sorry to say that we do have just one thing in common: I was once a bit of a seaman.

**Genius** Don't let it worry you, there's still an enormous difference: this Peter fished to provide food, whereas you plied your oars to get a paltry wage for yourself.

**Julius** In the second place, I was the nephew, by my mother, of Sixtus, a truly supreme pontiff ...

**Genius** Supremely sinful, he means.

**Julius** ... by whose special favour, and my own exertions, I first acquired wealth from the church and then rose gradually to the distinction of a cardinal's hat. After that I was tossed to and fro by many storms of misfortune and beset by appalling accidents; I was subject to epilepsy, among other maladies, and covered all over with what's called the French pox as well; finally I became an exile, hated, condemned, rejected by all, and more or less given up for lost. But I never lost hope of becoming supreme pontiff. That showed true strength of character, whereas you, scared by the words of a maidservant, gave up at once. A woman took your courage away, but it was a woman, a prophetess or fortune-teller, who increased my confidence; in the midst of all my troubles, she secretly whispered in my ear: 'Stand fast, son of the Julii! Do no be wearied by all that you must do and suffer: some day you shall be honoured with the triple crown. You shall be king of kings and lord of lords!' Well, neither my own hopes nor her prophecy misled me, for against all the odds I fought my way up to this position, partly with the help of the French, who took me in as a fugitive, and partly with the aid of an immense amount of money; I raised this both by paying high rates of interest and also by using my wits ...

**Peter** What does *that* mean?

**Julius** It means that I promised benefices in return for cash, and took great care to find guarantors for it, seeing that Crassus[8] himself could hardly have raised so much ready cash all at once. But it's no use telling you all this, when not even all the bankers understand it. Now you know how I reached my position. But since then, as pope, I have managed affairs so well that the church, and Christ himself, owe more to me than any previous pope, even the more recent ones, to say nothing of the early ones who, in my opinion, were popes in name only.

**Genius** The brute makes a fine Thraso,[9] doesn't he?

**Peter** I can hardly wait to hear the whole story.

**Julius** Well, I invented a lot of new offices, as they're called, and considerably enriched the papal treasury. Then I found a way of selling bishoprics without falling into the sin of simony. It had been established by my predecessors that anyone appointed to a bishopric must resign his other offices. I interpreted this as follows: 'You are told to resign, but you cannot resign something you don't possess, and so you must buy something to resign.' By this device single bishoprics used to bring in six or seven thousand ducats[10] each, apart from the usual extortions for the bulls. Again, I collected no mean profit from the new currency with which I flooded Italy. I've never missed an opportunity to pile up more money, because I understand only too well that nothing, sacred or profane, can be done properly without it.

But to come to greater achievements: Bologna had been taken over by the Bentivogli, but I restored it to the see of Rome. I crushed the previously invincible Venetians in battle. I almost lured the duke of Ferrara into a trap, after harassing him for years with war.[11] I cleverly frustrated a schismatic synod with a bogus counter-council[12] and, as the saying goes, used one nail to drive out another. Finally, I completely rid Italy of the French, at that time the terror of the whole world. I would have thrown the Spaniards[13] out too (I was on my way), had not the Fates snatched me from the earth.

In all this, too, I displayed my invincible courage, as you will see: when the French held the upper hand, I began to look for a place to hide. My situation was very nearly desperate, and I was growing a white beard, when suddenly the golden news was brought that several thousand Frenchmen had been slain at Ravenna. Julius breathed again. Another time I was virtually given up for dead, even by myself, for three days; but once again I recovered against all expectations, even my own. So either my authority or my cunning has proved so irresistible that today there is not one Christian king whom I have not incited to battle, after breaking, tearing, and shattering all the treaties by which they had painstakingly come to agreement among themselves; why, I so thoroughly ruined the most recent treaty, agreed at Cambrai[14] between myself, the French king, the king of the Romans, and some other princes, that it is never even mentioned now.

But my finest achievement: even though I maintained so great an army, organized magnificent triumphs, presented many spectacles, and put up buildings all over the place, yet at my death I left five million ducats, and would have gone on to greater things, if the skill of my Jewish doctor, which had already prolonged my life considerably, had been able to extend it still further. Ah, if only some wizard could restore me to life so that I could put the finishing touches to all my splendid plans! Mind you, on my deathbed I took great care to prevent any settlement of the wars I had stirred up throughout the world, and I saw to it that at least the money set aside for this purpose should be untouched: these were my last orders as I expired.

Can you now be reluctant to open the doors of heaven to a pope who has served Christ and the church so well? You'll admire me all the more when you realize that I achieved all this by the strength of my own character alone, having none of the advantages that most other people enjoy: no family connections, as not even I knew who my father was (which indeed adds to the glory of my achievement); no good looks, as everyone shuddered at my ghastly face; no learning, as that was something I never acquired; no physical strength – I've already described the state of my body to you; none of the advantages of youth, as I did all this in old age; no popular support, as everyone hated me; no mercy, since I was so ruthless myself that I even dealt harshly with those to whom other people usually show every indulgence ...

**Peter** What has this to do with your case?

**Genius** It seems hard, but it's really quite soft.

**Julius** ... but in the face of misfortune, of old age, of bodily weakness, in short, of gods and men, with only my courage and my money to help me, I achieved all this in a few years, and left enough unfinished business to my successors to keep them occupied for as much as ten years. This is the absolute truth about myself, though told with too much modesty; if one of my orators at Rome had embellished the tale with all the trimmings, I'd sound more like a god than a man.

**Peter** This whole story of yours, most invincible warrior, is so new and strange to me that I must ask you to forgive my simplicity or my inexperience, and not to resent answering some rather naive questions on individual points. Who are these fair and curly-haired youths?

**Julius** I was keeping them for my pleasure.

**Peter** And who are those dark and scarred veterans?

**Julius** My soldiers and captains, who met their deaths while fighting courageously for me and for the church, some in taking Bologna, many in the battle against Venice, and most of all at Ravenna; under our agreement, they all have a right to enter heaven, since some time ago I promised, in mighty bulls, that all who fought under Julius' banners should fly straight up to heaven, no matter what sort of life they had led before.

**Peter** So, as far as I can make out, it was some of these who gave me so much trouble before you arrived, stopping just short of violence in their efforts to get in here, and brandishing certain leaden bulls.

**Julius** Am I to understand that you didn't let them in?

**Peter** Let them in? Certainly not, none of that sort. Christ taught me that these doors are to be opened, not to those who bring along bulls heavy with lead, but to those who have clothed the naked, fed the hungry, given drink to the thirsty, visited the prisoner, and taken in the stranger. And if he wished even those who prophesied, cast out devils, and worked miracles in his name to be shut out, do you really think I should let in those who only bring a bull in the name of Julius?

**Julius** What if I'd found out?

**Peter** I see: if some refugees from hell told you about it, you'd have declared war on me?

**Julius** More than that: I'd have excommunicated you!

**Peter** But go on with your account: why do you bear arms yourself?

**Julius** Don't pretend that you didn't know that the supreme pontiff has *two* swords;[15] or would you like me to fight naked?

**Peter** But when I occupied the position, I knew of no sword but the sword of the spirit, the word of God.

**Julius** Malchus wouldn't agree that you cut off his ear without a sword,[16] I imagine.

**Peter** I remember and I admit it. But on that occasion I was fighting for Christ my master, not for myself; for the life of the Lord, not for money or temporal power; when I fought I was not yet pontiff; I had been promised the keys, but had not yet received them; I had not yet received the gift of the Holy Spirit. Even then, I was commanded to put up my sword, a public rebuke to show that such fighting was unworthy of a priest, and indeed of a Christian. But let's leave that for the moment. Why are you so particular about calling yourself a Ligurian, as if his nationality made any difference to a vicar of Christ?

**Julius** Of course it does: I consider it the height of loyalty to bring glory to my nation, and for that reason I put this title on all my coins, statues, arches, and walls.

**Peter** So he knows his fatherland but not his father! I thought for a moment that you were talking about the heavenly Jerusalem, fatherland of all believers, and its one Prince, whose name they wish to be hallowed, that is to be glorified. But why do you add 'nephew of Sixtus[17] by his sister'? I am astonished that no such Sixtus has ever arrived here, especially as he was supreme pontiff and a relative of such a brave general as yourself. So please tell me what kind of man he was: a priest?

**Julius** Yes, but a fine soldier too; and he was from a distinguished order – the Franciscans, no less.

**Peter** I once met a Francis, the best of laymen, but he held wealth, pleasure, and ambition in utter contempt. Does that humble pauper now have such mighty lieutenants?

**Julius** I can see that you don't like men to better themselves: Benedict was a poor man too, but his successors are now so rich that even we are jealous of them.

**Peter** Splendid! But to return to this business of being Sixtus' nephew ...

**Julius** I'm always careful to say that, to shut the mouths of those whose assert too freely that I'm his son.

**Peter** Freely, but perhaps truly?

**Julius** Perhaps, but such a thing isn't consistent with the dignity of the pope, which is always the first consideration.

**Peter** Well, it seems to me that this dignity can be best served if it never lays itself open to justifiable criticism. But now, by your pontifical majesty, would you please tell me truly if the method of obtaining the papacy that you described is now the common and accepted method?

**Julius** There's been no other for hundreds of years, unless perhaps my successor is elected in another way. As soon as I'd obtained the papacy, you see, I saw to it that a fearsome bull was published to prevent anyone from reaching the office by a similar route. I renewed the bull just before my death. It's up to other people now to see that it works.

**Peter** Yes, I suppose you were the best man to define the offence. But what surprises me is that anyone can be found willing to take up the post, especially since, as you inform me, it involves so many irksome duties and can only be obtained after an arduous struggle. When I was pontiff, hardly anyone could be pressed into service as an elder or a deacon.

**Julius** I'm not surprised: in those days the only revenue and rewards for the bishops were hardships, vigils, fasting, study, and, more often than not, death; but now they can get a kingdom and tyrannical power: and what man won't fight if he has the chance of a kingdom?

**Peter** All right: but what about Bologna? Had it renounced the faith, that it needed to be restored to the see of Rome?

**Julius** A pretty thought! No, nothing like that.

**Peter** Well, perhaps Bentivoglio's poor government was weakening the state?

**Julius** No, no, it was very prosperous; the city had been enlarged and improved by a lot of new building (all the more reason for me to hanker after it).

**Peter** I see: then had he seized power unlawfully?

**Julius** Not in the least: he was ruling by agreement.

**Peter** Then the citizens couldn't stand him as their prince?

**Julius** On the contrary, they were quite stubbornly attached to him; they were nearly all hostile to me.

**Peter** What *was* your reason then?

**Julius** Simply that, under his administration, our treasury got only a miserable few thousand out of all the enormous sums he collected from his citizens. But in any case, his deposition fitted in well with the plans I was making at the time. So the French, and some others who were intimidated by my thunderbolt, set to work with a will; Bentivoglio was overthrown, and I installed cardinals and bishops to run the city so that the whole of its revenue would be at the service of the Roman church. In addition, whereas previously it was he who enjoyed all the outward titles and honours due to a ruler, these days you can see our statues all over the city, read our inscriptions, salute our monuments; already Julius in stone or in bronze stands at every corner. Finally, if you'd seen the regal triumph with which I entered Bologna, I'm sure you'd pour scorn on the triumphs of such as Octavius and Scipio,[18] and understand that I had good reason to fight so hard for Bologna; indeed, you'd have seen, at one and the same time, the church militant and triumphant.

**Peter** So, if I'm not mistaken, you achieved during your reign what Christ taught us to pray for: 'Thy kingdom come.' Now then, what have the Venetians done wrong?

**Julius** First of all, they were talking Greek[19] to one another, and treating me more or less as a joke, hurling all sorts of accusations at me.

**Peter** Were they true or false?

**Julius** What's the difference? It's sacrilege even to whisper anything about the Roman pontiff, except in praise of him. Then again, they were handing out church livings as they thought fit; they would never allow court cases to be transferred to Rome, and would never purchase any dispensations. Need I say more? They were inflicting the most intolerable damage on the see of Rome, especially as they were also occupying a considerable portion of your patrimony.

**Peter** My patrimony? Whatever do you mean, patrimony? I forsook all and, naked, followed the naked Christ.

**Julius** I mean some towns belonging by right to the see of Rome: it was the term the most holy Fathers chose to describe that particular part of their possessions.

**Peter** Ah, so you take proper care of your own riches by dishonouring my memory? And you call this intolerable damage?

**Julius** Of course.

**Peter** But were their morals corrupt? Had their piety grown cold?

**Julius** Now, now, you're talking nonsense again. The point was that they were cheating us of countless thousands of ducats, enough to maintain a whole regiment of soldiers.

**Peter** Yes, of course, very damaging financially. But now, what had the duke of Ferrara[20] tried to do?

**Julius** That most ungrateful of men? The vicar of Christ Alexander[21] held him in such esteem that he gave him his younger daughter in marriage and also, as a dowry, invested him with the most glittering authority – the fellow was in other respects worthless. But, heedless of all this kindness, the duke was forever insulting me, accusing me of simony, pederasty, and even insanity. On top of all this, he laid claim to certain taxes – not very important ones, it's true, but by no means to be overlooked by a careful shepherd.

**Genius** Tycoon, he means.

**Julius** But the real truth of the matter is that by joining his territory, with its strategic position, to our own domains I could advance the plans I was making. After his expulsion, then, I planned to confer his duchy on a relative[22] of mine, a man of great energy and one willing to risk anything for the good of the church (as he showed not long ago when, with his own hands, he stabbed the cardinal of Pavia[23] for me); for my daughter's husband was satisfied with his lot.[24]

**Peter** What's this? Supreme pontiffs with wives and children?
**Julius** No, no, not wives of their own; but what's so odd about them having children, since they're men, not eunuchs?
**Peter** Well, finally, what provoked that schismatic synod?
**Julius** It would take too long to go back to the very beginning, but I'll give you the essentials. Certain individuals had been growing weary of the Roman curia. They said that all our doings were tainted by a shameful obsession with money, by monstrous and unspeakable vices, sorcery, sacrilege, murder, and graft and simony. They said that I myself was a simoniac, a drunkard, and a lecher, obsessed with the things of the world, an absolute disaster for the Christian commonwealth, and in every way unworthy to occupy my position. The only remedy for this wretched situation, they said, was a general council. They added that I'd sworn to call a general council within two years of my accession, and that I'd been elected on this condition.
**Peter** Was what they said true?
**Julius** Indeed it was. But I'd freed myself from the oath when the time was ripe. I mean, if there's a kingdom at stake, what man would hesitate to break any sort of oath? As my alter ego Julius so elegantly put it: 'Let piety be practised in everything else.'[25] But now, observe the audacity of men: listen to their next move. Nine cardinals desert; they announce a council to me; they invite me; they beg me to preside. When I refuse, they proclaim the council to the whole world, on the authority of Maximilian[26] as emperor (because, according to them, history tells us that at one time councils were usually proclaimed by the Roman emperors), and also (I shudder to think of it) on the authority of Louis XII of France;[27] in this way they try to tear the seamless coat of Christ, which even those who crucified him left in one piece.
**Peter** But were you as bad as they claimed?
**Julius** Does it matter? I was supreme pontiff. Suppose I were more vicious than the Cercopes, stupider than Morychus, more ignorant than a log, fouler than Lerna:[28] any holder of this key of power must be venerated as the vicar of Christ and looked on as most holy.
**Peter** Even an obvious scoundrel?
**Julius** As big a scoundrel as you like. And so of course it's insufferable that the man who stands in God's place on earth and is even a kind of god among men should be taken to task or insulted by some nonentity.

**Peter** But common sense rebels against admiring a man whom we can plainly see is a rogue or praising a man whom we feel to be evil.
**Julius** People can think what they like, so long as they speak well of us or at least hold their tongues. The supreme pontiff cannot be censured, even by a general council.
**Peter** I'm sure of one thing: the man who stands in Christ's place on earth must make every effort to be like him, and conduct his whole life in such a way that nothing in it can be censured, and that no one can justly speak ill of him. The papacy is in a bad way when popes must force men's approval by threats rather than win it by righteousness, when only liars can praise them, and when their highest achievement is to force silence upon their detractors. But answer me this: is there no way that a sinful and pestilent pope can be removed?
**Julius** Ridiculous! Who could remove the supreme power?
**Peter** But it is precisely because he *is* supreme that he must be removed: the greater he is, the more damage he can do. Civil laws can not only depose an emperor for misgovernment, but even sentence him to death; how unhappy is the condition of the church if it is obliged to tolerate a subversive pontiff at Rome and cannot by any means rid itself of such a public nuisance.
**Julius** Ah, but if a Roman pontiff needs correction, he must be corrected by a council; no council, however, can be convened against the pope's will, otherwise it isn't a council but a synod. Even if, under pressure, a council *is* convened, nothing can be decided without the pope's agreement, and in the end there is always the ultimate safeguard, the absolute power by virtue of which a pope on his own is far superior to a universal council. In fact, he cannot be deprived of his jurisdiction for any crime at all.
**Peter** Not for murder?
**Julius** Not for parricide.
**Peter** Not for fornication?
**Julius** Such language! No, not even for incest.
**Peter** Not for unholy simony?
**Julius** Not even for hundreds of simoniacal acts.
**Peter** Not for sorcery?
**Julius** Not even for sacrilege.
**Peter** Not for blasphemy?

**Julius** No, I tell you.
**Peter** Not for all these combined in one monstrous creature?
**Julius** Look, you can run through a thousand other crimes if you like, all more hideous than these: the Roman pontiff still cannot be deposed for them.
**Peter** This is certainly a strange new concept of the Roman pontiff's position that you're teaching me if, as you say, he alone is allowed to get away with every sort of crime; even stranger is the church's misfortune if it can find no way to rid itself of such a monster, and is compelled to venerate as pope the sort of man whom no one would tolerate as a brothel-keeper.
**Julius** Some people do say he can be deposed for just one thing ...
**Peter** And what's that, I wonder? A good deed? Since he obviously can't be deposed for evil deeds, if not for any of the things I mentioned.
**Julius** For heresy, but only if he's publicly convicted of it. But of course that's absurd too, and can't do the slightest harm to the pope's majesty. For one thing, he has the power to abrogate the law itself, if he finds it unsatisfactory; for another, who would dare to make accusations against the supreme pontiff, especially when he's so heavily armed and protected? In any case, if he should happen to be coerced by a council, he can easily recant, even if he can't disown his words. In the final analysis, unless he's a blockhead, not a man, there are always a thousand loopholes through which he'll find it easy to wriggle.
**Peter** But tell me, by the power of the pope, who made all these excellent laws?
**Julius** Who else but the fountain-head of all law, the supreme pontiff? But of course it is also his privilege to repeal, interpret, stretch, or limit them whenever it seems to be to his advantage.
**Peter** Now what quarrel *did* you have with the French and their king, whom your predecessors honoured with the title 'Most Christian,' especially as you admit that it was only under their protection that you survived at all, gained a crown greater than the emperor's, and even acquired Bologna and the other cities and subdued the invincible Venetians? How did the memory of so many recent good turns come to be lost? How were so many treaties broken?
**Julius** It would take a long time to tell the whole story. But to cut it short, I was entirely consistent in that I simply began to put into effect the ideas that I had formulated a long time before; I brought into the

open the plans that circumstances had forced me to keep quiet. As a matter of fact (and this is straight from the horse's mouth), I never really like the French; no Italian really feels kindly towards barbarians, any more, for heaven's sake, than a wolf does towards lambs. Well, I'm not just an Italian, but a Genoese, and so I used their friendship for as long as I needed their help; in such a case it is legitimate to use the service of barbarians. In the meantime, I put up with a lot, I concealed a lot, I promised a lot; in fact, there was nothing I didn't do, nothing I didn't suffer. But as soon as the situation had more or less reached the point that I wanted, all that was needed was to reveal the true Julius and throw all the barbarian scum out of Italy.

**Peter** These barbarians, as you call them: are they some sort of wild animal?

**Julius** No, they're human beings.

**Peter** Yes, human, but not Christians?

**Julius** Oh, they're Christians too, but what's that got to do with it?

**Peter** So they're Christians, in fact, but live like peasants, without laws or letters?

**Julius** No, they're very good at that sort of thing, and what's more – and this is what really annoys me – very rich.

**Peter** Then what does it mean when you call them barbarians? What's that you're muttering?

**Genius** I'll answer for him. Although Italy, like a sort of universal dustbin, is peopled by a chaotic mixture of all the dregs of the most barbaric nations, the Italians have acquired, from ancient literature, the ridiculous habit of calling anyone born outside Italy a barbarian; for them, the word is more insulting than if you said parricide or desecrator.

**Peter** So it appears. But seeing that Christ died for all men and that he was no respecter of persons, and since you claimed to be Christ's vicar, why didn't you welcome all men with equal enthusiasm? Christ himself never discriminated between them.

**Julius** I'd be quite willing to welcome Indians, Africans, Ethiopians, Greeks, so long as they paid up and acknowledged our supremacy by sending in their taxes. But we were quite right to cut them off from us, the Greeks most recently of all, because the obstinate fellows were slow to recognize the authority of the Roman pontiff.

**Peter** So the see of Rome is the tithe barn of the whole world, so to speak?
**Julius** Is it too much to expect that, having scattered our spiritual seed to all men, we should reap a worldly harvest from all men?
**Peter** What spiritual seed do you mean? All I've heard so far has been the story of a leader of the world, not of the church; not merely worldly, either, but pagan, and even more wicked than the pagans. Your proudest boast is your power to break treaties, to spark off wars, to provoke the slaughter of human beings. This is Satan's power, not the pope's. The man who makes himself vicar of Christ must model himself on him as closely as possible. In him is supreme power, but allied with supreme goodness; supreme wisdom, yet of the simplest kind. In you I see an illusory power combined with supreme wickedness and supreme folly. If the prince of evil, the devil, wanted to choose a vicar, whom better to appoint than a man like you? Tell me, when have you acted like an apostle?
**Julius** What could be more apostolic than to enlarge the church of Christ?
**Peter** But if the church is the Christian people, bound together by the spirit of Christ, you seem to me to have ruined the church by provoking hideous wars throughout the world, so that you could be evil and pestilent with impunity.
**Julius** What we call the church is the holy temples, the priests, particularly the Roman curia, and above all myself, the head of the church.
**Peter** But Christ made us his servants and himself the head. Has a second head grown now? How did you enlarge the church, anyway?
**Julius** Ah, now you're coming to it: listen. The church, once poor and starving, is now enriched with every possible ornament.
**Peter** What ornaments? Warm faith?
**Julius** You're talking nonsense again.
**Peter** Sacred learning?
**Julius** You don't give up, do you?
**Peter** Contempt for the world?
**Julius** Allow me to explain. I'm talking about real ornaments, not mere words like those.
**Peter** What then?
**Julius** Royal palaces, the most handsome horses and mules, hordes of servants, well-trained troops, dainty courtiers ...

**Genius** ... delicious harlots, grovelling pimps ...
**Julius** ... gold, purple, taxes; in fact, such is the wealth and splendour of the Roman pontiff that, by comparison, any king would seem a poor and insignificant fellow; any man, however ambitious, would admit defeat; any man, however extravagant, would condemn his own frugality; and any rich man – a money- lender, even – would look with envy on our wealth. These, I tell you, are the ornaments that I have protected and increased.
**Peter** You still talk of nothing but the world.
**Julius** You must still be dreaming of that ancient church in which, with a few starving bishops, you yourself, a pontiff shivering with cold, were exposed to poverty, sweat, dangers, and a thousand other trials. But now time has changed everything for the better. Now the Roman pontiff is something very different; you were pontiff in name and title only. Ah, if only you could see today the holy temples built for a king's ransom, the thousands of clerics in every country, most of them with enormous incomes, the bishops rivalling the greatest kings with their armies and wealth, the clerics' magnificent palaces! If you could only see, in particular, life in Rome today: all the cardinals in purple, attended by whole regiments of retainers, the horses more than fit for a king, the mules decked in fine cloth, gold and jewels, some even shod with gold and silver! If you could catch a glimpse of the supreme pontiff, carried aloft in a golden chair on the shoulders of his men, while the people on all sides pay homage at a wave of his hand; if you could hear the thunder of the cannon, the blare of the cornets, the blasting of the horns, see the flashes of the guns, and hear the applause of the people, the cheers, the whole scene lit by gleaming torches, even the greatest princes barely permitted to kiss the blessed feet; if you could watch the selfsame Roman priest, on foot this time, placing the golden crown on the head of the Roman emperor, who is the king of all kings (if written laws mean anything: in fact, he receives merely the shadow of a great name); if, I say, you could see and hear all this, what would you say?
**Peter** That I was looking at a tyrant worse than any in the world, the enemy of Christ, the bane of the church.
**Julius** You'd change your tune if you'd witnessed even one of my triumphs, such as my entry into Bologna, my celebrations at Rome after the defeat of Venice, my return to Rome after fleeing Bologna, or

the most recent one after the totally unexpected rout of the French at Ravenna; if you'd seen the ponies, the horses, the columns of armed soldiers, the panoply of the generals, the displays of hand-picked boys, the torches gleaming on all sides, the sumptuous litters, the processions of bishops, the stately cardinals, the trophies, the spoils; if you'd heard the cheers of people and soldiers resounding to the sky, the sound of applause echoing all round, the music of trumpets, the thunder of cornets, and seen the flashes of cannon, the coins thrown to the people, and myself, the leader and prime mover of the whole pageant, carried on high like some god: then you'd call the Scipios, the Aemilii, and the Augusti miserable skinflints compared to me.[29]

**Peter** Whoa! that's enough triumphs, General Braggart! I'd welcome those men, for all they were pagans, out of disgust for you, the most holy Father in Christ who celebrated triumphs after the slaughter of thousands of Christians for your sake, who caused the ruin of so many armies, who never won a single soul for Christ by word or by example. There's fatherly affection for you! O worthy vicar of the Christ who gave himself to save all men, while you have engineered the ruin of the whole world to save your own pestilent head!

**Julius** You're only saying that because you begrudge us our glory, realizing how insignificant your pontificate was compared to ours.

**Peter** Shameless man, do you dare to compare your glory with mine, although the glory is not mine, but Christ's? First of all, if you will allow that Christ is the best and true prince of the church, remember that he gave me the keys of the kingdom in person, that he gave me his sheep to feed, he sealed my faith with his approval. Bribery, fraud, and preoccupation with the things of the world made you pope, if indeed a man like you may be called pope. I won countless thousands of souls for Christ; you led as many to destruction. I was the first to teach Christ to pagan Rome; you have been a teacher of paganism in Christian Rome. I healed the sick with just the shadow of my body, I freed men possessed by devils, I restored the dead to life, and brought abundant blessings to every place I visited. What had your triumphs in common with all this? With one word I was able to consign to Satan anyone I wished: Sapphira and her husband both felt the extent of my power.[30] But whatever power I had, I used for the benefit of all; you benefitted no one, and if you had any power (and even in some cases when you hadn't) you aimed at the general ruin of the world.

**Julius** I'm surprised you don't include in your list of glories poverty, vigils, sweat, trials, prison, chains, abuse, stripes, and finally the cross.
**Peter** You do well to remind me, for I may more justly be proud of those things than of miracles. Christ commanded us to rejoice and exult because of such things; because of such things he called us blessed. In the same way my former colleague Paul, when boasting of his exploits, does not speak of cities taken by storm, of armies put to the sword, of princes of the world called to arms, of tyrannical splendour, but of shipwrecks, chains, scourges, dangers, snares; this is the true triumph of the apostle, this is the glory of the captain of Christ. He boasts of those he got for Christ, of those he called back from ungodliness, not of how many thousands of ducats he amassed. And now, at last, we celebrate an eternal triumph with Christ and even the wicked follow us with praises; there will be no one who will not revile you, except your own sort and your flatterers.
**Julius** I've never heard such things.
**Peter** I can believe it: after all, when did you have time to peruse the Gospels or to read through Paul's letters or mine, absorbed as you were by so many embassies, treaties, plots, armies, and triumphs? The other arts require a mind free from sordid concerns, but the teaching of Christ demands a heart wholly purged of the influence of worldly anxieties. Our great master did not come down from heaven to earth to give to men some easy or common philosophy. It is not a carefree or tranquil profession to be a Christian. To shun all pleasures like poison, to trample riches as if they were dirt, to hold one's life as of no account: this is the profession of the Christian man. Because such things seem intolerable to those who are not guided by the spirit of Christ, they take refuge in empty words and vain ritual, and they invent a false body of Christ to go with the false head of Christ.
**Julius** But what useful thing is left me, if you deprive me of my coin, rob me of my kingdom, strip me of my profit, forbid me my pleasures, if, in short, you take away my life?
**Peter** So you consider that Christ himself was unsuccessful because, although he was the master of all men, he became the butt of all? He spent his whole life in poverty, sweat, fasting, hunger, and thirst, until finally he died the most humiliating of deaths.
**Julius** Well, he may find some to praise him, but none to imitate him; at least, not in this day and age.

**Peter** And yet, in the end, to praise him is itself to imitate him. However, Christ does not deprive his followers of possessions, but enriches them with possessions true and eternal instead of false; none the less, he will not enrich them unless they have first repudiated and purged themselves of all worldly possessions. As he was himself wholly divine, so he wanted his body, that is his church, to be as like him as possible, in other words entirely detached from the evil influences of the world. Otherwise, how could it be like him who sits in heaven, if it is still wallowing in earthly mire? But when the church has shaken free from all the material comforts of the world and, more to the point, all its passions, then at last Christ displays his treasure and, in place of the honeyed pleasures (in fact tinged with much bitterness) left behind, he bestows a taste of heavenly delights, excelling by far those that have been abandoned ...
**Julius** What delights do you mean?
**Peter** Do you think that the gift of prophecy, the gift of knowledge, the gift of miracles are commonplace treasures? Do you think that Christ himself is worth little, when any man who receives him possesses all things in him? And do you think that we live like paupers here? Thus, the more each man suffers on earth, the richer is his joy in Christ; the poorer he is on earth, the wealthier in Christ; the humbler on earth, the more exalted and honoured in Christ; the less he lives in the world, the more he lives in Christ. But Christ not only wished his whole body to be thoroughly pure, but particularly his servants, that is the bishops, and whoever is greater among them, to be nearer to Christ and still less burdened and fettered by worldly possessions. But now I see the opposite of this: the man who wishes to be thought the closest to Christ, and even his equal, is involved with all the most sordid things, money, power, armies, wars, treaties, not to mention vices. And yet, although you are the furthest from Christ, you use the name of Christ to bolster your pride; you act like an earthly tyrant in the name of him who despised the kingdoms of earth, and you claim the honour due to Christ although you are truly Christ's enemy. You give your blessing to others, but are yourself accursed; you open heaven to others, but are yourself totally excluded from it. You consecrate, but are yourself execrated; you excommunicate, but have nothing in common with the saints yourself. What difference is there between you and the sultan of the Turks, except that you shelter behind the

name of Christ? You have the same mentality, the same disgusting way of life, and indeed you are the greater plague upon the world.
**Julius** But I wanted the church to be adorned with all good things. They say that Aristotle divided good things into three categories, those of fortune, those of the body, and those of the mind. I had no intention of changing his order; I began with those of fortune, and would perhaps have soon come to those of the mind, had I not been snatched from the earth by an untimely death.
**Peter** Untimely, indeed! you must be at least seventy. Still, why did you have to mix fire and water?
**Julius** Well, if we have no worldly possessions, the common people will take absolutely no notice of us, whereas now they both hate and fear us. What's more, the whole Christian commonwealth would collapse if it couldn't protect itself against the fury of its enemies.
**Peter** Not at all: if the common people of Christendom were to see in you the true gifts of Christ, such as holiness of life, sacred learning, fervent charity, prophecy, and miracles, they would recognize your greater detachment from worldly possessions and respect you the more for it. The Christian commonwealth would expand and flourish if the gentiles could admire in it purity of life and contempt for pleasures, wealth, power, and death. At the moment, not only is it confined within a tiny area, but if you examine it carefully, you will find many who are Christians in name only. Tell me: while you were supreme shepherd of the church, did you never reflect upon the way in which the church began, grew, and became established? Was it by wars, wealth, horses? Of course not: it was by suffering, the blood of martyrs (including mine), imprisonment, scourges. You claim that the church has grown, when its servants have to bear the burdens of temporal authority; you call it adorned, when it is sullied by the rewards and delights of the world; you call it well defended, when to further the petty interests of the clergy the entire world is embroiled in disastrous wars; you say that it is flourishing, when it is besotted with worldly pleasures; and that it is calm, because it enjoys its riches, or rather its vices, and no one protests. On these grounds you have imposed upon the princes, and under your tutelage they have learned to call their great robberies and mad battles 'the defence of Christ.'
**Julius** I never heard such things before.
**Peter** What did your preachers teach you?

**Julius** I never heard anything but pure praise from them; they roared out fine rhetorical eulogies of me; they declared that I was Jupiter shaking the world with my thunderbolts, that there was something truly divine about me, that I was the common saviour of the world, and a lot more in the same vein.

**Peter** No wonder there was no one to season you, since you were the salt that had lost its savour and a fool. The true role of the apostle is to preach Christ to others, in the purest possible way.

**Julius** You won't open up then?

**Peter** The last person I'd let in is a pestilent fellow like you. In any case, we're all excommunicated, according to you. But would you like some friendly advice? You have a band of energetic followers, an enormous fortune, and you yourself are a great architect; build some new paradise for yourself, but fortify it well to prevent the evil demons capturing it.

**Julius** Never! I shall be true to myself and wait a few months, increasing my army until I can throw you out by force, if you won't surrender. I've no doubt I shall soon be joined by several thousand more soldiers slaughtered in the wars.

**Peter** You pestilent fellow! Oh, unhappy church! Hey, Genius, come here; I'd rather talk to you than to that loathsome monster.

**Genius** What's up?

**Peter** Are the rest of the bishops like him?

**Genius** A good many are cast in the same mould, but he's the pacemaker.

**Peter** I suppose it was you who incited him to all these crimes?

**Genius** Nothing to do with me; in fact, he ran so far ahead that I had trouble keeping up, even with the aid of my wings.

**Peter** I'm really not surprised that so few men reach here, when scoundrels like him have seized the helm of the church. However, I may conclude even from all this, that there's some chance of curing the common people, if they will honour this sink of iniquity simply because he bears the title of pope.

**Genius** That's very true. But my master has been gesticulating at me for some time, and now he's waving his stick; so farewell.

# Shipwreck / *Naufragium*

The following dialogue is one of the *Colloquies*, a book designed to teach schoolboys good Latin. It was first published in 1518 under the title *Familiarium colloquiorum formulae* and became an instant success. In later editions Erasmus added a great deal of new material, often containing elements of social criticism. Consequently the book became controversial, was investigated by the faculty of theology at Paris, and condemned for its 'Lutheran' tendencies.

The dialogue presented here was first published in 1523. Its criticism of superstitious veneration of saints pleased reform- minded readers but caused indignation in conservative clerical circles who considered it irreverent.

This extract will be published in CWE 39–40, translated and annotated by Craig R. Thompson.

ANTONY, ADOLPH

**Antony** Terrible tales you tell! That's what going to sea is like? God forbid any such notion should ever enter my head!
**Adolph** Oh, no, what I've related up to this point is mere sport compared with what you'll hear now.
**Antony** I've heard more than enough of disasters. When you're recalling them I shudder as if I myself were sharing the danger.
**Adolph** To me, on the contrary, troubles over and done with are enjoyable. – On that same night something happened which in large part robbed the skipper of his hope of safety.
**Antony** What, I beseech you?
**Adolph** The night was partially clear, and on the topmast, in the 'crow's-nest' (as I think they call it), stood one of the crew, looking out for land. Suddenly a fiery ball appeared beside him – a very bad sign to sailors when it's a single flame, lucky when it's double. Antiquity believed these were Castor and Pollux.[1]
**Antony** What's their connection with sailors? One was a horseman, the other a boxer.
**Adolph** This is the poets' version. The skipper, who was by the helm,

spoke up: 'Mate' – that's what sailors call one another – 'see your company alongside there?' 'I see it,' the man replied, 'and I hope it's good luck!' Soon the fiery ball slid down the ropes and rolled straight up to the skipper.

**Antony** Wasn't he scared out of his wits?

**Adolph** Sailors get used to marvels. After stopping there a moment, it rolled the whole way round the ship, then dropped through the middle hatches and disappeared. Toward noon the storm began to rage more and more. – Ever seen the Alps?

**Antony** Yes, I've seen them.

**Adolph** Those mountains are warts compared with the waves of the sea. Whenever we were borne on the crest, we could have touched the moon with a finger; whenever we dipped, we seemed to plunge through the gaping earth straight down to hell.

**Antony** What fools they are who trust themselves to the sea!

**Adolph** Since the crew's struggle with the storm was hopeless, the skipper, pale as a ghost, at last came up to us.

**Antony** His pallor portends some great disaster.

**Adolph** 'Friends,' he says, 'I'm no longer master of my ship; the winds have won. The only thing left to do is to put our hope in God and each one prepare himself for the end.'

**Antony** Truly a Scythian speech.[2]

**Adolph** But first of all,' he says, 'the ship must be unloaded; deadly necessity compels it. Better to save life at the cost of goods than for both to perish together.' The plain fact convinced them. A lot of luggage filled with costly wares was tossed overboard.

**Antony** This was sacrificing for sure.

**Adolph** On board was a certain Italian who had served as legate to the king of Scotland. He had a chest full of silver plate, rings, cloth, and silk robes.

**Antony** He didn't want to come to terms with the sea?

**Adolph** No, instead he wanted to go down with his beloved treasures or else be saved along with them. So he protested.

**Antony** What did the skipper do?

**Adolph** 'We're quite willing to let you perish alone with your goods,' he said, 'but it's not fair for all of us to be endangered because of your chest. Rather, we'll throw you and the chest together into the sea.'

**Antony** True sailor's talk!

**Adolph** So the Italian, too, threw his goods overboard, cursing away by heaven and hell because he had entrusted his life to so barbarous an element.

**Antony** I recognize the Italian accent.

**Adolph** Soon afterward the winds, unappeased by our offerings, broke the ropes and tore the sails to pieces.

**Antony** Catastrophe!

**Adolph** At that moment the skipper comes to us again.

**Antony** To make a speech?

**Adolph** 'Friends' – he begins by way of greeting – 'the hour warns each of us to commend himself to God and prepare for death.' Questioned by some familiar with seamanship as to how many hours he thought he could keep the ship afloat, he answered that he couldn't promise anything, but not more than three hours.

**Antony** This speech was even sterner than the first one.

**Adolph** After saying this, he orders all the shrouds to be slashed and the mast sawn off down to its socket and thrown into the sea, together with the spars.

**Antony** Why this?

**Adolph** With the sail ruined or torn, the mast was a useless burden. Our whole hope was in the tiller.

**Antony** What about the passengers meanwhile?

**Adolph** There you'd have seen what a wretched plight we were in: the sailors singing *Salve Regina*, praying to the Virgin Mother, calling her Star of the Sea, Queen of Heaven, Mistress of the World, Port of Salvation, flattering her with many other titles the Sacred Scriptures nowhere assign to her.

**Antony** What has she to do with the sea? She never went voyaging, I believe.

**Adolph** Formerly Venus was protectress of sailors, because she was believed to have been born of the sea. Since she gave up guarding them, the Virgin Mother has succeeded this mother who was not a virgin.

**Antony** You're joking.

**Adolph** Prostrating themselves on the deck, some worshiped the sea, pouring whatever oil they had on the waves, flattering it no differently from the way we do a wrathful sovereign.

**Antony** What did they say?

**Adolph** 'O most merciful sea, O most kind sea, O most splendid sea, O most lovely sea, have pity on us! Save us!' Many songs of this kind they sang to the sea – which was deaf.

**Antony** Absurd superstition! What did the rest do?

**Adolph** Some did nothing but get sick. Many made vows. There was an Englishman who promised heaps of gold to the Virgin of Walsingham if he reached shore alive. Some promised many things to the wood of the Cross at such and such a place; others, again, to that in some other place. The same with respect to the Virgin Mary, who reigns in many places; and they think the vow worthless unless you specify the place.

**Antony** Ridiculous! As if saints don't dwell in heaven.

**Adolph** Some pledged themselves to become Carthusians. There was one who promised to journey to St James at Compostella barefoot, bareheaded, clad only in a coat of mail, begging his bread besides.

**Antony** Did nobody remember Christopher?

**Adolph** I couldn't help laughing as I listened to one chap, who in a loud voice (for fear he wouldn't be heard) promised a wax taper as big as himself to the Christopher in the tallest church in Paris – a mountain rather than a statue. While he was proclaiming this at the top of his lungs, insisting on it again and again, an acquaintance who chanced to be standing by nudged him with his elbow and cautioned: 'Be careful what you promise. Even if you sold all your goods at auction, you couldn't pay for it.' Then the other, lowering his voice – so Christopher wouldn't overhear him, of course – said, 'Shut up, you fool. Do you suppose I'm serious? If I once touch land, I won't give him a tallow candle.'

**Antony** Blockhead! Batavian, I suppose.[3]

**Adolph** No, a Zeelander.

**Antony** I'm surprised nobody thought of the apostle Paul, who was once on a voyage and when the ship broke leaped overboard and reached land. No stranger to misfortune, he knew how to help those in distress.

**Adolph** Paul wasn't mentioned.

**Antony** Did they pray all the while?

**Adolph** Strenuously. One chanted *Salve Regina*, another *Credo in Deum*. Some had certain queer beads, like charms, to ward off danger.

**Antony** How devout men are made by suffering! In prosperity the thought of God or saint never enters their heads. What were you doing all this time? Making vows to any of the saints?

**Adolph** Not at all.

**Antony** Why?

**Adolph** Because I don't make deals with saints. For what else is that but a bargain according to the form 'I'll give this if you do that' or 'I'll do this if you'll do that'; 'I'll give a taper if I can swim to safety'; 'I'll go to Rome if you rescue me.'

**Antony** But you called on some saint for help?

**Adolph** Not even that.

**Antony** But why?

**Adolph** Because heaven's a large place. If I entrust my safety to some saint – St Peter, for example, who perhaps will be first to hear, since he stands at the gate – I may be dead before he meets God and pleads my cause.

**Antony** What did you so, then?

**Adolph** Went straight to the Father himself, reciting the Our Father. No saint hears sooner than he or more willingly grants what is asked.

**Antony** But didn't your conscience accuse you when you did this? Weren't you afraid to entreat the Father, whom you had offended by so many sins?

**Adolph** To speak frankly, my conscience did deter me somewhat. But I soon recovered my spirits, thinking to myself, 'No father is so angry with his son that, if he sees him in danger in a stream or lake, he won't grasp him by the hair and pull him to shore.' Of all the passengers, none behaved more calmly than a certain woman who was suckling a baby.

**Antony** What did she do?

**Adolph** She was the only one who didn't scream, weep, or make promises; she simply prayed in silence, clasping her little boy. – While the ship was continually battered by the sea, the skipper girded it with ropes both fore and aft, for fear it might break to pieces.

**Antony** Miserable protection!

**Adolph** Meantime an old priest, a man of sixty named Adam, jumped up. Stripped to his underclothes, and with his shoes and leggings removed, he urged us all to prepare likewise for swimming. And standing so in the middle of the ship, he preached to us a sermon from Gerson[4] on the five truths concerning the benefit of confession, exhorting everyone to be ready both for life and for death. A Dominican was there, too. Those who wished confessed to these two.

**Antony** What did you do?

**Adolph** Seeing everything in an uproar, I confessed silently to God, condemning my unrighteousness before him and imploring his mercy.

**Antony** Where would you have gone had you died in that condition?

**Adolph** That I left to God the Judge, for I was unwilling to be judge of my own cause; nevertheless a strong hope possessed my mind the whole time. – While all this is going on, the captain returns to us in tears. 'Get ready,' says he, 'because the ship will be useless to us in a quarter of an hour.' It was already shattered in some places and drawing water. Soon afterward a sailor reports seeing a church tower in the distance and beseeches us to appeal to whichever saint took that church under his protection. Everyone falls to his knees and prays to the unknown saint.

**Antony** If you had invoked him by name, he might have heard.

**Adolph** We didn't know his name. As much as he could, meanwhile, the skipper steered the ship in that direction. By now it was breaking up, taking in water everywhere, and clearly about to fall to pieces had it not been undergirded with ropes.

**Antony** A bad state of affairs!

**Adolph** We were carried far enough in for the inhabitants of the place to see our plight. Groups of them rushed to the shore, and taking off hats and coats and sticking them on poles urged us toward themselves and by lifting their arms to heaven indicated their pity for our lot.

**Antony** I'm waiting to hear what happened.

**Adolph** The whole ship was filled with water now, so that thereafter we would be no safer in ship than in sea.

**Antony** At that moment you had to fall back on your last hope, your sacred anchor.

**Adolph** A miserable one. The crew bailed out the lifeboat and lowered it into the sea. Everyone tried to hurl himself into it, the sailors protesting in the uproar that the lifeboat would not hold such a crowd but that everybody should grab what he could and swim. The situation did not allow leisurely plans. One person snatches an oar, another a boathook, another a tub, another a bucket, another a plank; and, each relying on his own resources, they commit themselves to the waves.

**Antony** What happened during this time to that poor woman, the only one who did not weep and wail?
**Adolph** She was the first of them all to reach shore.
**Antony** How could she do that?
**Adolph** We had put her on a warped plank and tied her in such a way that she couldn't easily fall off. We gave her a small board to use as a paddle, wished her luck, and shoved her off into the waves, pushing with a pole to get her clear of the ship, where the danger lay. Holding her baby with her left hand, she paddled with the right.
**Antony** Brave woman!
**Adolph** Since nothing else remained, one man seized a wooden statue of the Virgin Mother, now rotten and mouse-eaten, and, putting his arms around it, began to swim.
**Antony** Did the lifeboat come through safely?
**Adolph** The first to go down. And thirty people had thrown themselves into it.
**Antony** What mishap caused that?
**Adolph** Before it could get away it was overturned by the lurching of the big ship.
**Antony** A cruel business! What then?
**Adolph** While looking out for others, I nearly perished myself.
**Antony** How so?
**Adolph** Because there was nothing left for me to swim on.
**Antony** Cork would have been useful there.
**Adolph** In that emergency I would rather have had plain cork tree than golden candlestick. Casting about, I finally thought of the stump of the mast. Since I couldn't pry it loose by myself, I enlisted the help of another man. Supporting ourselves on this, we put to sea, I holding the right end and he the left. While we were tossing about in this way, that priest who preached on board threw himself in our midst – on our shoulders. Big fellow, too. 'Who's the third?' we yell. 'He'll be the death of us all.' He, on the other hand, says calmly, 'Cheer up, there's plenty of room. God will help us.'
**Antony** Why was he so late in starting to swim?
**Adolph** Oh, he was to be in the lifeboat along with the Dominican (for everybody conceded this much honour to him), but although they had confessed to each other on the ship, nevertheless some condition –

I don't know what – had been forgotten. There on the edge of the ship they confess anew, and each lays his hand on the other. While they're doing this, the lifeboat goes down. Adam told me this.

**Antony** What became of the Dominican?

**Adolph** According to Adam, after entreating the aid of the saints he threw off his clothes and began to swim.

**Antony** Which saints did he invoke?

**Adolph** Dominic, Thomas, Vincent, and I don't know which Peter, but first and foremost he placed his trust in Catherine of Siena.[5]

**Antony** Christ didn't come to mind?

**Adolph** This is what the priest told me.

**Antony** He'd have swum better if he hadn't thrown off his sacred cowl. With that put aside, how could Catherine of Siena recognize him? – But go on with what happened to you.

**Adolph** While we were still tossing beside the ship, which was rolling from side to side at the will of the waves, the broken rudder smashed the thigh of the man who was holding on to the left end of the stump. So he was torn away. The priest, saying a prayer *Requiem aeternam*[6] for him, took his place, urging me to keep hold of my end with confidence and kick my feet vigorously. We were swallowing a lot of salt water all this while. Thus Neptune saw to it that we had not only a salty bath but even a salty drink, though the priest showed us a remedy for that.

**Antony** What, please?

**Adolph** Every time a wave came rushing upon us, he turned the back of his head to it and kept his mouth closed.

**Antony** That's a doughty old fellow you describe.

**Adolph** When we'd made some progress after swimming a while, the priest, who was very tall, said, 'Cheer up, I'm touching bottom.' I didn't dare hope for such great luck. 'We're too far from shore to hope for bottom.' 'Oh, no,' he replied, 'I feel land with my feet.' 'Maybe it's something from the chests that the sea has rolled this way.' 'No,' he said, 'I feel land plainly by the scraping of my toes.' After we had swum a while longer in this direction and he again touched bottom, 'Do what you think best,' he said, 'I'm giving up the whole mast to you and trusting myself to the bottom,' and thereupon, after waiting for the waves to subside, he went on foot as fast as he could. When the waves overtook him again, he resisted by clasping his knees with his hands and putting his head under water, as divers and ducks do; when the waves receded, up he popped and moved on. When I saw he was successful at this, I imitated him. Standing on the coast were men – hardy fellows and used to the water – who by means of long poles, held out from one to the other, braced themselves against the force of the waves; so that the one farthest out held his pole to the swimmer. When this was grasped, all heaved toward shore and the swimmer was hauled safely to dry land. A number were rescued by this device.

**Antony** How many?

**Adolph** Seven, but two of these died of exhaustion when brought to a fire.

**Antony** How many were you in the ship?

**Adolph** Fifty-eight.

**Antony** O cruel sea! At least it might have been satisfied with a tenth, which is enough for priests. From so large a number how few returned!

**Adolph** We were treated with wonderful kindness by the people there, who looked after our needs with astonishing eagerness: lodging, fire, food, clothing, money for travel.

**Antony** What people were they?

**Adolph** Hollanders.

**Antony** No people could be more kindly, though they do have savage neighbours. I guess you won't visit Neptune very soon again after this.

**Adolph** No, not unless God takes my reason from me.

**Antony** And I for my part would rather hear such tales than experience the events at first hard.

# *ERASMUS AND POLITICS* 5

## The Education of a Christian Prince / *Institutio principis christiani*

Published in May 1516, *The Education of a Christian Prince* was dedicated to Prince Charles, the future Emperor Charles v, to whose council Erasmus had been appointed a few months earlier. It belongs to a genre of advisory literature that has a long history, from Plato's *Republic* in antiquity to Machiavelli's *The Prince* and More's *Utopia* in Erasmus' own time. Erasmus' tract differed from these manuals of statecraft in that it focused on the Christian prince, that is, the ruler who would bear out the *philosophia Christi* outlined in *The Handbook of the Christian Soldier*. The *Education of a Christian Prince* saw ten editions during Erasmus' lifetime and was translated into a number of vernacular languages, which testifies to a general interest in the work. Of particular significance is the pacifist content of the last chapters which recurs in other 'peace classics,' such as the adage *War Is Sweet to Those Who Know It Not / Dulce bellum inexpertis* and *A Complaint of Peace*, which appears below 288–314.

This extract is taken from CWE 27 245–88, translated and annotated by Neil M. Cheshire and Michael J. Heath.

### The prince must avoid flatterers

The prince must avoid flatterers; but this cannot be brought about unless flatterers are kept at bay by every means, for the well-being of great princes is extremely vulnerable to this particular plague. Youthful innocence in itself is particularly exposed to this evil, partly because of the natural inclination to enjoy compliments more than the truth, and partly because of inexperience: the less suspicious the prince is of trickery, the less he knows about taking precautions.

And in case anyone thinks that this can be ignored as a trivial misfortune, he should realize that the most flourishing empires of the greatest kings have been overthrown by the flatterer's tongue. Nowhere do we read of a state oppressed by implacable tyranny without a flatterer playing a leading part in the tragedy.

Unless I am mistaken, this is what Diogenes[1] had in mind when he replied to the question 'What is the most dangerous animal of all?' 'If you mean wild animals,' he said 'the tyrant; if you mean tame ones, a flatterer.'

This pest has a certain attractive poison, but it acts so quickly that once the princes who rule the world are deranged by it they have allowed themselves to become the playthings of the most vile flatterers and to be taken for a ride by them; these repulsively depraved little men, and sometimes even slaves, were masters of the masters of the world.

In the first place, therefore, it will be necessary to see that nurses are employed who are either completely immune to this disease or at any rate the least susceptible to it. For their very sex tends to make them especially vulnerable to this evil; then again, most nurses take on the emotional tendencies of mothers, the majority of whom frequently spoil the characters of their children by over-indulgence. Indeed, this whole group should be kept away from the future prince as far as possible, since they have inherited more or less in their very nature the two great faults of foolishness and flattery.

The next concern will be to provide him with well-bred companions (though they will also need some grooming to this end from his tutor) to become his friends but not his flatterers and to create an atmosphere of civilized talk without ever using pretence or lies to gain favour. As to the choice of the tutor, I have already spoken about that.

The question of the prince's attendants is not an insignificant one either, for they often pander to a boy's predilections, either through stupidity or in the hope that some sort of recompense will come their way. It will therefore be necessary to fill these positions as far as possible with men who are prudent and honest, and beyond that to deter them by means of warnings and threats from being too permissive, and even further to use rewards to induce them to perform their function conscientiously. This cause will indeed be greatly advanced if anyone who has been caught giving encouragement and ignoble subservience in such a way as to spur the prince's mind toward things that are beneath the dignity of a prince is punished in public as an example to others (even by death if the nature of his offence requires it). Since we have the death penalty (and that beyond all the laws of the ancients) for a thief who steals a bit of money that he has come across, it ought not to seem cruel to anyone if the ultimate penalty is invoked for someone who has tried to corrupt the best and most precious thing that the country possesses. But the novelty of the idea may prevent its acceptance, although the Roman emperor Alexander ordered a seller of empty promises[2] called Thurinus to be bound to a stake and smoked to death by green logs set alight at his feet. In that case, it might be possible to construct an example artificially by finding a man who has already been convicted of some other capital offence and having it advertised that he was executed for contaminating the mind of the future prince with the plague of flattery.

If in fixing the penalty one is to take account of the harm done, then a plague of a flatterer does more damage to the state by corrupting and contaminating those first years of the prince with the ideas of a tyrant than does someone who steals from the public treasury. Anyone who has debased the prince's coinage is visited with ingeniously devised punishments, whereas there seem almost to be a reward for those who debase the prince's mind.

If only that dictum of Carneades[3] were less true at least among us Christians: he said that royal sons could not learn anything properly except horse-riding because in all other things everybody humoured and flattered them, but since a mere horse doesn't know whether he is being ridden by a nobleman or a commoner, by a rich man or a poor man, by a prince or a private individual, he throws off his back anyone who rides him incompetently. But it is a fact, as we too often see, that not only do nurses, companions, and attendants flatter a prince's children, but even the very tutor who has been trusted to form the boy's character conducts his business with a view not to passing out a better prince but to walking out a richer man himself. Quite often even those who preach on religious matters speak ingratiatingly, fishing for the favour of the prince and his court, or if they have some criticism to make, they mouth it in such a way that it becomes the greatest flattery. I do not say this because I think that the use of inflammatory language to rant against the lives of princes should be encouraged, but because I would like preachers to put forward a positive example of a good prince without abuse and not to approve in the Christian prince by obsequious connivance what the pagans have condemned in pagan princes. Officers of state do not give frank advice and counsellors do not consult with him with enough openness of heart. For since the nobility have rival interests among themselves, they all vie with one another in courting the prince's approval, either to put down an opponent or to avoid providing an enemy with a rod for their own backs. The priests are flatterers and the physicians are yes-men. It is now the custom everywhere to listen to undiluted praise from orators sent from abroad. There used to be one sheet-anchor remaining, but even that is now unreliable: I mean of course those whom the common people call 'royal confessors.' If they were sincere and prudent, surely they would be able to give the prince friendly and sincere advice in that uttermost privacy which they enjoy. And yet it very often happens that while each one is looking out for his own interests the means of serving the common good are neglected. Less harm indeed is done by poets and orators, who are all by now well versed in the practice of taking the measure for a prince's praise not from his deserts but from their own inspiration. Far more damaging are people like magicians and soothsayers who promise kings long life, victory, triumphs, pleasures, and kingdoms and then again threaten others with sudden death, disaster, affliction, and exile, trading upon hope and fear, the two chief tyrants of human life, in the process. Astrologers, who foretell the future from the stars, belong to the same class, but this is not the place to discuss whether theirs is a genuine science. Certainly, however, the hold they now have over the ordinary man presents no small problem to humanity.

But the most pernicious flatterers of all are those who operate with apparent frankness but in some remarkable way contrive to urge you on while seeming to restrain you and to praise you while seeming to criticize. Plutarch[4] has portrayed them marvellously in a short essay entitled 'How to Distinguish a Friend from a Flatterer.'

Now there are two times of life which are especially vulnerable to flattery: childhood because of inexperience and old age because of mental impairment. Folly, however, appears at any age and always brings self-love along with it. And Plato was right to warn us that the most dangerous kind of flattery is when someone is his own flatterer and as a result readily lays himself open to other people doing the same thing as he himself did of his own accord.

There is a certain implicit flattery in portraits, statues, and inscriptions. Thus Apelles[5] flattered Alexander the Great by painting him brandishing a thunderbolt; and Octavius[6] enjoyed being painted in the likeness of Apollo. The same thing goes for those huge 'colossus' statues, greater than life-size, which they used to erect to emperors in the past. A point that may seem trivial to some people, but is nevertheless of considerable importance here, is that artists should represent the prince in the dress and manner that is most worthy of a wise and distinguished prince. And it is preferable to depict him engaged in some aspect of state business rather than at leisure: for example, Alexander holding a hand over one ear while he attends to a trial, or Darius holding a pomegranate, or Scipio restoring to a young man his betrothed wife untouched and rejecting the gold which was offered to him.[7] It is right that the halls of princes should be decorated with fine pictures of this sort, and not with those that encourage debauchery, arrogance, or tyranny.

Now as regards honorary titles, I would not myself deny to the prince his tribute of respect, but I would prefer them to be of such a kind that they remind the prince in some way of his office: that is, I would prefer him to be called Most Honourable, Most Blameless, Most Wise, Most Merciful, Most Beneficent, Most Prudent, Most Watchful, Most Temperate, Most Patriotic; rather than the Famous, the Invincible, the Triumphant, the Ever-August, not to mention the 'Highnesses,' 'Sacred Majesties,' 'Divinities,' and even more flattering titles than these. I approve of the present custom honouring the Roman pontiff with the title 'his Holiness' because by hearing it continually he is reminded in what way he ought to excel and what is his finest quality: not having great wealth or a far-flung empire, but being pre-eminent in holiness.

But if it is inevitable that the prince should hear this sort of title sometimes, even against his will, nevertheless he ought not to hide his feelings about what would please him better. Alexander Severus[8] is said to have regarded all flatterers with such hatred that if anybody saluted him too obsequiously or bowed his head too humbly, he would at once noisily denounce the man and send him packing; and if a man's rank or office saved him from loud denunciation, he was rebuked by a grim countenance.

The boy must therefore be instructed in advance to turn those titles which he is forced to hear to his own advantage. When he hears 'Father of His Country,' let him reflect that no title given to princes more precisely squares with being a good prince than does 'Father of His Country'; consequently he must act in such a way that he is seen to be worthy of that title. If he thinks in this way, it will have been a reminder; if not, flattery.

When he is called 'Invincible,' let him think how absurd it is to call invincible a man who is conquered by anger, a slave to lust every single day, and the prisoner of ambition, which leads and drives him where it likes. He should think a man truly invincible only when he does not give in to any emotion and cannot be deflected from what is right by any circumstance.

When he is designated 'Serene,' let it come to mind that it is the prince's duty to keep everything peaceful and harmonious. But if anyone disrupts and confuses the order of things by revolts and the upheavals of war, whether out of ambition or anger, the title of 'the Serene' is no ornament for him but flings his crime in his face.

When he is called 'the Famous,' let him reflect that no accolade is valid except that which arises from integrity and good actions. For if anyone is depraved by desire, corrupted by greed, or defiled by ambition, then the title 'the Famous' is nothing but a warning if he is going astray inadvertently, or a condemnation if he knows he is doing wrong.

When he hears the names of his territories, let him not immediately swell with pride at being the master of such great affairs, but let him reflect what a multitude they are to whom he must be a good prince.

If anyone offers him 'your Highness,' 'your Majesty,' 'the Divine,' he will remember that these are valid only for someone who governs his realm according to the example of God with a kind of heavenly magnanimity.

When he listens to solemn eulogies, let him not immediately believe or approve of such praise of himself, but if he is not yet such a person as they make him out to be, let him regard it as an admonition and energetically pursue the goal of some day living up to that praise. If he already is such a person, he must strive to improve upon himself.

Indeed even the laws themselves will have to be held under suspicion, for even they sometimes collude with the prince; and no wonder, because they have been either collated or instituted by those who were under the thumb of kings or emperors. When they say that the prince is above the law, when they submit themselves to him; and when they accord him jurisdiction over all things, he must beware that he does not immediately get the idea that he is allowed to do whatever he pleases. To a good prince you can safely allow everything, to an average one not everything, to a bad one nothing.

Demetrius Phalereus[9] shrewdly recommends the prince to read books, because very often he may learn from these what his friends have not dared to bring to his attention. But in this matter he must be equipped in advance with an antidote, as it were, along these lines: 'This writer whom you are reading is a pagan and you are a Christian reader; although he has many excellent things to say, he nevertheless does not depict the ideal of a Christian prince quite accurately, and you must take care not to think that whatever you come across at any point is to be imitated straight away, but instead test everything against the standard of Christ.'

But first, indeed, comes the selection of authors, for it matters a great deal what books a boy reads and absorbs first. Bad conversation defiles the mind, and bad reading does so no less. For those silent letters are transformed into conduct and feelings, especially if they have taken hold of the mind which is prone to some defect; for example, it will take very little to incite a naturally wild and violent boy to tyranny if, without being equipped with an antidote, he reads about Achilles or Alexander the Great or Xerxes or Julius Caesar.

But today we see a great many people enjoying the stories of Arthur and Lancelot and other legends of that sort, which are not only tyrannical but also utterly illiterate, foolish, and on the level of old wives' tales, so that it would be more advisable to put one's reading time into the comedies or the myths of the poets rather than into that sort of drivel.

But if any tutor wants my advice, as soon as the boy has a grasp of language he should present the proverbs of Solomon, Ecclesiasticus, and the Book of Wisdom, not so that the lad is tormented by the notorious four senses at the hands of a meretricious interpreter, but so that he may be shown briefly and conveniently whatever is relevant to the office of a good prince. In the first place a liking for the writer and his work must be inculcated. 'You are destined for kingship,' one can say, 'this author teaches the art of being a king. You are the son of a king and a future king yourself; you will hear what the wisest king of all teaches his own son whom he is preparing for succession to the throne.' Next the Gospels; and here it is very important in what way you kindle a love of the author and the work in the boy's mind. For a good deal will depend upon the interpreter's ingenuity and fluency in communicating concisely, clearly, convincingly, and even excitingly not everything, but those things which are particularly relevant to the prince's role and which serve to rid his mind of the dangerous attitudes of commonplace princes. Thirdly, the *Apophthegms* of Plutarch and then his *Moralia*; for you can find nothing sounder than these, and I would prefer his *Lives* to be prescribed rather than those of anyone else. The next place after Plutarch I would readily assign to Seneca, for his writings excite and inspire the reader in a wonderful way to cultivate integrity and lift his spirit high above worldly concerns, especially in their repeated denunciation of tyranny. A good many extracts very worthy of attention can properly be taken from the *Politics* of Aristotle and the *Offices* of Cicero but, in my opinion, Plato has the purer message on this subject, and Cicero followed him to some extent in his book on *The Laws* (for the latter's *Republic* is lost).

Now I would not deny, to be sure, that very considerable wisdom can be gathered from reading the historians, but you will also take in the most destructive ideas from these same writers unless you are forearmed and read selectively.

## Revenue and taxation

If we scour the history of the Ancients we shall find that many revolts were occasioned by excessive taxation. Consequently the good prince will have to take care that the feelings of the populace are roused as little as possible on this account. He should rule without cost to the people if he can, for the position of prince is too noble to be commercialized with propriety. And the good prince has in his possession whatever his affectionate subjects possess.

There were many pagans who took nothing back home except glory from the good service they gave to the state. There were one or two, such as Fabius Maximus and Antoninus Pius,[10] who rejected the glory also. How much more ought a Christian prince to be content with the knowledge that he has done what is right, especially since he is in the service of one who does not fail to reward right actions richly?

There are some prince's agents whose only concern is to squeeze as much as possible out of the populace on one fresh pretext after another in the belief that they are properly serving the interests of their princes, as if the latter were the enemies of their people. But let anyone who chooses to pay attention to such men realize that he is a long way from the title of 'prince.'

Rather should his efforts and deliberations be directed to this end, that as little as possible should be exacted from the people. The most welcome way of increasing revenue would be for the prince to abolish superfluous expenditure, to disband redundant offices, to avoid wars and foreign tours (which are very like wars), to check the acquisitiveness of officialdom, and to pay more attention to the just administration of his territory than to its expansion.

Otherwise, if he assesses taxation to his greed or ambitions, what control or limit will there be in the end? For avarice is boundless, continually goading and putting pressure on what it has set afoot until, as the old proverb has it, the last straw breaks the camel's back and revolution eventually glares up when the people's patience is exhausted – a situation which has put an end to empires which were at one time highly prosperous.

So if necessity requires some taxation of the people, then it is the good prince's job to do it in such a way that the least possible hardship falls on the poor. For it is perhaps politic to summon the rich to austerity, but to reduce poor people to hunger and servitude is both very cruel and very risky.

When he is thinking of increasing his retinue, when he is anxious to make a brilliant marriage for his grand-daughter or sister, or to raise all his sons to his own status, or to make his nobles wealthy, or to display his substance to other countries while on foreign tours, then the conscientious ruler must continually remind himself how cruel it is that on these accounts so many thousands of men with their wives and children should be starving to death at home, getting into debt, and being driven to complete desperation. For those people who extort from the poor what they basely squander on women and gambling would not count in my judgment even as men, let alone as princes. Yet they do exist (or so rumour has it) and believe that they have the right to behave even in this way.

Indeed the prince should weigh up this further consideration, that it is impossible for a measure ever to be abolished, once it has been introduced to meet some temporary situation, if it seems to be to the financial advantage of the prince or the nobility. When the need for a tax has passed, not only should the people's burden be lifted but as far as possible their expenditure during that previous period should be reimbursed in compensation. Accordingly, someone who is well disposed to his people will beware of establishing an insidious precedent; for if he takes pleasure in the misfortunes of his people or neglects their interests, then he does not amount to a prince whatever his title may be.

Care must be taken meanwhile that discrepancies in wealth are not excessive: not that I would want anyone to be forcibly deprived of his goods, but some system should be operated to prevent the wealth of the many from being allocated to the few. Plato, for one, wants his citizens to be neither too rich nor on the other hand particularly poor, since the poor man is unable to make social contribution while the rich man is unwilling to do so by using his own talents. How is it that princes quite often do not even get rich from taxes of this sort? Anyone who wants to understand this may reflect on how much less our ancestors received from their subjects, and yet how much more generous they were and how much more profusely they were supplied with all things; the reason is that the best part of the revenue now slips through the fingers of these gatherers and receivers, mentioned above, and only a tiny part reaches the prince himself.

The good prince will therefore impose as little tax as possible on those things whose use is shared also by the poorest ranks of the people, such as corn, bread, beer, wine, clothes, and all the other things without which human life cannot be carried on. But these things at present carry a very heavy burden, and in more than one way: first by the very heavy taxes which the revenue agents extort (and which the people call 'assizes'), then by import duties, which even have their own agents to themselves, and lastly by the monopolies. In order that a very little income may get back to the prince from these sources, the poorer people are milked dry by this expenditure.

Much the best way, therefore, of increasing the value of the prince's income, as has been said, is to reduce his outgoing costs, and even in his case the proverb holds good that thrift is a great source of revenue. But if it is unavoidable that some levy be made, and the people's interests demand such action, then let the burden fall on those foreign and imported goods which are not so much necessities of life as luxurious and pleasurable refinements and whose use is confined to the rich, such as cotton, silk, dyed cloth, pepper, spices, ointments, jewels, and anything else of this kind. For in this way the inconvenience will be felt only by those who have the good fortune to be able to bear it; and the expense will not render them destitute but will perhaps make them less extravagant, so that what they lose in money is made good to them in a moral benefit.

In the coinage of money the good prince will display the trustworthiness he owes both to God and to the people, and will not allow himself to do things for which he punishes other people most harshly. The people are commonly robbed in four ways over this business, as we saw for some considerable time after the death of Charles, when a kind of protracted anarchy more dangerous than tyranny afflicted your kingdom: first, when the material for the coinage is contaminated by some sort of alloy; secondly, when it is underweight; next, when it is reduced by clipping round the edge; lastly, when it is constantly being devalued and revalued whenever it is seen to be to the advantage of the royal treasury.

## Generosity in the prince

If kindliness and generosity are the special glory of good princes, how can certain people lay claim to the title of prince when their whole policy is directed towards fostering their own interests at the expense of everyone else? The skilful and vigilant prince will therefore seek ways of helping everyone, and that does not mean simply by handing out gifts. He will assist some by his liberality and raise up others by his support; he will use his authority to restore those who are cast down and his advice to help others. In fact, he will be inclined to regard as wasted any day in which he has not used his power for good to help someone.

The prince's bounty must not be distributed recklessly, however. Some extort ruthlessly from good citizens what they squander on jesters, informers, and those who minister to their pleasures. The state should be aware that the prince will most often show kindness towards those who work hardest for the common good. Generosity should be the reward of virtue, not the result of a whim.

The prince must try especially to practise the sort of generosity that involves no disadvantage, or at least no harm, to anyone else. Robbing one group to enrich another, ruining some to advance others: far from being services, such actions are disservices twice over, particularly if what has been taken from worthy men is turned over to the unworthy.

Not for nothing do the myths of the poets tell us how the gods never visited a place without conferring some great benefit on those who received them. But if, at the approach of their prince, his citizens hide any elegant furniture, lock up their pretty daughters, send away their young sons, conceal their wealth, and do all they can to make themselves inconspicuous: is it not obvious what they think of him, since they act exactly as they would at the approach of an enemy or a robber? Since on their prince's arrival they fear for all the things it should be his duty to protect against the threat of treachery or violence? They fear treachery from the others, but they fear violence too from him: one man complains that he has been beaten up, another that his daughter had been abducted, another that his wife has been raped, and yet another that some trifling payment has been withheld. What a difference, indeed, between this prince's arrival and those descriptions of the gods! The more prosperous a city the more it suspects the prince, and on the prince's arrival all the more disreputable elements rush out, whereas all the best and wisest citizens are put on their guard and keep themselves to themselves; even if they say nothing, their actions proclaim their opinion of the prince. Someone may reply to this: 'I cannot keep a check on the activities of all my followers; I am doing my best.' Make your followers understand that you really have your heart set on this course, and I shall be very surprised if that will not keep them in check. In the end, you will convince the people that such crimes are committed against your will only if you do not allow them to go unpunished.

It was perhaps sufficient for a pagan prince to be generous towards his own citizens, but merely just towards foreigners. But it is the mark of a Christian prince to consider no one a foreigner except those who are strangers to the sacraments of Christ, and to avoid provoking even these by doing them injury. Of course he must fulfil his obligations towards his own citizens first, but for the rest, as far as possible, he should help all men.

Although it should be the prince's constant concern to protect everyone from harm, yet, as Plato suggests, he should make more diligent efforts to prevent harm befalling visitors than his own citizens, because visitors, bereft of the support of friends and relations, are more exposed to danger; for this reason they were thought to be under Jupiter's protection, and gave him the name *Xenios*.[11]

**Enacting or amending laws**

The principal method of making a city or kingdom prosperous is to have the best laws under the best of princes; the happiest situation arises when the prince is obeyed by all and himself obeys the laws, provided that these conform to the ideals of justice and honour and have no other purpose than to advance the interests of all.

The good, wise, and upright prince is simply a sort of embodiment of the law. He will therefore spare no effort to enact the best possible laws, those most beneficial to the state, rather than a great number. A very small number of laws will be sufficient in a well-ordered state under a good prince and honest magistrates, and if things are otherwise, no amount of laws will suffice. When an incompetent doctor tries one remedy after another, his patients tend to suffer.

In enacting laws, special care must be taken to ensure that they do not smell of profit for the privy purse or of special treatment for the nobility; everything should be related to an ideal standard of honour and to the public interest, and this should be defined, not by the opinion of the mob, but according to the precepts of wisdom, which should always be present at the councils of princes; in other words, as the pagans also agree, there will be no true law unless it is just, fair, and conducive to the common good. Nor does something become law simply because the prince has so decided, unless the decision is that of a wise and good prince, who will decide on nothing that is not honourable and in the best interests of the state. If the standards by which wrongdoing is to be judged are themselves distorted, the only result will be that even things that were just will be perverted by laws of this kind.

The law should not only prescribe penalties for wrongdoers but also provide rewards to encourage service to the state. We know that the Ancients had many laws of this kind: anyone who had distinguished himself in battle could hope for a reward, and if he fell, his children were brought up at public expense; anyone who had rescued a citizen, thrown down an enemy from the walls, or assisted the state with sound advice was entitled to a reward.

Of course the better sort of citizen will always follow the best course even if no reward is offered, but these inducements are useful to inspire the less well educated to pursue an honorable course.

Men of noble character are more interested in honour; the baser sort are attracted by money too. Thus a law will make use of all these methods to influence men: honour and disgrace, profit and loss. Finally, men of thoroughly servile, or rather bestial, disposition must be tamed by chains and the lash.

Citizens should be familiar with this sense of honour and disgrace from boyhood onwards, so that they know that rewards are given for good conduct rather than for wealth or connections.

In short, the vigilant prince should direct his best efforts, not simply to punishing crime, but to looking beyond that, and taking pains to ensure that no crime worthy of punishment is committed in the first place.

A doctor who prevents disease and keeps it away is better than one who expels it with medicine once it is established. Similarly, it is far better to ensure that no offenses at all are committed than to punish them once they have been perpetrated. This will be achieved if the prince can destroy, if possible, or at least check and reduce anything that he has noted as a likely source of criminal behaviour.

First, as we have said, the vast majority of crimes spring, as if from a muddy fountain, from perverted ideas about the state of things. Your first aim therefore should be to have citizens in whom the best of principles have been implanted, and your second, that the magistrates should be not only wise but uncorrupted.

Plato rightly warns that everything else must be tried, that no stone, as they say, should be left unturned, before the supreme penalty is invoked. To persuade men not to break the law, you must first use reasoned arguments, then, as a deterrent, the fear of divine vengeance against criminals, and in addition threats of punishment. If these are ineffective, you must resort to punishment, but of a comparatively light kind, more to cure the disease than to kill the patient. If none of this successful, then at last the law must reluctantly cut the criminal off, like a hopeless, incurable limb, to prevent the infection spreading to the healthy part.

A reliable and skilful doctor will not resort to amputation or cauterization if he can cure the disease by compresses or a draught of medicine, and will never fall back on them unless compelled by the illness to do so. In the same way, the prince will try all other remedies before resorting to capital punishment, remembering that the state is one body; no one cuts off a limb if it can be resorted to health in some other way.

In applying his treatment, the conscientious doctor concentrates on getting rid of the illness with the minimum of danger to his patient; similarly, in framing his laws, the good prince will consider nothing but the public interest and seek to remedy the ills of the people with the minimum of discomfort.

A good many crimes arise particularly from the fact that in every country riches are prized and poverty is scorned. The prince will therefore strive to ensure that his subjects are respected for good conduct and good character rather than for wealth, and he should apply this first to himself and his court. If the people see the prince flaunting his wealth, if they see that at his court the richest men are the most admired and that the road to the magistracy, honours, and public office is open to cash, then of course all this will incite the common people to acquire wealth by fair means or foul.

Now, to speak more generally, many of the pitfalls which exist in every state are the result of idleness, which everyone seeks in different ways. Once men have acquired a taste for it, they turn to the paths of evil if they lack the means to provide for it. The vigilant prince will therefore ensure that he has as few idlers as possible among his subjects, either making them work or banishing them from the state.

Plato thinks that all beggars must be driven out of his republic. But if there are men broken by illness or old age, with no family to care for them, they should be looked after in state institutions for the old and the sick. A man who is in good health and satisfied with little will not need to beg.

The inhabitants of Marseille refused entry to some priests who, in order to live in idleness and luxury under the guide of religion, used to hawk certain sacred relics from town to town. Perhaps, too, it would be to the state's advantage to limit the number of monasteries. For monastic life too is a kind of idleness, especially for those whose lives have been far from blameless and who now fritter away lethargic lives in idleness. My remarks about monasteries apply to colleges as well.

Under this heading too come tax farmers, pedlars, usurers, brokers, panders, estate managers, game wardens, the whole gang of agents and retainers whom some people keep purely for the sake of ostentation. When men like these cannot meet the demands of extravagance, the concomitant of idleness, they lapse into evil ways.

Soldiering, too, is a very energetic kind of idleness, and much the most dangerous, since it causes the total destruction of everything worthwhile and opens up a cesspit of everything that is evil. And so, if the prince will banish from his realm all such seed-beds of crime, there will be much less for his laws to punish.

Thus useful occupations must be held in high esteem and, I should add in passing, ineffective idleness should not go under the name of nobility. I would not wish to strip their honours from those of noble birth, if they upheld the standards of their forebears and excelled in those activities which originally created the aristocracy. But when we see so many of them these days grown soft with idleness, emasculated by their debauches, devoid of any useful talent, little more than jolly table-companions and devoted gamblers – I pass over their more revolting activities – why on earth should this sort of fellow be treated better than a cobbler or a farmer? In days gone by the aristocracy were excused the more menial tasks, not to allow them to waste time, but to learn those skills which help in the government of the state.

Therefore, rich or noble citizens should not be frowned on for instructing their sons in some sedentary occupation; for one thing, young men preoccupied with their studies will be kept away from many temptations, and for another, even if they have no need of their skills at least they harm no one. But, since human affairs are subject to the vagaries of fortune, if the need arises then skill will find its reward, not only in any land, as the proverb says, but in any station in life too.

The Ancients, recognizing that many problems arise from extravagance and luxurious living, counteracted them by sumptuary laws and appointed inspectors to control excessive expenditure on banquets, clothes, or buildings. If anyone thinks it harsh to prevent a man from using or abusing his own property as he pleases, let him reflect that it is much harsher to let social standards deteriorate, through luxurious living, to the point where capital punishment is required, and that it is less harsh to be compelled to live frugally than to be brought to perdition by vice.

There is nothing more harmful than for magistrates to make a profit out of convicting citizens. Who will exert himself to keep crime down to a minimum, if it is in his interest that there should be as many criminals as possible?

It is appropriate, and it was the custom among the Ancients, that money from fines should go primarily to the injured party, some part of it to public funds and, in the case of the most odious crimes, something also to the informer. But the degree of odiousness must be decided, not by the personal feelings of any one man, but according to the damage or benefit to the state.

The whole purpose of the law should be to protect everyone, rich or poor, noble or humble, serf or free man, public official or private citizen. But it should incline more towards helping the weaker elements, because the position of humble men exposes them more easily to danger. The law's indulgence should compensate for the privileges denied them by their station in life. There should thus be more severe punishment for a crime against a poor man than for offences against the rich, for a corrupt official than for a common criminal, and for a wicked nobleman than for a humble citizen.

According to Plato, there are two kinds of penalty. For the first, care must be taken that the punishment is not too harsh for the crime, and for this reason the supreme penalty must not be invoked lightly; nor must the gravity of the crime be measured by our greed, but fairly and honourably. Why is it that, contrary to the laws of all the Ancients, simple theft is generally punished by death, while adultery goes virtually unpunished? It is that everyone values money too highly, and so its loss is judged, not on the facts, but on emotional grounds? But this is not the place to discuss why adulterers, on whom the laws used to be very severe, are less severely treated today.

The other kind of penalty, which Plato calls exemplary, must be invoked very sparingly; it should act as a deterrent to others more by its rarity than by its frightfulness. For there is nothing so horrifying that familiarity does not breed contempt for it, nor anything so harmful as allowing one's subjects to become inured to a punishment.

Just as new remedies should not be tried out on a disease if the old ones will cure the illness, so new laws should not be enacted if the old ones will provide a means to treat the ills of the state.

If useless laws cannot be repealed without much trouble, they should be allowed gradually to lapse or else be amended. It is dangerous to alter laws without due consideration, but it is also necessary to adapt the law to the present circumstances of the state, just as treatment is adapted to suit the condition of the patient: some laws, appropriate enough when enacted, are still more appropriately repealed.

Many laws have been introduced quite justifiably but have been put to the worst uses by the corruption of officials; there is nothing so pernicious as a good law diverted to evil purposes. The prince must not be deterred from removing or amending such laws by any loss of revenue, for there is no profit to be made from the loss of honour, especially since the repeal of this kind of law will be much applauded. Nor should the prince be deceived by the fact that laws of this kind have grown up almost everywhere and are now firmly established by long custom; justice, essentially, is not a matter of mere numbers, and the more deeply rooted an evil practice the more thoroughly it needs to be extirpated.

Here are a few examples. In some places it is the practice that a prefect takes possession, in the king's name, of the property of anyone who dies while abroad. This was introduced, quite rightly, to prevent the property of a traveller being claimed by people who had no right to it; it remained in the hands of the prefect for a short time, until the true heirs came forward. But now the custom has been most unjustly perverted, so that whether the heir comes forward or not the traveller's property goes into the prince's treasury.

A law was rightly introduced to allow property found in the possession of a thief when arrested to be seized by the prince or by an officer in his name; obviously this was to prevent property going to the wrong person by some trick, if everyone had the right to claim. As soon as ownership was established, the property would be restored. But now anything found in a thief's possession is regarded by some princes as their own, as if it were part of their patrimony. They are well aware that this practice is shamefully unjust, but the profit motive overcomes honourable intentions.

It was a good idea, in days gone by, to provide officials on the frontiers of states to supervise imports and exports, to ensure, of course, that merchants and travellers could come and go free from the fear of bandits. If anything was stolen, each prince would ensure, within the boundaries of his realm, that the merchants should not suffer any loss and the robber not go unpunished; later, perhaps as a courtesy, merchants began to pay a small fee. But nowadays the traveller is held up at every turn by these customs duties, visitors are harassed, merchants are fleeced, and there is no longer any word of protecting them although the tolls increase from one day to the next. In this way the purpose for which the institution was first established has been totally lost, and what was a sound practice when introduced has been turned into utter tyranny by the fault of those who administer it.

It was established in days gone by that property washed ashore from a shipwreck should be held by the prefect of the sea, not so that it should pass into his hands or in the prince's but so that they could prevent it being seized by the wrong people; it would finally become public property if no one survived with a rightful claim on it. But today, in some places, anything which falls into the sea, no matter how, is taken as his own by the prefect, who is more merciless than the sea itself: for anything which was left to the miserable survivors he snatches away like a second storm.

You can see, then, how everything has gone wrong. The thief is punished for seizing another's property; but the magistrate, appointed to prevent theft, does the same, and the rightful owner is robbed twice over by the very man employed to spare him such loss. Merchants too are much harassed and robbed by those appointed specifically to prevent travellers being harassed and robbed. Property is withheld from its rightful owner by the very man appointed by law to prevent it getting into the wrong hands. In many lands there is a vast number of similar institutions, no less unjust than injustice itself. But it is not my purpose in this reproach any particular state, since these things are common to practically all – and are condemned by them all; I have listed them for the sake of instruction. It may be true that some of them cannot be abrogated without a great upheaval, but their abrogation will win the prince approval and – something more important than any financial gain – a good reputation.

Like the prince, the law must, more than anything else, be accessible and fair to all; otherwise, as the Greek philosopher[12] cleverly put it, the laws will be nothing but spiders' webs, which birds can easily break because of their size, and in which only flies will be entangled.

Like the prince, the law must always be more willing to forgive than to punish, either because it has a certain intrinsic mildness, or because it is a reflection of the ways of God, slow to be moved to anger and vengeance, or, again, because a man wrongly released can be recalled for punishment, but a man unjustly condemned cannot be helped; even if he is still alive, who can put a price on another man's suffering?

We read that in days gone by there was a kind of men, tyrants, not princes – and the conduct of the Christian prince must be entirely different – for whom the measure of a crime was the harm done to their personal interests; so they thought it mere petty theft to strip a pauper of his property and condemn him, with his wife and children, to slavery or to beggary, but a most serious theft, worthy of the sternest punishment, to cheat the privy purse or some rapacious official even of a few coins. Again, they would cry *lèse-majesté* if anyone murmured against a prince, however bad, or spoke a little too freely of some pestilent magistrate. But the pagan emperor Hadrian,[13] not normally included among good princes, never allowed a charge of *lèse majesté*, and not even the ruthless Nero set much store by accusations of this sort. Another one, who completely ignored charges of this kind, is supposed to have said: 'In a free state, tongues too should be free.'

It follows that the good prince will forgive no offences more easily and willingly than those which damage his personal interests: who will find it easier to overlook such things than the prince? The easier vengeance may be, the more it will appear invidious and unseemly, since vengeance is the mark of a weak and mean spirit, and nothing is less appropriate to the prince, whose spirit must be lofty and magnanimous.

It is not enough for the prince to keep clear of crime unless he is also free from any suspicion or taint of crime. For this reason he will consider not only the deserts of the man who has committed a crime against him, but also how other men will judge the prince, and he will sometimes show mercy in an undeserving case out of concern for his honour, and pardon a man unworthy of pardon to safeguard his reputation.

Let no one immediately cry out that this advice takes too little account of the majesty of a prince, which it should be the state's principal concern to keep sacrosanct and inviolate. On the contrary, there is no better safeguard for his greatness than that the people know him to be so vigilant that nothing escapes him, so wise that he understands the true sources of the prince's majesty, and so merciful that he will avenge no offence against himself unless the public interest demands it. The pardon granted to Cinna made the majesty of Augustus Caesar[14] both more glorious and more secure, when so many executions had had no effect.

*Lèse majesté* occurs only when a man has diminished those qualities which make the prince truly great; if his greatness lies in the excellence of his mind and the prosperity which his wisdom brings to his people, then anyone who undermines these must be accused of *lèse majesté*. It is a great mistake, and a complete misunderstanding of the true majesty of the prince, to suppose that this can be increased if the law and public liberties are little respected, as if prince and state were two separate entities. If a comparison must be made between things which nature has united, a king should not compare himself with any one of his subjects but with the whole body of the state: then he will realize that the latter, comprising so many distinguished men and women, is worth far more than the head alone, the prince. A state, even if it lacks a prince, will still be a state. Vast empires have flourished without a prince, such as Rome and Athens under democracy. But a prince simply cannot exist without a state, and in fact the state takes in the prince, rather than the reverse. What makes a prince a great man, except the consent of his subjects? On the other hand, if a man achieves greatness by goodness, that is, by his virtues, he will still be a great man even if deprived of his power.

It is obvious, therefore, that those who measure a prince's honour by standards unworthy of a prince's grandeur are quite wrong in their judgment. They call traitor (a word supposed by them to be the most loathsome of all) a man who, by advice freely given, recalls his prince to better paths when he strays and puts at risk his honour, his safety, and his country's welfare. But a man who corrupts the prince with ignoble ideas and launches him into a round of sordid pleasures, feasts, gambling, and similar indignities: surely such a man is not preserving the prince's honour? They call it loyalty to humour a foolish prince with constant flattery, and treason to oppose his shameful enterprises. But no one is less a friend to the prince than a man who deludes him and leads him astray by base flattery, who involves him in wars, advises him to pillage the people, teaches him the arts of the tyrant, and causes him to be hated by all decent people; this is real treason, and deserves no mean punishment.

Plato requires that the 'guardians of the law,' that is, those appointed to watch over the laws, be the least corruptible of men. The good prince should never act more severely than against those who administer the law corruptly, since the prince himself is the chief of the 'guardians of the law.'

To sum up: it is best to have as few laws as possible; these should be as just as possible and further the public interest; they should also be as familiar as possible to the people: for this reason the Ancients exhibited them in tables and on tablets in public places for all to see. It is disgraceful that certain men use the laws like a spider's web, plainly intending to entangle as many as possible, not in the interest of the state, but simply to catch their prey. Finally, the laws should be drafted in plain terms, with the minimum of complications, so that there is little need for that grasping sort who call themselves lawyers and advocates; once, in fact, this profession was the preserve of the best men in society, bringing little profit but much honour; but nowadays the profit motive has corrupted it, as it vitiates everything.

Plato says that there is no enemy more dangerous to the state than the man who subjects the laws to human eccentricity, whereas under the best princes the laws will possess supreme authority.

## Magistrates and their duties

The prince must demand from his officials the same standards of integrity, or very nearly, as he himself exhibits. He should not think it enough simply to have appointed magistrates; the manner of their appointment is of the greatest importance, and he must then see to it that they carry out scrupulously their appointed tasks.

Aristotle made the important and judicious observation that it is useless to establish good laws if there is no one who will labour to uphold what has been so well established; indeed, it sometimes happens that the best established laws are turned to the total ruin of the state through the fault of the magistrates.

Although magistrates must not be chosen for their wealth, their pedigree, or their age, but rather for their wisdom and integrity, yet it is better to appoint older men to this kind of post, on which the well-being of the state depends, not only because old men have acquired prudence with experience and are more temperate in their appetites, but also because their advancing years confer on them a kind of authority in the minds of the people. For this reason Plato forbids the appointment of men younger than fifty or older than seventy as guardians of the laws. He would not have a priest younger than sixty because, just as there is a certain point in life when a man reaches maturity, so there is a certain decline in life which requires retirement and a rest from all duties.

A choral dance makes an elegant spectacle so long as it is performed with order and harmony, but it becomes farcical if the gestures and voices get confused; similarly, a kingdom or city is an excellent institution if everyone is assigned a place and performs his proper function, that is, if the prince acts like a prince, the magistrates play their parts, and the people submit to good laws and upright magistrates. But where the prince acts in his own interest and the magistrates simply plunder the people, where the people do not submit to honourable laws but flatter prince and magistrates, whatever they do – there, the most appalling confusion must reign.

The first and chief concern of the prince must be to serve the state to the best of his ability: he can do it no greater service than to ensure that the magistrature and its duties are entrusted to the most upright men, those most devoted to the common good.

What is the prince but a physician to the state? But it is not enough for a physician to have skilful assistants; he must himself be the most skilful and careful of all. Similarly, it is not enough for the prince to have virtuous magistrates; he must himself be the most virtuous of all, since it is he who chooses and corrects them.

The parts of the mind are not all equals: some give instructions, others carry them out, while the body does no more than carry out instructions. In the same way the prince, the highest part of the state, must be the most discerning, and entirely free from all gross passions. Next to him stand the magistrates, partly carrying out and partly giving instructions; they obey the prince but command the people.

Thus the happiness of the state depends particularly on its magistrates being impartially appointed and impartially performing their duties. There should therefore be provisions against maladministration, just as the Ancients had them against extortion. Finally, if they are convicted, the most severe punishment should be decreed against them.

They will be appointed impartially if the prince nominates, not the highest bidder, the most brazen lobbyist, his closest relatives, or those most adept at pandering to his character, passions, and desires, but rather those most upright in character and best suited to perform the appointed tasks.

Otherwise, when a prince merely sells appointments for the best price he can get, what else can he expect but that his appointees will resell them, making good their own outlay as best they can, and trading on their office, since they acquired it by a business deal? This practice should not be thought any the less dangerous to the state just because by long and wretched usage, it has won acceptance with a number of nations, since it was frowned on even by the pagans, and the laws of the Caesars lay down that those who preside over the courts must be given the inducement of a princely salary so that they have no excuse for graft.

In days gone by, the charge of giving a corrupt verdict was treated very seriously; but on what grounds can a prince punish a judge for taking bribes to give of withhold a verdict, if the prince himself has sold off the job of making judgments and was in fact the first to instruct the judge in the ways of corruption? Let the prince treat the magistrates as he would have them treat the people.

In the *Politics*, Aristotle wisely remarks that, above all, care must be taken that magistrates do not make money out of their duties; otherwise, two disadvantages occur: first, it will mean that the magistracy will be sought after, or should I say be attacked and overwhelmed, by the most grasping and corrupt of men, and, second, the people will suffer the double blow of being excluded from office and robbed of their money.

**Treaties**

In making treaties, as in everything else, the good prince will pursue only the public interest. Otherwise, if they are arranged to benefit the princes at the expense of the people, they should be called conspiracies, not treaties. Anyone who acts like this makes one people into two, nobility and commons, and one of them profits only from the other's loss; but where this happens, there is no state.

There is a most binding and holy contract between all Christian princes, simply from the fact that they are Christians. What, then, is the point of negotiating treaties day after day, as if everyone were the enemy of everyone else, as if human contracts could achieve what Christ cannot? When business is done by means of a lot of bits of paper, it suggests that there is little trust present, and we often see that a great deal of litigation arises from the very things that were supposed to preclude litigation. Where mutual trust exists and business is being done between honest men, there is no need for a lot of these niggling bits of paper, but when business is being done between dishonest and untrustworthy men the bits of paper actually provide raw material for the courts. Similarly, friendship will exist between good and wise princes even if there is no treaty between them, but war will arise between bad and foolish princes out of the very treaties designed to prevent war, when one of them complains that one or other of the innumerable clauses has not been observed. Treaties are supposed to be made to put an end to war, but nowadays an agreement to start war is called a treaty. Alliances of this kind are no more than stratagems of war, and as the situation develops, the treaties fall into line with it.

The good faith of princes in fulfilling their agreements must be such that a simple promise from them will be more sacred than any oath sworn by other men. How shameful it is, then, to fail to fulfil the conditions of a solemn treaty, one sworn by those things which Christians hold most sacred! Yet every day we can see this becoming the custom; I will not say who is at fault, but it certainly could not happen unless someone is at fault.

If some clause of a treaty has apparently not been observed, this must not be taken at once as evidence that the treaty as a whole is null and void, because this will suggest that a pretext has been found for breaking off friendly relations. On the contrary, great efforts should be made to repair the breach with as little damage as possible; indeed the best course sometimes is to connive at something like this, since even an understanding between private citizens will not hold together for long if they take everything, as it were, too literally. Do not immediately follow the course dictated by anger, but rather that suggested by the public interest.

The good and wise prince will try to be at peace with all nations but particularly with his neighbours, who can do much harm if they are hostile and much good if they are friendly; no state can survive for long without good relations with them. In addition, it is easy for friendship to be made and kept between those who are linked by a common language, by the proximity of their lands, and by similarities of temperament and character. Certain nations are so different from one another in every way that it would be advisable to refrain from any contact with them rather than be linked to them even by the most binding of treaties. Others are so distant that even if they are well disposed they can be of no help. There are others, finally, who are so capricious, so insolent, such habitual breakers of treaties, that even if they are neighbours they are useless as friends. With this sort the best plan is neither to break with them by open war nor to be linked to them by any very binding treaties or marriage alliances, because war is always disastrous, and certain people's friendship is not much better than war.

One element of wise government will therefore be a knowledge of the character and temperament of all races, gathered partly from books and partly from the accounts of wise and well-travelled men; do not imagine that, with Ulysses,[15] you must travel across all lands and seas. Beyond this, it may not be easy to lay down hard and fast rules. One may state as a general rule that it is not advisable to be too closely allied with those, such as the heathen, who are divided from us by a difference of religion, and we should neither encourage nor reject those whom natural obstacles, such as mountain barriers or seas, separate from us, or those who are totally cut off from us by vast distances. There are many examples of this, but one will suffice for all, since it is closest at hand: the kingdom of France is by far and in every way the most prosperous of all; but she would have been still more prosperous had she refrained from invading Italy.[16]

**The marriage alliances of princes**

In my judgment it would be most beneficial to the state if marriage alliances of princes were confined within the boundaries of their kingdom; if they must go beyond their frontiers, they should be united only with near neighbours and then only with those best suited to a pact of friendship. But, people will say, it is unseemly for the daughter of a king to be joined with any but a king or a king's son. But bettering one's family whenever possible is an ambition for private citizens, and the prince must be as different as possible from them. What does it matter if a prince's sister marries a man less powerful than he, if it is for the greater good of all? A prince will win more honour by disregarding rank in his sister's marriage than by putting the whim of a mere woman before the public interest.

To a certain extent the marriage of princes is a private affair, but we must acknowledge that sometimes the whole course of events may come to depend almost entirely on this one point, so that what happened long ago to the Greeks and Trojans over Helen[17] often happens to us. If a choice worthy of the prince is to be made, let a woman be chosen who is distinguished among her fellows by her honesty, modesty, and prudence, who will make an obedient wife for the best of princes, and will bear him children worthy of both parents and of their country. Whatever her parentage, she will be noble enough if she makes a good wife for a good prince.

It is generally agreed that nothing is so beneficial to everyone as that the prince should warmly love his people and be loved by them in return. In this area a common fatherland, similar characteristics of body and mind, and a sort of national aura arising from some secret affinity of temperament are of enormous importance, but most of this is bound to disappear if it is disturbed by the wrong sort of marriage. It is hardly likely that children born of such a marriage will be accepted whole-heartedly by the country, nor will they themselves be whole-heartedly devoted to the country.

Yet the common opinion is that such marriages are like iron chains of concord between states, although experience has shown that the greatest upheavals in human affairs arise from them; for example, it is alleged that some article in the marriage contract has been overlooked, or the bride is taken back because of some slight she is said to have received, or a prince changes his mind, renounces his first choice, and takes another to wife, or dissatisfaction arises in some other way. But what does this mean to the state? If marriage alliances between princes could guarantee peace in the world, I should be glad to see them all joined by a thousand marriage alliances. But did his marriage stop James king of Scots from invading England a few years ago? It sometimes happens, too, that after many years of war's upheavals, after countless disasters, the quarrel is finally patched up by arranging a marriage, but only when both sides are already exhausted by their misfortunes.

The princes must set out to establish a perpetual peace among themselves and make common plans for it. Even if a marriage brings about peace, it certainly cannot be perpetual. When one party dies, the chain of concord is broken. But if a peace were to be based on true principles, it would be stable and lasting. Someone will object that the begetting of children will perpetuate an alliance. But why then are wars most often fought between those who are the closest kin? No, it is the birth of children in particular which causes changes of ruler, when the right to rule is transferred from one place to another or when some territory is taken away from one state and given to another; the greatest upheavals usually arise from this sort of thing.

So these devices do not succeed in preventing wars but succeed only in making wars more frequent and more frightful. For if kingdoms are linked to one another by marriage, whenever one prince has been offended he calls in all the rest, invoking the laws of kinship, so that for some trifling offence the best part of Christendom is immediately brought to arms, and one man's pique is mollified by an immense outpouring of Christian blood. I shall refrain, with good reason, from giving examples, to avoid offending anyone.

To sum up, the fortunes of princes may be improved by alliances of this kind, but the fortunes of the people suffer and are diminished. The good prince, however, should consider that his own affairs are prospering only if this is compatible with the interests of the state. I shall pass over the fact that it is no way to treat one's daughters – to send them away, sometimes to remote regions, to men entirely different in language, appearance, character, and thought, as if they were being sent into exile – when they would be happier to live in their own land, even with somewhat less pomp.

However, I can see that this custom is too well established for me to hope that it can be uprooted; but I thought it right to speak out, just in case things should turn out contrary to my expectations.

**The business of princes in peacetime**

So the prince who is schooled in the doctrine of Christ and in the precepts of wisdom will hold nothing more dear than the happiness of his people: indeed, he will hold nothing else dear, and must both love and cherish them as one body with himself. He will devote all his thoughts, all his actions, all his energies to a single purpose, that of ruling the province entrusted to him in such a way that on the day of reckoning he will satisfy Christ and will leave a most honourable memory of himself among mortals.

Even if he is at home or in retreat the Prince should imitate the worthy Scipio,[18] who used to say that he was never less alone than when he was on his own and never less idle than when he had time to spare; for whenever he was free of public business, he would always be pondering some idea concerning the security or dignity of the state. Let the prince imitate Virgil's Aeneas,[19] whom the excellent poet often portrays turning over in his mind throughout the night, while others sleep, some way of helping his people. Then there is this thought of Homer's, which should be inscribed on every wall of the palace, but most of all in the prince's heart; the sense of the verses, more of less, is: 'The man entrusted with a nation and its heavy business / Should not expect to enjoy a full night's sleep.'[20] Or, if he is out in public, he should always be contributing something to the common weal; in other words, he should never cease to be the prince.

It is better for the prince to be engaged in public duties than to spend his life hidden from sight. But whenever he goes out, he should take care that his face, his bearing, and above all his speech are such that they will set his people an example, bearing in mind that whatever he says or does will be seen by all and known to all. Wise men have criticized the custom of the Persian kings who spent their lives hidden away in their palaces. They sought the esteem of their subjects simply by never being seen in public, and by very rarely giving the people access to them. But if ever they did go out, it was to flaunt their barbaric arrogance and their immoderate wealth at the expense of the people. They used to fritter away the rest of their time in games or mad military adventures, as if the noble prince had nothing to do in time of peace, when in fact a whole crop of good works lies open to him, if only he thinks like a prince.

Some people today think that it is not very regal to be engaged in public duties, whereas in fact this is the only worthwhile occupation for a king. Similarly, some bishops consider that instructing the people, the one occupation worthy of a bishop, is the last of their duties, and for some strange reason they delegate to others the special duties of a bishop as unworthy of them and claim as their own all the most worldly affairs. But Mithridates,[21] a king ennobled no less by his learning than by his empire, was not ashamed to dispense justice to his people from his own lips, with no interpreter: we read that he learned twenty-two languages thoroughly for the purpose. Again, Philip of Macedon[22] thought it no disgrace for a king to sit and listen to cases every day, and they say that his son Alexander the Great, though ambitious to the point of madness in other ways, had a custom of covering one ear with his hand while hearing cases, saying that he was keeping it free for the other party.

The fact that some princes take no part in these duties can be explained by their perverse upbringing. As the old proverb says, every man likes to practise the skill he has learned but avoids those for which he knows he has no aptitude. When a man has spent his early years among toadies and women, gambling, dancing, and hunting, corrupted first by perverse ideas and then by debauchery, how can he be expected afterwards to enjoy carrying out duties whose performance requires very careful consideration?

Homer says that a prince hasn't time to sleep all night; but this kind have only one aim, to cheat the boredom of their lives by constantly finding new pleasures, as if the prince had absolutely nothing else to do. How can a prince, with his vast domains, find nothing to do, when the head of a family is kept busy enough by just one household?

There are bad customs to be counteracted by good laws, corrupted laws to be amended and bad ones repealed, honest magistrates to be sought out and corrupt ones punished or restrained. The prince has to find ways to lighten the burden of the weakest classes, to rid his domain of robbery and crime with the least possible bloodshed, and to establish and secure lasting concord among his people. there are other tasks, less pressing but not unworthy of a prince, however great: he can inspect his cities, so long as his object is to see how they can be improved; he can fortify those which are vulnerable, enhance them with public buildings, such as bridges, colonnades, churches, embankments, and aqueducts, and clean up plague-spots, either by rebuilding or by draining swamps. He can divert rivers whose course is inconvenient, and let in or keep out the sea according to the needs of the town. He can ensure that abandoned fields are tilled to increase the food supply, and he can direct that those producing useless crops be used differently, for example prohibiting vineyards where the wine is not worth making and where corn can be grown. There are a thousand similar tasks, whose supervision is an admirable job for the prince, and even a pleasant one for the good prince, so that he will never feel the need, bored by inactivity, to seek war or to waste the night gambling.

In his public acts, for example in public building or the games, or in receiving embassies if they involve the people's welfare, the prince should aim at a certain splendour, but without ostentation or extravagance. In his private life he will be more frugal and restrained, partly to avoid appearing to live at the public expense, and partly to avoid teaching his subjects extravagance, the father of many ills.

There was one error, I see, into which a great many of the Ancients fell – and I wish that there were none of our contemporaries doing the same – namely, that they directed all their efforts, not to improving the realm, but to increasing it; we can see that it often turned out that in striving to extend their power they lost even what they already had. Not without reason have Theopompus'[23] words been much praised; he said that he was not interested in how large a kingdom he left to his sons, only in how much better and more secure it was. It seems to me that that Laconic proverb 'You have drawn Sparta, now enhance it' might be inscribed on the arms of every prince.[24]

The good prince will be fully convinced that he can have no more worthwhile task than that of increasing the prosperity of the realm which fate gave him, and of enhancing it in every way. The conduct of General Epaminondas[25] has been praised by learned men; when he was appointed, through envy, to a lowly office, one held in public contempt, he carried out its duties so well that it was regarded afterwards as one of the most honourable of positions and the greatest men vied for it; thus he showed that it is not the office that brings honour to the man, but the man to the office.

It follows that if, as we have tried to show, the prince gives particular attention to things which strengthen and ennoble the state, he will thereby drive out and keep out things which weaken the state. All this will be much assisted by the example, wisdom, and vigilance of the good prince, the integrity of magistrates and officials, the piety of priests, the choice of schoolmasters, by just laws, and devotion to the pursuit of virtue. Therefore the good prince should devote all his attention to increasing and supporting these things. But the state is harmed by their opposites, which can be eliminated more easily if we try first to remove the roots and sources from which we know that they spring. The philosophy of the Christian prince involves dealing with things of this kind carefully and intelligently. It is entirely fitting for Christian princes to conspire, in good sense, and to make common plans, against such things as these.

If the heavenly bodies are disturbed even for a short while or deflected from their true courses, it brings grave dangers to the world, as is obvious from eclipses of sun and moon. In the same way, if great princes stray from the path of honour, or sin through ambition, anger, or foolishness, they at once cause enormous trouble throughout the world. No eclipse ever afflicted mankind so gravely as the dispute between Pope Julius[26] and King Louis of France, which we have witnessed and wept over only recently.

## On starting war

Although the prince will never make any decision hastily, he will never be more hesitant or more circumspect than in starting a war; other actions have their different disadvantages, but war always brings about the wreck of everything that is good, and the tide of war overflows with everything that is worst; what is more, there is no evil that persists so stubbornly. War breeds war; from a small war a greater is born, from one, two; a war that begins as a game becomes bloody and serious; the plague of war, breaking out in one place, infects neighbours too and, indeed, even those far from the scene.

The good prince will never start a war at all unless, after everything else has been tried, it cannot by any means be avoided. If we were all agreed on this, there would hardly ever be a war among men. In the end, if so pernicious a thing cannot be avoided, the prince's first concern should be to fight with the least possible harm to his subjects, at the lowest cost in Christian blood, and to end it as quickly as possible.

The truly Christian prince will first ponder how much difference there is between man, a creature born to peace and good will, and wild animals and beasts, born to pillage and war, and in addition how much difference there is between a man and a Christian. He should then consider how desirable, how honourable, how wholesome a thing is peace; on the other hand, how calamitous as well as wicked a thing is war, and how even the most just of wars brings with it a train of evils – if indeed any war can really be called just. Finally, putting aside all emotion, let him apply just a little reason to the problem by counting up the true cost of the war and deciding whether the object he seeks to achieve by it is worth that much, even if he were certain of victory, which does not always favour even the best of causes. Weigh up the anxieties, expense, dangers, the long and difficult preparations. You must call in a barbarian rabble, made up of all the worst scoundrels, and, if you want to be thought more of a man than the rival prince, you have to flatter and defer to these mercenaries, even after paying them, although there is no class of men more abject and indeed more damnable. Nothing is more precious to the good prince than that his people should be as virtuous as possible. But could there be a greater and more immediate threat to morality than war? The prince should pray for nothing more fervently than to see his subjects secure and prosperous in every way. But while he is learning to wage war, he is compelled to expose young men to all kinds of peril and to make countless orphans, widows, and childless old people, and to reduce countless others to beggary and misery, often in a single hour.

The world will have paid too high a price to make princes wise, if they insist on learning by experience how dreadful war is, so that as old men they can say: 'I never thought war could be so pernicious.' But, immortal God! what incalculable suffering has it cost the whole world to teach you that truism! One day the prince will realize that it was pointless to extend the frontiers of his kingdom and that what seemed at the outset to be a profitable enterprise has resulted in terrible loss to him; but before then many thousands of men have been either killed or maimed. These things would be better learned from books, from the reminiscences of old men, or from the tribulations of neighbours. For years now this prince or that has been fighting for this or that realm: how much greater are their losses than their gains!

The good prince will arrange these matters so that they will be settled once and for all. A policy adopted on impulse will seem satisfactory for as long as the impulse has hold of you; a policy adopted after due consideration, and which satisfies you as a young man, will satisfy you as an old man too. This is never more relevant than when starting a war.

Plato calls it sedition, not war, when Greek fights Greek, and advises that, if this does occur, the war must be fought with the utmost restraint. What word, then, do we think should be used when Christian draws the sword against Christian, since they are bound to one another by so many ties? What shall we say when the cruellest wars, prolonged for year after year, are fought on some slender pretext, some private quarrel, a foolish or immature ambition?

Some princes deceive themselves as follows: 'Some wars are entirely just, and I have just cause for starting one.' First, I will suspend judgment on whether any war is entirely just; but who is there who does not think his cause just? Amid so many shifts and changes in human affairs, amid the making and breaking of so many agreements and treaties, how could anyone not find a pretext, if any sort of pretext is enough to start a war?

It can be argued that papal laws do not condemn all war. Augustine too approves it somewhere. Again, St Bernard praises some soldiers. True enough, but Christ himself, and Peter, and Paul, always teach the opposite. Why does their authority carry less weight than that of Augustine or Bernard? Augustine does not disapprove of war in one or two passages, but the whole philosophy of Christ argues against war. Nowhere do the Apostles approve it, and as for those holy doctors who are alleged to have approved of war in one or two passages, how many passages are there where they condemn and curse it? Why do we gloss over all these and seize on the bits which support our wickedness? In fact, anyone who examines the matter more closely will find that none of them approves of the kind of war which is usually fought today.

Certain arts, such as astrology and what is called alchemy, were banned by law because they were too close to fraud and were generally managed by trickery, even if it were possible for a man to practise them honestly. This would be far more justifiable in the case of wars, even if some of them might be just – although with the world in its present state, I am not sure that any of that kind could be found, that is, wars not caused by ambition, anger, arrogance, lust, or greed. It often happens that the leaders of men, more extravagant than their private resources will allow, will take a chance to stir up war in order to boost their own finances, even by pillaging their own people. This is sometimes done by princes in collusion with one another, on some trumped-up pretext, in order to weaken the people and to strengthen their own position at the expense of the state. For these reasons the good Christian prince must be suspicious of all wars, however just.

Some, of course, will protest that they cannot give up their rights. First of all, these 'rights,' if acquired by marriage, are largely the prince's private concern; how unjust it would be while pursuing these rights, to inflict enormous damage on the people, and to pillage the whole kingdom, bringing it to the brink of disaster, while pursuing some small addition to his own possessions. Why should it affect the population as a whole when one prince offends another in some trifling matter, and a personal one at that, connected with a marriage or something similar?

The good prince uses the public interest as a yardstick in every field, otherwise he is no prince. He has not the same rights over men as over cattle. Government depends to a large extent on the consent of the people, which was what created kings in the first place. If some dispute arises between princes, why do they not take it to arbitration instead? There are plenty of bishops, abbots, scholars, plenty of grave magistrates whose verdict would settle the matter more satisfactorily than all this carnage, pillaging, and universal calamity.

First of all, the Christian prince must be suspicious about his 'rights,' and then, if they are established beyond doubt, he must ask himself whether they have to be vindicated to the great detriment of the whole world. Wise men prefer sometimes to lose a case rather than pursue it, because they see that it will cost less to do so. I believe that the emperor would prefer to give up rather than pursue the rights to the ancient monarchy which jurists have conferred on him in their writings.

But, people will say, if no one pursues his rights will anything be safe? Let the prince pursue his rights by all means, if it is to the state's advantage, so long as his rights do not cost his subjects too dear. After all, is anything ever safe nowadays when everyone pursues his rights to the letter? We see wars causing wars, wars following wars, and no limit or end to these upheavals. It is clear enough that nothing is achieved by these methods, and so other remedies should be tried. Even between the best of friends the relationship will not last long without some give and take. A husband often overlooks some fault in his wife to avoid disturbing their harmony. What can war produce except war? But consideration breeds consideration, and fairness, fairness.

The godly and merciful prince will also be influenced by seeing that the greatest part of all the great evils which every war entails falls on people unconnected with the war, who least deserve to suffer these calamities.

When the prince has made his calculations and reckoned up the total of all these woes (if indeed they could ever be reckoned up), then let him say to himself: 'Shall I alone be the cause of so much woe? Shall so much human blood, so many widows, so many grief-stricken households, so many childless old people, so many made undeservedly poor, the total ruin of morality, law, and religion: shall all this be laid at my door? Must I atone for all this before Christ?'

A prince cannot revenge himself on his enemy without first opening hostilities against his own subjects. The people will have to be pillaged, the soldier (not for nothing called 'godless' by Virgil)[27] will have to be called in. Citizens must be expelled from places where they have been accustomed to enjoy their property; citizens must be shut in in order to shut in the enemy. It happens all too often that we commit worse atrocities against our own citizens than against the enemy.

It is more difficult, and so more admirable, to build a fine city than to demolish one. We observe, however, that the most prosperous cities are built by private citizens, simple men, but are demolished by the wrath of princes. All too often we go to more trouble and expense to demolish a town than would be needed to build a new one, and we fight wars with such extravagance, at such expense, and with such enthusiasm and diligence, that peace could have been preserved for a tenth of all that.

The good prince should always seek the kind of glory that is bloodless and involves no harm to anyone. However well a war may turn out, there can be success only on one side, and on the other is ruin. Very often the victor too laments a victory bought too dearly.

If religion does not move us, or the misfortunes of the world, at least the honour of the Christian name should move us. What do we imagine the Turks and Saracens say about us, when they see that for hundreds of years the Christian princes have been utterly unable to agree among themselves? That peace never lasts, despite all the treaties? That there is no limit to the shedding of blood? And that there are fewer upheavals among the pagans than among those who preach perfect concord according to the doctrine of Christ?

How fleeting, how brief, how fragile is the life of a man, and how subject to misfortune, assailed already by a multitude of diseases and accidents, buildings which collapse, shipwrecks, earthquakes, lightning! We do not need to add war to our woes, and yet it causes more woe than all the others.

It used to be the task of preachers to root out all hostile feelings from the hearts of the common people. Nowadays the Englishman generally hates the Frenchman, for no better reason than that he is French. The Scot, simply because he is a Scot, hates the Englishman, the Italian hates the German, the Swabian the Swiss, and so on; province hates province, city hates city. Why do these ridiculous labels do more to separate us than the name of Christ, common to us all, can do to reconcile us?

Even if we allow that some wars are just, yet since we see that all mankind is plagued by this madness, it should be the role of wise priests to turn the minds of people and princes to other things. Nowadays we often see them as very firebrands of war. Bishops are not ashamed to frequent the camp; the cross is here, the body of Christ is there, the heavenly sacraments become mixed up in this worse than hellish business, and the symbols of perfect charity are brought into these bloody conflicts. Still more absurd, Christ is present in both camps, as if fighting against himself. It is not enough for war to be permitted between Christians; it must also be accorded the supreme honour.

If the teaching of Christ does not always and everywhere attack warfare, if my opponents can find one passage approving war, then let us fight as Christians. The Hebrews were allowed to engage in war, but with God's permission. On the other hand, our oracle, which re-echoes again and again in the pages of the Gospel, argues against war – and yet we make war with more wild enthusiasm than the Hebrews. David was beloved of God for his other virtues, and yet he was forbidden to build his temple for the simple reason that he was a man of blood, that is, a warrior. God chose the peaceful Solomon for this task. If such things happened among the Jews, what will become of us Christians? They had only the shadow of Solomon, we have the true Solomon, Christ, the lover of peace, who reconciles all things in heaven and on earth.

However, I do not think, either, that war against the Turks should be hastily undertaken, remembering first of all that the kingdom of Christ was created, spread, and secured by very different means. Perhaps it should not be defended by other means than those which created and spread it. In addition we can see that wars of this kind have too frequently been made an excuse to fleece the Christian people – and then nothing else has been done. If it is done for the faith, this has been increased and enhanced by the suffering of martyrs, not by military force; if the battle is for power, wealth, and possessions, we must constantly consider whether such a course does not savour too little of Christianity. Indeed, judging by the people who fight this kind of war nowadays, it is more likely that we shall turn into Turks than that our efforts will make them into Christians. Let us first make sure that we are truly Christian ourselves and then, if it seems appropriate, let us attack the Turks.

But I have written a great deal elsewhere on the evils of war, and this is not the place to repeat it. I would merely exhort the princes who bear the name of Christian to set aside all trumped-up claims and spurious pretexts and apply themselves seriously and whole-heartedly to making an end of this long-standing and terrible mania among Christians for war, and to establishing peace and harmony among those who are united by so many common interests. To achieve this, they should exercise their talents, deploy their resources, draw up common plans, and stretch every sinew. It is in this way that those whose ambition it is to be considered great will prove their greatness. Anyone who can achieve this will have performed a far more dazzling deed than if he had subdued all Africa by arms. Nor should it prove too difficult to achieve, if each of us will cease to urge his own case, if we will set aside our personal feelings and work for the common cause, if our guide is Christ, not the world. At present, while each man looks out for himself, while popes and bishops are preoccupied with power and wealth, while princes are made reckless by ambition or anger, and while everyone else finds it to his advantage to defer to them, we are running headlong into the storm with folly as our guide. But if we acted with common purpose in our common affairs, even our private business would prosper. At the moment, even the things we are fighting for are destroyed.

I have no doubt, most illustrious Prince, that you are of one mind with me, by your birth and by your upbringing at the hands of the best and most upright of men. For the rest, I pray that Christ, perfect and supreme, will continue to favour your noble enterprises. He left a kingdom unstained by blood and he would have it remain unstained. He rejoices to be called the Prince of Peace;[28] may he do the same for you, that your goodness and wisdom may at last give us relief from these insane wars. Even the memory of past troubles will commend peace to us, and the misfortunes of days gone by will make your good deeds doubly welcome.

# A Complaint of Peace / *Querela pacis*

*A Complaint of Peace* is Erasmus' most celebrated plea for peace. It is dedicated to Philip of Burgundy, bishop of Utrecht, in a prefatory letter urging a reconciliation between France and the empire. Erasmus had already spoken out against war in several works, in the *Panegyric for Archduke Philip of Austria*, in the adages *War Is Sweet to Those Who Know It Not*, and *One Ought to Be Born a King or a Fool* (see below 334), and in the *Education of a Christian Prince* (see above 249).

In this prosopopoeiac composition, Peace appeals to man's better nature, his capacity for humanity and rationality. Erasmus draws his arguments from both the Christian and the classical tradition, quoting the New Testament as well as Plato and Cicero. The treatise attacks not only secular rulers and their wars of greed and ambition but also the warmongering clergy and their promotion of so-called 'holy wars.' He puts in a strong plea for arbitration and calls for adherence to the Christian teaching that all men are brothers.

*A Complaint of Peace* was first published in 1517 and reprinted twice within a year. Further editions followed rapidly. There were more than thirty editions during the sixteenth century and translations into French, Spanish, Dutch, German, and English. The fact that José Chapiro dedicated his version of 1950 to the United Nations attests to the contemporary appeal of the work.

This extract is taken from CWE 27 293–322, translated and annotated by Betty Radice.

## A COMPLAINT OF PEACE SPURNED AND REJECTED BY THE WHOLE WORLD

Peace speaks: If it were to their advantage for men to shun, spurn, and reject me, although I have done nothing to deserve it, I would only lament the wrong done me and their injustice; but since in rejecting me they deny themselves the source of all human happiness and bring on themselves a sea of disasters of every kind, I must shed tears rather for the misery they suffer than for any wrong they do me. I should have liked simply to be angry with them, but I am driven to feel pity and sorrow for their plight. To repel in any way one who loves you is cruel, to reject a benefactor is ungrateful, to distress your universal provider and guardian is wicked; but for men to deny themselves all the many remarkable benefits I bring with me, and deliberately to prefer instead a foul morass of manifold evils must surely look like the height of madness. Anger is the proper reaction to criminals, but for men thus hounded by the Furies what can we do but shed tears? They need our tears for no better reason than that they shed none for themselves; they have no greater unhappiness than in being unaware that they are unhappy, for the mere recognition of the gravity of a disease is a step towards recovery of health.

If then I am Peace, praised aloud by gods and men, the fount and source, the sustainer, amplifier, and preserver of all the good things of heaven or earth; if without me there can be no prosperity, no security, nothing sacred or undefiled, nothing pleasurable for men or acceptable to the gods; if on the other hand war is a kind of encircling ocean of all the evils in the world, if through its inherent wickedness prosperity immediately declines, increase dwindles, towers are undermined, sound foundations are destroyed, and sweetness is embittered; in short, if war is so unholy a thing that it is the greatest immediate destroyer of all piety and religion, if nothing is so unfortunate for men and hateful to the gods, in the name of immortal God I must say this: who would believe those beings to be human or possessed of any spark of sanity when they devote so much expenditure and application, such great effort and artifice, amid so many anxieties and dangers, to rid themselves of me – such as I am – while they are willing to pay the heavy price they do for such a burden of evils?

If I were rejected by wild animals in this way, I could bear it more easily and attribute their hostility towards me to nature, which endowed them with a savage disposition; if I were hateful to dumb cattle I would forgive their ignorance because they have been denied the intelligence which alone can discern my qualities. The shameful and monstrous truth is that Nature has produced only one animal gifted with reasoning power and possessed of divine insight, and created only one fitted for good will and concord, and yet you could put me amongst any wild beasts or dumb cattle and I should find a place there sooner than amongst men.

Even between the many celestial bodies, different as they are in motion and power, throughout so many centuries treaties have been established and maintained. The conflicting forces of the elements are evenly balanced so as to preserve unbroken peace, and despite their fundamental opposition they maintain concord by mutual consent and communication. In the bodies of living creatures we see how faithfully the limbs support each other and how ready they are to provide mutual assistance. And what can be so dissimilar as body and soul? Yet the closeness of the tie with which Nature has bound them together is indeed revealed when they are torn apart. Just as life is nothing other than the union of body and soul, so health is the harmony between all the parts of the body.

Animals, though they lack the faculty of reason, live together peacefully and harmoniously according to their different species; elephants, for example, live in herds, pigs and sheep graze together, cranes and rooks fly in flocks. Storks form their own communities and give us lessons in loyalty, dolphins protect each other with mutual services, and the harmony prevailing in colonies of ants and bees is well known. Shall I give further instances, where reason is lacking but not feeling? You can find friendliness in trees and plants. Some are barren unless they have a male nearby; the vine embraces the elm and the peach welcomes the vine. Even where things lack sense perception of the benefit of peace; though they have no power to perceive, yet they come very close to those having perception because they have life. Nothing could be so insensible as a stone, and yet you could say that stones too have a sense of peace and concord; thus the magnet draws iron to itself and holds it when attracted. Moreover, is there not some agreement between the fiercest of animals? Savage lions do not fight each other, nor does a boar threaten a fellow boar with his murderous tusks; there is peace amongst lynxes, no fighting between snakes, and the concord between wolves has won fame in proverbs. Furthermore, what is even more amazing, the evil spirits who first destroyed the harmony between heavenly beings and mortal men and continue to do so today can still observe a truce amongst themselves and maintain their tyranny by agreement, such as it is.

Only men, for whom concord was so fitting and who have the greatest need of it, are not reconciled to each other by Nature, so powerful and effective in other respects, or united by education; they can be neither bound together by the many advantages of agreement nor persuaded to love each other through their awareness and experience of many powerful evils. All men have the same shape and voice, whereas all other kinds of animal differ very widely in bodily shape; to man alone has been given the power of reason, which is common to all and shared with no other living creature. He is the only animal with the gift of speech, the chief promoter of friendly relationships; the seeds of learning and the virtues alike are implanted in him, along with a mild and gentle disposition which is inclined towards good will between him and his fellows, so that he delights in being loved for himself and takes pleasure in being of service to others – so long as he has not been corrupted by base desires, as if by Circe's potions,[1] and degenerated from man to beast. Hence it is, I believe, that the word 'humane' is generally applied to anything to do with mutual good will. Man has also the capacity for tears, proof of a disposition which is readily persuaded, so that if some difference has arisen and a cloud has overcast the clear sky of friendship, a reconciliation can easily be achieved.

Now take a look at all the reasons Nature has provided for concord. She was not satisfied simply with the attractions of mutual good will; she wanted friendship to be not only enjoyable for man but also essential. So she shared out the gifts of mind and body in a way that would ensure that no one should be provided with everything and not need on occasion the assistance of the lowly; she gave men different and unequal capacities, so that their inequality could be evened out by mutual friendships. Different regions provided different products, the very advantage of which taught exchange between them. To all other creatures she assigned their own armour and weapons for self-protection, but man alone she made weak and unarmed and unable to find safety except in treaties and the need of one man for another. Need created cities, need taught the value of alliance between them, so that with combined forces they could repel the attacks of wild beasts or brigands.

Indeed, there is nothing in human affairs which can be self-sufficient. At the very start of life, the human race would have died out at once if it had not been propagated by conjugal harmony; for man would not be born at all, or would die immediately at birth and lose life as he entered it, if the tiny infant were not helped by the kind hand of the midwife and the kind care of his nurse. To meet the same need, Nature has implanted the glowing spark of family affection, so that parents can love the child they have not yet seen; and to this she has added the reciprocal love of children for their parents, so that in their turn they can relieve the helplessness of the old by their support; and we have what all alike find praiseworthy and the Greeks name so aptly 'mutual affection.'[2] Then there are the ties of kinship and affinity, and similarity of disposition, interests, and appearance amongst several people which is certain to foster good will; many too possess a mysterious kind of spiritual perceptiveness and a marvellous propensity towards reciprocal love, something which the Ancients attributed in admiration to a man's godhead.[3]

So Nature provided all these arguments for peace and concord, so many lures and inducements to draw us towards peace, so many means of coercion. But then what Fury appeared with such harmful powers, to scatter, demolish, and destroy them all and to sow an insatiable lust for fighting in the human heart? If custom did not blunt first our sense of amazement and then our awareness of evil, who would believe that there are men endowed with human reason who thus fight, brawl, and rage against each other in perpetual discord, strife, and war? Finally, they confound everything, sacred and profane, with pillaging, bloodshed, disaster, and destruction; no bond is sufficiently sacred to check them in their frenzy for mutual extinction. Were there nothing else, the common name of 'man' should be sufficient to ensure concord amongst men. But granted that Nature, who is such a powerful influence even on wild animals, can do nothing for men, has Christ no influence at all on Christians? And granted that Nature's teaching may well prove inadequate, although it is highly effective even where there is no perception, since the teaching of Christ is so far superior to Nature's, why does it not bring home to those who profess to follow it the importance of what is especially trying to promote, namely peace and mutual good will? Or at least dissuade men from the wickedness, savagery, and madness of waging war?

When I hear the word 'man,' I run to him at once, as if to an animal specially created for me, confident that with him I shall be permitted to rest; when I hear the name 'Christian' I hurry all the faster, full of hope that I shall certainly come into my kingdom. But here too, I am ashamed and reluctant to say, assemblies, lawcourts, secretariats, and churches everywhere resound with strife, more so than among the heathen, and so much so that even though a good part of human misfortune is due to the number of advocates, there is a positive scarcity of them and an empty desert compared with the swarms of litigants. I see a city, and my hopes are raised at once; here at least there will be agreement among men who are enclosed by the same walls and regulated by the same laws, held together by shared hazards like passengers in a single ship. Alas! Here too I find everything marred by dissension, so that I can scarcely find a single house where I can stay even for a few days.

I leave out the common people, who are swayed by their passions like a stormy sea, and seek the courts of princes, expecting to find a haven. There will surely be a place for Peace there, I tell myself, for they are wiser than ordinary men, being the mind of their subjects and eye of their people. Besides, they represent him who is the Teacher and Prince of concord, who commends me to all men and especially to princes. And all promises well. I see polite greetings, friendly embraces, cheerful conviviality, and all the other courtesies of civilized conduct. Yet, shameful to say, not even a shadow of genuine concord could be seen amongst them; all was false and counterfeit, everything corrupted by open factions and secret dissension and rivalry. In fact I was far from finding a place for Peace in their courts; instead, there were the sources and seeds of every kind of war.

My hopes have been dashed so often; where then shall poor Peace go now? Well, princes are powerful rather than learned, and moved more by their desires than by true rational judgment. I shall seek refuge in the company of scholars, for good learning makes men, philosophy makes superior men, theology makes holy men. Surely I shall be allowed to settle down amongst them after all my wanderings. But woe is me! Here too there is warfare, another kind and not so bloody, but just as insane. Scholar argues with scholar, and, apparently, factual truth is altered by a change of place; some dogmas don't cross the sea or climb over the Alps or swim the Rhine, and indeed, in the same seat of learning logicians war with rhetoricians and theologians argue with lawyers. Even in the same profession, Scotist battles with Thomist, Nominalist with Realist, Platonist with Peripatetic,[4] so fiercely that there is no agreement amongst them even on the smallest points, and often enough they fight with the utmost fury on the subject of goat's wool. Then the heat of the debate mounts from argument to insult, from insult to fisticuffs, and if they don't settle the matter by daggers or spears they take to stabbing with poisoned pens, tear one another with barbed wit, and attack each other's reputation with the deadly darts of their tongues.

Where shall I turn now, after being so often deceived? What remains but the single sheet-anchor of religion? All Christians are one in the profession of their faith, but some have special ways of showing it in their title, dress, and ceremonies, and these are generally distinguished by the name of priest. At first sight everything makes me hope that there is a haven awaiting me with them. Their white garments are my own colour, so they encourage me; I can see crosses, symbols of peace, and the name of brother, a sure indication of close affection, sounds sweet in my ears; I hear the welcome greeting 'Peace,' a happy omen, and I note that all property is held in common, that there is a united college of clergy, and a single church, the same rules for all and daily assemblies. Who would not be confident that there will be a place for Peace here? But, for shame, scarcely anywhere does a college agree with the bishop, though this would not matter much if its members were not also divided into factions amongst themselves. Is there a single priest who is not involved in a dispute with some fellow priest? Paul says it is intolerable that one Christian should take another to court; so is priest to confront priest or bishop a fellow bishop? But this might perhaps be forgiven them, seeing that they have long become accustomed to consorting with non-clergy, after they have begun to own the same sort of property. Well, let them enjoy on their own authority what they claim for themselves as if by right of usage.

There remains one class of men who are so closely bound to religion that they cannot cast it off even if they wish, any more than a tortoise can its shell. I should expect there would be a place for me among them, if my hopes had not been belied so often and disillusionment had not taught me to despair altogether. Still, I don't want to leave any stone unturned, and I shall try. What happened, you ask. I was never more glad to jump back! For what could I hope for, when the religious orders are at loggerheads amongst themselves? There are as many factions as communities, Dominicans wrangling with Franciscans, Benedictines with Bernardines, and in addition innumerable names and rites and ceremonies with different aims which are designed to prevent any agreement at all; everyone delights in his own practices and damns and hates everyone else's. There are, besides, internal factions which split up a community: the Observants abuse the Colettines, and both combine against a third lot, who take their name from uniting together though there is no united spirit among them.

After this I lost confidence in everything, as was to be expected, and all I wanted was to bury myself in one humble monastery of any order, so long as it should be truly peaceful. What I have to say is spoken with reluctance, and I wish it were not true, but I have not yet found a single one which has not fallen a victim to internal feuds and quarrels. I am ashamed to recount what furious battles about silly trifles, with nothing to be gained, are provoked by old men who expect reverence for their beards and habit, and in their own eyes are paragons of wisdom and piety.

Then I was encouraged to hope that there would be some sort of a place for me somewhere among all the married couples; for a joint home and fortune and a common bed and children certainly look highly promising. And isn't there a law binding two bodies together so that you might suppose they merge into one instead of remaining two? But here too the evil monster strife finds a way in, and introducing conflicts of will divides those who have so many ties to hold them together. And yet I should find a place with these people more easily than amongst those who display their perfect love through all their many titles, trappings, and ceremonies. Finally I could only pray that there would at least be somewhere for me in the heart of a single individual, but even there I was unsuccessful. Man is a battlefield within himself: reason is at war with the passions and these are in conflict with each other, when duty calls him in one direction and desire pulls him in another, and in addition he is swayed this way and that by lust, anger, ambition, and service. But though they are like this, such men have no scruple about being called Christians, although they are in complete disharmony with what is specially important to Christ.

Survey the life of Christ from start to finish, and what else is it but a lesson in concord and mutual love? What do all his commandments and parables teach if not peace and love for one another? Think of the mighty prophet Isaiah: when he was inspired by the divine spirit and prophesied that Christ would come to unite the world, did he promise a tyrant, a sacker of cities, a warrior, a conqueror? He did not. What then did he promise? A prince of peace. Isaiah wished it to be understood that his Prince was the best of all princes, and so he named him after that quality which he judged to be best. Nor indeed is that surprising of him, seeing that the pagan poet Silius[5] has written of me in these words: 'Peace the best of the gifts / Which Nature has given to man.' The sacred Psalmist[6] agrees, saying that 'his place is prepared in peace.' Note that he spoke of peace, not of tents and army camps. He is the Prince of peace, he loves peace and is offended by discord. Again, Isaiah[7] calls peace 'a work of righteousness,' and his view, if I am not mistaken, is that of Paul, who found serenity after his change from the violence of Saul, and taught the value of peace when he made love the greatest of the gifts of the Holy Spirit. How he thundered out my praise to the Corinthians with heartfelt eloquence! (Why shouldn't I take pride in being thus praised by a man so praised himself?) Sometimes he speaks of the God of peace, sometimes calls for the peace of God, clearly indicating that the two are so closely united that there can be no peace where God is absent, and God cannot be where there is no peace.

In the same way we read in holy books of the faithful and the ministers of God being called 'messengers of peace,'[8] so that it is plain who must be understood as messengers of war. Hear that, you restless warmongers, see under whose standard you serve – that of him who first sowed discord between God and man. Every calamity known to mortal man must be attributed to this discord, for it is foolish to argue as some do that in the Old Testament God is called the Lord of hosts and of vengeance. There is a great difference between the God of the Jews and the God of the Christians, even though by his very nature he is one and the same God. But if we wish to retain old titles, well, let there be a God of hosts, so long as you understand by hosts the virtues united in concord to provide protection for good men who wish to destroy the vices. Let there be a God of vengeance, provided you take revenge to mean the correction of vices, so that you interpret the bloody slaughters which fill the pages of the Hebrew Scriptures not as the mangling of human bodies but as the tearing of wicked inclinations out of the heart. But to continue as we began: whenever the Old Testament indicates perfect happiness it does so with reference to peace. Isaiah, for example, says that 'my people shall sit in the beauty of peace,' and another prophet says, 'Peace be over Israel.'[9] Again, Isaiah marvels at the beauty of the feet of those who bring tidings of peace and prosperity. Whoever brings tidings of Christ brings tidings of peace. Whoever preaches war preaches one who is the very opposite of Christ.

Tell me, what induced the Son of God to come to earth if not his wish to reconcile the world with the Father, to bind men together with mutual and indestructible love, and, finally, to make man his own friend? He was an envoy on my behalf, he did my business. And it was because the name of Solomon means 'peace-making' or 'man of peace' that he was chosen to prefigure him; for though David was a great king, since he was a warrior and defiled with blood he was not permitted to build the house of the Lord – in this respect he was unworthy to prefigure a peace-making Christ. Now consider this, warrior: if wars undertaken and fought by God's command desecrate the fighter, what will be the effect of wars prompted by ambition, anger, or madness? If the shedding of pagan blood pollutes a god-fearing king, what will result from wholesale Christian bloodshed? I implore you, Christian prince, if you are truly a Christian, to look at the example of your Prince, behold the manner of his entry upon his reign on earth, his passage through it, his departure thence, and then you will understand how he wishes you to rule in such a manner that peace and concord are the chief of your concerns.

When Christ was born, did the angels sound trumpets of war? The Jews heard the noise of the trumpet, for they were permitted to wage war, and this was the appropriate sign for men whose law told them to hate their enemies. But the angels of peace sing a very different song in the ears of a people seeking peace. They do not sound the war-trumpet or promise victories, triumphs, and spoils of war. No, it is peace they proclaim, in accordance with the pronouncements of the prophets, and they proclaim it not to those who breathe war and slaughter, who are filled with fury and longing for arms, but to men of good will whose inclination is towards concord. Men may suggest what reasons they like for their own malady, but if they did not love war they would not engage in perpetual warfare amongst themselves in the way they do.

Then when Christ reached manhood, what else did he teach and expound but peace? He repeatedly greeted his disciples with an assurance of peace, saying 'Peace be with you,' and bade them use that form of greeting as the only one worthy of Christians. The apostles also remember this command when they start their letters with words of peace, wishing peace to those whom they especially love. To wish good health for anyone is an excellent thing, but a prayer for peace is a prayer for the sum total of happiness. Now see how at the hour of his death Christ is deeply concerned to commend peace to his hearers, as he had so often done throughout his lifetime. 'Love one another,' he says, 'as I have loved you'; and again, 'I give you my peace, I leave you peace.'[10] You hear what he leaves his people? Not horses, bodyguards, empire, or riches – none of these. What then? He gives peace, leaves peace – peace with friends, peace with enemies. Now please consider what he begged from his Father at the Last Supper, in his final prayers as the hour of death drew near. He knew he would be granted whatever he asked and so, I think, he sought no ordinary thing. 'Holy Father,' he said, 'keep them through thy name, that they may be one as we are.'[11] Please note that Christ asks for his people a special sort of concord: he said not that they should be of one mind but that they might be one, and not just in any way, but, as he said, we are one who are united in the most perfect and inexpressible way; and incidentally he indicated that there is only one way for men to be preserved – if they unite among themselves to foster peace.

The princes of this world mark their men by distinctive attire so that they can be picked out from the others, especially in time of war; but look at the mark Christ has used to indicate his followers – none other than that of mutual love. 'By this sign,' he said, 'men shall know that you are my disciples,' not if you are dressed in a special way or eat special food, not if you spend your time on excessive fasting or exhaustive study of the Psalms, but 'if you love one another' – and in no common manner, but 'as I have loved you.'[12] The precepts of the philosophers are without end, the pronouncements of Moses and the kings are many and various, but Christ said only: 'This is my sole commandment: love one another.[13] And in prescribing a form of prayer for his disciples, does he not give in its opening words a wonderful suggestion of Christian concord? 'Our Father,' he says. The spoken prayer is for one God, the petition is one which is common to all men, for they are all one household, one family, dependents of one Father; how then is it right for them to contend amongst themselves in continual warfare? How can you call on a common father if you are drawing a sword to thrust in your brother's vitals? And as Christ wished this one concept to be deeply implanted in the minds of his followers, he drove home his concern for concord with so many signs, parables, and commandments.

He calls himself a shepherd and his disciples sheep. I ask you, who has ever seen sheep fighting sheep? What is left for the wolves to do if the flock tears itself to pieces? When he calls himself the stock of the vine and his people the branches, what else does he mean but that they are of one mind? It would seem a strange portent demanding propitiation if branch warred on branch on the same vine, but isn't this to be seen if Christian fights Christian? Finally, if anything at all is sacrosanct for Christians, one thing should surely be sacrosanct and deep-seated in their hearts, that is, the message given in Christ's last instructions, his final testament, as it were, in which he commended to his sons what he hoped they would never come to forget. What was the sum of his teaching, instruction, commandment, and prayer, if not that they should love one another? What did the communion of holy bread and loving-cup ratify but a kind of new concord which should never be broken?

But as he knew that peace could not be established where there is rivalry for office, fame, wealth, and vengeance, he removed these passions completely from the hearts of his people, he absolutely forbade them to resist evil and ordered them to return good for evil and, if they could, pray for good for those who wished them harm. Can men believe themselves to be Christians if for some trifling injury they plunge a great part of the world into war? Christ commands the prince to be the servant of his people and to excel them only in being a better man and doing good to more. Yet there are men who are not ashamed to create widespread chaos simply in order to make some tiny little addition to the territories they rule. He tells us to live for the day, like birds and lilies; he forbids us to worry about the next day, he wants all to depend on heaven, and he excludes the rich from the kingdom of heaven. But some men have no scruples about shedding human blood on account of a trifling sum not paid them, and perhaps not even owed. In these days indeed, these seem pre-eminently just reasons for starting a war!

What is so frail and fleeting as the life of man, exposed to so many hazards and infirmities? Yet although it is burdened with more inherent misery that can be borne, men in their madness still bring down the worst of it on their own heads. The minds of mortals are so blind that they perceive none of this. They rush on headlong to break, sunder, and shatter every bond and covenant of Nature and of Christ. They fight everywhere and endlessly, with neither measure nor limit; nation battles with nation, city with city, faction with faction, prince against prince; and because of the folly or ambition of two wretched little men who are destined soon to perish like creatures of a day, human affairs are turned upside-down in confusion.

I will pass over the tragedies of bygone wars; let us just recall events of the past ten years. Where in the world has there not been savage warfare on land and sea? What land has not been soaked in Christian blood, what river or sea not stained with human gore? And (shameful to say) the cruelty of the fighting exceeds that of the Jews, of the heathen, and of wild beasts. The kind of wars the Jews carried on against their foreign foes should have been fought by the Christians against evil, but as things are they ally themselves with evil to make war on their fellow men. Yet the Jews were led to battle by God's command, whereas, if you look at the true facts, putting pretexts aside, the Christians are led astray by ambition, swayed by anger (worst of counsellors), and seduced by insatiable greed. Moreover, the Jews were mainly involved with non-Jews, while Christians have a treaty with the Turks and are at war amongst themselves. It was generally thirst for glory which roused heathen tyrants to war, yet their subjugation of barbarous and savage peoples brought benefits with conquest, and the victor was concerned to treat the defeated fairly. Their aim was to win as bloodless a victory as possible, so that the reward for the conqueror should be fame with honour, and his benevolence should bring consolation to the vanquished.

But I am ashamed to recount the disgraceful and frivolous pretexts Christian princes find for calling the whole world to arms. One discovers or invents some mouldering, obsolete title to support his claim, as if it really matters much who rules a kingdom so long as there is proper concern for the welfare of the people. Another pleads some trifling omission in a treaty covering a hundred clauses, or has a personal grievance against his neighbour over the interception of an intended spouse or a careless word of slander. Most criminally wicked of all, there are rulers who believe that their authority is undermined by harmony amongst their people and strengthened by discord, so they use their despotic power to suborn persons who will set about stirring up war; this gives them an opportunity to divide those who were previously united, and at the same time greater freedom to pillage their unhappy subjects. They are the worst sort of criminals, men who thrive on the sufferings of the people, and in time of peace find little to do in society.

What Fury from hell could have implanted this poison in a Christian heart? Who taught the followers of Christ a tyranny such as no Dionysius nor Mezentius[14] ever knew? They are beasts, not men, princes only in the tyranny they wield, using their wits only to do harm, never united except to damage the public interest. Yet in spite of their conduct are they held to be Christians, and although everywhere polluted with human blood, do they dare to approach holy churches and altars. Such monsters should be banished to islands at the far corners of the world! If Christians are members of one body, why is there no rejoicing at another's good fortune? Today if a neighbouring kingdom is rather more prosperous throughout, it seems almost a just cause for starting a war.

For if we are willing to admit the truth, what has stirred so many in the past and still stirs them today to take up arms against the kingdom of France except the knowledge that it is the most prosperous of all powers? There is no larger territory, nowhere a senate more highly honoured or an Academy of greater distinction, and nowhere is there greater concord. The consequence of all this is that France is supremely powerful. The law flourishes as nowhere else, nowhere has religion so retained its purity without being corrupted by commerce carried on by the Jews, as in Italy, or infected by the proximity of the Turks or marraños,[15] as in Hungary and Spain. Germany, to say nothing of Bohemia, is divided between so many petty princes that it cannot present even the appearance of a kingdom. France alone – the unspotted flower of Christendom and an impregnable fortress, should any storm assail it – is the target for attacks of so many kinds, for so many assaults and stratagems, and all for what would have been cause for congratulation if there had been any glimmer of Christian mentality in those responsible. Thus a holy pretext is named for these unholy deeds, and a road is laid for enlarging the empire of Christ. How monstrous – to hold that the Christian realm is ill served unless the most beautiful and fortunate part of Christendom is destroyed! ...

At the time when the Romans still followed pagan beliefs, it was the custom for the high priest on entering office to swear an oath that he would keep his hands clean of all blood, to the extent that he would not retaliate even if he were attacked. The heathen emperor Titus Vespasian held steadfastly to this oath, and is praised for so doing by his heathen biographer.[16] How the world has lost all sense of shame today, when amongst Christians, priests dedicated to God, and monks who boast of greater holiness than theirs fan the flames of bloodshed and carnage and turn the herald's trumpet of the Gospel into the battle trumpet of Mars. They rush to and fro, forgetful of their calling, prepared to do and suffer anything so long as they can stir up war. Through them, princes who would otherwise perhaps remain at peace are fired to enter battle, though their influence would have been better directed towards calming men's passions. What is even more monstrous, the clergy go to war themselves, and for the same causes, causes which even among the pagans were despised by the philosophers and should seem especially contemptible to men who follow the apostles.

A few years ago, when a kind of fatal madness was hurrying on the whole world to take up arms, the preachers of the Gospel, that is, certain Franciscans and Dominicans, sounded the trumpet of war from the pulpit and fired their hearers, who were all ready for violent action, to further atrocities. In England they stirred up feeling against the French, in France against the English; all called for war, none appealed for peace except one or two whom I could not so much as name: it would be their death-sentence. Holy bishops, unmindful of their profession and calling, hurried hither and thither making every effort to aggravate the general fever of the world, and now inciting the Roman pontiff Julius,[17] now the ruling kings, to hurry on the war, as if they had not already completely lost their wits unaided. Yet we have concealed their obvious insanity behind fine-sounding titles. For this end we misrepresent the laws of our fathers, the writings of pious men, and the words of Holy Scripture with supreme shamelessness, to say nothing of irreverence. It has almost come to the point that it is foolish and irreverent to open one's mouth against war or to speak in favour of what alone found favour on the lips of Christ. Apparently it is not enough to act in the people's interests, to support the Prince who preached the one thing which can be our salvation, and who sought to dissuade us from the most noxious course of all. Already the priests are making for the army camps where the bishops preside, their churches abandoned for the service of Bellona.[18] Indeed, war breeds priests, bishops, and cardinals, for whom the title of Legate in the Field is believed honourable and worthy of the apostles' successors. So it is small wonder if those whom war begat breathe the spirit of war; and to make the evil harder to remedy, they conceal their impious ways behind a facade of piety. They carry the cross as their standard; the godless soldier, the mercenary paid a fixed sum in cash for butchery and slaughter, bears the sign of the cross, so that what alone could lead man away from war has become its symbol.

What is the cross to you, villanous soldier? Serpents, wolves, and tigers were better suited to your spirit and conduct. The cross is the symbol of him who won his victory not by fighting, but by dying, who when he came did not destroy, but saved; the cross could teach you better than anything the enemies with whom you have to deal, if you are truly a Christian, and how they must be overcome. But you carry the banner of salvation as you hasten to destroy your brother, to kill in the name of the cross one who was saved by it. Worse still, think how men take part in the mystery of the holy sacraments (for these too are brought into the camps), which all should revere and which are the special symbol of the closest union between Christians, and then run straight into battle, cruel swords drawn to plunge into their brothers' vitals; and how they make Christ the witness (if Christ can bring himself to be present) of the wickedest of all crimes, the one most acceptable to the spirits of evil. Finally, and what is most absurd of all, the cross is displayed in both camps, in both battle-lines, and the sacraments are administered on both sides. What anomaly is this, when the cross fights the cross and Christ makes war on Christ! This symbol is one to strike terror into the enemies of the name of Christ. Why do they now attack what they should revere – these men who deserve not the crucifix but crucifixion?

Tell me, how can the soldier during divine worship pray in the words 'Our Father'? What impudence, to dare call on God as Father, when you are making for your brother's throat! 'Hallowed by thy name.' How could the name of God be less hallowed than by your violence towards each other? 'Thy kingdom come.' Is this how you pray, when you are planning so much bloodshed to get a kingdom for yourself? 'Thy will be done, on earth as it is in heaven.' But God's will is for peace, and you are preparing for war. Do you ask for daily bread from our common Father when you burn your brother's crops and would prefer them to be lost to you rather than to benefit him? And then, how can you say 'Forgive us the debts we owe, as we forgive those who are indebted to us,' you who are hurrying to murder your kin? You pray to be spared the danger of being put to the test, but you risk danger to yourself so that you can endanger your brother. Do you beg to be delivered from the evil one while you are plotting the worst of evils against your brother at his prompting?

Plato declares that a war provoked by Greeks against Greeks must not be called a war but says it is a civil war. Then are men to speak of a war as holy – a war which Christian wages with Christian, on any pretexts, with soldiery and arms such as we have now? According to pagan law, anyone who stained his sword with his brother's blood was sewn into a sack and thrown into a river. Are men less than blood brothers when they are united in Christ? Yet amongst us parricide is rewarded. What misery war brings! The victor commits parricide, the vanquished dies, none the less guilty of parricide because he also attempted it. They they curse the Turks for being godless and unchristian, as if they could be Christians themselves while committing these crimes or as if there could be anything more agreeable for the Turks than the sight of Christians putting each other to the sword. The Turks, so they say, offer sacrifice to demons, but these spirits find no victim so acceptable as one Christian killed by another; so aren't you doing the same as the Turks? The wicked demons then enjoy a double sacrifice, since the killer and the killed are both equally their victims. Anyone who favours the Turks and is a friend to their demons should always be offering sacrifices of this kind.

But I have long been hearing the sort of excuse clever men produce for their own wrongdoing. They protest that they act under compulsion and are dragged unwillingly into war. Pull off your mask, drop your pretences, examine your own heart, and you will find that anger, ambition, and folly brought you to war, not any constraint – unless you define constraint as something not altogether to your liking! Such trappings are for the people; God is not to be fooled by pretence. Yet meanwhile solemn prayers are offered, and peace is sought with noisy clamour and deafening roar of voices: 'Grant us peace, we beseech you, hear us!'[19] Surely God could justly answer: 'Why do you mock me? You are asking me to remove what you bring on yourselves of your own choice. You pray to be let off what is your own responsibility.'

If any sort of affront can start a war – why, who has nothing to complain of? Incidents arise between husband and wife which are best overlooked, unless you want their mutual good will to be destroyed. If something of the same sort arises between princes, why need there be an immediate rush to arms? There are laws, there are learned men, venerable abbots, and reverend bishops whose sound advice could have calmed a stormy situation. Why do the princes not ask them to arbitrate? They could hardly pick out any so partisan that they would not depart with a better solution than they would achieve by arms. Hardly any peace is so unjust that it is not preferable to a war, however just that may be. First count all the separate demands and concomitants of war, and then you will see how much you profit by it!

The supreme authority is that of the pontiff of Rome. But when nations and princes are violently engaged in wicked wars which may go on for years, what has become of papal authority then? Where is the power second only to Christ's? It should surely have been exercised, were its holders not gripped by the same passions as the people. When the pontiff calls for war, he is obeyed. If he calls for peace, why is there not the same obedience to his call? If men prefer peace, why were they so eager to answer the summons of Julius as a war leader, though scarcely anyone responds to Leo's appeal for peace and concord?[20] If the authority of the pontiff is truly sacrosanct, it should surely most prevail whenever it appeals for what was the special message of Christ. But when those whom Julius could rouse to engage in a war of deadly destruction cannot be similarly stirred when the most holy pontiff Leo appeals in so many ways for Christian concord, they make it clear that under pretext of serving the church they are the slaves of their own desires, to say nothing harsher than that.

If you are genuinely tired of war, let me give you a word of advice on how you can maintain concord. A sound peace does not rest on alliances and treaties between men, which, as we see, can often lead to wars. The very sources from which the evil springs and the base passions which give rise to your conflicts must be cleansed. And while each individual is the slave of his desires, the state suffers; nor does any individual attain the very end he pursues with his evil designs. The princes must learn wisdom and use it for their subjects, not for themselves, and they should be truly wise, measuring their majesty, happiness, wealth, and magnificence by the factors which make them truly great and glorious. Their intention towards their country should be that of a father towards his family. A king should think himself great if the subjects he rules are of the very best, happy if he makes his people happy, exalted if the men he governs enjoy the greatest measure of freedom, wealthy if they are wealthy, prosperous if his cities prosper in unbroken peace. And the nobles and holders of office should model their attitude on that of their prince, judging everything by the country's interests; by this means they will also have acted properly in their own interests.

If a king is of this intention, will he be easily persuaded to extort money from his subjects in order to pay barbarian mercenaries? Will he reduce his people to famine to enrich some godless army leaders? Will he expose the lives of his people to so many hazards? I think not. He should exercise his power within limits, remembering that he is a human being and a free man ruling over men who are also human and free and, finally, that he is a Christian ruler of Christians. The people in their turn should defer to him only so far as is in the public interest. A good prince should demand no more, and a bad one will in fact have his desires held in check by the combined will of the citizens. Neither side should consider personal interests.

All honour to those who have used their talents or wisdom for the prevention of war and the establishment of concord; in short, to the man who has directed all his efforts, not to procuring the greatest force of fighting men and engines of war, but to ensuring that there shall be no need of them. Yet out of so many Roman emperors, only Diocletian is recorded as having conceived this noblest of designs.[21] But if war is unavoidable, it should be conducted in such a way that the full force of its calamities must fall on the heads of those who gave cause for it. As things are now, princes wage war unscathed and their generals thrive on it, while the main flood of misfortune sweeps over the peasants and humble citizens, who have no interest in war and gave no occasion for it. Where is a prince's wisdom, if he takes no thought of this, or his heart, if he reckons it of small consequence? Some plan must be devised whereby the power to rule shall not change hands so frequently and be forever on the move, because every innovation in affairs creates disturbance, and disturbance creates war. It could easily be achieved if royal children had to marry within the bounds of their own territory, or if, when an alliance between neighbours was desirable, all parties should renounce their expectations of succession. Nor should a prince be permitted to sell or transfer any part of his realm, as if free cities were his personal property: for the cities subject to a king's rule are free, unlike those which are slaves under a tyrant's domination.

In the kind of intermarriage we have today it may happen that a native Irishman suddenly becomes emperor of the Indies, or the previous ruler of Syria unexpectedly finds himself king of Britain. As a result of this, neither country will have a ruler; someone will have abandoned his old country and not be recognized by his new one, as he is wholly unknown and born in a different world. Meanwhile, as he tries to consolidate his position and establish himself by conquest, he drains away and exhausts the resources of one of the countries, and while struggling to retain his hold on two places, though he is hardly fit to administer one, more often than not he loses them both.

There should be agreement between princes once and for all on what each of them should rule, and once territories have been assigned them, no alliance should extend or diminish these and no treaty tear them apart. Thus each ruler will try to make every improvement he can in his own portion, and by applying all his energies to one territory, he will try to leave it to his children enriched in the best way he can. By this means the future could be one of universal prosperity everywhere. It remains for the princes to be bound together not by marriage alliances or artificial associations, but by friendship which is genuine and disinterested, and above all by a like and common desire to be of service to mankind. A prince should be succeeded either by his next of kin or by one judged most suitable by vote of the people; for the others, it should be enough if they rank amongst eminent members of the nobility.

It is royalty's duty to know nothing of personal inclinations and to judge everything by the common good. Accordingly, the prince should avoid distant journeys; indeed, he should never be willing to go beyond the bounds of his own realm, and should keep in mind the saying tested and proved throughout the centuries: 'Better master's face than the back of his head.'[22] He should think himself enriched not if he has robbed others but if he has improved what is his own. When war is under discussion, he should not seek counsel from young men, who like the idea of war simply because they have no experience of the evils it brings, or from those who gain control by general disturbances of the peace, who flourish and fatten on the miseries of the people. He should call on older men of prudence and integrity, whose devotion to their country is proved. Nor should a war be rashly started to suit the whim of one individual or another, for a war once begun is difficult to end. Something so highly dangerous, more so than anything, must not be undertaken except by the consent of the whole people.

The causes of war must be removed immediately. Some things must be overlooked; such courtesy will encourage courtesy. There are times when peace has to be paid for. If you calculate all a war would have cost and the number of citizens you will save from death, peace will seem cheap at the price, however much you paid for it; the cost of war would have been greater, quite apart from the blood lost by your subjects. You must work out how much evil you avoid and how much good you can preserve, and you will not regret the cost. Meanwhile the bishops should carry out their duties, the priests be true priests, the monks be mindful of their profession, and the theologians teach what is worthy of Christ. Let all combine against war, all be watchdogs and speak out against it. In private and in public they must preach, proclaim, and inculcate one thing: peace. Then if they cannot prevent a conflict to settle the issue, they must certainly not approve or take part, lest they should be responsible for giving a good name to so criminal or at least so questionable a practice.

It should be sufficient for men killed in war to be buried in unconsecrated ground. If there are any good men amongst them, they will certainly be very few in number, and will not be denied their reward because of this. But the godless, who are the largest number, will be less satisfied with themselves if their privilege is withdrawn. I am speaking about the wars which Christians generally fight against Christians; I take a different view of men who repel the violent attacks of barbarian invaders by their wholehearted and loyal determination, and protect the peace and security of their country at their own peril.

Today the trophies stained with the blood of those whom Christ shed his own blood to save are set up in churches between the statues of the apostles and martyrs, as if in future it will be an act of piety to create a martyr, not to become one. It would have been quite sufficient to set these up and preserve them in the market-place or some armoury; it is wholly improper for what has been polluted by bloodshed to be received into holy churches which should be kept pure and undefiled. Priests dedicated to God should intervene in wars only to put a stop to them. If they were united on this, if they would drive the same lesson home everywhere, it would be something of the greatest importance. But perhaps it is the fatal malady of human nature to be quite unable to carry on without wars. If so, why is this evil passion not let loose upon the Turks? Of course it used to be thought preferable, even in their case, to win them over to the religion of Christ by teaching and by the example of good deeds and a blameless life rather than by mounting an armed attack. But if war, as we said, is not wholly avoidable, that kind would be a lesser evil than the present unholy conflicts and clashes between Christians. If mutual love does not bind them together, a common enemy will surely unite them after a fashion, and there will be some sort of common purpose, even if true harmony is lacking.

Finally, the greatest element in peace is a heartfelt desire for it. Those who truly have peace at heart snatch at every opportunity for it; they ignore or remove the obstacles in the way and put up with a lot, so long as this greatest of blessings is unimpaired. Yet today men seek out the breeding-grounds for wars, disparaging or even concealing what makes for peace while going out of their way to exaggerate and aggravate what leads to war. I am ashamed to mention the kind of trivial incident they exploit in order to create widespread tragedy, and what a tiny spark can set such a holocaust ablaze. It is then that they recall a whole host of wrongs they have suffered, and everyone makes the most of his misfortune. Meanwhile, any benefits received are completely forgotten; you'd swear their only aspiration was war. And there is often some personal grievance between princes which forces the whole world to take up arms, though any grounds for starting on a war ought to be a fully public concern, if anything is.

Are you longing for war? First take a look at what peace and war really are, the gains brought by one and the losses by the other; this will enable you to calculate whether there is anything to be achieved by exchanging peace for war. If it is something for admiration when a kingdom is prosperous throughout, with its cities soundly established, lands well cultivated, excellent laws, the best teaching, and the highest moral standards, consider how you will necessarily destroy all this happiness if you go to war. By contrast, if you have ever seen towns in ruins, villages destroyed, churches burnt, and farmland abandoned and have found it a pitiable spectacle, as indeed it is, reflect that all this is the consequence of war.

If you judge it a serious thing to introduce the criminal dregs of hired mercenaries into your country, to feed them on your people's misery, to submit to them, fawn on them, indeed, to entrust yourself and your safety to their will, you must realize that this is a condition of war. If you abominate robbery, this is what war teaches; if you abhor murder, this is the lesson of war. For who will shrink from killing one man in hot blood when he has been hired for a pittance to slaughter so many? If neglect of the law is the most imminent threat to civil authority, why, 'the law says nothing when arms hold sway.'[23] If you believe that fornication, incest, and worse are loathsome evils, war is the school where these are taught. If irreverence for and neglect of religion is the source of every evil, religion is entirely swept away by the storm of war. If you judge the state of your country to be worst when the worst people in it have the most power, in time of war the lowest kinds of criminal are the rulers; war has most need of those whom in time of peace you would nail to the cross. For who will be better at leading troops through hidden tracks than a trained brigand? Who will be bolder at plundering houses and despoiling churches than a housebreaker or tomb-robber? Who will be so eager to strike down and disembowel a foe as a gladiator or murderer? Or so suitable for setting fire to cities and engines of war as an incendiary? Who will defy the waves and hazards at sea like a pirate trained by a lifetime of plundering? If you want to see clearly how immoral a thing is war, you have only to look at the agents it employs.

If nothing should be so important to the conscientious prince as the welfare of his subjects, it is essential that war should be particularly hateful to him; if his happiness is to rule a happy people, he must cherish peace above all. If the chief desire of a good prince should be that his subjects are as good as they can be, he ought to loathe war as the cesspool of every iniquity. If he would believe that his personal wealth resides in the possessions of the citizens, he must avoid war by every possible means, for it will certainly wear down everyone's resources if it is to have a successful outcome, and what was won by honest skill must be squandered on individuals who are no more than murderers and monsters.

Then too, princes must consider over and over again that every man is won over by his own cause and smiled on by his own expectations, and that what seems perfectly just in the heat of the moment may often prove the opposite; self-deception of this kind is not infrequent. However, imagine a cause which is undoubtedly just and a war which is wholly successful in outcome, and them make sure you weigh up all the disadvantages of actually fighting the war against the advantages won by victory, and see if the victory was worth while. It can scarcely ever be bloodless, so now you have your people defiled by human blood. Then reckon the damage to individual morals and public discipline, for which no gain can compensate. You empty your purse, plunder your people, burden the just, and incite the unjust to further crimes, and even when you have ended the war, its legacy remains with you. Skilled crafts will have fallen into disuse and trade and business been interrupted, for you will have been forced to cut yourself off from many places in order to blockade your enemy. Before the war, all neighbouring regions were yours, for peace makes everything common to all through trade. See what you have done: even the country which is especially yours can now hardly be called your own.

When you set out to destroy a small town, how many siege engines and tents do you need? You have to make a sham city to demolish the real one, but you could have built another real town at less cost. If the enemy is to have no advantage from this town, then you must sleep without a roof over your head, an exile far from home. It would have cost less to build new town walls than to use engines to pull down those already built. I am not reckoning here the money which has slipped through the fingers of the army captains and of those who exact and receive it; it will certainly form no small part of the total. But if you sum up all these separate items accurately and don't find that you could have secured peace for a tenth of the cost, you can all make an end of me: I shan't protest.

You may suppose you are weak-spirited if you forgive any wrong done you, but in fact nothing is surer proof of a mean spirit far removed from any noble-mindedness than a desire for revenge. You think there is some loss of dignity on your part if you renounce a tiny portion of your rights when dealing with a fellow prince who is a near neighbour, and perhaps a kinsman or relative by marriage, maybe someone who has done something for you on another occasion. But it is far more humiliating to your dignity when you are repeatedly compelled to use your gold to propitiate barbarian mercenaries and the lowest dregs of criminal society, who are insatiable in their demands; far more humiliating when you send envoys to the Carians,[24] the vilest and most pernicious of men, to seek their support with honeyed words, when you entrust your own life and the fortunes of your subjects to the word of a people totally lacking in scruple and integrity.

Then if ever peace appears to be a hard bargain, you must look at it like this: 'I'm paying a price, but what I'm getting is peace.' Of course you could argue against this with the quibble 'I'd pay up readily if it were a personal matter, but I am a prince and must concern myself with the public interest whether I want to or not.' Yet a man who looks only to the public interest will not easily embark on war; in fact all the causes of war can be seen to arise from matters which are none of the people's concern. Do you intend to establish your claim to some part of your realm? That is not the people's affair. Do you want to take action against the man who has abandoned your daughter? It is not your country's concern. The ability to judge and discriminate between public and private interest is the mark of the truly wise man and the truly great prince. ... Oh, there has been more than enough shedding of blood – and not just human blood but Christian blood – enough frenzy ending in mutual destruction, enough sacrifices by now even to hell and the Furies – there has long been enough to gladden the eyes of the Turks. The play is ended. The miseries of war have been endured far too long; now at least return to your senses. Let all previous madness be blamed on the Fates, and Christians agree, as the pagans agreed before us, to forget their evil ways. Then unite in counsel, press on and be zealous for peace, and do so in such a way that it will be established never to be broken, held together not by ties of rope but by firm bonds of adamant.[25]

I call on you, princes, on whose assent especially the affairs of the world depend, who bear amongst men the image of Christ the Prince: heed the voice of your King, who summons you to peace. Consider that the whole world is exhausted by a long period of misfortune and demands it of you. If any grievance is still outstanding, it must be endured as a proper concession to the general happiness of all. The matter is too serious to be delayed for frivolous reasons. I call on you, priests, dedicated to God, to express in all your endeavours what you know is most pleasing to God, and to cut out what is most hateful to him. I call on you, theologians, to preach the gospel of peace and to make your message ring unceasingly in the ears of the people. I call on you, bishops, and you others who are high in the offices of the church, to see that your authority prevails and peace is held firm in bonds which will last for all time. I call on you, nobles and magistrates, to ensure that your will supports the wisdom of kings and the piety of pontiffs. I call on you all alike who are counted Christians to work together with united hearts. Here you must show how the combined will of the people can prevail against the tyranny of the powerful; here must be the focal point of all endeavour. Eternal concord should unite those whom nature has made one in many things and whom Christ has unified in more, and all should join in a united effort to bring about what concerns the happiness of one and all.

Everything points the way, first natural instinct and what we might call the human principle itself, then the Prince and Author of all human happiness, Christ. In addition, there are all the advantages of peace and many disasters of war. The very wills of the ruling princes, which are inclined toward concord as if inspired by God, summon you to peace. See how the great Leo, peacemaker and lover of peace, has raised his standard with a general call for peace, proving himself a true vicar of Christ. If you are truly his sheep, follow your shepherd. If you are his sons, listen to your father. Francis,[26] the most Christian king of France (and not in title alone), summons you hither; he is ready to buy peace, and sets aside consideration of his majesty in the interests of general peace, proving that true glory and royalty lie in the possible service to the human race. The most noble Prince Charles, a young man of pure and upright character, summons you. The emperor Maximilian raises no objection, the illustrious King Henry of England[27] does not refuse his support. When the greatest princes set an example, it is only right that all other men should gladly follow it.

The majority of the common people loathe war and pray for peace; only a handful of individuals, whose evil joys depend on general misery, desire war. Whether it is right or not for their wickedness to prevail over the will of all honest men is for you yourselves to judge.

You see that hitherto nothing has been achieved by treaties, nothing advanced by alliances, nothing by violence or revenge. Now try instead what conciliation and kindness can do. War springs from war, revenge brings further revenge. Now let generosity breed generosity, kind actions invite further kindness, and true royalty be measured by willingness to concede sovereignty.

Our human endeavours alone have not brought success; but Christ himself will bless sincere negotiations which he sees are undertaken with his own guidance and support. He will stand at our right hand as our inspiration, he will give his aid to those who assist the cause he has himself so much at heart, so that personal interests will yield to general welfare. And yet while this is our concern, every man will see his own fortunes advanced: princes will win more respect for their authority if their subjects are loyal and happy, under a rule of law rather than of arms; nobles will have a greater and truer nobility; priests a life of greater tranquillity; the people a more prosperous peace and more peaceful prosperity; and the name of Christian will be more to be feared by enemies of the cross. Finally, you will all be loving and kindly, one to another and all to all; and above everything you will be dear to Christ, in pleasing whom is the sum of happiness. I have said my say.

# On the War against the Turks / *De bello turcico*

The Turkish army abandoned the siege of Vienna on 14 October 1529, having failed to force the gateway to the Habsburg Empire. For the next few months, dire prophecies and nervous uncertainty abounded in the West. In this atmosphere of fearful anticipation, Erasmus spoke his mind on the principle of war against the infidel.

The work should be read in light of the controversy over Luther's views on the subject. In 1518 Luther had proclaimed that the Turks were a scourge of God and must not be resisted – statements that were condemned in the papal bull *Exsurge Domine* of 1520. In 1529 Luther had a change of heart, brought about by alterations in political circumstances. He was as adamant as ever that the clergy must not become involved in war, but now allowed that the emperor had the right to lead an army against the Turks in a defensive motion. His conclusion of *Vom Kriege / On War*, published in 1529, is strikingly similar to that of Erasmus: 'I would not urge or bid anyone to fight against the Turk unless the first method, mentioned above, that men had first repented and been reconciled to God, etc, had been followed. If anyone wants to go to war in another way, let him take his chances.'

Erasmus composed his treatise on the eve of the Diet of Augsburg in 1530. He was expected to attend in person but was prevented from doing so by poor health. This work was published a number of times in or just after 1530, twice more in 1547, and in a partial German version not long after the first publication.

This extract is taken from the translation by Michael J. Heath to be published in CWE 64.

Let us not turn a deaf ear to the repeated warnings of the Lord;[1] He is now calling out once again through the cruelty of the Turks, to which we have almost become accustomed; but this only makes our deafness the more unpardonable, in that, despite the frequency of these warnings, we have still not awoken to the danger. How many defeats have the Christian peoples suffered at the hands of this race of barbarians, whose very origin is obscure? What atrocities have they not committed against us? For how many cities, how many islands, how many provinces have they snatched away from the domain of Christ? See how they have confined the once world-wide power and influence of our religion to a narrow strip of land! These early successes seem to suggest that, unless we are shielded by the right hand of God, in a few years the remainder of the Christian world will also be absorbed. Even if all these calamities occurred through no fault of our own, the whole body of Christendom should be moved by Christian sympathy to grieve for one of its members in distress; but now there can be no doubt that the Turks have won an immense empire less by their own merits than because of our sins, whose just reward has been the destruction of our empire. In view of this, all who acknowledge the name of Christ must now do more than grieve: we must give assistance to our brother nations in their time of distress. It is no longer a case of sharing these disasters because of our common religion, but because there is a danger now that we may soon share them in reality. 'When your neighbour's wall is on fire, it becomes your business'; in fact, it becomes the business of the whole city, whenever a single house catches fire. Therefore we must give assistance if we are truly anxious to rid ourselves of this peril; but assistance of two kinds. Of course, we must make all the preparations necessary for such an arduous war, but before that we must make the preparations without which military strength will be in vain. We have frequently taken the field against the Turks, but so far with little success; either because we have still clung to all the things which have angered God and caused him to send the Turks against us, just as he sent frogs, lice, and locusts upon the Egyptians long ago, or perhaps because we have relied upon our own strength for victory, and have forgotten that the battle is fought in the name of Christ, and conducted ourselves like Turks against the Turks. This situation therefore demands that we should say something about both kinds of preparation, if it can first be demonstrated to us that the Turks have increased their empire up to now as a result of our negligence rather than their own virtue or valour. ...

It is easy to see how profitable their false religion has been to them, as long as we have neglected the duties of true piety. While we have been endlessly fighting among ourselves over some useless plot of ground in what are worse than civil wars, the Turks have vastly extended their empire or, rather, their reign of terror. To the north, it stretches to the Black Sea; to the east, it extends to the Euphrates, and to the south, to Ethiopia. For within the last few years the Turks have conquered the whole of Egypt and Syria as well as Phoenicia and Palestinian Judaea. In the west, their boundaries stretch to the Ionian Sea and, turning from there towards the north, they extend as far as the Danube, although, in fact, they have recently passed far beyond that barrier and reached the river Dnieper.

Can we attribute these successes to the Turks' piety? Of course not. To their valour? They are a race softened by debauchery and fearsome only as brigands. What, then, is the answer? They owe their victories to our sins; we have opposed them but, as the results plainly show, God has been angered against us. We assail the Turks with the selfsame eagerness with which they invade the lands of others. We are betrayed by our lust for power; we covet riches; in short, we fight the Turks like Turks. For the chronicle of these events shows clearly enough that it was our treachery, our ambition, our inherent faithlessness which provoked all these dreadful disasters. ... Now, if we had undertaken this legitimate war against the Turks in harmony among ourselves, with purer hearts, beneath the banners of Christ, and relying on his aid alone, Christendom would never have been reduced to its present straits. But I shall say more of this in its proper place.

Before that I must briefly take issue with two sets of opponents, those who are eager for a Turkish war for the wrong reasons, and those who, also wrongly, argue against making war on the Turks. Both groups seem to me equally wrong, though for different reasons. Of course, not all wars against the Turks are legitimate and holy, yet there are times when failure to resist the Turks simply means the surrender of part of Christendom to these barbaric enemies, and the abandonment of those of our brethren who are already enslaved beneath their foul yoke.

On the other hand, whenever the ignorant mob hear the name 'Turk,' they immediately fly into a rage and clamour for blood, calling them dogs and enemies to the name of Christian; it does not occur to them that, in the first place, the Turks are men, and, what is more, half-Christian; they never stop to consider whether the occasion of the war is just, nor whether it is practical to take up arms and thereby to provoke an enemy who will strike back with redoubled fury. They do not realize that the Church has no more dangerous enemies than sinners in high places, especially if they are in holy orders; finally, they do not understand that God, offended by our wickedness, from time to time uses the outrages committed by these barbarians to reform us. For instance, pictures are painted showing examples of Turkish cruelty, but these ought in fact to remind us how reluctant we should be to make war against anyone at all, since similar 'amusements' have been common in all the wars in which, over so many years, Christian has wickedly fought Christian. These paintings condemn their cruelty, yet worse crimes were perpetrated at Asperen,[2] not by Turks, but by my own countrymen, many of them even my friends. The memory of that calamity is too fresh; I need not reopen the wound. If the subjects of these paintings truly shock us, we should curb our own impetuosity, which so easily leads us headlong into war. For however cruel the deeds of the Turks, the same deeds committed against his fellow by a Christian are still more cruel. What a sight it would be if men were confronted with paintings of the atrocities which Christians have committed against Christians in the last forty years! This is all I have to say to those who do no more than scream 'War on the Turks! War on the Turks!'

Now I shall deal with the errors of those whose arguments for the opposite point of view, though perhaps more plausible, are no less dangerous; for there are those who claim that the right to make war is totally denied to Christians.[3] I find this idea too absurd to need refutation, although there has been no lack of people ready to contrive accusations against me because of this, in that in my writings I am lavish in my praise of peace and fierce in my hatred of war. But honest men reading my works will recognise, without any prompting from me, the obvious impertinence of these slanderers. My message is that war must never be undertaken unless, as a last resort, it cannot be avoided; war is by its nature such a plague to man that even if it is undertaken by a just prince in a totally just cause, the wickedness of captains and soldiers results in almost more evil than good. St Bernard goes further, in calling 'malicious' the 'militia' of this world; he designates it 'of this world' because so often the call to arms is provoked by ambition, anger or the hope of plunder; the man who falls in wars of this kind, he says, is dead for all eternity, while he who kills and conquers lives on – as a murderer.

Now I come to those who agree with Luther's contention that those who make war on the Turks rebel against God, who is punishing our sins through them. The theologians of Paris have censured this opinion in the following sentence: This proposition is universally understood to be false, and does not conform to Holy Writ.[4] They attack it as false, not as heretical, and they do not simply condemn it but declare that it is universally false. Their meaning is, I believe, that sometimes war against the Turks is rightly undertaken, sometimes not, according to the circumstances. As for the Scriptures, it is beyond dispute that the Israelites once fought a bloody war with the Allophyli at God's bidding, and, again, Moses himself, with the aid of the sons of Levi, executed 23,000 of his own people because of the molten calf.[5] But here another objector will raise the question whether this right was transferred to Christians, especially since the Israelites almost never went to war without specific orders from the Almighty. But if Christians are to be entirely denied the right to make war, by the same reasoning magistrates will have to lose the right to punish offenders. For war is no more than judicial retribution meted out on a large scale, if there is no other way of punishing the crime. Now, although in the Gospel the woman taken in adultery was set free, Jesus never denies the civil powers their legitimate rights, even if he never openly approves them. Besides, Paul appears to commend the sword which is used to punish the wicked and to reward the virtuous. Someone may quibble, and say that here Paul is only referring to a pagan magistracy, to which he wanted Christians to submit, on the grounds that if Christians were to seem to undermine the statutes and ordinances of the state, the Gospel would be brought into disrepute. My reply is that since, among Christians, there is no other way of keeping the peace, secular magistrates are necessary to deter criminals who do not observe the laws and customs of the state with the threat of punishment. Now, if we allow the magistrates this rights, we must also allow princes the right to make war.

However, although I am quite convinced of this, I also think that all other expedients must be tried before war is begun between Christians; no matter how serious nor how just the cause, war must not be undertaken unless all possible remedies have been exhausted and it has become inevitable. And, of course, if the war is inspired by such motives as the lust for power, ambition, private grievances, or the desire for revenge, it is clearly not a war, but mere brigandage. What is more, although it is primarily the function of the Christian princes themselves to carry on wars, they must not resort to this most dangerous of expedients without the consent of their citizens and of the whole country. Finally, if absolute necessity dictates that a war must be fought, Christian clemency demands that every effort be made to confine the numbers involved to the minimum and to end the war, with the least possible bloodshed, as quickly as may be. The Emperor Theodosius is praised on this count, and the praise comes from no less a man than St Ambrose, because he abstained from communion of the sacraments as a result of winning a bloody battle in which there had been much slaughter of the enemy.[6] On the other hand, the Romans determined the splendour of statues and triumphs according to the number of enemies slain.

Ambrose, who publicly praised this action of Theodosius, does not approve any war simply because it is necessary or just; it must also be accompanied by a religious spirit which places all its hopes of victory in God, and aims only at the peace of the state. When one asks how the Christian commonwealth can survive if there is no one to defend it by laws and by arms, there is always someone who will reply with another question: how did the Christian commonwealth survive, and increase, at a time when it possessed no secular magistrates, no arms, no means of fighting? But, I reply, although it was fitting that the church should rise initially from such foundations, it does not follow that things must always remain unchanged. The church owed its rise to a series of miracles, which is not to be expected now. But even at that time, pagan magistrates used to protect the peace of the church, and no man was allowed to kill a Christian.

As far as Luther's argument is concerned, I may add that if it is not lawful to resist the Turks, because God is punishing the sins of his people through them, it is no more lawful to call in a doctor during illness, because God also sends diseases to purge his people of their sins. He uses the wiles of Satan for the same purpose, and yet we are commanded to resist them. It is therefore lawful to fight off the Turks, unless God manifestly prohibits it.

However, it is clear that this war will be fought in the face of God's anger if we are moved by the desire for greater power, the lust for wealth, or any similar reason, rather than by concern for the peace of Christendom; or if, on meeting the enemy, we rely on our own strength rather than on God's protection, or fight without regard for our Christian principles. What is more, since God sends the Turks so frequently against us to call us to reform our lives, all the omens will be against us in this war if we take up arms without correcting the errors which have provoked God to punish us through their barbaric cruelty. It is obvious that this has been the case up to now; I am afraid that in the future things will get worse unless we turn wholeheartedly towards the Lord, and offer to him the sacrifice which the psalm suggested.

Someone will intervene here to say that it is lawful for Christian to fight Christian, but that it is not lawful to fight the Turks, since Paul declares that it is not his business to judge outsiders, and that he has enough to judge those within the community; the Turks are outsiders, and do not belong to the church; if we are permitted to kill Turks, why did not the church arm herself long ago against the Gentiles who cruelly persecuted all who confessed the name of Christ? But Augustine refused to authorise this, even at a time when our numbers and our wealth were greater than theirs; in fact, he appealed to the emperor not to execute certain men who had murdered some Christians, his reason being that in this way the glory of the martyrs would not be sullied. We read that certain idolatrous emperors instituted merciless persecution against the property and lives of Christians, but we never read that the Christians defended themselves by force of arms or planned revenge. They sought refuge in flight, the one relief which God allowed them. Some writers, including Tertullian,[7] declare that flight was not simply permitted, but allowed for a time as part of God's plan, since there were as yet few to proclaim the teaching of the Gospel, and the flight of the persecuted would spread the Word more widely. But once the Word had been spread throughout the city, flight became a kind of denial. Now, if it is not even right to flee, still less is it right to rush to arms.

The mass of Christians are wrong, on the other hand, in thinking that anyone is allowed to kill a Turk, as one would a mad dog, for no better reason than that he is a Turk. If this were true then anyone would be allowed to kill a Jew; but if he dared to do so he would not escape punishment by the civil authorities. The Christian magistrate punishes Jews who break the state's laws, to which they are subject, but they are not put to death because of their religion; Christianity is spread by persuasion, not by force; by careful cultivation, not by destruction. This right, by which Jews are punished in the same way as Christians, was also exercised by pagan rulers against their Christian subjects; if, God forbid, we were living under the laws of the Turkish empire, they too could exercise this right. So any who believe that they will fly straight up to heaven, if they happen to fall in battle against the Turks, are sadly deluding themselves; they will reach heaven only if their conscience be pure, even though, for Christ's sake, they expose their lives to a tyrant who calls them to worship idols. ...

But to take away the power of the sword from secular princes and magistrates is simply to undermine the whole foundation of the state, and to expose the lives and property of the citizens to the violence of criminals. There is, on the other hand, no good precedent for priests becoming involved in the business of war, to say nothing of actually fighting themselves. Their fight is for the Lord, and they must not be involved in the struggles of this world. War is such a soulless business that it should really be called pagan. If it is right for priests to make war, it is equally right for them to play the executioner. Now, when papal decrees forbid the priest to practise medicine, on what grounds is he permitted to turn to war, since all the energies and skill of the doctor go to preserving life, and those of the warrior to taking it? But this analogy of curing sickness does not entirely fit the present case, for the use of drugs does not entail loss or injury to anyone, whereas anyone using war as a cure applies it in such a way that he contrives the death of others. Anyone who makes war with too little justice on his side, or who conducts the campaign improperly, is no more acceptable than a man trying to ward off illness by witchcraft.

Another question which should be considered here is this: should a man, who is aware of his sin and recognises that his illness is visited upon him by an angry God, be allowed to use all permitted remedies to cure his illness, while still persistently committing the same sins as before? For such a man appears to be clearly resisting the will of God. But, although it may be allowed that the first law of nature permits each man to look after his health, if there is any hope of improvement, yet, even if he does not lapse into danger again because of his care for his health, it is clear that he sins grievously in rejecting God's clemency which has urged him to reform; he plunges himself into the greatest danger, namely that his illness will not be eased and that he may expose himself to even worse trouble. For it is the height of impiety to think that the doctor's art can cure illness without God's blessing. Now, we are in a similar condition if, while recognising that the Turkish invasion is sent to persuade us to reform our lives and to live in harmony with one another, we persist in our sins and continue to believe that we can ward off disaster, in the face of God's anger, by our own efforts. If we attack the Turks after breaking faith and violating our oath and covenant, we are like an invalid seeking help from a sorcerer rather than a doctor. The best advice that could be given to the invalid would be that first of all he should make his peace with God, acknowledge that God's treatment of him is less harsh than he deserves, and beg God's forgiveness while agreeing to mend his ways. Similarly, the soundest advice that could be given to our Christian princes now would be to persuade them that, before rushing into battle, they should eradicate all those evils which offend God and cause him to send the Turks against us so often. Otherwise, if we promise ourselves victory by our own efforts, we merely delude ourselves and anger the Lord still further, fighting against God more than against the Turks themselves.

There is no need for me to make a list of all the things which turn God away from us; let every man examine his own conscience and he will find enough there. ... We all have our different faults, and some sin more obviously than others; but we all need the mercy of God. Yet the principal and most glaring faults are those which are disguised the most cunningly. What are they? How I wish that what I have to say, reluctantly and with a heavy heart, concerned fewer men, or none at all! How far the church's ministers have fallen below the ideals of their predecessors! How completely the worst of cankers, ambition and profit, have corrupted all our dealings! How long have we seen foreign princes battling with implacable hatred against one another! The Greeks and Trojans fought over Helen for ten years. How much longer than that have we been fighting over the 'Helen' of Milan?[8] What misfortunes has Italy not suffered? What troubles has France not endured? Even the lands of the victors are in mourning. It is better not to touch upon our private struggle in the war which we fought so many years with the Gelders, which is a most sensitive point with us;[9] without listing individual events, one may ask what province there is now where the poor are not miserably oppressed by an extraordinary scarcity of every commodity? Where now is to be found a vestige of true faith, of Christian charity, of peace and harmony? What age ever saw fraud, violence, rapine and imposture practised so freely? And yet, all the while, like good Christians, we hate the Turks! If we wish to succeed in ridding ourselves of the Turks, we must first cast out from ourselves all our loathsome 'Turkish' vices: avarice, ambition, power-lust, self-satisfaction, impiousness, luxury, love of pleasure, fraudulence, anger, hatred, envy. If, after destroying these vices with the sword of the spirit, we resume the Christian way of life, we may then, if the situation requires it, fight beneath the banners of Christ against the flesh-and-blood Turks and, under his protection, defeat them. God promised this in Leviticus, but only to those who observe his law: 'You shall put your enemies to flight and they shall fall in battle before you: five of you shall pursue a hundred, and a hundred of you ten thousand.'[10]

However, this triumph will be all the more acceptable to Christ if, instead of slaughtering the Turks, we manage to join them to us in a common faith and observance. For he who glories in the name of Saviour, who kills in order to give life, and wounds in order to heal, delights in victories of this sort; to destroy a Turk in order to make a Christian, to hurl down an infidel in order to make a true believer: such 'slaughter' as this is the work of piety, and will be pleasing to God. This must be our only aim, our principal preoccupation: to extend the kingdom of Christ rather than our own. Otherwise, to slaughter Turks is simply to increase the kingdom of the dead. To possess the Turk's possessions, to rule his subjects, and to look no further, may make us prouder and still more covetous, but it cannot make us happier; and there is the danger that we ourselves shall degenerate into Turks rather than bring them into Christ's fold.

Anyone who contemplates, besides Syria and Palestine, all the kingdoms of Greece, all the provinces of Asia Minor (in which the apostles preached the Gospel), which are now virtually deserts, beneath the tyrannical rule of these barbarians, cannot fail to grieve with all his heart, and pray that the name of Christ, now confined within such narrow bounds, will one day be acknowledged, praised and worshipped throughout the world, as the psalm declares; that all nations will sing his glory with a single voice, though in many tongues, within his temple, which is the unity of the Church of our Redeemer. St Paul gives us good reason to hope that one day the stubborn Jewish race will be gathered into the fold and will acknowledge our one shepherd, Jesus. There is even more reason to hope for this from the Turks and other barbarian nations, none of whom, I hear, worships idols; on the contrary, their beliefs are half-Christian. If so few disciples were able to cause the whole world to serve Christ, using no other weapon than their confidence in God's promises and the sword of the spirit, why cannot we, with the aid of Christ, do the same? For, besides our Christian princes, we have so many doctors of theology, so many excellent prelates, so many cardinals: so many, in fact, who profess the perfection of the Gospel. The Lord's arm is not short unless we have lost his favour. The outcome of the whole undertaking depends upon the will of him who said: 'Without me you can do nothing.'[11] Under his protection, one man may rout a thousand, but without his aid, however large the army, however meticulous the preparations, all will be in vain. But, provided that our hopes are first founded on him, there is then nothing to prevent us going on to consider purely human counsels; nevertheless, even these are to be applied in such a way that we still depend completely upon the protection of the eternal deity. We cannot hope to enjoy his favour if we appear to fight in his name but, in reality, make war against his will.

Someone will perhaps deduce from all this that I have undertaken the task of arguing *against* a Turkish war. Not at all; on the contrary, my purpose is to ensure that we make war against them successfully and win truly splendid victories for Christ. Merely to clamour for war against the Turks, calling them inhuman monsters, traitors to the Church and a race tainted with all kinds of crime and villainy, is simply to betray the ignorant mob to the enemy.

We have been hearing from close at hand of the recurrent misfortunes of Hungary, and most recently of the wretched death of Louis, the pitiable fate of Queen Mary, and now, besides the occupation of the kingdom of Hungary, the merciless devastation of Austria;[12] during all these events, I have more than once been astonished by the nonchalance of other Christian lands, and especially of Germany herself, as if these things in no affected the rest of us. We become tight-fisted, and spend on pleasures and trivialities what we do not wish to spend on rescuing Christians. I am well aware of the excuses that some apologists for this attitude put forward. This charade, they say, has been played too often by the various popes, and the outcome has always been farcical. Either nothing gets done at all, or the situation takes a turn for the worse. The money collected has stuck fast in the hands of the popes, cardinals, monks, princes, and dukes, and the common soldiers are given permission to plunder, instead of receiving pay. We have heard so often, they say, of crusading expeditions, of recovering the Holy Land; we have seen so often the red cross adorned with the triple crown, together with the red wallet;[13] we have heard so often the holy sermons promising us the earth; we have heard so often of valiant deeds and boundless hopes – but the only thing that has triumphed has been money. How can we, who have been misled thirty times over, believe any more promises, however splendid? We have been plainly tricked so often and as the proverb says: Once bitten, twice shy. This very question almost led men to reject indulgences altogether. We had come to realise, they say, that these were a pure money transaction; suddenly the name was changed. One minute it was a campaign against the Turks, the next the pope himself was in difficulty in a war; then it was a jubilee, which turned into a double jubilee, to bring in double the profit. In Alexander's pontificate, there was even a triple jubilee, perhaps because he was disappointed with sales.[14] Then again, we were offered plenary powers, or even more, and purgatory was in danger of losing all its inmates. Another time, there was the building of St Peter's in the Vatican.[15] On other occasions, St James of Compostela[16] was in need, the Holy Spirit, the giver of all things, was begging for aid, the monks on Mount Sinai needed help, and finally those owing restitution were mercifully given the chance to make amends, and to obtain pardon for their thefts, even of the property taken from looted churches. In short, there was no limit nor end to these indemnities. ...

It seemed right to say all this, in fact our present situation made it imperative, to show that we must not imagine that it is enough merely to bellow for war against these Turkish 'brutes,' but that we must adopt a course of action which will enable us to fight them more successfully in the future, if we have to, than has been the case up to now. I also wanted to remind men of their duty to their religion (although their distraction from this duty has not been without cause). Today the anger is even more pressing, and now our princes are men of immense power but also of great devotion to religion: the emperor Charles, his brother Ferdinand, and the most Christian king of France, Francis, their ally at last;[17] if only it had been sooner. The illustrious king of England, Henry, will not desert this cause, both out of piety and to uphold his title, for he has won the right to be called Defender of the Catholic Faith.[18] We must hope and pray that our Lord Jesus, in his compassion for us, will inspire his vicar, Clement VII, with good intentions, and will strengthen and favour the resolution which he is said, and believed by all good Christians, to have adopted.

I have already sufficiently described the conditions which will ensure a successful outcome to this war, namely that, first of all, God's anger be appeased, that our intentions be pure and honourable, and all our trust placed in Christ; that we fight beneath his standard, that he triumph in us, and that we obey the commandments of our God and attack the enemy as if he were watching over our every movement. For if the whole nation of Israel was defeated in battle to punish the thefts of one man, Achan,[19] what can we hope for if we are encumbered with the sins of all our sinful soldiers? Their mercenary outlook incites them to commit every outrage, as they set out for war intent on plunder and return to plunder more, sometimes more ruthless towards their own people than towards the enemy; they cart their whores round with them, they get drunk in camp, play dice, forswear themselves, quarrel, fight; in fact, they are only attracted to war by the freedom it confers to commit crimes and pay the hope of booty. Perhaps we cannot hope to be the kind of soldiers described by St Bernard, who was not sure whether to call them soldiers or monks, such were their uprightness of character and bravery in battle; but, if we wish to have God as our shield, at least let our consciences be free of guilt, and let us not provoke the Lord, under whose banners we fight, by our wickedness. Much of the responsibility for ensuring that our soldiers are as they should be falls upon their commanders, especially upon our monarchs. If the latter are concerned with acquiring new wealth, and enjoying increased power, rather than with advancing the interests of Christendom (although, in my opinion, this is hardly to be suspected of our present rulers), all our efforts, however strenuous, will only lead to an unsuccessful end. Again, heaven forbid that the pope should reason in the following way: I shall extend my temporal domain, my revenue from first-fruits will grow with the foundation of new churches, I shall establish my power more securely, I shall appoint my cardinals and my trusted servants to govern cities and provinces, and by means of this war I shall rule the monarchs themselves. I am afraid that such a campaign would do great harm to Christendom.

But it is in our power to prevent all this; it is our responsibility to prepare our minds, and then God will grant us a happy outcome. Now, if some idiot laughs at all this, and calls it nonsense, I advise him to look at it very carefully, or he may have to laugh on the other side of his face. I would not mind being accused of talking nonsense, if our campaigns against the Turks had not so often been unsuccessful. We cannot complain if our efforts have come to nothing, since up to now we have been doing Satan's work in the name of Christ, making war despite the anger of God. The Lord cries out to us through Isaiah; He cries out to us every day, in the verses which read: 'Put away the evil of your deeds, away out of my sight; cease to do evil and learn to do right ... come, let us argue it out.'[20]

It remains for me to say something about the method of winning back the hearts of men. My own opinion is that the people will be rather more enthusiastic about this war if they see that it is being undertaken in a spirit of true harmony by their supreme and legitimate lords. The first place in this undertaking must go to the emperor, with his lieutenants; the second to the most Christian king, the third to King Ferdinand,[21] who is most closely threatened by these barbarians, and after them the other princes. For, to tell the truth, it is not proper that cardinals, bishops, abbots, and priests should be involved in affairs of this sort; such involvement is not consistent with the teaching of the Scriptures, nor with the statutes of the church, and, finally, it has never so far been successful. For some reason Mars is always more hostile to those who have pledged themselves to higher things, and soldiers always obey secular captains more willingly than priestly ones. In addition, the necessities of the moment rather than the rules of honour often dictate the tactics used in war; such things are better left to men who do not profess the perfection of the Gospel. War is a business governed by necessity rather than by honour, even though it seems to have been the original source of almost all such titles of nobility as Count, Duke, Baron, Marshal and Landgrave. Those titles were evidently once either the authorisation or the reward of those who exposed their lives to danger to preserve the peace of the state. But all such titles and offices, even kingdoms for that matter, are far beneath the dignity of those who are the successors of Christ, although they in their turn owe honour and obedience to all princes who perform their duties properly. Princes who normally recognise the pope only when it suits them will, in their justice, still tolerate the man who tells them the truth. God alone judges the merits of our lives, but, as far as the ordering of the commonwealth is concerned, there is no bishop so humble that he does not surpass any monarch by virtue of his honourable calling. Ambrose was bishop of a single city, yet he ruled Theodosius, an emperor who had not bought his title and the ruler of a broad empire.[22]

We read that Christ never made war, but he handed down to us a heavenly philosophy; he showed us the way of immortality, he counselled sinners, rebuked unbelievers, encouraged the faint-hearted, supported the weak and strove to win as many as possible to his father. By his goodness he won over the worthy and the unworthy, and cured all manner of sickness. These are truly sublime and princely deeds, and beside them all the military functions of the nobility seem mean and servile. I am not taking from princes the honour due to them, which Paul too allows them; I am simply drawing up an order of precedence. And yet for some reason many churchmen, putting aside these more honourable duties, turn to the lower sort, like a man silly enough to take delight in lead and iron and despise his gold and jewels. Such combinations as 'cardinal-marshal,' 'bishop-general,' 'abbot-lieutenant' and 'priest-sergeant' simply do not fit together, like a statue made half of precious stone and half of clay, or a centaur, a mixture of man and horse. ...

To sum up, the people will be less distrustful if they see their lawful sovereigns embark on this war in a spirit of harmony, and if most of the money collected for the purpose is entrusted to the leading cities, so that it is ready for use whenever the need arises. All suspicion must be avoided; the expedition must not be made an excuse to undermine the freedoms and laws of the various states, or of Christian kings and princes; as far as is possible, the immunity of the churches must be preserved so that, while we try by ill-conceived plans to ensure peace on the Turkish front, we do not allow the whole of Christendom to be ravaged by civil war; while overthrowing the tyranny of the Turks, we must not bring a new and worse tyranny upon ourselves.

Similarly, there are those who complain that some of the Christian princes seem to be aiming at the sort of tyranny formerly called 'Turkish,' by oppressing their peoples with intolerable impositions, and adding to the burden every day; although this allegation is not entirely false, I hope that in the future it will prove groundless. Our predecessors describe the state of things seventy years ago, and if one compares that with present conditions, it is incredible how the freedom of the people, the power of the towns, the authority of parliaments, and reverence towards the ecclesiastical hierarchy have all diminished. On the other hand, the powers of the princes, and their exactions, have increased enormously and, in short, have provided new confirmation of that too-famous dictum that princes are a law unto themselves. Even where our predecessors do not mention this aspect, it is abundantly clear from reading annals and documents which are not particularly old. I am not making accusations against the princes; perhaps, because of our obstinate ways, we have deserved to be treated more severely; but my complaint is more serious against the princes of the church, especially those who manage the pope's affairs. A comparison between their decisions and those published in the annals and papal decrees of previous generations will reveal an enormous difference. If the Lord would consent to turn the thoughts of our spiritual fathers to matters more exalted than money, honours, and worldly pleasure, many who at the moment shrink from them as from tyrants and robbers would willingly submit to them once more. To lift suspicion from men's minds, the princes of the church must renounce all kinds of luxury, ambition, avarice, and tyranny.

It is an old complaint that the number of cardinals has much increased; if the pope could provide them with ambitions worthy of Christ as well as with their red hats, the church would have cause for celebration. Cardinals were so called because, by the sanctity of their lives, the purity of their learning, and the earnestness of their Christian piety, they should be the principal supports of the Lord's house. They owe their authority to their outstanding virtue, and their powers of persuasion, if accompanied by Christian sincerity, can be considerable. It is hoped that there are some such among them, and it may well happen that the Lord, moved by the prayers of the people, will make them all of this quality, but in these turbulent times it is also practical to bring some redress to men's grievances. There are murmurs against the venality of the title, and although there are so many affluent bishops, archbishops, and abbots in the world, men complain that the cardinals' property passes into the pope's control. Three or four bishoprics, three or four abbeys, and a host of other benefices, they say, go towards sustaining the dignity of a cardinal, and, associating with kings as they do, they aspire in some degree to be esteemed above kings, which is why some of them do all they can to rival, and even to surpass, the ostentatious pageantry of kings. Some critics are afraid that from such beginnings, if their ambition overcomes their piety, they will go on from being kings' associates to become kings in their own right, and eventually the masters of kings. Someone may answer that there is no harm in such honour being paid to the church. But these critics will immediately retort: You perfect fools, Christendom already has enough rulers and potentates, without any increase in the ranks of the princes; we need spiritual leaders, the flock of Christ needs fatherly guidance, and everywhere there is a dearth of such men. Indeed, the more impudent among these critics are now not afraid to attack their morals, which is contrary to the Scriptures, which forbid the people to revile their leaders. At this point, although we may stop their mouths as regards their other charges, by disproving some and explaining away others, they will retort: We are simply saying what everyone knows, and these are not vague and ambiguous charges. They cannot disguise facts that are notorious throughout Christendom: they themselves parade their luxury and pomp before us. Among their numbers we see the author of schisms;[23] we see some stripped of their office, others of their riches by means of fines; many have been thrown into prison, some banished, a few even executed![24]

Arguments can be found to counter this sort of malicious talk, but it is nonetheless true that we would find the people far more willing to contribute money and give help if the princes of the church could make their office conform more nearly to the principles of Christian moderation. What is really required is that all of us, from the highest to the lowest, and including all those in between, should remove from our hearts and lives the things that are hateful in the sight of God. If in Isaiah's time he rejected the offerings of those whose hands were stained with blood, still less will he countenance this war of ours, if we march off more laden with sins than with arms. All these considerations mean that we must expect to come to grief and to end up in total and miserable confusion if we attack the Turks while God is still angry, and if we have not carried through that necessary reformation of our lives which will win us God's mercy. The princes must give a lead, for it is hardly to be hoped that there should be no wicked man among the people, however desirable this may be. But it does not matter quite so much what the common soldiers are like, if our kings and generals are working together for good. We must all, with constant prayers and entreaties, beg the Lord to consent to accomplish this.

There are also some people who suspect that the princes are being very cunning in this matter; under the pretext of a Turkish war, a tiny clique will seize power, after plundering towns, countryside, and people, overthrowing the rule of law, suppressing the liberties of the states, removing the authority of parliaments, and crushing the ecclesiastical hierarchy; government will be carried on in the Turkish fashion, by force of arms rather than by the rule of reason. In this way, they say, after a few spurious disturbances, a treaty will be made and the pope, emperor and sultan will betray Christendom, just as Octavius, Lepidus and Antony joined forces to suppress the liberties of the Roman people. I am quite sure that such impious and seditious suspicions can be utterly rejected and condemned. The good qualities of Pope Clement, the emperor's piety, King Ferdinand's integrity, the goodness of the most Christian king and the loyalty of the German princes: all these in my eyes guarantee a happier outcome than that. The idea of universal monarchy, at which certain princes are supposed to be aiming, frightens some. Even if we capture all the Turkish possessions, they say, look at the map and you will see how little this is beside the rest of the world; when can we hope to see an end to this campaign? The same ambition defeated Alexander, and he failed in his design; it cost the Romans dearly, and yet they never fulfilled this troublesome ambition. In fact, I think that such a monarchy is the best kind, if it be granted a godlike ruler, but, such is human frailty, probably the safest solution lies in a number of modest dominions, linked together by the bonds of Christianity.

Others fear that the commodities which come to us from Turkish lands will cost more than they do now. They give the example of sugar,[25] which now costs four times more, and is adulterated into the bargain, and they feel that there is a danger that the same will happen to all the rest. But, again, I have no doubt that the emperor's sense of justice will take care of this. For it is unjust that all should bear the cost, and few take the profit.

Someone may press me here and say: why such a long speech? Tell us plainly, do you think we should make war or not? Now, if the Lord had spoken to me, I should readily speak out; it is very easy now to say what I should like to see done, but what will actually happen is a different matter. I cannot predict the outcome nor do I know enough details about the enterprise; I am merely giving our rulers a warning to consider this undertaking with greater care. I am not against such a war, but I am doing my best to show how it may be successfully begun and continued. For when we finally set about this most dangerous of all tasks, it must result either in complete success for Christendom, or in total disaster. What, you may say, must we therefore endure all the evils which Turkish cruelty has inflicted upon us for centuries past, the evils which continue to afflict us and threaten us in the future, without striking back? I agree that it is hard, but it is better to endure this hardship, if it be God's will, then to invite utter ruin. The best solution of all would be to conquer the Turkish empire in the way in which the apostles conquered all the peoples of the earth for their master, Christ; but the best alternative must be to have as the chief object of an armed campaign that the Turks will be glad to have been defeated. This task will be made easier if, firstly, they see that Christianity is not mere words, and can observe that our deeds are worthy of the Gospel; secondly, if honest preachers are sent in to reap the harvest, men will further Christ's interests, not their own. Thirdly, if any infidel cannot so quickly be persuaded, he should be allowed for a time to live under his own laws, until gradually he comes to agree with us. Long ago, Christian emperors used this method to abolish paganism by degrees. At first they allowed the pagans to live on equal terms with our Christians, in such a way that neither interfered with the other. Then they deprived the idolaters' temples of their privileges, and finally, after forbidding the sacrifice of victims in public, they abolished the worship of idols completely. In this way our religion gradually grew stronger, paganism was stamped out, and the signs of Christ's triumph filled the world.

# One Ought to Be Born a King or a Fool / *Aut regem aut fatuum nasci oportere*

The following text is taken from Erasmus' *Adages*, a collection of classical proverbs, first published under the title *Adagiorum collectanea* in 1500, and greatly enlarged in subsequent editions. For each proverb Erasmus listed the classical sources, then explained the context in which the phrase in question could be used by contemporary writers. This often led him to muse about the social and political conditions of his time and occasionally prompted him to embark on lengthy digressions. *One Ought to Be Born a King or a Fool*, which was first published in the 1515 edition, is an example of such an excursus.

This extract is taken from CWE 31 227–36, translated by Margaret Mann Phillips, annotated by R.A.B. Mynors.

Annaeus Seneca was a man, as Tacitus said, of a very pleasant wit; this is clear from that amusing skit which he wrote against Claudius Caesar, and which has recently come to light in Germany.[1] In this short work he mentions an adage, One ought to be born a king or a fool. It is best to give his very words: 'As for me,' he says, 'I know I have gained my freedom from the fact that the end has come for that man who proved the truth of the proverb, One ought to be born a king or a fool.' And again in the same book, 'He killed in one and the same house Crassus, Magnus, Scribonia, Bassionia, the Assarii, although they were noble, while Crassus was such a fool that he might have reigned.' In another place, though the allusion is less clear, he refers to the same thing in his line 'He snapped the royal thread of a stupid life.' If Hesiod[2] is right in the view that a popular saying is never meaningless, perhaps it would not be beside the point to inquire what can have given rise to this proverb, uniting as it does two such dissimilar things – a king and a fool – with the obvious intention of drawing a parallel between the two. Especially as it is the particular distinction of kings (and the only true royal one) to surpass all others in wisdom, prudence, and watchfulness.

Well, everyone agrees that those famous kings of old time were for the most part well endowed with stark stupidity; one can see this in the fables of the poets on the one hand, in the writings of the historians on the other. Homer, for instance (and the writers of tragedy after him), makes his Agamemnon[3] ambitious rather than wise. ...

The whole of the *Iliad*, long as it is, has nothing in it, as Horace says in an elegant line, but 'the passions of foolish kings and foolish peoples.'[4] The *Odyssey* also has its dense and stupid suitors and characters like Alcinous. Even Hercules himself is described as sturdy and spirited, but heavy and doltish in mind. Indeed Hesiod (whom some think older than Homer) calls princes 'gift-greedy' and 'childish' – I suppose on account of their small wisdom in government, and the way they strained after the accumulation of riches by fair means and foul, rather than after the public good. So they imagine old Midas,[5] wearing his asses' ears as a mark of stupidity. And I think perhaps this is the place to mention how the earliest theologians – that is, the poets – attribute wisdom to Apollo and to Minerva,[6] but to Jove, the ruler of gods and men, they leave nothing but the three-forked lightning, and that nod and that eyebrow which makes all Olympus tremble. Moreover, what profligate, what buffoon ever fooled so foolishly, or was more vilely vile, than this character whom they make ruler of the world? He deceives his wife with tricks, turning himself into a swan, a bull, a shower of gold; he rigs up traps for women, suborns his Ganymedes,[7] fills heaven with bastards. In the same way Neptune and Pluto[8] are painted as fierce and ruthless, but they are not credited with wisdom.

But suppose we dismiss the legends and turn to more recent times, to history: how much sense do you think Croesus King of Lydia had, if he was truly such as Herodotus paints him, so relying on his treasure of jewels and gold that he was angry with Solon for refusing him the name of 'fortunate'?[9] Or what could be imagined more idiotic than Xerxes, when he sent messengers to Mount Athos, to terrify it with most scornful and threatening letters, or ordered so many lashes to be given to the Hellespont?[10] Alexander the Great showed a no less kingly stupidity when he renounced his father and took pleasure in being greeted as the son of Jove, when he competed in drinking to excess, when he allowed himself to be worshipped as god by the flatterers in his banquets, when he complained that this world was too small for his victories, and took to the ocean to find other worlds to conquer. I leave aside all the others, the Dionysiuses, the Ptolemies, the Juliuses, the Neros, the Tiberiuses, the Caligulas, the Heliogabaluses, the Commoduses, and the Domitians[11] – among whom one arrogated to himself the name of god when he was unworthy of the name of man, another exposed himself to be laughed to scorn by his very flatterers, another urged by ambition shook the whole world with meaningless wars.

But I look rather silly myself when I embark on this catalogue, and as they say, seek water in the sea. You merely have to turn over the chronicles of both the ancients and the moderns, and you will find that in several centuries there have been barely one or two princes who did not by sheer stupidity bring disaster to human affairs. A prince, indeed, is either a fool to the immense detriment of the whole world, or a wise man to the immense benefit of all; although it is easier to do badly than well, and the harm he does spreads or rather pervades everything more quickly than the good. But nowadays we see some princes who aspire to anything except the one thing which would make them deserve the name of prince; and stupid subjects, who admire everything in their kings except the one thing needful. 'He is young'; that would recommend him as a bridegroom to a bride, not as a prince to the state. 'He is good-looking'; that is the right praise for a woman. 'He is broad-shouldered, broad-flanked'; if you were praising an athlete, that would be the way to do it. 'He is strong and can stand hard toil'; that is a testimonial for a batman or a houseboy. 'He has a large store of gold'; you are describing an active moneylender. 'He is eloquent'; that's what dazzles me in a sophist. 'He sings well, he dances well'; that is the way to praise flute-players and actors, not kings. 'He has no equal in drinking' – for former princes actually delighted in this commendation! It would be fitter praise for a sponge. 'He is tall, and stands head and shoulders above the rest'; that's splendid, if one wants to reach something down from a high place. As for saying 'He's a skilled dice player, he's good at chess,' that is praise shared with the lowest idlers, and a prince should be ashamed of it. You may heap up everything – public refinement, gold and jewels, ancestral images, a pedigree drawn from Hercules (or from Codrus or Cecrops if you prefer),[12] but unless you tell me of a mind far removed from vulgar foolishness, free from sordid desires for worthless things, and from the prejudices of the herd, I have not heard any praise worthy of a king.

For it was not ill-advisedly that the divine Plato wrote that the only way for a state to attain happiness was for the supreme command to be given to philosophers, or else, inversely, that those who govern should themselves follow philosophy. And to follow philosophy is not just to wear a mantle and to carry a bag round, or let your beard grow.[13] What is it then? It is to despise those things which the common herd goggles at, and to think quite differently from the opinions of the majority. And I don't see how it is possible for a man who thinks he is free to do just what he likes, who marvels at riches as if they were important, who thinks even a sworn oath may be set aside for the sake of power, who is captivated by empty glory, who is a slave to shameful lust, who is terrified of death – I just can't see how such a man can play the part of a beneficent king.

The first requisite is to judge rightly about each matter, because opinions are like springs from which all the actions of life flow, and when they are contaminated everything must needs be mismanaged. The next essential is to recoil from evil and to be led towards good. For true wisdom consists not only in the knowledge of truth, but in the love and eager striving for what is good. You may well find among rulers one who can see that it is not possible to go to war without grave disaster to human affairs, and that an obsolete claim to sovereignty is not very important – and yet he will plunge everything into war merely out of ambition. There may be one who can see that the greatest curse of a state comes from appointing as magistrates, not those who can be of the most use to the public weal by their prudence, experience and integrity, but those who can bid the highest sums – and yet he will be impelled by avarice to look after the treasury and let the abuse go on. And there is another who understands that the duty of a prince, who takes taxes from all, is to look after everyone's interest, to preside over trials, to stamp out crime, to watch the magistrature, to amend useless laws. And yet he is called away from this business by pleasures, which do not give him the time to attend to matters worthy of a ruler. Another is conscious that he has it in his power to confer a great benefit on the human race, but at the risk of his life; and anyone who thinks it is the most terrible thing to die, will fail in duty to the state at this point. And so first of all the mind of the prince must be freed from all false ideas, so that he can see what is truly good, truly glorious, truly splendid. The next thing is to instil the hatred of what is base, the love of what is good, so that he can see clearly what is becoming to a prince, and wish for nothing but what is worthy of a good and beneficent ruler. Let him recognize the good where it may be found, and always measure everything by it, never varying from this aim. This is what is meant by wisdom, and it is in this that the prince must so far excel other mortals, as he excels them in dignity, in wealth, in splendour, and in power.

If only all Christian princes would copy that wisest of all kings,[14] who when he was given a free choice of a boon from him to whom nothing is impossible, wished for wisdom alone, and that wisdom by which he might rightly govern his people! And pray what did he teach his own son, but the love and following of wisdom? It is for this reason that the Egyptians make a symbolic representation of a prince by drawing an eye and a sceptre. Indeed what the eye is to the body, so is a true prince to the people; the sun is the eye of the world, the prince the eye of the multitude. As the mind is to the body, so is the prince to the state; the minds knows, the body obeys. And if the mind commands the body, it is for the body's good; it does not rule for itself like a tyrant, but for that which is in its charge. Above all, the good ruler is the living portrayal of God, who rules the universe. And the closer the prince conforms to the lines of the original, the more magnificent he is. God is all-seeing, all-feeling, and swayed by no passions. He is greatest in power, but at the same time greatest in goodness. He does good to all, even the unworthy. He deals no punishments, except rarely and when he must. He governs this world for us and not for himself. All the reward he asks is to do good. But the evil prince, on the contrary, seems to be the copy of the devil, and to act in his stead. Either he knows nothing, or what he knows is how to bring about public disaster. What power he has, he uses to harm the state. And though it is in his power to do a great deal of harm to everybody, he would like to do even more than he can.

Nothing is nobler than a good king, nothing better, nothing nearer God; equally, nothing is worse than a bad prince, nothing viler, nothing more like the devil. There is something divine about a beneficent prince, but no wild beast is more destructive than a tyrant. And a tyrant is whoever wields power for himself, whatever name his paintings and statues give him. It is not for us to pass judgment, as it were, upon the great ones of the earth, but yet we are obliged – not without sorrow – to feel the lack in Christian princes of that high wisdom of which we have spoken. All these revolutions, treaties made and broken, frequent risings, battle and slaughter, all these threats and quarrels, what do they arise from but stupidity? And I rather think that some part of this is due to our own fault. We do not hand over the rudder of the ship to anyone but a skilled steersman, when nothing is at stake but four passengers or a small cargo; but we hand over the state, in which so many thousands of people are in peril, to the first comer. If anyone is to be a coachman, he learns the art, spends care and practice; but for anyone to be a king, we think it is enough for him to be born. And yet to rule a kingdom well, as it is the finest of all functions, is also the most difficult by far. You choose the man who is to have charge of a ship; but you do not choose the man to whom you are entrusting so many cities, so many human lives? But there it is, the thing is so established that it is impossible to root it out. Kings are born, and whoever may have been picked out by chance, whether he be good or bad, stupid or wise, sane or clouded in mind, as long as he looks like a human being, he is to be entrusted with supreme power in the state. By his will the world is to be thrown into an uproar with wars and slaughter, all things sacred and profane are to be turned upside down.

But if this is a thing which we cannot change, the next best plan would be to improve matters by careful education; and if we may not choose a suitable person to be our ruler, we must strive to try to make that person suitable whom fate has given us. We see with what care and solicitude and watchfulness a father brings up his son, who is the future master of one estate. How much more care, then, should be spent on the education of one who, if good, will be so to the immense benefit of all, and if bad, will bring about the ruin of all – one on whose nod hangs the safety or the destruction of the world? With what rules and precepts of philosophy must that mind be fortified, not only against such great calamities as may arise in a state, but against the favour of fortune, so often accompanied by pride and stupidity; against pleasures, which can corrupt the best natures; still more against the dangerous fawning of flatterers, and that poisonous 'Bravo!' which they chant – particularly when the prince is acting most like a madman. It seems to me that he should have attached to him, while still an infant, some skilful educator; for no one can truly be fashioned into a prince, except long before he knows that he is what he is. In the early days, I say, a preceptor should be appointed, and we should take all the more care in choosing him because we are not free to choose our prince – but we are free to educate him. Let him instil into this childish mind, as yet blank and malleable, opinions worthy of a prince; arm it with the best principles of conduct, show it the difference between a true prince and a tyrant, and lay before its very eyes what a god-like thing is a beneficent ruler, what a loathsome hateful brute is a tyrant. He will explain that a ruler who wields power for himself and not for the state is no prince, but a robber; that there is no difference between pirates and pirate-minded princes, except that the latter are more powerful and can bring so much more disaster on human affairs. He will impress on his pupil that he can be of use to so many thousands of people – nay, to the whole world, by simply behaving as one good and wise man. He will teach that among Christians supreme rule means administration of the state, and not dominion. It may bear the name of supreme rule, but he must remember that he is ruling over free men, and over Christians, that is, people who are twice free. In addition, for a person to be a prince it is not enough to be born, to have ancestral statues, the sceptre and the crown. What makes a prince is a mind distinguished for its wisdom, a mind always occupied with the safety of the state, and looking to nothing but the common good. He will warn his pupil not to judge himself by the plaudits of the stupid populace or the praise of flatterers, not to do anything on the impulsion of hatred, love, or anger, or at the urge of any passion. When he appoints magistrates, creates laws, or in his other duties, he must work for one end only, for good, and for the people's benefit. It is not enough if he himself does harm to no one – the prince is also the guarantor of the uprightness of his officials. The glory of a prince does not lie in extending his sway, in removing his neighbours by force of arms; but if he happens to acquire the sovereignty of a region, he must make it flourish by justice, by wise economy, and the other arts of peace. The teacher will recommend him to be particularly inclined to serve the cause of good men, to be ready to pardon, and with the attitude towards punishment of a friendly doctor, who amputates or cauterizes the limb which he despairs of healing; to be careful to avoid everything from which he can foresee the danger of evil to the state. Above all, he is to shun war in every way; other things give rise to this or that calamity, but war lets loose at one go a whole army of wrongs. These principles and others like them should be impressed on the child's mind, with the help of the maxims of the wise and the examples of esteemed princes.

What actually happens is that no kind of man is more corruptly or carelessly brought up than those whose education is of such importance to so many people. The baby who is to rule the world is handed over to the stupidest of womenkind who are so far from instilling anything in his mind worthy of a prince, that they discourage whatever the tutor rightly advises, or whatever inclination to gentleness the child may have in himself – and they teach him to act like a prince, that is like a tyrant. Then no one fails to fawn and flatter. The courtiers applaud, the servants obey his every whim, even the tutor is obsequious; and he is not doing this to make the prince more beneficial to his country, but to ensure a splendid future for himself. The cleric who is popularly called his confessor, is obsequious too – he has some bishopric in mind. There is flattery from the judges, flattery from playmates and companions; so that Carneades[15] was right when he said that the only art kings could learn properly was the art of riding, because only a horse makes no distinction between prince and peasant and is unable to flatter. He just tosses off the rider who is not skilful enough to stay on his back, no matter who it may be.

One of the earliest lessons is pomp and pride; he is taught that whatever he wants, he can have. He hears that the property of everyone belongs to the prince, that he is above the law; that the whole paraphernalia of government, laws and policies exist stored in the prince's mind. He hears the terms *sacred majesty, serene highness, divinity, god on earth,* and other such superb titles. In short, while he is yet a boy, all he learns to play at is being a tyrant. Then he is caught up among the girls; they all allure and admire and defer to him. The effeminate crew of young friends is there, and they have no other topic for jokes or conversation but girls. Next there are other diversions – gaming, dancing, feasting, lute-playing, gadding about; the best years of his life are used up like this. If he takes a fancy to beguile his leisure by reading, he reads old wives' tales, or what is worse, historical romances. His mind is not in the least equipped with any antidote, and he imbibes from them an enthusiasm – what the Greeks call *zeal* – for some pernicious hero, say Julius Caesar or Xerxes or Alexander the Great. And what suits him best in them is the worst. They furnish the worst example, they foster the craziest urges. Now imagine, if you please, an intelligence not selected from among many, as should be the case, but a very ordinary mind, and an education so corrupt that it would corrupt the mentality of an Aristides;[16] then imagine the poison of flattery, frolic and pleasure (which don't agree very well with wisdom), luxurious living, wealth and magnificence, the sense of power; all this at an age of ruthlessness and inclined naturally to bad courses. Add finally the tainting of the mind by false ideas. And can you wonder if, coming from this early environment to the administration of a kingdom, he doesn't do it very wisely?

'But never mind,' they say, 'he's young, he'll learn by experience.' But the prince must never be young, even if he is young in years. Any prudence which is won from experience is of a sorry kind, and sorriest of all in a prince. The prince's prudence will be too dearly bought by the country, if he only learns by waging war that war is the thing he must avoid at all costs; or if he fails to understand that public offices must be given to upright men, until he sees the state tottering through the audacity of evildoers. Don't tell me that those who wish to learn to sing to the lute will spoil several lutes in the process, before they learn the art, as Xenophon said;[17] that would mean that the prince would only learn to administer his state by the ruin of the state.

It is not therefore much to be wondered at, if we see things going absolutely contrary to the way they should; when instead of the passions which arise from the body being controlled by the mind the disturbances in the mind spread out into the body, when the eyes see less than the rest of the body sees, when the person who is most pernicious and harmful to the public is the very person who should be beneficial to all, acting in place of God. Do we not see fine cities, created by the people, overthrown by the princes? Or a state enriched by the toil of its citizens, and looted by the princes' greed? Plebeian lawyers make good laws, princes violate them; the people seek for peace, the princes stir up war.

I think these are the things which give rise to this adage, from which somehow or other we have digressed a long way; but now we return to it. So it is said, One ought to be born a king or a fool, because the primitive kings were of that sort, as the ancients tell – and may the princes of our day be altogether different! For everything is permitted to fools, because of the weakness of their minds. And everything is praised in kings, because of their power. There is perhaps another way of understanding the saying, in reference to the equal happiness of kings and fools; because whatever a king wants is provided by fortune, and fools are no less fortunate because of their self-satisfaction, it allows them to think they have no lack of good gifts. And in fact the proverb seems to have originated among the Romans, who hated the name of king as barbaric and tyrannous, and contrary to political freedom, of which they at that time were the most enthusiastic supporters.

# Notes

**Introduction**

1 See Erasmus' autobiographical sketch, *Brief Outline of His Life*, below 16.
2 For the text of this treatise, see the *Collected Works of Erasmus*, Vol 66 135–75. Hereafter the *Collected Works of Erasmus* (Toronto 1974–) is cited as CWE.
3 For selections from the *Praise of Folly* and *The Handbook of the Christian Soldier* see below 140–54 and 156–68.
4 Erasmus' first published work was a poem, which appeared on a blank leaf at the end of Robert Gaguin's *Compendium de origine et gestis Francorum* (Paris 1497). Classical literature was Erasmus' first love. 'A sort of inspiration fired me with devotion to the Muses,' he wrote (Ep 1110:8–9). In references throughout this book, 'Ep' ('Epistle') refers to letter and line numbers in the CWE. 'Allen Ep' refers to letter and line numbers in the Latin edition of the letters of Erasmus (see Bibliography Ep 47:14–17).
5 For Erasmus' poems see C. Reedijk ed *The Poems of Desiderius Erasmus* (Leiden 1956). An English and Latin edition of the poems is forthcoming in CWE 85.
6 For selections from Erasmus' educational writings see below 51–121.
7 For *On the Method of Study* see CWE 24 661–91. For selections from *On Education for Children*, see below 65–100.
8 For selections from the *Praise of Folly*, see below 156–68. For a defence of the *Folly*, see Erasmus' letter to Dorp, below 169–94.
9 For a chronology of Erasmus' travels, see the chart below 367–8.
10 The text of Erasmus' *Annotations on the New Testament* will appear in CWE 51–60.
11 For a selection from these works, see below 249–333.
12 See the letters to and concerning Luther, below 195–215.
13 He edited and translated a wide range of patristic authors, among them Jerome, Augustine, Ambrose, Chrysostom, and Origen.
14 For the text of the *Paraphrases* on Mark, Romans, and Galatians see CWE 42 and 49. Translations of other paraphrases are forthcoming in volumes 43–50.
15 Quoted by Roland H. Bainton in *Erasmus of Christendom* 176

16 For selections from *The Ciceronian* see below 124–37. The text of *The Tongue* is in CWE 29 257–412. *Ecclesiastes* will appear in CWE 67–8.
17 Quoted by Bruce Mansfield in *Phoenix of His Age* 65
18 The *Opera omnia* of 1538–40 were edited by the Amerbach brothers for the Froben Press in Basel. The Leiden edition is the work of J. Leclerc (see Bibliography 369).
19 P.S. Allen ed *Opus epistolarum Des. Erasmi Roterodami* (Oxford 1906–58) 12 vols
20 *Opera omnia Desiderii Erasmi Roterodami* (Amsterdam 1969–)
21 *Collected Works of Erasmus* (CWE) (Toronto 1974–).
22 Erasmus von Rotterdam *Ausgewählte Schriften* ed W. Welzig (Darmstadt 1967–80) 8 vols
23 *La Correspondance d'Erasme* (Brussels 1967–84) 12 vols
24 For fuller information the reader is referred to the introductions and notes in the CWE. Volume and page numbers are indicated in the running heads.

**Brief Outline of His Life**

1 Erasmus was born during the night of 27–28 October c 1469.
2 On the much-discussed issue of the year of his birth see CWE 4 400–1 n1.
3 A younger brother of the famous Guarino d' Guarini of Verona who was teaching at Ferrara
4 The *Pater meus* was probably an elementary Latin grammar. Eberhard of Bethune, a twelfth-century grammarian, was the author of *Graecismus*, a Latin grammar in verse. John of Garland (c 1180–1258), an Englishman who taught in Paris, was the author of several standard textbooks.
5 Alexander Hegius (1433–98), a German scholar and student of Rudolph Agricola, was rector of the school at Deventer from 1483 to 1498. Johannes Synthen (d 1498) was the author of a commentary on the *Doctrinale* of Alexander de Villa Dei.
6 Rombold is not otherwise known.
7 A guarded reference to Erasmus' brother Pieter. The author's reticence about the existence of his brother is regarded by some as a serious objection to accepting the authenticity of the *Brief Outline*, but the omission may simply be discretion. There was no reason for Erasmus to involve his brother in this potentially embarrassing account.
8 In 1488
9 William Blount, Baron of Mountjoy (c 1478–1534)
10 Being unaware that it was against English law to export gold coins, Erasmus had his money confiscated by customs.

11 William Warham (1456–1532)

12 Erasmus stayed with the famous printer Aldo Manuzio who published his *Adages* in 1508. For a selection from this work, see below 239–47.

13 Raffaele Riario (1461–1521), who made Erasmus welcome at Rome in 1509

14 In 1509

15 Jean Le Sauvage (1455–1518)

16 A controversy developed when the French scholar Jacques Lefèvre (c 1460–1536) took issue with Erasmus' interpretation of Hebrews 2:7. For Dorp see below 169.

17 For the relationship between Luther and Erasmus see below 195–215.

**Catalogue of His Works**

1 Botzheim used this cognomen from 1507 on, perhaps out of admiration for the Italian humanist Lorenzo Astemio, but it is more likely that he acquired the name for his notably temperate habits.

2 The celebrated German humanist (1444–85) and pioneer of New Learning in Northern Europe

3 Fausto Andrelini (1462–1518) lectured at the University of Paris. He was made royal poet by Charles VIII.

4 Either St Michael's at Hem, if the poem was composed before Erasmus' departure for Paris, or a church near Paris

5 The *Epigrammata* of Erasmus and More were published, together with More's *Utopia*, in Basel in March 1518.

6 A native of Basel (c 1466–1532) and a distinguished physician, later court physician to Louis XII and Francis I

7 Erasmus was accompanying the sons of Giovanni Battista Boerio, physician to Henry VII. Their tutor was a man named Clyfton.

8 Grocyn (c 1449–1519) taught Greek at Oxford.

9 See above 346 n11.

10 Josse Bade (1461–1535), Paris printer

11 Erasmus presented the panegyric in 1504 to Archduke Philip the Handsome of Burgundy.

12 Among them the future Henry VIII, who became a patron of Erasmus

13 See above 346 n9. Erasmus tutored him in Paris and accompanied him on a journey to England in 1499.

14 John Colet (1467–1519) lectured on the Epistles of St Paul at Oxford. In 1510 he founded a school at St Paul's Cathedral.

15 Teacher of Greek at Paris from 1476 to about 1505. Among his pupils were Johann Reuchlin, Guillaume Budé, and Beatus Rhenanus.

16 Aldo Manuzio, the famous Venetian printer, of whose household Erasmus was a member in 1508
17 *De duplici copia verborum ac rerum commentarii duo*, a manual of style, which appears in English in CWE 24 279– 659
18 See above note 14.
19 William Lily (d c 1522), first master of St Paul's School
20 *De ratione studii ac legendi interpretandique auctores* appears in English in CWE 24 661–91. Vitré (d 1540) taught at Lombard College and the Collège de Navarre from 1516.
21 Teacher of Greek in Italy from c 1435
22 For an early draft see CWE 25 258–67.
23 See 239 below, introduction to the Colloquy *Shipwreck*.
24 Nicholaas Baechem Egmondanus, a Carmelite (d 1526), later appointed inquisitor by Charles V. Egmondanus was a lifelong enemy of Erasmus.
25 The adulterated version of the *Colloquies* described here was the work of a German Dominican, Lambertus Campester (d c 1538).
26 A popular collection of maxims ascribed to Cato
27 Like the *Cato*, a collection of sayings used in schools
28 John More (c 1509–47), the youngest child of Thomas More
29 Thomas More's eldest daughter (c 1504–44), who was married to William Roper
30 Lorenzo Valla (1406–57) wrote notes on the New Testament, of which Erasmus discovered a manuscript in 1504. He published it the following year.
31 Suetonius Tranquillus (c 69–c 140), Roman biographer
32 Cyprian (d 258), Church Father
33 Arnobius, fifth-century exegete; Pope Adrian VI (1454–1523)
34 Hilary of Poitiers (d 366), Church Father; Jean Carondelet (1469–1545)
35 The first edition of the *Adagia*, *Adagiorum collectanea*, was actually published in 1500. A fuller version was published under the title *Adagiorum chiliades* in 1508. On the Dover incident, see also 246 n10.
36 See the table of money and coinage in CWE 1 336–47.
37 See note 10 above.
38 Matthias Schürer (d 1520), printer at Strasbourg
39 Johann Froben (1460–1527), printer at Basel
40 *Parabolae sive similia* appears in English in CWE 23 123–277. Gillis (1486/7–1533), chief secretary of Antwerp from 1510, was one of Erasmus' closest friends.
41 The friendship between Orestes and Pylades was proverbial.
42 Ie someone on the fringe of society, according to sixteenth-century values

43 See below 288.
44 Richard Croke (c 1489–1558) was a pupil of Erasmus. In 1518 he became Greek lecturer at Cambridge.
45 Gerardus Listrius (c 1492–after 1522) was rector of the school at Zwolle.
46 The *Antibarborum liber* appears in English in CWE 23 1–122. See the selection below 249–87.
47 See above note 11.
48 Desmarez (d 1526) was Erasmus' host at Louvain in 1504. The letter referred to here is Ep 180.
49 The *Institutio principis christiani* appears in English in CWE 27 199–288. It was dedicated to the future Charles V.
50 The *Enchiridion militis christiani* appears in English in CWE 66 1–127. See the selection below 136–54.
51 Johann Poppenruyter, a gunsmith in Nürnberg. Jacob Batt was a schoolteacher and town secretary in Bergen; see headnote to *The Antibarbarians* (below 51), in which he figures as one of the speakers.
52 Warden of the Franciscan convent at Saint-Omer, whom Erasmus admired greatly. He wrote a biographical sketch of Vitrier and Colet in Ep 1211.
53 Matthaeus Schiner (1465–1522)
54 Henry VIII (1491–1547), Francis I (1494–1547), Pope Clement VII (1478–1534)
55 Michael Vianden (d before Feb 1535), a Louvain scholar, who also taught briefly at the trilingual college at Tournai
56 Justus Ludovicus Decius (Jost Ludwig Dietz, c 1485–1545) who wrote treatises on economics and history
57 Christoph of Utenheim (d 1527), Erasmus' protector in Basel. See also below 000.
58 Helius Marcaeus, warden of a convent of Benedictine nuns. It took its name from relics of the Maccabees possessed by the house.
59 See above note 14. The speech was to be recited by a pupil of St Paul's School.
60 The *Method* was included among the introductory material of the New Testament edition of 1516. It was amplified and published separately in 1518 under the title *Ratio verae theologiae*.
61 Maarten Dorp was a theologian at the University of Louvain. See below 169.
62 A French biblical scholar; see above 346 n16.
63 Lee (d 1544), an Englishman who studied in Louvain, attacked Erasmus' *Annotations on the New Testament* and provoked an acrimonious controversy.

64 Latomus (Jacques Masson, d 1544) attacked Erasmus on the issue of language studies.
65 Atensis (Jan Briart of Ath, 1460–1520) attacked Erasmus' rhetorical speech in praise of matrimony.
66 Gillis van Delft (d 1524) had taught at Paris until 1515 and returned there in 1520. Erasmus often mentions his metrifications of biblical material.
67 Ie, because Erasmus had changed the wording of the Vulgate at John 1:1, using *sermo* rather than *verbum* to translate Greek *logos*, 'word.'
68 Not identified
69 Zúñiga (d 1531) first attacked Erasmus' New Testament edition in 1520. The controversy between the two men was carried on in a series of apologiae and antapologiae between 1520 and 1529. After Zúñiga's death the executor of his will conveyed to Erasmus a further set of critical notes.
70 Sancho Carranza de Miranda (d 1531)
71 It was a custom to attach anonymous satirical verses to an ancient statue in Rome which was called Pasquin or Pasquil.
72 Pope Leo X died in December 1521. The newly elected pope, Adrian VI, arrived in Rome in August 1522.
73 Adrian died in September 1523 and was followed by Clement VII.
74 Nicolaas Baechem; see above note 24.
75 Ie, to lick the arse and the sandals of a peasant: Catullus 98.3–4
76 The reference is to the Dominican Vincentius Theoderici, who attacked Erasmus' treatise on confession.
77 Ulrich von Hutten (1488–1523) was originally an admirer of Erasmus, but was disappointed in the latter because he refused to come out openly in favour of Luther. Erasmus in turn was appalled by Hutten's advocacy of an armed attack on the church. When Hutten arrived in Basel in 1522 sick and destitute, Erasmus refused to receive him. Hutten remonstrated with him in his *Expostulation*, published in 1523, and Erasmus answered that same year with the *Sponge*.
78 Albert of Brandenburg; see below 195.
79 Hutten declared a private war against the Carthusians who bought peace at the cost of two thousand Rhenish florins. The other crimes related here by Erasmus took place in 1522 and were punished by Ludwig V, count Palatine.
80 See below 355 n1.
81 See note 57 above.
82 See above note 17.
83 Richard Pace (d 1536), an English scholar and diplomat
84 The commentaries were never published and are considered lost, unless

one is to assume that they were worked into Erasmus' *Annotations* or *Paraphrases on the Pauline Epistles.*
85 *Ecclesiastes,* published in 1535
86 Ie, Pope Julius II. See below 216.
87 The wealth of King Midas was proverbial.
88 Cf the table of money and coinage in CWE 1 342–7.
89 Erasmus' longtime publisher in Basel
90 See note 88 above.
91 See note 88 above.
92 Margaret of Austria (1480–1530)

**The Antibarbarians**

1 Scythian tribe
2 Diogenes (c 400–325 BC) was the founder of the Cynic school of philosophy. The story is told by Diogenes Laertius 6.32.
3 Horace *Epistles* 2.1.31
4 The *Andabatae* were proverbial for thrashing around with their eyes closed (*Adages* II iv 33); for the 'stentorian' voice see Homer *Iliad* 5.785; the enormous size of the army of the Persian king Xerxes was proverbial (Herodotus 7.60).
5 Wool or fluff
6 Vergil *Georgics* 4.441
7 Phaeton borrowed the chariot of the sun, and by his loss of control brought drought and destruction upon the earth before he was finally burned to death.
8 Pyrrhus, king of Epirus, was famous for his talents as a general.
9 Midas was given asses' ears for being an incompetent judge in the song contest between Apollo and Marsyas.
10 An imaginary flower that never fades
11 Aristotle
12 Ie a precious jewel
13 The Battus of legend was a shepherd of Pylos turned to stone by the God Mercury.
14 Probably Livy 39.16.6–7
15 Augean stable. One of Hercules' labours was to clear the Augean stable, ie a 'Herculean task.'
16 12.10.15. For Quintilian see below 354 n6.
17 Dionysius, tyrant of Syracuse, and Clodius Pulcher, the enemy of Cicero, exemplify dissolute life. Numa Pompilius, the early ruler of Rome (seventh century BC), typifies beneficient and wise government.

18 Thersites, a character in Homer's *Iliad*, stands for ugliness and baseness; the arms of the Homeric hero Achilles were put up as a prize after his death.
19 Sharp critics named after the Roman statesman Cato the Censor (second century BC) who was famous for his temperate life
20 Chrysippus was a Stoic philosopher.
21 Ie, nuns
22 Greek Church Fathers, just as Augustine and Jerome are used as representatives of the Latin Fathers
23 A reference to the God Mercury, the escort of the dead in Greek mythology
24 A Greek Church Father, some of whose works were considered dangerous because of his Montanist leanings
25 Sardanapalus, king of ancient Assyria, was notorious for luxury; Thraso is the braggart soldier in Terence's *Eunuchus*; Gnatho is his flattering parasite.
26 Followers of the medieval scholastics Albertus Magnus, Thomas Aquinas, Duns Scotus, William of Occam, and Durandus

**On Education for Children**

1 A medical author of late antiquity (c 130–99) who was popular with Renaissance readers. Erasmus translated three of his essays from Greek into Latin. See CWE 29 219–48.
2 Demosthenes, the great Greek orator; this is related by Quintilian 2.3.6.
3 Lycurgus, the Spartan law-giver; the anecdote is related by Plutarch *Moralia* 3A–B.
4 For Diogenes see above 351 n2.
5 Cynic philosopher (c 365–285BC). The story is told by Plutarch *Moralia* 4A where the saying is attributed Socrates, however.
6 Fl c 400 BC, founder of the Hedonist school; the anecdote is told by Diogenes Laertius 2.72.
7 See above note 4. The anecdotes come from Diogenes Laertius 6.41 and 6.32.
8 An adaption of 1 Timothy 2:15
9 Son of the Syracusan tyrant by the same name who succeeded his father in 367/66 BC. Dion was a relative of his.
10 Proverbs 10:1
11 Types of fish
12 1 Corinthians 15.33

13 King of Macedon, cf Plutarch *Lives* Alexander 7.
14 Juvenal 7.187–8
15 See above note 5. The quotation comes from Diogenes Laertius 6.86.
16 See above note 6.
17 Diogenes (see note 4 above). The anecdote is in Plutarch *Moralia* 2A.
18 Roman general, cf Plutarch *Lives* Paulus Aemilius 6.
19 Pliny the Younger (61–c 112) published his correspondence. The information about his involvement comes from this source; cf *Epistles* 2.18.
20 Minerva was the goddess of wisdom; cf *Adages* I i 60.
21 *Georgics* 3.51–2
22 Ibidem 3.75–6
23 Perhaps Periander. See Diogenes Laertius 1.7.99.
24 *Georgics* 3.166–73 paraphrased
25 According to Diogenes Laertius 3.38
26 *Epistles* 1.10.24
27 King of Pontus in Asia Minor during the first century BC
28 Athenian leader and statesman (c 528–462BC). He was accused of pro-Persian activities, whereupon he fled to the Persian court.
29 Ie, M. Porcius Cato (d 146BC). See above 352 n19.
30 The great-grandson of the above, who led the republican opposition to Caesar
31 A family of Dutch scholars in the fifteenth and sixteenth centuries
32 Isabella of Castile, grandmother of Charles V
33 Erasmus describes More's efforts to educate his family in his famous character sketch in Ep 999. See CWE 7 15–25.
34 Ie, a slave
35 Proverbial for keen sight
36 Isocrates was a Greek orator and educator (c 436– 338BC). The saying comes from his essay *To Demonicus* 18.
37 Ie, syphilis
38 For Erasmus' own connections with the Brethren of the Common Life see above 17.
39 See above note 4. The anecdote is in Diogenes Laertius 6.74.
40 Cf *Adages* I viii 36.
41 Tribes that were a byword for savagery
42 This anecdote was told of the Greek athlete Milo.
43 *Epistles* 8.12
44 See above note 19.
45 *Works and Days* 11–12
46 1.1.19

## On Good Manners

1 1 Corinthians 4:19–25
2 In 1528 Erasmus had dedicated a work on the pronunciation of Greek to Maximilian. Henry and Maximilian were the grandsons of Anna of Borssele, Erasmus' patroness until 1501/2.
3 Jan van der Cruyce (d 1533)
4 A classical notion. See Athenaeus *Deipnosophistae* 7.303.
5 A character in Terence's *Heautontimorumenos*, who is told by his slave: 'Avoid twisting your neck, sighing, spitting, coughing, and laughing' (lines 372–3)
6 Quintilian, the author of a manual on rhetoric, *Institutio oratoria* 1.11.9
7 Literally, 'walking around' – Aristotle's school was called 'peripatetic' because teacher and pupil walked up and down while discussing.
8 Matthew 27:29
9 Odyssey 1.149
10 Terence *Heautontimorumenos* 1062
11 Odes 1.18.13
12 Martial 1.27.7, a proverbial saying
13 Romans 12:12
14 A mythological bull whose look sufficed to kill a man
15 Proteus, a mythological figure, whose ability to change shape was proverbial

## The Ciceronian

1 Tommaso Fedra Inghirami (1470–1516), Vatican librarian, was called the Cicero of his age (Erasmus is mistaken about his first name); Giulio Camillo Delminio (1480–1544) was an extreme Ciceronian who had a room full of lexica, phrase inventories, and subject indices to Cicero's works.
2 Jewish feast in preparation for Passover
3 For Pope Julius II, see headnote to the *Julius exclusus* below 216.
4 Publius Decius and his son of the same name and Quintus Curtius, another Roman hero, sacrificed themselves for their fatherland; Menoecus sacrificed himself for the Boeotian city of Thebes; Cecrops must be a mistake for Codrus, an Athenian king who sacrificed his life to ensure the city's victory over the Spartans.
5 The Athenian thinker Socrates and the statesman Phocion were put to death in 399 and 317 BC respectively. In both cases the citizens soon repented of the executions and raised statues to the victims.

6 In the course of delivering his native city Thebes from Spartan domination, Epaminondas retained his command beyond the legal date and was impeached, but honourably acquitted (in 369 BC).
7 Scipio Africanus, conqueror of Hannibal, was attacked by political opponents and went into exile where he died (in 183 BC).
8 An Athenian statesman in the fifth century BC whose honesty became proverbial; he was ostracized (that is, sent into exile) for ten years.
9 Scipio (see above note 7), Aemilius Paulus, and Julius Caesar were famous Roman generals from the second and first century BC.
10 *Partitiones* 79
11 Horace *Ars poetica* 309
12 Demosthenes was the most famous Greek orator, Marcus Tullius (Cicero) the most famous Roman orator. For Cato and Phocion see above note 5 and 352 n19.
13 A Roman gourmet of the first century AD
14 Cf Terence *Heautontimorumenos* 1035–6.
15 They were scientific writers, not representative of *belles-lettres*. Aristotle wrote on cosmology, zoology, plants, etc; Theophrastus, his successor, on weather, plants, etc; Pliny is the author of the encyclopaedic *Natural History*.
16 *Amores* 2.4

**The Handbook of the Christian Soldier**

1 For Colet see above 347 n14. In Erasmus' mind the Jewish religion was associated with rigid formalism. He often used 'Jews' and 'Jewish' metaphorically to denote strict observance of rituals.
2 The inner and the outer man
3 2 Corinthians 4:6
4 Plato *Phaedo* 64A–68B, 80D–81A
5 Psalms 44:22
6 Colossians 3:1–2
7 Renowned painter of antiquity
8 Egyptian hermits of the fourth century
9 Terence *Adelphi* 98
10 See above n1.
11 Luke 18:11
12 Romans 8:1–8
13 Luke 6:44
14 Ie between two unpleasant alternatives
15 *Disticha Catonis* 1.1

16 Psalms 51:17
17 Ezekiel 8:8
18 Jeremiah 13:17
19 Luke 8:10, Matthew 13:14
20 Isaiah 6:9, Jeremiah 5:21
21 Psalms 45 45:10–14
22 Ie on papal indulgences and dispensations
23 Ezekiel 37:4
24 Isaiah 59:4
25 Romans 10:2
26 Isaiah 5:13
27 John 7:38
28 Plato *Phaedrus* 251A, B
29 Genesis 28:12

**Praise of Folly**

1 Thersites and Nestor stand for ugliness and old age; Nireus and Phaon for beauty and youth; the pig and Minerva for stupidity and wisdom respectively.
2 Thracians and Scythians stand for barbarous and inhospitable people.
3 A swamp that was drained against Apollo's orders, with the result that the disobedient city was sacked by enemy troops.
4 According to Homer, Vulcan trapped his wife Venus with her lover Mars in an invisible net (*Odyssey* 8.270ff).
5 Proverbial for cutting through ambiguities and arguments
6 Proverbial for keen sight
7 Followers of scholastic theologians
8 Hebrews 11:1
9 John 4:24
10 I Timothy 1:4
11 Chrysippus, a Stoic philosopher of the third century BC, set forth an elaborate system of tenets.
12 Chrysostom and Basil were Fathers of the Greek church; Erasmus edited their works as well as those of Jerome.
13 See above 355 n1.
14 A subject chosen for disputation from a free range of theological problems; theology students were required to take part in such disputations. Erasmus uses Scotus as representative of scholastic theology.
15 Ie undoing one's own work
16 Mythological figure

17 Greek lawgiver, sixth century BC
18 Vulcan split Jupiter's head with an axe so that he could give birth to the goddess Athene.
19 Probably a reference to the doctoral bonnet
20 The four Hebrew consonants in the name of Jahweh
21 Latin for 'our master' – denoting a professor on the faculty of theology
22 The word 'monk' is derived from Greek *monos*, 'alone.'
23 Coarse and fine wool respectively
24 A Gnostic sect who believed in 365 heavens
25 Ie, taken on too big a task
26 Cf Plato *Gorgias* 493A.
27 Cf Plato *Republic* 7.514A–17A.
28 Said in the *Golden Legend* to have happened to St Bernard when meditating on the Scriptures
29 Supreme good
30 Cf Plato *Phaedrus* 245B.
31 Isaiah 64:4
32 The traditional concluding phrase in Roman comedy

**Letter to Dorp (Ep 337)**

1 The *Praise of Folly* had been published in 1511; Froben's edition of the works of Jerome on which Erasmus had collaborated was about to be published; work on his edition of the New Testament was at an advanced stage.
2 1 Corinthians 13:4–5
3 Two boastful soldiers in Terence's and Plautus' comedies
4 See the selection from this work above 138.
5 *The Education of a Christian Prince*: see the selection from this work below 249–87.
6 See above 347 n11.
7 *Satires* 1.1.24–5
8 In 1509. See above 34.
9 Athenian judges renowned for their severity
10 Latin farces; the players wore masks.
11 In *Phaedrus* 237A
12 A proverbial monster
13 A Greek expression, meaning 'sacred bitter things'
14 2 Timothy 4:2
15 King Pyrrhus of Epirus; the story is told in Plutarch *Moralia* 184D.
16 Roman emperor 69–79 AD

17 A mischievous slave in Latin comedy
18 See above 346 n9.
19 See above 347 n11.
20 Alexandre de Ville-Dieu (fl c 1200), the author of a widely used grammar
21 Possibly Jan Briart of Ath (Atensis), the leading theologian at the University of Louvain; see above 350 n65.
22 1 Timothy 6:4
23 Quintilian in his rhetorical textbook, *Institutio oratoria* 5.13.23
24 In *Phaedrus* 244A–45C Plato speaks of three positive forms of 'madness,' those of prophets, lovers, and poets.
25 1 Corinthians 1:23–5
26 *Commentary on Matthew* 17.5
27 *Adages* III iii 1; the Sileni were statues that were ugly on the outside, but when opened revealed golden images.
28 Plutarch *Moralia* 15D. Simonides (c 556–468 BC) was a Greek lyric and elegiac poet.
29 Herostratus, who set fire to the temple of Diana in Ephesus in 356 BC
30 Greek Church Fathers
31 Guillaume Le Breton, the famous thirteenth-century Franciscan, who wrote a work on St Jerome's biblical prologues
32 A reference to the Constitution of Clement V, promulgated at the Council of Vienne
33 Collection of papal letters that have the force of law
34 Customary title of theology professors
35 Ie the union in one person of the divine and human natures
36 See above 348 n30.
37 See above 347 n16.

**Ep 980**

1 Of Louvain, where Erasmus was residing at this time
2 Erard de la Marck (1472–1538). The passage caused the bishop considerable embarrassment. He was questioned by three members of the faculty of theology at Louvain and had to declare that he was not a supporter of Luther.
3 Jacob Probst (1486–1562). His efforts to propagate the new faith ended with the suppression of his convent in 1522.
4 Philippus Melanchthon (1498–1560) was at the time professor of Greek at Wittenberg and eventually became Luther's right-hand man.

**Ep 1033**

1 Johann Reuchlin (1454/5–1522), the well-known Hebrew scholar, came under suspicion of heterodoxy. He was investigated by the inquisitor Jacob of Hoogstraten and put on trial, but Pope Leo x halted the proceedings. Another tribunal in 1520 found him guilty, but Reuchlin appealed and was acquitted.
2 The Cabbala is a system of Jewish theosophy; the Talmud is a compilation of Jewish traditions.
3 The twelfth-century scholastic doctor and author of the *Sentences*
4 Isaiah 36:6, 42:3
5 Nicolaus Baechem; see above 348 n24.
6 Schismatic group, fourth century
7 See above 355 n1.
8 Alvar Pelayo (d 1349), Silvester Prierias (c 1456–1523) and Cajetanus, cardinal of San Sisto (1469–1534)
9 *Georgics* 1.514
10 See above note 8.
11 Savaronella is a corruption of Girolamo Savonarola's name. The Dominican (1452–98) had great influence in Florence at the time – he was eventually burned at the stake. The reference to Bern concerns a certain Johann Jetzer, a Dominican novice, who claimed that the Virgin Mary had appeared to him. The discovery that his claims were fraudulent led to a widely publicized scandal.
12 For the *Method*, see above 349 n60.

**Ep 1202**

1 The Diet of Worms (1520) where Luther refused to recant
2 Ie Aristotelian
3 Cf Acts 2:16–21, Joel 3:1–5.
4 Acts 2:29
5 Acts 17:30, 22
6 Cf Acts 17:23.
7 A Stoic philosopher of the third century BC; cf Acts 17:28.
8 Cf Acts 26.
9 For the Donatists see above 359 n6; the Manichaeans were a Gnostic sect founded in the third century.
10 Cf Cicero *Epistulae ad Brutum* 25.
11 *Republic* 3.389B, 459C–D

12 Galatians 5:13–14
13 A fox who has fallen into a well persuades a goat to jump in as well. The story is told by Phaedrus 4.9.
14 See above note 1 (Ep 1033).
15 The letter to Luther is Ep 980 (text above 196–7).
16 The letter to the cardinal is Ep 1033 (text above 198–205).
17 Willibald Pirckheimer, the Nürnberg counsellor, but the letter referred to here appears to be lost.
18 Santiago de Compostela, a famous centre of pilgrimage in Spain
19 *The Divine Names, Mystical Theology,* and *The Celestial and Ecclesiastical Hierarchy*
20 For Hutten see above 350 n77.
21 For Melanchthon see above n4 (Ep 980).

**Julius Excluded from Heaven**

1 Julius' family crest
2 Ie from Liguria, the region around Genoa
3 'Supreme Plague'
4 'Supreme Pontiff'
5 Julius Caesar
6 There are several possible interpretations: in Italian the words mean 'but come on, say yes'; in Greek they mean 'yes, by Zeus!'
7 The underworld
8 A Roman statesman proverbial for wealth
9 The braggart soldier in Terence's play *Eunuchus*
10 Cf CWE 1 336–47.
11 Giovanni Bentivoglio made himself master of Bologna in 1462; the Venetians were defeated at Agnadello in 1509; the duke of Ferrara, Alfonso d'Este, was imprisoned by the pope but managed to escape.
12 A schismatic council opened at Pisa in 1511; Julius countered by calling his own council in Rome.
13 Julius had to rely on Spanish help to drive out the French, which resulted in an increase of their influence in Italy.
14 Concluded in 1508
15 Temporal and spiritual, according to medieval exegesis of Luke 22:38
16 Cf John 18:10.
17 Pope Sixtus IV (1414–84)
18 The Roman emperor Augustus and the famous conqueror of Carthage
19 The reference is cryptic; perhaps it means 'act like the Greeks,' a reference

to the Greek Orthodox schism which refused to recognize the supremacy of the pope.

20 Alfonso d'Este, the husband of Pope Alexander VI's daughter Lucrezia Borgia, who ruled Ferrara until his death in 1534
21 Pope Alexander VI (1430–1503)
22 Julius' nephew Francesco Maria della Rovere (1490–1538)
23 Francesco Alidosi who was murdered in the streets of Ravenna in 1511; Julius most likely did not order the murder.
24 Giangiordano Orsini
25 Attributed to Caesar by Suetonius *Julius* 1.30.5
26 Maximilian I (1459–1519)
27 Louis XII (1462–1515) had sponsored the schismatic Council of Pisa.
28 Proverbial names; the Cercopes were renowned for their cunning and were changed into monkeys by Jupiter; Morychus is an alternative name for Bacchus; the Lerna is an ill-smelling swamp.
29 Distinguished Roman families; Erasmus witnessed the triumphal entry of Julius into Bologna.
30 Cf Acts 5:1–10.

**Shipwreck**

1 In ancient mythology the twin sons of Zeus and Leda. Ancient seamen regarded the electrical discharge, called today St Elmo's fire, a sign of the heavenly twins.
2 Ie, severe
3 Batavians (ie Dutchmen) were proverbial for dull wits.
4 Jean Gerson (1363–1429), an outstanding theologian and author of many writings on moral and mystical theology
5 St Dominic (1170–1221) was the founder of the Dominicans (Preachers); St Thomas Aquinas was a member of this order; 'Vincent' probably refers to the Dominican St Vincent Ferrer (c 1350–1419); 'St Peter' could be Peter Martyr (1205–52).
6 Opening words of the introit in the mass for the dead

**The Education of a Christian Prince**

1 Perhaps a slip – The remark is attributed to Bias in Plutarch's *Moralia* 61C and in Erasmus' own *Apophthegms* (LB IV 324F).
2 Literally 'a seller of smoke'; thus the punishment was particularly appropriate. Alexander Severus was Roman emperor from 222 to 235AD.

3 Carneades was the leading philosopher of the Middle Academy (mid-second century BC). The story is told in Plutarch *Moralia* 58F.
4 Erasmus translated the essay into Latin and dedicated the version to Henry VIII.
5 The most famous painter of antiquity
6 Ie, the emperor Augustus. The historian Suetonius (*Augustus* 70) describes a banquet at which the emperor appeared dressed as Apollo.
7 For the full story concerning Alexander the Great, see below 278. On being presented with a pomegranate the Persian king Darius expressed the wish that for every seed in it he could have another man like his trusted counsellor Zopyrus. The great Roman general Scipio Africanus captured New Carthage in Spain in 209BC; on hearing that a captive was betrothed to an honourable youth, he had her released and handed over to the couple the ransom paid by relatives for the bride.
8 See above note 2.
9 Governor of Athens under the Macedonians in the fourth century BC.
10 Fabius Maximus, the celebrated adversary of Hannibal, 'valued safety more than the mob's applause' according to Cicero *De senectute* 4.10 – that is, he persevered in his unpopular delaying tactics, exhausted Hannibal, and saved Rome. Antoninus Pius, Roman emperor 137–61AD, refused to take an unmerited share in his brother's glory.
11 Ie, 'protector of hospitality'
12 Anacharsis, quoted by Plutarch *Solon* 5.2
13 Hadrian, Roman emperor from 117 to 138AD
14 Cinna, son of the conspirator against Julius Caesar, plotted to assassinate Augustus during a sacrifice.
15 The Homeric hero; his adventures were proverbial.
16 Charles VII and Louis XII had both carried on unsuccessful and costly campaigns.
17 Ie, wars being fought over a love affair
18 For Scipio see above note 7. The saying is quoted by Cicero *De officiis* 3.1.
19 The hero of Virgil's Aeneid; cf eg *Aeneid* 1.305.
20 *Iliad* 2.24–5
21 Mithridates VI, king of Pontus (120–63BC)
22 Macedonian king, father of Alexander the Great
23 Spartan king (eighth century BC)
24 *Adages* II V 1
25 Theban general (fourth century BC)
26 Julius II; see above 216.
27 *Eclogues* 1.70

28 Isaiah 9:6

### A Complaint of Peace

1 The sorceress Circe changed Odysseus' men into pigs (*Odyssey* 10.235ff).
2 *Antipelargosis*, a rare word denoting love between parents and children
3 A Neoplatonic tenet
4 References to scholastic disputes and the classical dispute between Platonists and Aristotelians
5 Silius Italicus in *Punica* 11.592
6 Psalms 76:2 explained in Hebrews 7:2
7 Isaiah 32:17
8 Isaiah 33:7
9 Isaiah 32:18, Psalms 125:5
10 John 13:35 and 14:27
11 John 17:11
12 John 13:34–5, 15:12
13 John 15:12
14 Dionysius, tyrant of Syracuse (d 367BC), often cited as a symbol of tyranny; Mezentius, King of Caere in Etruria, whose cruelty is described by Virgil in *Aeneid* 8.485ff
15 Spanish Jews baptized after Ferdinand's edict of 1492 but secretly adhering to Judaism
16 Titus Vespasian, Roman emperor 68–79 AD; the reference is to his biographer Suetonius (*Titus* 9).
17 Julius II; see above 216.
18 Roman goddess of war
19 The common refrain in litanies of the Latin liturgy
20 Leo X, who succeeded Julius II in 1513, was active in arranging peace between England and France in 1514.
21 Diocletian (Roman emperor, abdicated 305 AD) pursued a defensive policy. This tribute by Erasmus is somewhat surprising since he is remembered primarily for his persecutions of Christians.
22 Cato *On Agriculture* 4.1
23 Cicero *Pro Milone* 4.11
24 Proverbial for treachery
25 Diamond or other hard substance
26 Francis I, king of France 1515–47; 'Rex christianissimus' was one of his official titles.
27 Charles, later Charles V (d 1559); Maximilian his grandfather, emperor 1493–1519; Henry VIII of England (d 1547)

**On the War against the Turks**

1 Erasmus set his advice on war against the Turks within his exegesis of Psalm 29, which refers to the warning voice of the Lord: 'The voice of the Lord is powerful. The voice of the Lord is full of majesty. The voice of the Lord breaketh the cedars. ... The voice of the Lord divideth the flames of fire' (Psalms 29:4–7).

2 The sack of Asperen occurred in July 1517 when atrocities were committed by the 'Black Band' organized by the Duke of Gelders.

3 This was Luther's opinion. See below 318–20.

4 Erasmus quotes literally from the condemnation of Lutheran doctrine issued by the Sorbonne in 1521.

5 The Philistines: 1 Samuel 7:10–13

6 The massacre occurred at Salonika in 390. Ambrose imposed a penance on the emperor. He praised Theodosius' submission in his funeral oration.

7 Tertullian, a Father of the Church (160–c 240)

8 The French claim to the duchy of Milan was the major point at issue in the series of wars between the Hapsburg and Valois dynasties, 1494–1559. See also the references in *Julius Excluded* (above 230–1) and *A Complaint of Peace* (above 305).

9 'Us,' that is, Hollanders. Karel Egmont, Duke of Gelders, had persistently and violently resisted the efforts of the Hapsburgs to dominate the Netherlands.

10 Leviticus 26:7–8

11 John 15:5

12 Mary's husband, Louis of Hungary, was killed in the battle of Mohacz in 1526; by 1529 the Turks had advanced to Vienna, where their march was halted.

13 In which indulgences (that is, papal documents releasing a soul from purgatory) were carried

14 Alexander VI, the notorious Borgia pope (1492–1503)

15 Begun by Julius II in 1506

16 In Spain, see above 360 n18.

17 The Peace of Cambrai of 1529 brought a temporary lull in the Hapsburg-Valois struggle.

18 Awarded by Leo X to Henry VIII in 1521

19 Cf Joshua 7.

20 Isaiah 1:16–18

21 Brother of Charles V, who had ceded to him the Austrian lands. What Erasmus says here is no idle speculation. In 1529 Francis proposed an

expedition to relieve Vienna in which the emperor was to be the 'chef de toute l'armée' and he himself 'come le principal après icelle.'

22 See above note 6.

23 Probably a reference to the schismatic council at Pisa in 1511

24 Erasmus may be thinking of Cardinal Wolsey who fell from power in October 1529. Rumours circulated in 1530 that the cardinal faced execution (see Ep 2253:322).

25 Since the loss to Europe of Syrian sugar supplies as a result of Turkish conquests in 1516, the commodity had become a Spanish monopoly, being produced principally in Sicily and the new Spanish colonies of the Caribbean.

**One Ought to Be Born a King or a Fool**

1 Seneca (c 4BC–65AD), whose life and career is described by the Roman historian Tacitus, had written a satire about the emperor Claudius, entitled *Apocolocyntosis*. It was published as a new discovery by Erasmus in his edition of Seneca of 1515 (ie, the year in which this adage made its first appearance).

2 Hesiod (fl 700BC), Greek epic poet

3 The leader of the Greeks in Homer's *Iliad*

4 *Epistles* 1.2.8

5 For Midas see above 351 n9.

6 Patrons of the arts

7 Ganymedes, cup-bearer of Zeus

8 Gods of the sea and of the underworld, respectively

9 The meeting between the Athenian statesman Solon and the Lydian king is described by the historian Herodotus 1.30–3.

10 The Persian king wished to punish the Hellespont whose stormy waters had destroyed his bridge. The story is told by Herodotus.

11 Ancient rulers renowned for their cruel tyranny

12 Codrus was the last, Cecrops according to the legend the earliest king of Athens; both therefore are legendary figures typical of remote antiquity.

13 Considered the trade-marks of the 'Greek philosopher' or those who affected to be considered philosophers.

14 Ie Solomon

15 See above 362 n3.

16 Athenian politician (fifth century BC)

17 *Oeconomicus* 2.13

# Chronology

| Date | Biographical Data | Work: Year of Publication |
|---|---|---|
| c1469 | 27 Oct: Erasmus' birth | |
| c1478–83 | Attends school of the Brethren of the Common Life at Deventer | |
| c1483–86 | Attends school at 's Hertogenbosch | |
| 1486 | Enters the Augustinian monastery at Steyn as a novice | |
| 1492 | Ordained priest | |
| 1492/3 | Enters the service of Henry of Bergen, Bishop of Cambrai | |
| 1495–99 | First stay in Paris, studying theology | |
| 1499 | First visit to England: association with More, Colet | |
| 1500–02 | Second stay in Paris, sojourns in Orléans and Holland | *Adagia* (prototype) |
| 1502–4 | First stay in Louvain; refuses offer to teach at university | *The Handbook of the Christian Soldier / Panegyric for Archduke Philip of Austria* |
| 1504–5 | Third stay in Paris | |
| 1505/6 | Second visit to England, staying at More's house | |
| 1506–9 | Travels in Italy, 1507/8 staying at Aldo Manuzio's house in Venice | *Praise of Folly / Copia: Foundations of the Abundant Style* |
| 1509–14 | Third stay in England; visit to Paris in 1511; lecturing at Cambridge 1511–14 | *Julius Excluded from Heaven /* Ep 337 |
| 1514–16 | First visit to Basel; association with Froben press; sojourns in England (1515) and the Netherlands (1516); Erasmus | *New Testament / The Education of a Christian Prince* |

| | | |
|---|---|---|
| | appointed councillor to Charles v | |
| 1517 | Antwerp, staying with Pieter Gillis; visit to England; move to Louvain | *A Complaint of Peace* |
| 1517–21 | Second stay in Louvain, with trips to Calais (1520, audience with Henry VIII), Basel (1518, to supervise revision of NT), and Cologne (1520, discusses Luther with Frederick the Wise); Erasmus co-opted into the faculty of theology at Louvain | Epp 980, 1033, 1202 / *The Colloquies* (prototype) / *The Antibarbarians* |
| end of 1521–29 | move to Basel; attempts to mediate between Protestants and Catholics | *Paraphrases* / *On Free Will* / *Catalogue* / *The Ciceronian* |
| 1529 | Basel turns Protestant; Erasmus emigrates to Catholic Freiburg | *On Education for Children* / *On Good Manners* / *On the War against the Turks* |
| 1535 | Return to Basel | |
| 1536 | 12 July: death of Erasmus | |

# Bibliography

## 1 Editions of Erasmus' Works

Allen, P.S., H.M. Allen, and H.W. Garrod eds *Opus epistolarum Des. Erasmi Roterodami* (Oxford 1906–58) 11 vols and Index: ALLEN

*Collected Works of Erasmus* (Toronto 1974–): CWE

Ferguson, W.K. ed *Erasmi opuscula: A Supplement to the Opera Omnia* (The Hague 1933): FERGUSON

Holborn, Hajo, and Annemarie Holborn *Desiderius Erasmus Roterodamus. Ausgewählte Werke* (Munich 1933, 1964): HOLBORN

*La Correspondance d'Erasme* (Brussels 1967–) 11 vols and index

Leclerc, J. ed *Desiderii Erasmi Roterodami opera omnia* (Leiden 1703–6) 10 vols: LB

*Opera omnia Desiderii Erasmi Roterodami* (Amsterdam 1969–): ASD

Reedijk, C. ed *The Poems of Desiderius Erasmus* (Leiden 1956): REEDIJK

Welzig, Werner ed *Erasmus von Rotterdam: Ausgewählte Schriften, lateinisch und deutsch* 8 vols (Darmstadt 1967–80): WELZIG

## 2 Bibliographical Aids

For the period prior to 1970 see J.-C. Margolin's compilations *Douze années de bibliographie érasmienne (1950–1961)* (Paris 1969); *Neuf années de bibliographie érasmienne (1962–1970)* (Paris and Toronto 1977).

For the period after 1970 see the reviews and bibliographical notes in two periodicals exclusively dedicated to Erasmus: *Erasmus in English* (1970–88) and *Erasmus of Rotterdam Society Yearbook* (1981–).

For biographical and bibliographical information on Erasmus' contemporaries see P.G. Bietenholz and T.B. Deutscher eds *Contemporaries of Erasmus: A Biographical Register of the Renaissance and Reformation* 3 vols (Toronto 1985–7): CEBR

## 3 Basic Books

Augustijn, C. *Erasmus: His Life, Work, and Influence* (Toronto 1991)

Bainton, R.H. *Erasmus of Christendom* (New York 1969)

Bouyer, L. *Erasmus and His Times* tr F.X. Murphy (Westminster 1959)

Faludy, G. *Erasmus of Rotterdam* (London 1970)
Huizinga, J. *Erasmus of Rotterdam* tr F. Hopman (New York 1952)
McConica, J.K. *Erasmus* Past Masters Series (Oxford 1991)
Phillips, Margaret Mann *Erasmus and the Northern Renaissance* (London 1949)
Smith, P. *Erasmus: A Study of His Life, Ideals and Place in History* (New York 1923)
Sowards, J.K. *Desiderius Erasmus* (Boston 1975)

## 4 Further Reading

Adams, R.P. *The Better Part of Valor* (Seattle 1962)
Bataillon, M. *Erasme et l'Espagne* (Paris 1937); Spanish version: *Erasmo y España* (Mexico 1950)
Bentley, J. *Humanists and Holy Writ* (Princeton 1983)
Bierlaire, F. *Les Colloques d'Erasme* (Paris 1978)
Boyle, M. O'Rourke *Erasmus on Language and Method in Theology* (Toronto 1977)
Chomarat, J. *Grammaire et rhétorique chez Erasme* 2 vols (Paris 1981)
Etienne, J. *Spiritualisme érasmien et theologiens louvanistes* (Louvain 1956)
McConica, J.K. *English Humanists and Reformation Politics under Henry* VIII and Edward VI (Oxford 1969)
Mansfield, B. *Phoenix of His Age: Interpretations of Erasmus c 1550–1750* (Toronto 1979)
Markish, Sh. *Erasmus and the Jews*, tr A. Olcott (Chicago 1986)
Murray, *Erasmus and Luther* (London 1920)
Olin, J.C. *Six Essays on Erasmus* (New York 1979)
Payne, J. *Erasmus: His Theology of the Sacraments* (Richmond 1969)
Rabil, A. *Erasmus and the New Testament; The Mind of a Christian Humanist* (San Antonio 1972)
Renaudet, A. *Erasme: Sa pensée religieuse, d'après sa correspondance (1518–1521)* (Paris 1926)
– *Erasme et l'Italie* (Geneva 1954)
Rummel, E. *Erasmus and His Catholic Critics* 2 vols (Nieuwkoop 1989)
Screech, M.A. *Ecstasy and the Praise of Folly* (London 1980)
Seidel-Menchi, S. *Erasmo in Italia* (Milan 1986)
Thompson, C.R. *Inquisitio de Fide* (New Haven 1950)
Thompson, G. *Under Pretext of Praise* (Toronto 1973)
Tracy, J.D. *Erasmus: The Growth of a Mind* (Geneva 1972)
– *The Politics of Erasmus* (Toronto 1977)
Woodward, W.H. *Desiderius Erasmus Concerning the Aim and Method of Education* (Cambridge, Mass 1904)

# English and Latin Titles

## OF ERASMUS' WORKS MENTIONED IN THE ERASMUS READER

Adages / *Adagiorum chiliades*
Annotations on the New Testament / *Annotationes in Novum Testamentum*
The Antibarbarians / *Antibarbarorum liber*
Apophthegms / *Apophthegmata*
The Ciceronian / *Dialogus Ciceronianus*
Comparison between Virgin and Martyr / *Virginis et martyris comparatio*
A Complaint of Peace / *Querela pacis*
Brief Outline of His Life / *Compendium vitae*
Catalogue of Works / *Catalogus lucubrationum*
Colloquies / *Colloquia*
Copia: Foundations of the Abundant Style / *De duplici copia verborum et rerum commentarii duo*
Ecclesiastes / *Ecclesiastes sive de ratione concionandi*
The Education of a Christian Prince / *Institutio principis christiani*
The Handbook of the Christian Soldier / *Enchiridion militis christiani*
The Homily on the Child Jesus / *Concio de puero Iesu*
Julius Excluded from Heaven / *Dialogus Julius exclusus e coelis*
Method of True Theology / *Ratio verae theologiae*
On Disdaining the World / *De contemptu mundi*
On Education for Children / *De pueris statim ac liberaliter instituendis*
On Establishing Concord in the Church / *De sarcienda ecclesiae concordia*
On Free Will / *De libero arbitrio diatribe*
On Good Manners / *De civilitate morum puerilium*
On the Method of Study / *De ratione studii ac legendi interpretandique auctores*
On the War against the Turks / *Consultatio de bello Turcis inferendo et obiter ennarratus Psalmus XXVIII*
Panegyricus / *Panegyricus ad Philippum Austriae ducem*
Parallels / *Parabolae sive similia*
Paraphrases / *Paraphrasis in Novum Testamentum*
Praise of Folly / *Moriae encomium*
Sermon on the Mercy of the Lord / *De immensa Dei misericordia concio*
The Tongue / *Lingua*

# Index

This book

was designed by

Antje Lingner

University of

Toronto Press